Dana Facaros and Michael Pauls

flying visits
SPAIN

CADOGANguides

Contents

About the authors

Dana Facaros and **Michael Pauls** have written over 30 books for Cadogan Guides, including all the Spain series. They have lived all over Europe, but have recently hung up their castanets in a farmhouse surrounded by vineyards in the Lot Valley.

Cadogan Guides
165 The Broadway,
Wimbledon, London
SW19 1NE, UK
info.cadogan@virgin.net
www.cadoganguides.com

The Globe Pequot Press
246 Goose Lane, PO Box 480, Guilford,
Connecticut 06437–0480, USA

Copyright © Dana Facaros and
   Michael Pauls 2003

Cover design by Jodi Louw
Book design by Andrew Barker
Cover photographs by John Miller, Beth Evans and
   Alan Copson (front), and Beth Evans (back).
Maps © Cadogan Guides,
   drawn by Map Creation Ltd
Managing Editor: Christine Stroyan
Series Editor: Linda McQueen
Editor: Nick Rider
Design: Sarah Gardner
Proofreading: Gill Paul
Indexing: Isobel McLean
Production: Navigator Guides Ltd

Printed in Italy by Legoprint
A catalogue record for this book is available
   from the British Library
ISBN 1-86011-897-6

The author and publishers have made every effort to ensure the accuracy of the information in this book at the time of going to press. However, they cannot accept any responsibility for any loss, injury or inconvenience resulting from the use of information contained in this guide.

Please help us to keep this guide up to date. We have done our best to ensure that the information in this guide is correct at the time of going to press. But places and facilities are constantly changing, and standards and prices in hotels and restaurants fluctuate. We would be delighted to receive any comments concerning existing entries or omissions. Authors of the best letters will receive a copy of the Cadogan Guide of their choice.

Introduction and Themes

01

Spain is a country of strong flavours – rich red wines, dry-cured hams, piled-high platters of succulent seafood, sharp contrasts of whitewashed walls and azure-blue skies, the full-on energy of a night bar- and club-hopping in Madrid or Barcelona. It's also a place of very diverse flavours, a sub-continent in itself. Every part of Spain has its own special character, history and identity, which nowadays is expressed vigorously – through distinctive cuisines, folklore and fiestas, attitudes to going out, ways of serving wines or coffee or architectural and artistic traditions, right up, in places like the Basque Country and Catalonia, to different languages and a sense of being separate countries altogether. Within Spain there is a greater diversity of landscape than in almost any other European country, from green-wooded hills to dry-stone deserts. This huge variety means that a visit to one part of Spain can be a wholly different experience from a visit to another.

In the last few years the emergence of a string of new cheap flight destinations has put a range of Spain's experiences, from cities to beaches, at your fingertips. And they're only a couple of hours from Britain, ideal for a flying visit, a short break... or more, should you find that the place has stolen your heart.

Spain has been Europe's most popular holiday destination for many years now, so some of its attractions – its beach *costas* – could hardly be better-known. Recently, too, fashionable and stylish cities like Barcelona, Madrid and Bilbao have taken their places as must-see places on any modern traveller's map. Spain's most famous and apparently familiar attractions – the great art museums of Madrid and Bilbao's Guggenheim, the constant parade on the Ramblas and the Gaudí buildings in Barcelona, the Alhambra in Granada, the prime beach-spots of the Costa Blanca or the hill villages of Andalucía – are all featured in this guide. Around them, though, we also point to many more, less publicized things to discover – uncrowded beaches in sheltered bays, fabulous mountains and walking country in the Catalan Pyrenees or Madrid's sierras, tiny Basque fishing villages offering superb seafood right by the quay, impenetrably sleepy rustic towns just a few miles away from major modern cities. For every cliché there are a hundred surprises.

Flying Visits Spain provides the perfect opportunity to rediscover old favourites and open your eyes to new places. We've divided Spain into regional chapters, each one structured around the cities that can be reached directly from Britain by low-cost flights or in some cases – Bilbao and Santander – by sea, by overnight ferry. Each main destination, as well as being an attraction in itself, thus acts as a gateway to the towns, coun tryside and beaches of the surrounding region. Several pages introduce the key sights, monuments and museums in the gateway city, while a practical section provides the essentials on how to get around, where to stay, eat and shop while you're there. Then come suggestions for day or overnight trips that you can make from the city by public transport, a chance to experience some of the highlights of each region even if you only have a few days in which to travel. And with most cities we've also included a five- or six-day touring itinerary you can do from the city by hiring a car, picking out some of the hidden and not-so-hidden gems of Spain's small towns and countryside for you to explore at your own pace and take advantage of mobility to get a little more off-track.

What to Go For...

	Art City	Beaches	Gastronomy	Scenery	Shopping	Architecture	History
Alicante		●	●	★		★	★
Barcelona	●	●	●	●	●	●	●
Bilbao	●	★	●	●		●	●
Girona	★	★	●	★		●	
Jerez		★	●	★		★	★
Madrid	●		●	●	●	●	●
Málaga		●		★			★
Murcia		★		★			
Santander		●		★			

● In the gateway city itself   ★ Within easy reach of the gateway city

We begin with **Catalonia**, one of the parts of Spanish that is the least 'Spanish' at all. Its capital **Barcelona** has built up a legend all of its own as perhaps the most charismatic city in Europe today, a place where tradition, style, hip street-fashion and hugely imaginative official policies have all combined in a heady, creative urban mix. Barcelona has the extraordinary architectural creations of Antoni Gaudí, the Picasso museum with relics of the great artist's youth, medieval marvels like the church of Santa Maria del Mar or the narrow streets of the Gothic Quarter, the constant energy of the Ramblas and the view from Tibidabo; it has slick, elegant shops and fabulous restaurants; most of all, though, it's a place that people just like to *be* in for a while. Another of its attractions is that it's a beach city, and we also show you the way to Sitges, traditionally the city's favourite seaside escape route. With a car, Barcelona is also an excellent base for exploring the Catalan countryside, with wine regions like the Penedès – home of *cava* sparkling wine – or the empty wetlands of the Ebro Delta. Catalonia's second city, **Girona** (or Gerona, in Spanish), is much smaller but also has a great deal of charm, with treasures of Catalan Gothic architecture and relics of its medieval Jewish community. It's most popular, though, as a gateway to superb coastline and landscapes: the exquisite coves and cliffs of the Costa Brava – with, in Figueres and Cadaqués, the sites most associated with the greatest 20th-century eccentric from a region that's known for them, Salvador Dalí – and magnificent mountain scenery in the Pyrenees and Pre-Pyrenees.

Next comes an area even more idiosyncratic – certainly in its language – the **Basque Country**. Its main city, **Bilbao**, has been catapulted from an old and smoky industrial hub into an art capital above all by Frank Gehry's astonishing Guggenheim museum; around it, too, the old town has been spruced up, to reveal it as a lively, elegant city. Basques like to do things their own way: their subtle cuisine has the reputation of being the best in Spain, and their *tapas* bars are spectacular, so that for eating, large- or small-scale, Bilbao and its gracious neighbour San Sebastián are hard to beat. Around them, the green, cool Basque countryside is full of characterful places to explore, from clifftops to mountains. Just west is Cantabria, another area that's green and cool, but different again. **Santander** is another of Spain's 19th-century seaside resorts, which still gets buzzing every summer; just a short distance away are villages preserved from Spain's Golden Age, and superb scenery in the Cantabrian mountains.

It's only natural to compare Spain's capital, **Madrid**, with its chalk-and-cheese rival Barcelona. They're like very different meals that are equally enjoyable. Madrid's bar and nightlife is not as stylish as that of the Catalan city, but often has a more down-to-earth energy, and can be more fun; and cranky Madrid has few rivals as an art destination, with the three grand treasure-houses of the Prado, the Reina Sofía and the Thyssen museum all within a short walk of each other. Around Madrid there is also a truly spectacular ring of historic towns – the austere grandeur of El Escorial, charming Segovia with its earthy roast-meat restaurants, the elegant gardens of Aranjuez, matchless, mysterious Toledo – and more high mountains than can be found within an hour's distance of any other European capital.

Then we head back to the sea and two *costas*, the **Costa Blanca** and **Costa Cálida**. **Alicante**, gateway to the Blanca, is another city that, like Barcelona, combines beaches and a historic old centre within its limits, in a very enjoyable cocktail. It is most popular, though, as an entry point to all the coast to the north, whether brash and noisy Benidorm or the more discreet pleasures of Altea and Dénia. It's also only a short hop from Valencia, one of Spain's liveliest cities. A little to the south, **Murcia** is growing fast as a gateway to some of Spain's most popular beach-zones around La Manga and Torrevieja, with superb facilities, above all, for golf and every kind of sport.

Last but not least comes **Andalucía**, not a separate nationality but one of the regions with most character of all, the home of whitewashed villages, bullfighting, flamenco and many other things considered 'essentially Spanish'. Its main modern gateway is **Málaga**, another beach-and-city town, the capital of the Costa del Sol. From here you can head for big, celebrated resorts like Fuengirola or Marbella, or just as easily make for classic Andaluz hill towns like Ronda, surprisingly secluded beaches east of the city or one of humanity's greatest sights, Granada. And in western Andalucía is a final gateway in **Jerez de la Frontera**, the gracious home of sherry, and also an excellent jumping-off point for exploring the famous 'White Villages' of Cádiz, the funky little towns on the Guadalquivir river famous for seafood and flamenco, or the unmissable old Moorish cities of Andalucía like Córdoba and Seville.

Wherever you land, the possibilities are myriad.

Travel

Who Goes Where?

	page	easyJet (inc. Go)	Buzz	mytravellite	Bmibaby	Monarch	Ryanair	Brittany Ferries	P&O Portsmouth
Alicante	174	•		•	•	•			
Barcelona	41	•		•					
Bilbao	94	•							•
Girona	74			•			•		
Jerez	222			•					
Madrid	128	•							
Málaga	200	•		•	•	•			
Murcia	189			•	•				
Santander	117							•	

Getting There

By Air: the Lowdown on Low-cost Flights

In the last few years the airline industry has undergone a revolution. Inspired by the success of Stelios Haji-Ioannou's 'upstart' easyJet company, other airlines – Buzz, Go, Ryanair, Bmibaby – flocked to join him in breaking all the conventions of air travel to offer fares at rock-bottom prices. After September 11th, while long-haul carriers hit the ropes in a big way, these budget airlines experienced unprecedented sales, and responded by expanding their list of destinations throughout Europe. As regards flights between Britain and Spain in partic-ular, the absorption of Go by easyJet at the end of 2002 threatened to reduce the level of price competition once again on the most popular routes, but new airlines are still starting up with an eye on expanding the no-frills cake. Whereas in their first years no-frills airlines had an undoubted 'backpackerish' feel, this has become an increasingly main-stream way to travel. October 2002 saw the first flights of yet another all-new airline, mytravellite, set up by the huge My Travel tour operator and with its operating base in Birmingham.

No Frills, No Thrills

The ways in which low prices are achieved sometimes have a negative effect on the experience of travellers, but can sometimes be a bonus too. First, these airlines often use **smaller regional airports**, where landing fees and tarmac-time charges are at a minimum:

easyJet flies out of Luton and Liverpool, and, with the former Go routes, from Stansted and Bristol, as well as Gatwick; Buzz flies from Stansted, Bmibaby from East Midlands, and so on. At the other end, Buzz especially flies to small, uncongested airports that are close to some very attractive destinations.

The **planes** (nearly always Boeing 737s) are all one-class only and with the maximum seating configuration. For anyone remotely tall it's worth checking in early and being assertive in asking for an aisle seat or by an emergency exit; if the airline doesn't give assigned seats, just check in early.

Fares are one-way – so no need to stay over on a Saturday night to qualify for the lowest fares – and can vary enormously on the same route, according to when you travel and how far in advance you book: the most widely advertised, rock-bottom deals are generally for seats on very early-morning, early-in-the-week flights, and on the most popular routes (such as any to Barcelona) while you might get a price of £40 for a 6am Monday flight, the same route can cost you £140 on a Friday evening. Because of this constantly changing price system it is important to note that **no-frills airlines are not always the cheapest**, above all on the very popular routes at peak times (Barcelona again). One of the benefits of the no-frills revolution that is not always appreciated is not as much in their own prices as in the concessions they have forced on the older, mainstream carriers (British Airways, British Midland, Aer Lingus and Iberia, between the UK, Ireland and Spain). Obliged to compete, Iberia in particular has responded with a programme of flight offers often at very good prices, especially off-peak. It is **always** worth comparing no-frills prices with those of the main airlines, and checking out what special offers are going.

No-frills airline tickets are only sold direct, by phone or online, not through travel agents. To get the lowest prices you must book online, not by phone. You will not be issued with an actual **ticket** when you book, but given a reference number to show with your ID at check-in (some form of photographic ID, such as a driving licence, is now required even for UK domestic flights where no passport is needed). With some airlines you are not issued with an **assigned seat** at check-in either, but will board on a first-come, first-served basis.

There are no 'air miles' schemes, and no **meal** will be included, though there will be (fairly expensive) snacks for sale on-board. There are no refunds if you miss your flight for any reason, although some of the airlines will allow you to **change** your destination, date of travel or the named traveller for a fee of around £15. There are also charges for **excess baggage**.

Another way in which prices are kept down is by keeping **staffing levels** very low, especially on the ground. This means that check-in can take a lot longer than for main-carrier flights, especially for the most popular routes and at peak times. Be warned.

What's the Worst that Can Happen?

From time to time the press ripples with stories of 'holiday hell' in low-cost air travel, from people ending up a four-hour journey from their destination to lost baggage and

Airlines

UK and Ireland

Aer Lingus, t (Irish Republic) 0818 365000, (UK) 0845 084 444, www.aerlingus.ie.
Bmibaby, t 0870 264 2229, www.flybmi.com. From East Midlands.
British Airways, t 0845 77 333 77, www.britishairways.com.
British Midland, t 0870 6070 555, www.flybmi.com. From East Midlands and Heathrow.
Buzz, t 0870 240 7070, www.buzzaway.com. From Stansted.
easyJet, t 0870 600 0000, www.easyjet.com. From Luton, Gatwick, Stansted, Bristol, East Midlands and Liverpool.
Go, operating from Stansted, Bristol and East Midlands, was taken over by easyJet in 2002.
Iberia, t 0845 6012 854, www.iberia.com.
Monarch, t 0870 0405 040, www.fly-monarch.com. From Luton and Manchester.
mytravellite, t 0870 1564 564, www.mytravelite.com. From Birmingham.
Ryanair, t (0871) 246 0000, www.ryanair.com. From Stansted.

Making it Work for You: 10 Tips to Remember

1 Whichever airline you travel with, the earlier you book, the cheaper seats will be.

2 Book on-line for the best prices, as there are often discounts of £2.50 to £5 per journey for on-line sales. Always compare the no-frills lines' prices with those of main carriers on the route you want to travel.

3 Be ready to travel at less convenient times. Very early morning and late night flights, and those early in the week (Mon–Wed) will always be the cheapest. But be sure to check there is a means of getting from your destination airport if you arrive at night, allowing for at least an hour's delay – if you have to fork out for a taxi rather than a shuttle bus or local bus service, this could eat up the saving you make by travelling late.

4 Think hard whether you want to book by credit card. You will have the consumer protection that offers, but there is likely to be a supplement of anything up to £5. Consider using a debit card instead.

5 Check whether airport taxes are included in the quoted price; they are usually extra.

6 If you intend to travel often and can go at short notice, sign up for airlines' e-mail mailing lists to hear news of special offers.

7 Check the baggage allowance and don't take any excess. If you can travel light, take hand baggage only, as at some airports your airline will be low priority for the baggage handlers and this can cause a long wait.

8 Take your own food and drink, allowing for possible delays, to avoid paying for over-priced airport food or on-board snacks.

9 Make sure you take your booking reference and confirmation with you to check in (this will have been emailed or posted to you). You must of course also show your passport for international flights.

10 Never ignore the advised check-in times, which are generally two hours. Don't be tempted to cut it fine, as check-in takes longer with budget airlines than with traditional carriers (*see* above), and at the same time the airlines try to keep boarding times short to meet their fast turn-around times. If you care where you sit, or are travelling in a group, check in even earlier or, if the airline doesn't give assigned seats, get to the departure gate as early as possible to be ahead of the bunch.

no one to look for it, queues, cancellations and so many hidden extras – taxes, expensive food, travel to and from outlying airports – that any old main-carrier flight could have been better value. Essentially, with no-frills flights, you're supposed to get what you pay for. If you pay a really low fare and get to your destination without a hitch, you think, hey, this is great. It's when a problem does arise, though, that you start to notice the downside of no-frills operations. Since every plane is used to the limit, there are no 'spare' aircraft, so if one has a technical problem somewhere the day's schedules can collapse like a house of cards; since there are so few ground staff, when bags gets lost there's scarcely anyone available to look for them, or even show an interest. And all the budget operators accept far fewer obligations towards customers in the event of lost bags, delays and so on than

main carriers traditionally have; this is stated in the small print of their terms and conditions (all there, on the websites), but many people don't read this until after their problem has come up. The companies' explanation is always that this is what 'no-frills' is all about, and that this level of service is what permits the price levels the public have shown they want – which is all well and good if you do pay £40 to get to Málaga, but can be annoying when you're paying £250 return, as much as a main-carrier fare, for a weekend trip to Barcelona.

Disasters, of course, can always happen, but an awareness of the way the system works and why fares are cheap can go a good way to avoiding mishaps or being caught out – *see* the tips in the box left. And, while corners are cut in many ways, there is no evidence that those corners affect safety.

Getting to Spain Cheaply from North America

US and Canadian citizens will be able to find flights direct to some of the larger Spanish cities listed in this guide. But it is also possible for North Americans to take advantage of the explosion of cheap inter-European flights, by taking a charter to London, and booking a UK–Spain budget flight in advance on the budget airline's website (*see* p.11).

This will need careful planning: you're looking at an 8hr flight followed by a 3hr journey across London and another 2–2½hr hop to Spain; it can certainly be done, especially if you are a person who is able to sleep on a night flight, but you may prefer to spend a night or two in London.

Direct to Spain

There are frequent flights to Madrid, Spain's main gateway airport, on Iberia, Air Canada and several US airlines, and Iberia and Delta also fly direct to Barcelona from New York. During off-peak periods (the winter months and fall) you should be able to get a scheduled economy flight from New York to Madrid for as little as around $380–$500, and for an extra $100 or so a transfer to one of the regional airports (such as Málaga, Bilbao or Alicante).

In the summer you may also be able to get non-stop charters to Madrid or Barcelona.

Air Canada, t 1 800 247 2262, *www.aircanada.ca*.

American Airlines, t 1 800 433 7300, *www.aa.com*.

British Airways, t 1 800 AIRWAYS, *www.britishairways.com*.

Continental, t 800 231 0856, Canada t 800 525 0280, *www.continental.com*.

Delta, t 1 800 241 4141, *www.delta.com*.

Iberia, t 1 800 772 4642, *www.iberia.com*. Offices, 6100 Blue Lagoon Drive, Suite 200, Miami, FL 33126, t (305) 267 7747; 655 Madison Ave, 20th Floor, New York, NY 10022, t (718) 553 6708; 333 North MIchigan Ave, Suite 2131, Chicago, IL 60601, t (773) 686 3812.

United Airlines, t 1 800 538 2929, *www.ual.com*.

Via London

Start by finding a cheap charter flight or discounted scheduled flight to London; check the Sunday-paper travel sections for the latest deals, and if possble research your fare initially on some of the US cheap-flight websites: *www.priceline.com* (bid for tickets), *www.expedia.com*, *www.hotwire.com*, *www.bestfares.com*, *www.travelocity.com*, *www.eurovacations.com*, *www.cheaptrips.com*, *www.courier.com* (courier flights), *www.fool.com* (advice on booking over the net) or *www.ricksteves.com*.

When you have the availablity and arrival times for London flights, match up a convenient flight time on the website of the budget airline that flies to your chosen Spanish city (*see* p.11).

Be careful if using easyJet to opt for its flights from Luton, not Liverpool, and note also that Bmibaby's hub, East Midlands airport, and also Birmingham and Manchester, are not near London and would be fairly impractical for a single day's journey.

You will most likely be arriving at Heathrow terminals 3 or 4 (possibly Gatwick), and may be flying out from Stansted (Ryanair, easyJet/Go and Buzz), Luton (easyJet/go) or Gatwick (some easyJet flights), all of which are in different directions and will mean travelling through central London, so leaving enough time is essential. Add together the journey times and prices for Heathrow into central London and back out again to your departure airport. You could mix and match – the Tube to Victoria and the Gatwick Express, or a taxi from Heathrow to King's Cross Thameslink and a train to Luton – but don't even think of using a bus or taxi at rush hours (7–10am and 4–7pm); train and/or Underground (Tube) are the only sensible choices. Always add on waiting times and delays in London's notoriously creaky transport system; and finally, although the cheapest budget airline fares are early morning and late at night, make sure your chosen transport is still operating.

Note also that as the market for cheap travel takes off, major carriers such as BA and British Midland have begun to compete directly, offering one-way fares that do not require a Saturday night stay. For North

American visitors they have the singular advantage of sometimes leaving from Heathrow.

Airport to Airport Taxis

A taxi directly between airports might avoid central London but is an expensive option:
Heathrow–Gatwick: 1hr 30mins, £85–£100.
Heathrow–Stansted: 2hrs 15mins, £140–£160.
Heathrow–Luton: 1hr 15mins, £80–£90.

Heathrow

Heathrow is about 15 miles west of the centre. **Airport information:** t 0870 0000 123.

By Tube: Heathrow is on the Piccadilly Line. Tube trains depart every 5–9 minutes from 6am to midnight and the journey time to the centre is 55mins. A single fare into the city centre costs £3.60.

By bus: The Airbus A2 (**t** 0870 575 7747) departs from all terminals every 30mins and makes several stops before terminating at King's Cross. Tickets cost £8 single. It's a long ride: at least 1hr 45mins.

By train: The Heathrow Express is the fastest option: trains every 15mins between 5.10am and 11.40pm to Paddington Station, which is on the Tube's Bakerloo, Circle and District Lines, taking 15mins. Tickets cost £13 single.

By taxi: There are taxi ranks at all terminals. Fares into central London are about £35–£50.

Gatwick

Gatwick is about 20 miles south of London. There are two terminals, North and South, linked by a shuttle service. **Airport information:** t 0870 000 2468.

By train: The fastest service is the Gatwick Express (**t** 0870 530 1530), which runs from Victoria Station to the South Terminal to every 15 minutes and takes about 30mins. Tickets cost £11 for a single. There are two other slower train services: another from Victoria, and one from London Bridge.

By taxi: Fares from central London with a black cab are about £40–£60.

Luton

30 miles north of London. **Airport information:** t (01582) 405 100.

By bus: Greenline bus 757 (**t** 0870 608 7261) runs roughly every half-hour between Luton Airport and stop 6 in Buckingham Palace Road, Victoria, via Marble Arch. Tickets cost £7 single. The journey takes 1hr 15mins.

By train: Between 8am and 10pm, Thameslink (**t** 0845 330 6333) run frequent trains from King's Cross Thameslink Station (10mins' walk from the King's Cross Station), via Blackfriars, London Bridge and Farringdon, to Luton Airport Parkway. Tickets cost £10 single. At Luton a free shuttle bus takes you on to the airport; the journey takes 55mins.

By taxi: A black cab will cost you around £40–£60 from central London.

Stansted

Stansted is the furthest from London, about 35 miles to the northeast. **Airport information:** t 0870 000 0303.

By bus: Airbus A6 and Jetlink coaches (**t** 0870 575 7747) run every 30mins from Victoria Station, Marble Arch and Hyde Park Corner, taking 1hr 40mins. There are less frequent services all night. Tickets cost £8 single.

By train: The Stansted Express (**t** 0870 530 1530) runs every 30mins (15mins during peak times) between 5am and 11pm to and from Liverpool Street Station, in the City, taking 45mins. Tickets cost £13 single.

By taxi: A black cab from central London will cost £45–£65.

Sample Journeys

Heathrow–Luton: get to Heathrow Express from terminal 15mins; wait for train 10mins; journey 15mins; go from Paddington Station down into Tube 10mins; Tube to Farringdon 15mins; go up and buy Thameslink ticket 10mins including queueing; train and shuttle to Luton 55mins. **Total journey time** 2hrs 10mins, plus 45mins for delays and hitches, so 3hrs would be safest.

Heathrow–Stansted: get to Tube station from terminal 10mins, wait for Tube 5mins, Piccadilly Line to King's Cross 1hr 10mins, change to Circle Line and continue to Liverpool Street Tube Station 15mins, up into main line station and buy Stansted Express ticket 10mins, wait for train 20mins, train journey 45mins. **Total journey time** 2hrs 55mins, plus 45mins for delays and hitches, so 3hrs 40mins would be safest.

By Sea

There are two direct ferry services between Britain and Spain. **P&O Portsmouth** has regular ferries between Portsmouth and Bilbao, with two sailings each way, each week (Portsmouth–Bilbao, Tuesday, Saturday; Bilbao–Portsmouth, Monday, Thursday). Each trip takes about 27 hours. **Brittany Ferries** runs between Plymouth and Santander, also with two sailings a week (Plymouth–Santander, Monday, Wednesday; Santander–Plymouth, Tuesday, Thursday). The journey is a little shorter, at about 24 hours. Both companies have certain 'gaps' during the year when services are less frequent or suspended completely, mainly in January and February.

These are real, overnight ocean crossings, so the ships are larger and more comfortable than cross-Channel ferries, with a range of entertainments and amenities on board, and both companies try to give the trips a bit of a feel of a cruise rather than just a car ferry. Consequently fares – although they vary a good deal according to when you want to travel – are quite high, especially in peak seasons: a standard (over five days) return for a car and four people, cabin included, can cost around £550–£750 in summer. In early spring or autumn, on the other hand, the same journey might cost under £400, and both companies now offer a variety of off-peak short-term offers, such as £340 for a one-week trip for two people with a car in October. Both also offer off-peak 'minicruises' for foot passengers only for about £70–£100 return per person; you come back on the next sailing, and so have about a day to a day and a half in Spain. In the holiday seasons these ferries are popular with people who own second homes in Spain, and summer sailings, despite the cost, need to be booked well in advance.

Ferry Operators

Brittany Ferries, The Brittany Centre, Millbay, Plymouth PL1 3EW, **t** 08705 665 333, *www.brittany-ferries.com*.
P&O Portsmouth, Peninsular House, Wharf Rd, Portsmouth PO2 8TA, **t** 0870 242 4999, *www.poportsmouth.com*.

Another option is to drive straight down to Spain from the French Channel crossings, but this hardly qualifies as a short break. Driving on motorways with as few stops as possible, it's possible to get down to the Spanish border from the Tunnel or any of the French Channel ports in about 17 hours. Once you're at the border, Barcelona is only about another two hours away, but getting to Alicante or Andalucía will require many more hours' hard driving.

Entry Formalities

Passports and Visas

Holders of full EU, US and Canadian passports can enter Spain freely without any kind of visa for stays of up to three months. If they intend to stay longer, EU citizens are required to register with the police and obtain a *tarjeta de residente comunitario*, a resident's card. Non-EU citizens who wish to stay more than three months should apply for a special visa at a Spanish consulate before leaving home.

Customs

Duty-free allowances have been abolished within the EU. For those arriving from outside the EU, duty-free limits are 1 litre of spirits or 2 litres of fortified wine (port, sherry, brandy), plus 2 litres of wine and 200 cigarettes.

Much larger quantities – up to 10 litres of spirits, 90 litres of wine, 110 litres of beer and 800 cigarettes – bought locally, can be taken through customs provided you are travelling between EU countries, and if you can prove that they are for private consumption only.

For more information, US citizens can phone the US Customs Service, **t** (202) 354 1000, or consult *www.customs.gov*.

Getting Around

By Air

Spain has an ample domestic air network. **Iberia** has flights to every part of the country from Madrid and regional hubs in Barcelona, Seville and other cities (some routes are flown by **Air Nostrum**, a wholly owned subsidiary). Their main challengers are **Air Europa** and **Spanair**, which offer very competitive prices. If you're travelling from North America, Iberia domestic flights can be booked at the same time as transatlantic tickets; Air Europa has route sharing and ticketing arrangements with Continental and some other US carriers.

Air Europa, t (Spain) 902 401 501, *www.air-europa.com*.

Iberia/Air Nostrum, t (Spain) 902 400 500, *www.iberia. com, www.airnostrum.es*.

Spanair, t (Spain) 902 131 415, *www.spanair.com*.

By Rail

Spain's national rail corporation, **RENFE**, has had a huge amount invested in it over the last two decades, and service has improved beyond recognition. Trains, especially on long-distance routes, are modern and comfortable; punctuality is also good (and positively spectacular for anyone used to modern British standards), and RENFE's safety record is also among the best in Europe. The network still has its quirks, often stemming from features built into it when the tracks were laid years ago by different private companies. Some areas are much better served by rail than others, and in some regions (notably Andalucía) lines can follow apparently inexplicable routes, or connect up only via strange little junctions in the middle of nowhere. Where a good rail service is available, this will generally be the most attractive way of getting from main towns to smaller places.

RENFE operates several different categories of train. *Grandes Líneas* (long-distance routes), are themselves divided into several groups. Jewel in the RENFE crown are the AVE high-speed trains, which run between Madrid and Seville in 2½ hours; by about 2008 AVE lines should be extended to Barcelona and the French border, to connect with the French TGV network. For the moment, the most comfortable trains for long-distance journeys in most of Spain are *Talgos*, which are now almost as fast (at 220kph/137mph) and luxurious as the AVE. Some *Talgos* have their own 'identities', such as the *Alaris* between Madrid and Valencia. Slower, less comfortable and so

cheaper long-distance trains that stop more frequently are known by the English tag *Intercity*, and there are also two categories of sleeper (*Trenhoteles* and *Tren Estrella*).

The next big category is that of *Regionales* services, which stop at all or nearly all stations on each route, and are an essential aid for exploring the countryside. When *semidirecto* appears next to any train on timetables this means it only stops at some stations en route, so check which they are (they will nearly always be listed next to the time).

Lastly, Madrid, Barcelona, Bilbao and other cities have *Cercanías* or local rail networks serving the suburbs and surrounding towns. At main stations *Cercanías* (or in Catalan-speaking areas, *Rodalies*) ticket windows and platforms are signposted separately, with a distinctive red and white logo.

Fares are generally very reasonable – such as €37 for a second-class ticket on a fast train from Barcelona to Alicante. Fares, though, vary according to the speed and comfort-level of the train, so a *Talgo* will be significantly more expensive than an *Intercity* or *Regional* train on the same route. On most trains there are two classes, now called *Preferente* (first) and *Turista* (second). Children under four travel free, and there are reductions of 40% on all tickets for children aged 4–12 and anyone over 60. Return tickets are always cheaper than two singles, and there are other discounts for frequent travellers, groups and so on.

There are also some lines not operated by RENFE. Most important is the **FGC**, Catalan government railways, which has lines from Barcelona out to some of its suburbs and Montserrat (*see* p.64). In the Basque Country there is the **FEVE** from Bilbao to Oviedo via Santander and the **Euskotren** between Bilbao and San Sebastián, but, while picturesque, these are generally less efficient than buses as a means of getting from A to B (*see* p.98). And Barcelona, Bilbao and Madrid all have city **Metro** (underground/subway) systems, which provide the quickest and most trouble-free way of getting around each city.

RENFE information and reservations, **t** in Spain, 902 24 02 02, from outside, Spain 34 934 901 122, *www.renfe.es*.

Many tickets can be booked on-line or by phone; there are English-speaking operators.

By Bus

Just about everywhere that does not have a rail service in Spain is still connected to the outside world by bus. There are long-distance coaches (*autocares*) between most main towns, and a huge web of regional and local services (*autobuses*). There is no national bus network (or central information service), as services are operated by many different companies, most based in a particular region.

Provincial capitals and other towns act as hubs for bus routes to their surrounding areas, and most villages have a bus at least once a day, and often more frequently. In most larger towns there is a central bus station (*estación de autobuses*), but in some cities there may be more than one, or companies may operate from their own depots. In small towns and villages, buses will nearly always stop on or near to the main square. Local tourist offices are the best sources of information on the layout of bus services in any specific area.

By Car

Virtually all the day trips we propose are accessible by public transport, but if you plan to follow the touring itineraries suggested in this guide a car will be an enormous asset.

Hiring a Car

Car hire is a competitive business in Spain, which keeps costs low: basic rates are reasonable, and most companies provide a steady stream of special offers, especially for weekends, which are worth looking out for. Every company has its own pricing structure and special deals, but it's usually possible to get a small car for under €200 a week. There are branches of major rental chains (*see* p.17) throughout the country, and to get a reasonable deal with the minimum inconvenience it can be a good idea to book a car ahead with one of the majors on-line, or as part of a flight package. In Spain, though, there are also many small, locally based car-hire agencies, which are generally perfectly reliable and often cheaper than the big chains (even with pre-booking) and readier to offer bargain deals. Selected local car-hire firms are listed for each of the main destinations in this book.

Car Hire

Listed here are the main car rental chains that operate in Spain. For local companies, *see* under each chapter.

Avis, Spain, **t** 902 135 131, *www.avis.es*; UK, **t** 0870 6060 100, *www.avis.co.uk*; North America, **t** (US) 800 230 4898, **t** (Canada) 800 272 5871, *www.avis.com*.

Budget, **t** (UK) 01442 280 181, **t** (US and Canada) 800 404 8033, *www.budget.com*.

Europcar, Spain, **t** 902 405 020, *www.europcar.es*; UK, **t** 0870 607 5000, *www.europcar.co.uk*; US and Canada, **t** 877 940 6900, *www.europcar.com*.

Europe by Car, New York, **t** 800 223 1516, **t** (212) 581 3040, *www.europebycar.com*. Europe-wide US discount booking service.

Hertz, Spain, **t** 902 402 405, *www.hertz.es*; UK, **t** 08708 448 844, *www.hertz.co.uk*; US and Canada, **t** 800 654 3001, *www.hertz.com*.

National-Atesa, Spain, **t** 902 100 101, *www.atesa.es*; UK, **t** 08704 004 581, *www.nationalcar.co.uk*; US and Canada, **t** 800 227 7368, *www.nationalcar.com*. The Spanish Atesa chain is affiliated to the worldwide National car-hire network.

To hire a car in Spain you must be at least 21 years old and have had a licence for at least a year. Valid licences from any EU country, Canada or the USA are acceptable in Spain, with no need for an international driving licence. Some companies have a minimum age of 25, and some also have an upper limit of 65, 70 or 75. When hiring, check that the price quoted includes insurance, tax (*IVA*, VAT, at 16%) and unlimited mileage (*kilometraje ilimitado*). Most agencies now give unlimited mileage as standard, and any deals that do not are a waste of money. All contracts must by law include third-party insurance (*seguro obligatorio*), but check whether your agency will add in comprehensive cover, including Collision Damage Waiver (CDW or *cobertura de daños*), theft cover (*cobertura contra robos*) and personal accident insurance (*daños personales*). If not, it's worth paying extra to have them, for peace of mind. To hire a car you will also, in practice, need a credit card.

Driving in Spain

Spain's roads, like its trains, have had a great deal spent on them since the 1970s, and most are now in very good condition. Backbone of the system are *Carreteras Nacionales*, comparable to British A-roads and identified by *N* and a number. Motorways (*autopistas*, A-1, A-2, and so on) serve some parts of the country; they are toll roads, and quite expensive. Many N-roads have been upgraded to *autovías*, which are toll-free but dual carriageways of near-motorway standard, and a great help in cutting delays when you're in a hurry.

Away from the main routes, the many regional and provincial roads have also been improved lately, and while there are still a few bumpy dirt tracks about, in general even the most hair-raising twister of a mountain road now has a good surface and modern crash barriers on its brake-testing bends. Driving along these roads can be wonderful, a near-traffic-free cruise through stunning scenery.

On country roads traffic is generally quite light, but a big contrast comes whenever you approach any major town. In general, driving is simply **not worth the trouble** inside Madrid, Barcelona or any of Spain's major cities: the Metro or local buses will always get you there quicker, and even if you rely on taxis you will avoid the modern Spanish urbanite's constant dilemma, of where the hell to park. It's best to use cars only for out-of-town travelling, and, if you do go into a city, to park near a convenient train or Metro station and carry on by public transport. Car parks (quite expensive in city centres) are indicated by a blue 'P' sign.

Petrol/gas stations are plentiful around towns, less so in back-country areas. Petrol in Spain is currently a little cheaper than in Britain. The same EU-recognized fuel grades are on sale: unleaded is *sin plomo* (or *sense plom* in Catalan), regular, lead-replacement petrol is *super*, and diesel is *gas-oil*.

Spain's frequently abused official **speed limits** are 120kph (75 mph) on *autopistas* and *autovías*, 100 or 90kph (62 or 56 mph) on most N and country roads, and 50kph (30 mph), or sometimes less, in towns. Spain has a bad road safety record, and locals often seem to drive pretty carelessly; caution is advisable, especially on blind corners on country roads. In response to local habits a far more severe set of traffic laws was introduced in 2002. Police checks on drivers are frequent, and note that the legal alcohol limit for drivers is now lower than in Britain. Fines can be levied on the spot. It is illegal to use a mobile phone while driving, and compulsory to wear front and rear seatbelts at all times, while children under 12 cannot travel in the front of a car except in a child's car seat. It is also obligatory to have a warning triangle, basic spares (tyre, fanbelt, headlamp bulbs), and to have your insurance documentation with you at all times.

Details of current traffic laws and other information (including *autopista* tolls) can be found on Spain's highways agency website, *www.dgt.es* (partly in English).

Practical A–Z

Children

Spaniards love children, and will welcome yours almost everywhere. Baby foods and so on are widely available, but don't expect to find babysitters except at really smart hotels; Spaniards always take their children with them, even if they're up till 4am. Nor have there traditionally been many special amusements for kids – Spaniards never thought of their children as separate little creatures who ought to be amused – but these have multiplied with Spain's new prosperity. In particular, around many cities there are **waterparks**, where kids (and elders) can cool off on spectacular slides each summer, and on the Mediterranean coast there are two of Europe's largest theme parks, **Universal Mediterrània** near Tarragona and **Terra Mítica** outside Benidorm (*see* pp.70 and 181). Ask at tourist offices for lists of kid-friendly attractions.

Climate and When to Go

Spain is hot and sunny in summer, brisk and sunny in winter, with little variation among the regions except in the matter of rainfall. The northern coast, especially Euskadi and Galicia, fairly drowns all year, which is why it's so green. Catalonia has a more moderate rainfall, but nearly everywhere else rain is pretty scarce, and every locality brags in its brochures about so many 'hours of guaranteed sunshine' each year. Statistically, the champion for the best holiday climate is Alicante, with Europe's mildest winter temperatures and hardly any rain, but most of the southern and eastern coasts are nearly as good.

Spring and autumn are by far the best times to visit; the winter can be pleasant, although it's damp and chill in the north, and temperatures can fall very low across Castile and Aragón. Teruel and Soria provinces traditionally have the worst winter climate.

Average Maximum Temperatures in °C

	Jan	April	July	Oct
Alicante	21	31	34	29
Barcelona	7	25	33	24
Madrid	7	27	39	29
San Sebastián	15	27	34	24
Seville	20	31	35	31

Disabled Travellers

Facilities for disabled travellers are limited within Spain and public transport is not particularly wheelchair-friendly, although most cities now have accessible buses and RENFE usually provides wheelchairs at main city stations. Spanish Tourist Offices (*see* p.26) provide a factsheet and general information on accessible accommodation. Alternatively, contact one of the organizations listed below.

Specialist Organizations in the UK

Holiday Care Service, 2 Old Bank Chambers, Station Rd, Horley, Surrey RH6 9HW, **t** (01293) 774 535, *www.holidaycare.org.uk*. For travel information and details of accessible accommodation and care holidays.

RADAR, 250 City Rd, London EC1V 8AF, **t** (020) 7259 3222, *www.radar.org.uk*. Has a wide range of travel information.

Royal National Institute for the Blind, 224 Great Portland St, London W15 5TB, **t** (020) 7388 1266, *www.rnib.org.uk*. Its mobility unit offers a 'Plane Easy' audio-cassette which advises blind people on travelling by plane.

Specialist Organizations in the USA

American Foundation for the Blind, 11 Penn Plaza, Suite 300, New York, NY 10001, **t** 800 232 5463, *www.afm.org*. The best source of information for visually impaired travellers.

Mobility International USA, PO Box 10767, Eugene, OR 97440, **t** (541) 343 1284, **f** (541) 343 6812, *www.miusa.org*. Information on volunteer services for the disabled.

SATH, 347 5th Avenue, Suite 610, New York, NY 10016, **t** (212) 447 7284, **f** (212) 725 8253, *www.sath.org*. Travel and access information, and links to other web resources.

Electricity

Current is 220v, the same as most of Europe. Plugs are the standard European, two-pin style, and British travellers will need adapters, while North Americans with any 110v appliances will also need a current transformer. A declining few corners of Spain still have wiring for an older 125v system, and if you stay in any old buildings it's worth checking before you plug in any 220–240v equipment.

Embassies and Consulates

Australia: Pza Descubridor Diego Ordaz 3, Madrid, **t** 914 419 300.
Canada: C/Núñez de Balboa 35, Madrid, **t** 914 233 250.
Ireland: Paseo de la Castellana 46, Madrid, **t** 915 763 500.
New Zealand: Pza de la Lealtad 2, Madrid, **t** 915 230 226.
UK: (Embassy) C/Fernando el Santo 16, Madrid, **t** 913 190 200, *www.ukinspain.com*; (Consulate-General) C/Marqués de la Ensenada 16, Madrid, **t** 913 085 201.
USA: C/Serrano 75, Madrid, **t** 915 872 200, *www.embusa.es*.

Festivals

Local and regional fiestas – many of which were revived and 'modified' after years of drab regimentation in the Franco era – are celebrated with gusto, and if you can arrange your trip to include one or two you'll be guaranteed an unforgettable holiday. Besides those listed on p.22–3, there are thousands of others; tourist offices provide full lists and dates.

Big holidays that are celebrated in most of Spain are Holy Week (*Semana Santa*) at Easter; 15 August (the Feast of the Assumption), and 25 July, feast day of Spain's patron, Santiago. Fiestas, though, are very local, and some of the most impressive are found in some places and not others. Madrid's main event is San Isidro, in May, while St John (*Sant Joan*, 23–4 June) is one of the biggest nights of the year in Catalonia and Menorca, but is ignored in large parts of the country. Festival dates tend to be fluid, flowing towards the nearest weekend; if the actual calendar date falls on a Thursday or a Tuesday, Spaniards 'bridge' the fiesta with the weekend to create a four-day whoopee.

The most extravagant, folkloric fiestas tend to be in Andalucía and the south. Music, dancing, food, wine and fireworks are all necessary ingredients of a proper fiesta, while bigger ones often include bullfights, funfairs and competitions. City fiestas like San Isidro include all kinds of cultural events, free concerts and so on as well as more trad folklore. *See* the 'Calendar of Events' overleaf for some of Spain's most spectacular festivities.

Food and Drink

See also **Food and Drink** chapter, pp.29–38.

Spaniards are notoriously late diners; traditionally, the way to eat has been to start the day just with a coffee and a roll, then go for a huge lunch at around 2pm, followed by a few tapas at a bar after work at 8pm to hold you over until dinner at 9 or 10pm. Hours get later the further south you go, and as temperatures rise in summer. In July, young *Madrileños* might think of going for a bite at midnight or 1am. In cities, at least on weekdays, hours are now often more flexible, and on the coasts restaurants tend to open earlier to accommodate foreigners (some as early as 5pm) but in most of the country it's best just to do as the Spaniards do, and enjoy it. A few rounds of tapas – available all day – will fill in the gaps.

Almost every restaurant offers a *menú del día* or *menú turístico*, which includes two or three courses, bread and drink for a set price. This is always the best-value way to eat, and much cheaper than ordering straight from the *carta*, the main menu. Many restaurants, though, only offer their bargain set *menús* for lunch, not in the evenings, so have your main meal at midday if you want to save money.

Tipping: Unless it's stated on the bill (*la cuenta*), service is not usually included in the total. Spaniards are modest tippers, and while 10% is appreciated there's no set rule.

Price categories quoted in the 'Eating Out' sections throughout this book and shown below are based on set menus or a three-course meal with drinks, per person. However, the price categories for Madrid and Barcelona differ slightly from those used in the rest of the guide, because the range of prices in these cities, as in any large city, tends to be more extreme than elsewhere in Spain.

Restaurant Price Categories

In Madrid and Barcelona
expensive   over €30
moderate   €15–30
inexpensive   up to €15

Elsewhere in Spain
expensive   over €30
moderate   €18–30
inexpensive   up to €18

Calendar of Events

January
First week Granada: commemoration of the city's capture by the Catholic kings.
6 (Epiphany) parades throughout Spain to welcome the *Reyes Magos* (Three Wise Men).

February
Jan–Feb *Carnaval* is celebrated throughout Spain (dates, as for Easter, change each year). Cádiz has perhaps the best in the country, and the oldest: parades, masquerades, music and fireworks in abundance. Modern, urban parties feature in Madrid and Barcelona, and at Solsona, near Lleída, *Carnaval* features the explosive 'marriage of the mad giant'.
First weekend Bocairente, near Valencia: mock battles between Moors and Christians.
Lent During Lent there are Passion Play performances at Ulldecona (Tarragona), Cervera and Esparraguera (Barcelona).

March
15–19 Valencia's *Las Fallas*: one of Spain's great fiestas, with the gaudiest bonfires and the best fireworks west of China.
Semana Santa (Easter Week) The most important celebrations are in Seville, with over 100 processions, broken by the singing of *saetas* (weird laments). Murcia has the most charming *pasos*.

April
All month Seville's *Feria de Abril*: originally a horse-fair, now the greatest festival of Andalucía. Costumed parades, lots of flamenco, bullfights, eating and drinking.

23 Barcelona and Catalonia: St Jordi's day, when people exchange books and roses. Around this time Alcoi (València) has the best of the 'battles' between Moors and Christians with pageantry and fireworks.

May
First week Jerez de la Frontera has a *feria* much like the April Fair in Seville. Almeria: *Peña de Taranto* Cultural Week. One of the most prestigious flamenco festivals.
Second week Córdoba: every third year the *Concurso Nacional de Arte Flamenco* takes place on the seventh Sun after *Pentecost*. El Rocío (Huelva): the biggest *romería*, or horseback pilgrimage, in Spain.
15 *San Isidro*, Patron Saint of Madrid. For a week or so around the day the city puts on a constant programme of entertainment, street events and concerts. It also hosts one of the most important bullfighting festivals.
End May *Corpus Cristi*: four days of festivities, especially in Toledo, Sitges (where streets are covered with flower carpets), Berga (Barcelona) and Zahara de la Sierra (Cádiz).

June
Mid-month Granada: *Festival Internacional de Música y Danza* attracts famous names in classical music, jazz and ballet, with a flamenco festival in odd-numbered years.
21–4 Alicante celebrates St John's day (*San Juanes*) with a huge *Fallas* bonfire similar to València's. More celebrations for St John are held throughout Catalonia, and in Segovia.
End of month Hita, near Guadalajara: Festival of Medieval Theatre; food, dance, bullfights and falconry, all set to flutes and bagpipes.

Health and Insurance

Ambulance: t 112
Fire Brigade: t 080
Police: t 091

All EU citizens are entitled to free basic medical care through the Spanish national health service, provided they have an E111 form, available in the UK from health centres and main post offices. In a medical emergency, the best place to go is the *Urgencias* department of the nearest main hospital; in smaller towns there will usually be a health centre (called an *ambulatorio, centro de salud* or *casa de socorro*).

The E111 will not cover you for dental care, nor will it allow you to choose your doctor, and many medicines will still be charged for, at least in part. Hence, for short-term trips most visitors find it more convenient to take out private travel insurance, and use private clinics for any non-emergency medical needs. Similarly, non-EU nationals should have with them a travel insurance policy with full health cover, with which they can use private clinics or the state system on a paying basis. Consulates and sometimes local tourist offices have lists of English-speaking doctors and clinics in each area.

July

First 2 weeks Córdoba: International Guitar Festival; classical, flamenco and Latino.

6–7 Nava, Asturias: cider festival.

6–14 Pamplona: the famous running of the bulls and party for San Fermín.

Second week València, *Feria*: lots of entertainment and the Valencian speciality, fireworks. Segovia has a chamber music festival.

Mid-July–mid-Aug Cadaqués (Girona): International Music and Art Festival.

25 Santiago: celebrations throughout Spain.

Last week San Sebastián: International Jazz Festival, the biggest in Spain.

August

All month Santander: International Music Festival.

3–9 Estella (Navarra): the only *encierro* where women run with the bulls.

4–9 Vitoria: giants, music, bonfires and more for the Virgen Blanca.

5 Trevélez (Granada): a midnight pilgrimage up mainland Spain's highest mountain.

First week Torrevieja (Alicante): Habaneras International Music Festival.

11–18 San Sebastián: Fireworks contest.

15–16 Assumption of the Virgin and San Roque festivities at Amer (Girona): with Sardana dancing. Llanes (Asturias): bagpipes and ancient dances. Bilbao: Basque sports and races. Vejar (Cádiz): with flamenco.

Mid-month Málaga: *feria*, with concerts, bullfights, dancing and singing in the old town.

Third week La Unión (Murcia): festival of *Cante de Las Minas*, flamenco competition, specializing in miners' songs.

Last Sunday Ontinyent (València): four-day Christian and Moor battles.

Last week Sanlúcar de Barrameda (Cádiz): exaltation of the Río Guadalquivir and major flamenco events.

31 Loiola (Euskadi): St Ignatius de Loiola Day.

September

8 Virgin's birthday, with celebrations in many places. Ronda: 18th-century-style bullfight in its historic ring. Ceremonies at Montserrat.

12 Murcia: International Mediterranean Music Festival.

19–28 San Sebastián: Film Festival.

24 Barcelona: music, human towers, fire-breathing dragons, and tons of other entertainments for its patroness, the Virgin of *la Mercè*.

October–November

31 Oct–1 Nov *Todos Santos*, All Saint's Day (1 Nov), is the day to remember the dead, and the night before it's traditional to eat special cakes in Catalonia and many other regions.

December

21 Santo Tomás fair, with processions, in San Sebastián, Bilbao, Azpeitia.

Last week *Olentzero* processions in many Basque villages.

Christmas For the whole season (roughly all Dec and up to Three Kings, 6 Jan) most cities host lovely Christmas fairs in main squares, where you can buy handmade figures for traditional cribs, and all sorts of other gifts. In most of Spain the big family feast-time is late on Christmas Eve, not on the 25th.

Chemists/pharmacies (*farmacias*) are plentiful, usually indicated by a big green cross. Pharmacists are highly skilled and can advise on minor complaints. Local papers list *farmacias* open outside normal hours. Tap water is safe to drink, but in most places bottled water tastes better.

It is, in any case, always advisable to have **travel insurance**, which apart from covering you for medical needs will cover your bags, money and such things as cancelled flights as well. If you need to use your insurance, be sure to save all doctors' receipts and police documents (if you are reporting a theft).

Internet

Checking your email is easy and cheap. Every city of any size has a clutch of Internet cafés or Net centres, while big cities and heavily visited towns are likely to be infested with *cibers*, as the Spanish call Net cafés. Even the most unlikely country towns sometimes have Internet facilities – if you can get past the local kids locked in chatrooms or indulging their aggression on digital baddies. The average price in most of the country is €1–2 per hour, although getting online can be more expensive in the cities.

Maps

Local tourist offices hand out detailed maps of each town, and the national tourist office's *Mapa de Comunicaciones* is an excellent general map. Good local maps and walking maps for hikers and mountaineers can be obtained in Spain from the following:

Desnivel, Pza Matute 6, Madrid, **t** 914 299 740, *www.libreriadesnivel.com*.

Instituto Geográfico Nacional, C/General Ibáñez de Ibero 3, Madrid, **t** 915 333 121.

Llibreria Quera, Petritxol 2, Barcelona, **t** 933 180 743.

Specialist shops in the UK and USA include:

UK: Stanford's, 12 Long Acre, London WC2, **t** (020) 7836 1321, *www.stanfords.co.uk*.

USA: The Complete Traveler, 199 Madison Ave, New York, NY 10022, **t** (212) 685 9007.

Money

Spain is one of the 12 European countries that since the beginning of 2002 have had the **euro** as their sole, common currency. The standard symbol for the euro is €, and each one is divided into 100 cents (also called *céntimos* in Spain). There are notes for 5, 10, 20, 50, 100, 200 and 500 euros, and coins for 1, 2, 5, 10, 20 and 50 cents and 1 and 2 euros. All the notes are entirely the same throughout the Eurozone, but coins have a common design on one side and another specific to each country on the other (Spain's have the face of King Juan Carlos). Coins and notes, though, can all be used equally in any of the 12 countries. While currency values can of course go up and down, lately the value of the euro has been fairly steady, with a slight tendency to rise; €1 is usually worth roughly **US$1** or **UK 65p**, and **UK £1** is worth around **€1.55–€1.60**.

The currency changeover has gone ahead pretty smoothly, barring a certain tendency to round up prices, but many Spaniards show a perverse determination to continue working out prices, especially larger ones, in the now non-existent *peseta*, and go back and forth between the two. If you ever need to convert, €1 is (or was) equivalent to 166.386 *pesetas*.

Spain's city centres seem to have a bank or savings bank (*caja de ahorros*, or *caixa d'estalvis* in Catalan-speaking areas) on every corner, and both kinds exchange money. Differences in rates from bank to bank are not usually enough to justify shopping around. Private exchange offices (*cambios*) tend to charge hefty commissions. There are 24-hour bank exchange counters at airports and the main train stations in Barcelona and Madrid.

Traveller's cheques are readily accepted by banks if they are from one of the major issuing companies. **Credit cards** are widely accepted, and all but essential for hiring a car. ATM cash machines are easy to find too. Debit cards are also useful ways of obtaining money, but check with your bank before leaving to ensure your card can be used in Spain. Using cards and hole-in-the-wall machines is often one of the most economical ways of getting money, as you miss local bank commissions (although you will still be charged by your card company back home), but it's best not to rely on them as your sole source of cash, in case you ever have a problem with your card.

Opening Hours

Banks: Most are open Mon–Thurs 8.30–4.30, Fri 8.30–2 and Sat (sometimes) 8.30–1.

Churches: Many smaller ones are kept locked. If you're determined to see one, it will never be hard to find the *sacristán* or caretaker. Usually they live close by, and are glad to show you around for a tip.

Shops: Most smaller shops open roughly from 9–2, close for a long lunch and then reopen from 4/5–8/9pm, Mon–Sat, and are closed on Sundays. Bigger stores, shopping malls and a growing number of city shops open without a break 10am–9pm Mon–Sat, and on an ever-increasing number of Sundays. In the south, more shops keep to the traditional *siesta*, and throughout the country shops are likely to open later in the afternoon in summer, or may not reopen at all after lunch, especially on Saturdays. Markets, especially smaller ones, get going early, by 8am, and are often finished by 2pm.

Museums and **historical sites**: These tend to follow shop opening times, but hours are shorter in winter months; nearly all close on Mondays. Seldom-visited ones have a raffish disregard for their official hours. Don't be discouraged: bang on doors and ask around.

Police Business

Crime is not really a huge problem in Spain and Spaniards and foreign visitors perhaps talk about it more than is warranted. Bag-snatching, pickpocketing and robbing parked cars are the specialities. Street crime has been getting more common and cities like Madrid, Barcelona, Málaga or Seville are places to be careful, although, except for some parts of the largest cities, walking around at night is not a problem – primarily because everybody does it. Crime is also spreading in tourist areas like the Costa del Sol, but even there by international standards the dangers are pretty low.

Wherever you are, there are some basics to follow to minimize the threat of street crime:

• Avoid dark, empty streets in the old quarters of cities at night.

• If you sit at a café table, above all outdoors, **never** leave your bag where you cannot see it, on the ground or on the back of the chair. Place it on the table, or on your lap.

• Keep shoulder bags closed and at the front, not on your back; keep a hand on the bag.

• Be aware, and wary, of the famous Spanish 'street scams' such as people who try to distract you (by starting a conversation, shaking your hand, or pointing to a supposed stain on your back) while their 'associate' moves in to steal your bag.

The several species of **police** have differing areas of authority. The *Policía Nacional*, in dark blue and white uniforms (or blue overalls, in riot gear), is the main force responsible for dealing with crime in most areas; if you are robbed, the nearest *Policía* station (*Comisaría*) is usually the best place to go. Every city and town also has its own *Policía Municipal* (or *Guardia Urbana*), usually in dark and pale blue, who also take on crime control in some cities, although their main responsibility is as urban traffic cops. The *Guardia Civil*, in green (but now usually minus their sinister black patent-leather tricorn hats) are usually only seen in rural areas, and are most conspicuous as a highway patrol. Two regions have their own forces. In Catalonia, the *Mossos d'Esquadra* have taken over many *Guardia Civil* roles in rural and highway policing. In the Basque Country, the regional government's police, the *Ertzaintza*, recognizable by their red berets, have more wide-ranging responsibilities.

Post Offices and Faxes

Every city, regardless of size, seems to have one main **post office** (*correos*) and a few, hard-to-find smaller ones. Unless you have packages to post, though, you may not need ever to visit them. Tobacco shops (*estancos*, recognizable by the *Tabacos* sign) sell **stamps** (*sellos*) and their staff usually know the correct postage for whatever you're sending.

Postboxes are bright yellow, with two horizontal red stripes around them; there are also a few red boxes for urgent mail, which have more frequent collections. Stationery shops are the best places from which to send **faxes**.

Telephones

Despite the huge popularity of cellphones across the nation Spain still has plenty of public phones, operated by its main phone company, *Telefónica*. Most now only work with phonecards, sold in *estancos* and post offices in denominations of €6 and €12. You can make long-distance and international calls from any booth, but this may eat up your card pretty quickly. In addition, there are phone company offices and private phone centres in cities (often at main train stations) where you call from metered booths, and pay when you're finished. They are indispensable for making long international calls and above all reversed charge or collect calls (*cobro revertido*).

Most UK **mobile phones** will work in Spain provided they have a roaming facility; check with your phone company before travelling. North American cellphones operate on a different signal band, and so will not work in Spain unless they have a triband facility.

Overseas calls from Spain are expensive: calls to the UK cost about €1–2 a minute, to the USA substantially more. Cheap rate for international calls is Mon–Fri 10pm–8am and all day weekends and public holidays. Use hotel phones as little as possible, as most hotels impose surcharges of around 100%.

For international calls from Spain, dial 00 and then the country code (44 for the UK, 353 for the Irish Republic, 1 for the US and Canada). For calls to Spain, dial 00 followed by the country code (34) and the number.

All conventional **phone numbers** in Spain now have nine digits, as since 1998 the former area codes (91 for Madrid, 93 Barcelona, and so on) have been incorporated into the number and must be dialled even for local calls. Numbers given in this guide are listed as they must be dialled. Telephone numbers in Spain beginning 900 are free, but those beginning with 901, 902 and 903 carry higher rates. **National directory enquiries: t** 1003. **International directory enquiries: t** 025.

Toilets

Outside bus and train stations, public facilities are quite rare. On the other hand, every bar on every corner has a toilet; don't feel uncomfortable using it without purchasing something. Ask for *los servicios*.

Tourist Information

All cities and many towns have tourist offices, run by national or, more often, regional and municipal authorities, and most have at least some staff who speak English. As well as providing brochures on all sorts of local activities they are an invaluable source of town maps, and the best organized (as in Barcelona) also have accommodation booking services. Most offices are open Monday to Friday, 9.30–1.30 and 4–7, and many are also open on Saturday mornings, and sometimes Sundays.

> **Spanish National Tourist Offices**
> **Canada:** 102 Bloor Street West, 34th Floor, Toronto, Ontario M4W 3E2, **t** (416) 961 3131, **f** (416) 961 1992, *www.tourspain. toronto.on.ca*.
> **UK/Ireland:** 22–3 Manchester Square, London W1U 3PX, **t** (020) 7486 8077, **f** (020) 7486 8034; 24hr brochure request **t** 09063 640 630, *www.tourspain.es*.
> **USA:** Water Tower Place, Suite 915, East 845, North Michigan Avenue, Chicago, IL 60611, **t** (312) 642 1992, **f** (312) 642 9817; 8383 Wilshire Blvd, Suite 960, Beverly Hills, CA 90211, **t** (323) 658 7188, **f** (323) 658 1061; 666 Fifth Avenue, New York, NY 10103, **t** (212) 265 8822, **f** (212) 265 8864, *www.okspain.org*.

Where to Stay

Hotels in Spain are no longer the bargains they once were, especially in places most in demand (Barcelona stands out). However, overall rates are still pretty reasonable – above all by comparison with Britain – and, while some city hotels can seem frankly overpriced, there are also still great bargains to be found.

The **prices** given in this guide are for double rooms with bath (unless stated otherwise) in high season, but **do not include VAT** (IVA), charged at 7% on all accommodation. Prices for single rooms will average about 60% of a double, while triples or an extra bed cost around 35% more. Prices listed in 'Where to Stay' sections of the guide have been divided into five categories (*see* box right). Those for Madrid and Barcelona vary a little from those for other areas, because the range of prices found in these cities, as in any large city, tends to be more extreme than elsewhere. In the major resort areas – such as La Manga in Murcia, or the big Costa del Sol towns – many big hotels expect to do their business through tour operators in Britain, Germany and so on rather than deal with guests directly. Hence you often find that you get a far better rate if you book these hotels as part of a package rather than by contacting the hotel yourself. However, this is no longer always the case, as even big resort hotels, if they have room, are now happy to take clients wherever they find them, so it's often worth checking, especially off-season.

All accommodation in Spain is now regulated by the various regional authorities, although most follow the same system. Perhaps surprisingly, most of the many traditional names for accommodation in Spain (*fondas*, *pensiones* and more) no longer mean anything, officially, even though many individual establishments still use them, for old times' sake. The only categories that are now officially recognized are *hoteles* and *hostales*: a *hotel*, star-rated one to five, must have ensuite bathrooms in every room; a *hostal*, star-rated from one to three, need not, although many do have several rooms with bathrooms.

Paradores

This much-celebrated, nationwide chain of state-owned, classy hotels was inaugurated in the 1920s, as part of a plan to develop tourism and preserve historic buildings at the same time. Old palaces, castles and monasteries were restored for the purpose, furnished with antiques and provided with fine restaurants featuring local specialities.

Not all *paradores* are historical landmarks; in resort areas, they are often cleanly designed modern buildings, usually in a great location with a pool and sports facilities. As their popularity has increased, so have prices, but the best *paradores* offer a really memorable experience, and so still count as a bargain. Rates range from about €70 (out of season) in remote provincial towns to €200 and upwards (high season) for the most popular. Many offer out-of-season or promotional weekend rates.

To book a *parador* in advance, contact:
Spain: Central Reservations, C/Requena 3, 28013 Madrid, **t** 915 166 666, *www.parador.es*.

You will get better rates booking *paradores* direct rather than through agents abroad.
UK: Keytel International, 402 Edgware Road, London W2 1ED, **t** (020) 7616 0300.
USA: Marketing Ahead, 433 Fifth Avenue, New York, NY 10016, **t** (212) 686 9213.

Hoteles

Hoteles (H) are rated from one to five stars, according to the services they offer, which is not always the same as their level of comfort

---

Accommodation Price Ranges
Prices are for a double room with bathroom.

In Madrid and Barcelona
luxury   over €180
expensive   €100–180
moderate   €40–100
inexpensive   €20–40
cheap   under €20

Elsewhere in Spain
luxury   over €132
expensive   €78–132
moderate   €48–78
inexpensive   €30–48
cheap   under €30

---

or attractiveness – many business hotels, for example, offer loads of services and so get a high star rating, but are cold, charmless places. *Hotel-Residencias* (HR) are the same as hotels, but without a restaurant. Many hotels offer discounts off-season – and it's always worth enquiring about special offers, particularly for city hotels at weekends – but conversely higher rates will apply during important festivals. These are supposedly regulated, but in practice hotels often charge whatever they can get. If you want to attend a big event, book as far in advance as possible.

Hostales and Others

Hostales (HS) are usually more modest than hotels, often just a floor in an apartment block; a three-star *hostal* is roughly equivalent to a one-star hotel. Some still have the blue plaques next to their doors indicating their status in the old and incomprehensible traditional classification system, like *F* for *fonda*, *CH* for *Casa de Huespedes* and so on. These names may now be officially defunct, but in general anywhere that has ever been an *F*, *P* or *CH* will be more basic than an *HS*. Most *hostales* do not offer any meals except maybe breakfast, and often not even that. On the other hand, there are many *hostales* that are bright and comfortable, with showers ensuite or good shared bathrooms.

The really basic Spanish cheap hotel, crammed into one floor of a 19th-century apartment block, is now an increasingly scarce bird in most areas. This rise in comfort levels, though, means that it's also much harder to find real rock-bottom prices than it once was. In country towns you might still be able to find signs advertising *camas* or *habitaciones* on private houses, indicating rooms available that are often spotlessly clean, but at very low rates. In cities, anyone looking for a cheap room is advised to look right in the centre, not around bus and train stations, where cheap hotels are most likely to be dingy and noisy.

Camping

Campsites are rated with from one to three stars, depending on facilities, and in addition to the ones listed in the official government handbook there are always others, rather primitive, that are unlisted. On the whole, camping is a good deal in Spain, and facilities in most first-class sites include shops, restaurants, bars, laundries, hot showers, first aid, swimming pools and phones. If you just want to pitch your tent or sleep out in some quiet field, ask around in bars or at likely farms. Camping is forbidden in many forest areas because of fears of fire, and on beaches. If you're doing any hiking, bring a sleeping bag and stay in the free *refugios* by the main trails.

An official handbook of all sites in Spain, *Guía de Campings*, can be found in most travel bookshops and at Spanish Tourist Offices.

Self-Catering Accommodation

This is an increasingly popular way of holidaying in Spain. Write to provincial tourist offices for the area you're interested in; most will send full listings, often with photos. Some firms that arrange self-catering holidays are listed in the box right.

Self-Catering Organizations

In the UK

Casas Cantabricas, 31 Arbury Road, Cambridge, CB4 2JB, **t** (01223) 328 721, **f** 322 711.

Individual Travellers, Bignor, nr Pulborough, West Sussex, RH20 1QD, **t** (01798) 869 461, **f** 869 381. Village and rural accommodation.

International Chapters, 47–51 St John's Wood High St, London NW8 7NJ, **t** (020) 7722 0722, **f** (020) 7722 9140, *www.villa-rentals.com*. A wide range of high-quality farmhouses, châteaux and villas.

Magic of Spain, 227 Shepherd's Bush Road, London W6 7AS, **t** (020) 8741 4440. Apartments and hotels along the coast.

Travellers' Way, Hewell Lane, Tardebigge, Bromsgrove, Worcs B60 1LP, **t** (01527) 836 791, **f** 836 159. Self-catering and hotels along the coast, in mountain villages and in cities.

In the USA

EC Tours, 10153 1/2 Riverside, Toluca Lake, CA 91602, **t** (800) 388 0877. Pilgrimages and city accommodation.

Ibero Travel, 6924 Loubet Street, Forest Hills, NY 11375, **t** (718) 263 0200. Apartments and fly-drive offers.

Women Travellers

On the whole, the horror stories of sexual harassment in Spain are a thing of the past, unless you dress provocatively and hang out by the bus station after dark. It often seems that most Spanish women sunbathe topless these days at *costa* resorts, but be discreet elsewhere. Apart from on the coast, it tends to be older men who comment on your appearance. Whether you can understand them or not, they are best ignored.

Food and Drink

Read an old guidebook to Spain, and when the author gets around to the local cooking, expressions like 'eggs in a sea of rancid oil' and 'mysterious pork parts' pop up with alarming frequency. One traveller in the 18th century fell ill from a local concoction and was given a purge 'known on the comic stage as angelic water. On top of that followed four hundred catholic pills, and a few days later...they gave me *escordero* water, whose efficacy or devilry is of such double effect that the doctors call it ambidexter. From this I suffered agony.'

You will fare better; in fact, the chances are you'll eat some of the tastiest food you've ever had, often at half the price you would have paid for it at home.

Restaurant Generalities

Learning to Eat the Spanish Way

Going to Spain, you may have to learn to eat all over again; dining is a much more complex affair here than in many countries. It may seem as if they eat at absurd hours, but the essential fact to learn is that Spaniards like to eat *all day long*; this scheme spreads the gratification evenly through the day, and facilitates digestion, which in Spain can be problematic. Give it some consideration. Start out with a big coffee, a *doble in vaso* and a pastry (mostly French clones, with extra sugar) or find a progressive-looking **bar** where you might find a more fitting breakfast: a glass of wine or brandy, and a salami sandwich or *pincho*, or maybe a glazed American doughnut. These bars will be around all day, their piles of treats under the glass cases on the bar growing by the hour, an eternal alternative to a heavy sit-down dinner. Ask around for the one that does seafood *tapas*. As if the bars weren't enough, there are **pastelerías** serving all sorts of savoury pastries in the towns, **merenderos** (snack stands) in the countryside, and **ice cream** everywhere. For a mid-morning, mid-afternoon or just-before-dawn energizer, there are sweet 'n' greasy *churros*, sticks of deep-fried, sweet batter, sold in bars and *churrerías* and dipped in cups of thick, rich chocolate – for most non-Spaniards a once-in-a-lifetime gut-gurgling experience.

Spanish cooking as a whole still tends to come a bit on the heavy side, but at the upmarket end of the scale you'll find plenty of modern **restaurants** creating innovative dishes. There are, however, still thousands of old-fashioned restaurants around – and many of the sort that travellers have been complaining about for centuries. Spain has its share of poor restaurants, and you will need luck as well as judgement, but the worst offenders are often those with the little flags and 10-language menus found in very touristy areas, and common sense will warn you off these. If you dine where the locals do, you'll be assured of a good deal, if not necessarily a special meal.

One step down from a restaurant are **comedores** (literally, dining-rooms), often tacked on to the backs of bars, where the food and décor are usually drab but cheap, and **cafeterías**, usually those places that feature photographs of their offerings of *platos combinados* (mixed, one-course platters of chops, salad, chips and so on) to eliminate any ordering problems. **Asadores** specialize in roast meat or fish;

marisquerías serve only fish and shellfish – you'll usually see the sign for '*pescados y mariscos*' on the awning. In country areas keep an eye out for **ventas**, usually modest, family-run establishments offering excellent set *menús del día* for working people. Try and visit one on a Sunday lunchtime, when Spanish families go out and make merry.

There are also many Chinese restaurants in Spain, which can be fairly good and inexpensive (though all pretty much the same), and American fast-food outlets in the big cities and resort areas; while Italian restaurants are 98 per cent dismal in Spain, you can get a good pizza in many places. Don't neglect the rapidly disappearing shacks on the beach; they often serve up roast sardines that are out of this world. Vegetarians are catered for in the cities, which always manage to come up with one or two veggie restaurants, and usually rather good ones at that. In the countryside and away from the main resorts, proper vegetarians and vegans will find it hard going, though *tapas* make life easier than it would be in some other southern European countries. Fish-eaters will manage just about everywhere.

Throughout the guide, restaurants in the 'Eating Out' sections are grouped together according to how expensive they are. For a guide to these price categories and more practical advice on eating out, *see* **Practical A–Z**, 'Food and Drink', p.21.

Tapas Bars

If you are travelling on a budget, you may want to eat one of your daily meals at a **tapas bar**. *Tapas* means 'lids'; they started out simply as little saucers of goodies served on top of a drink to keep the dust off, and have evolved over the years to play a major role in the world's greatest snack culture. Bars that specialize in them have platter after platter of delectable titbits, from shellfish to slices of omelette, mushrooms baked in garlic, or vegetables in vinaigrette or stews. All you have to do is pick out what looks best and order a *pincho* or *tapa* (an hors-d'œuvre) or a *ración* (a big helping) if it looks really good. It's hard to generalize about prices, but take on board that *tapas*-sampling is not necessarily an economical way of eating: all those little dishes, with drinks, soon mount up, and if you let your ordering run on a set of *tapas* in a bar can easily cost more than a full meal in a restaurant. You can always save money in bars by standing up; sit at that charming table on the terrace and prices can jump considerably. Another advantage of *tapas* is that they're available at what most Britons or Americans might consider normal dining hours.

Regional Specialities

The massive influx of tourists has had its effect on Spanish kitchens, but so has Spaniards' own increased prosperity and, perhaps most significantly, the new federalism. Each region, each town even, has come to feel a new interest and pride in the things that set it apart, and food is definitely one of them. The best restaurants are nearly always those that specialize in regional cuisine, and no regions pride themselves on their own cooking as much as the Basque Country, Catalonia or Galicia – and with good reason (*see* 'The Three Kings', overleaf).

Along the coast, **seafood** is undoubtedly the star of the show; and in any coastal town or village, you'll find the best seafood restaurants dotted around the harbour. The fancier ones will post set menus, while at the rest you'll find only a chalkboard with prices listed for a plate of grilled fish or whatever else came in that day. On the whole, Spaniards try to keep their seafood simple: **Galicians** like to cook fish with potatoes and garlic; **Basques** do it with simple garlic and parsley sauces; in **Asturias** it's hake in *sidra* (the ubiquitous local cider) or *fabada*, an enchanting mess of pork and beans. Inland, though you'll still find plenty of seafood, the cuisine would seem to come from an entirely different world. In **Castile**, it's almost medieval, and here tureen-sized bowls of soup and roast suckling pig (*cochinillo asado*), lamb or game have pride of place. Over to the east, you can order one of the famous *paellas* or a dozen other rice dishes in **Valencia**, the land of rice, while down in **Andalucía**, several

The Three Kings

Basque Cuisine

By popular acclaim, the champion cooks of Spain are the Basques who, coincidentally, are also the most legendary eaters. Like the Greeks, the well-travelled Basques take their culinary skill with them everywhere. Marseille may have its bouillabaisse, but the Basques stoutly maintain that their version, called *ttoro* (pronounced *tioro*), is the king of them all. A proper one requires a pound of mussels and a mess of crayfish and congers, as well as the head of a codfish and three different kinds of other fish. Basque cuisine relishes imaginative yet simple sauces, including the legendary *pil pil* (named for the sound it makes while frying), where olive oil, garlic and chillies, sizzling hot, magically meld with the cooking juices of salt cod. Another delight is fresh tuna cooked with tomatoes, garlic, aubergine and spices and *chipirones* (squid) – reputedly the only one in the world that's all black, and better than it sounds. Each Basque chef knows how to work wonders with elvers (*angulas* or *txitxardin*) in garlic sauce, salmon and the famous *txangurro* (spider crab) – flaked, seasoned, stuffed and served in its own shell. Gourmets especially recommend *kokotxas a la Donostiarra*, hake cheeks with a garlic and parsley green sauce, clams and slightly piquant red *guindilla* peppers. Peppers are another icon of the Basque kitchen: housewives hang strings of them on the walls of their houses, and they turn up everywhere: in omelettes, in sauces for seafood, or in the common stewed chicken. Basques like to wash it down with *txakoli*, a tangy green wine produced on the coast with just a modicum of sunlight.

Catalan Cuisine

Like the Basque kitchen, Catalan food has enjoyed considerable influence from beyond the Pyrenees and is rated one of the best in Spain. Not surprisingly, seafood is a main ingredient, in such well-known dishes as *zarzuela*, a seafood casserole; lobster with chicken; *suquet* (similar to bouillabaisse); any fish with *romesco* sauce (toasted hazelnuts, wine, nutmeg, paprika, garlic and olive oil); or *xapada*, with dried eels from varieties of *gazpacho* (chilled tomato, cucumber and onion soup) compete with sizzling fried fish and *rabo de toro* (a spicy concoction of oxtail, tomatoes and onions) for champion status.

Wine and Other Tipples

Wine

No matter how much other costs have risen in Spain, most **wine** (*vino*) has remained happily inexpensive by northern European or American standards; what's more, it's mostly very good, and there's enough variety for you to try something different every day. There are over 40 areas in Spain under the control of the *Instituto*

the Ebro delta. *Botifarra* – pork sausage, black or white, with beans – is a staple, as is *escudella*, a hearty pork and chicken stew. In the autumn a Catalan's mouth waters for partridge with grapes, or goose with pears, or rabbit cooked with almonds or garlic sauce, and wonderful use is made of many *bolets* (wild mushrooms). Near Tarragona in the very early spring outdoor *calçotada* feasts are the rage, featuring lamb cutlets, sausage, wine and, the star ingredient, a special local type of tender green onions (*calçots*) grilled over the fire, which diners slurp down dressed in aprons and bibs. Excellent red wine and *cava* (champagne) are also produced in Catalonia.

Galician Cuisine

When it comes to seafood, Galicians claim to have the best of the best, including delicacies found nowhere else in the world. The estuaries boast an extraordinary array of riches, from the famous scallops of Santiago to creatures unique to Galicia such as *zamburiña* scallops, lobster-like *santiaguiños*, and ugly *percebes*, which have no names in English. Quantity is matched by quality, and has been exported throughout the country, for *Gallego* restaurants are found in every town in Spain, and command as much respect as Basque ones do. Preparation is kept as simple as possible. In every town you'll come across *empanadas*, large flat flaky pies filled with eels or lamprey (the most sought after; try it before you knock it), sardines, pork, or veal. Turnip greens (*grelos*) are a staple, especially in *caldo gallego*, a broth that also features turnips and white beans; in winter, many also opt for *lacón con grelos*, pork shoulder with greens, sausages and potatoes. Galicia also produces fine cheeses, such as *gamonedo* (mainly from cow's milk, mixed with ewe's or goat's milk); birch-smoked, pear-shaped *San Simón*; or mild, soft *ulloa* or *pasiego*. A tapas meal to make a Gallego weep would include grilled sardines, *pulpo a la gallega* (tender octopus with peppers and paprika), roasted small green peppers (*pimientos de Padrón*), with chewy hunks of bread and lightly salted *tetilla* cheese, washed down with white Ribeiro wine. For dessert try *tarta de Santiago* (almond tart) and, to top it off, a glass of Galician firewater, *orujo* – served at night after a meal to ward off evil spirits – properly burned (*queimada*), with lemon peel and sugar.

Nacional de Denominaciones de Origen (INDO), which acts as a guide to the consumer and keeps a strict eye on the quality of Spanish wine (DO, or *denominación de origen*, is the same as French AOC). A restaurant's *vino de la casa*, house wine, is always your least expensive option while dining out; in rustic places it often comes out of a barrel or glass jug, and may be a surprise either way. Much of the inexpensive wine sold throughout central Spain comes from La Mancha or the neighbouring Valdepeñas DO regions. Anyone with more than a passing interest in wine will want to visit a *bodega* or two. If you take an empty bottle with you, you can usually bring it out filled with the wine that suits your palate that day. A *bodega* can be a bar, wine cellar or ware-house, and is worth a visit whatever its guise. Two of the best areas for vineyard and bodega-visiting are the Penedès southwest of Barcelona, home of sparkling *cava* and many fine Catalan wines (*see* p.65) and Jerez, the great home of sherry (*see* p.222).

What to Drink Where

Every region has its wine and liqueur specialities. **Catalonia** is best known for its wines from Penedès and Priorat, the former producing excellent whites and some fine reds (try Gran Caus '87). One of the most typical Catalan whites is Blancs en Noirs, which, like the dry white wines of Tarragona, is excellent with fish, or as an *aperitivo*. The Penedès and more specifically the town of Sant Sadurní d'Anoia is also the origin of Catalonia's own champagne, or *cava*. The principal house, Cordoniú, is always a safe bet, but there are also very fine smaller producers, such as Mestres Mas Vía, whose bottles can rival any standard champagne. Elsewhere in Catalonia, the Priorat produces wonderful rich reds. **Navarra** also has some excellent reds and young *tempranillo* wines, while its neighbour, **La Rioja**, is the best known and richest area for wine in all Spain (*see* box, opposite). In **La Mancha**, Valdepeñas is Spain's most prolific area; its young, inexpensive table wines are sold everywhere, and make even a potato *tortilla* something special. **Valencia** has some fresh, dry whites and a distinctive rosé (Castillo de Liria). Euskadi is known for its very palatable young 'green' wine called *Txacoli* (since 1994 a DO or *denominación de origen*), which is poured into the glass with bravura from a height, like cider, while **Galicia**'s excellent Ribeiro resembles the delicate *vinho verde* of neighbouring Portugal; other good wines from the region are *Rías Baixas* (areas on the coast near Pontevedra, and south of Vigo on the Portuguese border) and *Valdeorros* (east of Ourense), pleasant light vintages that complement the regional seafood dishes perfectly. In many parts of **Andalucía** you may have diffi-culty ordering a simple bottle of white wine, as, on requesting *una botella de vino blanco de la casa*, you will often be served something resembling diluted sherry. To make things clear, specify a wine by name or by region, or ask for *un vino seco*, and the problem should be solved. Some *andaluz* wines have achieved an international repu-tation for high quality. The best known of course is *jerez*, or what we in English call **sherry**. It comes in a wide range of varieties: Andalucíans nearly always drink only very dry *manzanillas*, or dry, light and young *fino* (the famous Tío Pepe), served chilled; rich and sweet *amontillados* and still sweeter *olorosos*, which can be either brown, cream or *amoroso*, are mainly made for foreign consumption.

Rioja in the Bottle

Rioja tastes like no other: soft, warm, mellow, full-bodied, with a distinct vanilla bouquet; its *vino de gran reserva* spends three years ageing in American oak barrels, and then another in bottles, before its release to the public. Look for the fine Viña Cumbrero '85, Monte Real '85 or Valdemar '97, and the aristocratic Marqués de Villamanga '73. It was the Phoenicians who introduced the first vines to the region, which after various invasions and empires were replanted under the auspices of the Church; the first law concerning wine here was decreed by Bishop Abilio in the 9th century. The arrival of masses of thirsty medieval pilgrims along the Camino de Santiago proved a big boost to business, much as mass tourism would do from the 1960s and 1970s onwards.

Despite a long pedigree, the Rioja we drink today dates from the 1860s, when growers from Bordeaux, their own vineyards wiped out by the phylloxera plague, brought their techniques south of the border and wrought immense improvements on the native varieties. By the time the plague reached La Rioja in 1899, the owners were prepared for it with disease-resistant stock. During the First World War, when the vineyards of Champagne were badly damaged, the French returned to buy up *bodegas*, sticking French labels on the bottles and trucking them over the Pyrenees. Rioja finally received the respect it deserved after Franco passed on to the great fascist parade ground in the sky. In the last 25 years, *bodegas* have attracted buyers from around the world and prices have skyrocketed. La Rioja's growing area covers 48,000 hectares, comprising three zones: Rioja Alta, home of the best red and white wines, followed by Rioja Alavesa (on the left bank of the Ebro in Alava province) known for its lighter, perfumed wines, and the decidedly more arid Rioja Baja, where the wines are coarse and mostly used for blending – a common practice in La Rioja. The varieties used for the reds are mostly spicy, fruity Tempranillo (alone covering some 24,000 hectares), followed by Garnacha Tinta (a third of the red production, a good alcohol booster) with smaller quantities of Graciano (for the bouquet) and high-tannin Mazuela (for acidity and tone). Traditional Rioja whites, although they remain relatively unknown, are excellent, golden and vanilla-scented like the reds: Viura are the dominant grapes, with smaller doses of Malvasía and Garnacha Blanca. Unlike French wines, Riojas are never sold until they're ready to drink (although you can, of course, keep the better wines for even longer). DOC rules specify that La Rioja's *Gran Reserva*, which accounts for only three per cent of the production, spends a minimum of two years maturing in American oak barrels (six months for whites and rosés) then four more in the *bodega* before it's sold. *Reservas* (six per cent of the production) spend at least one year in oak and three in the *bodega*. *Crianzas* (30 per cent of the production) spends at least a year in the barrel and another in the bottle. The other 61 per cent of La Rioja is *sin crianza* and labelled CVC (*conjunto de varias cosechas*, combination of various vintages): this includes the new young white wines and light red wines (*claretes*) fermented at cool temperatures in stainless steel vats, skipping the oak barrels altogether and losing most of the vanilla tones.

Menu Decoder

Appetizers and First Courses (*Entremeses y Primeros*)

aceitunas olives
alcachofas con mahonesa artichokes with mayonnaise
ancas de rana frogs' legs
caldo broth
entremeses variados assorted hors d'œuvres
gambas al pil pil shrimps in hot garlic sauce
gazpacho chilled tomato soup
huevos a la flamenca eggs poached in tomato sauce
huevos al plato poached eggs with peppers
huevos revueltos scrambled eggs
sopa de ajo garlic soup
sopa de arroz rice soup
sopa de espárragos asparagus soup
sopa de fideos noodle soup
sopa de garbanzos chickpea soup
sopa de lentejas lentil soup
sopa de verduras vegetable soup
tortilla Spanish omelette, with potatoes
tortilla francesa French omelette

Fish and Seafood (*Pescado y Mariscos*)

acedías small plaice
adobo fish marinated in white wine
almejas clams
anchoas anchovies
anguilas eels
angulas baby eels
atún tuna
bacalao salt cod
besugo sea bream
bogavante lobster
bonito tuna
boquerones anchovies
caballa mackerel
calamares squid
cangrejo crab
centollo spider crab
chanquetes whitebait
chipirones cuttlefish
  ... en su tinta ...in its own ink
chirlas baby clams
cigalas crayfish
escabeche pickled or marinated fish
gambas prawns
langosta lobster
langostinos langoustines
lenguado sole
lubina sea bass
mejillones mussels
merluza hake
mero grouper
navajas razor-shell clams
ostras oysters
pejesapo monkfish
percebes sea barnacles
pescadilla whiting
pez espada swordfish
platija plaice
pulpo octopus
rape monkfish
raya skate
rodaballo turbot
salmón salmon
salmonete red mullet
sardinas sardines
trucha trout
vieiras/veneras scallops
zarzuela fish stew

Meat and Fowl (*Carnes y Aves*)

albóndigas meatballs
asado roast
bistec beefsteak
buey ox
callos tripe
cerdo pork
chorizo spiced sausage
chuletas chops
cochinillo suckling pig
conejo rabbit
corazón heart
cordero lamb
faisán pheasant
fiambres cold meats
filete fillet
hígado liver
jabalí wild boar
jamón de York baked ham
jamón serrano dry-cured ham
lengua tongue
lomo pork loin
morcilla blood sausage
paloma pigeon
pato duck
pavo turkey
perdiz partridge
pinchitos spicy mini kebabs
pollo chicken

rabo/cola de toro oxtail with onions
and tomatoes
riñones kidneys
salchicha sausage
salchichón salami-like sausage
sesos brains
solomillo fillet steak
ternera veal

Note: *potajes, cocidos, guisados, estofados, fabadas* and *cazuelas* are all varieties of stew.

Vegetables (*Verduras y Legumbres*)
ajo garlic
alcachofas artichokes
apio celery
arroz rice
arroz marinera rice with saffron and seafood
berenjena aubergine (eggplant)
cebolla onion
champiñones mushrooms
col, repollo cabbage
coliflor cauliflower
endivias endives
ensalada salad
espárragos asparagus
espinacas spinach
garbanzos chickpeas
judías (verdes) French beans
lechuga lettuce
lentejas lentils
patatas potatoes
...*fritas* ...fried
...*salteadas* ...sautéed
...*al horno* ...baked
pepino cucumber
pimiento pepper
puerros leeks
remolachas beetroots (beets)
setas Spanish mushrooms
zanahorias carrots

Fruits (*Frutas*)
albaricoque apricot
almendras almonds
cerezas cherries
ciruelas plums
ciruelas pasas prunes
frambuesas raspberries
fresas strawberries
...*con nata* ...with cream
higos figs
limón lemon

manzana apple
melocotón peach
melón melon
naranja orange
pasas raisins
pera pear
piña pineapple
plátano banana
pomelo grapefruit
sandía watermelon
uvas grapes

Desserts (*Postres*)
arroz con leche rice pudding
bizcocho/pastel/torta cake
blanco y negro ice cream and coffee float
flan crème caramel
galletas biscuits (cookies)
helados ice creams
pajama flan with ice cream
pasteles pastries
queso cheese
requesón cottage cheese
tarta de frutas fruit pie
turrón nougat

Drinks (*Bebidas*)
agua water
...*con hielo* ...with ice
agua mineral mineral water
...*sin gas* ...still
...*con gas* ...sparkling
batido de leche milkshake
café coffee
...*solo* ...black
...*con leche* ...with milk
cava Spanish sparkling wine
cerveza beer
chocolate hot chocolate
granizado fruit or coffee in crushed ice
jerez sherry
leche milk
té tea
...*con limón* ...with lemon
vino wine
...*tinto* ...red
...*rosado* ...rosé
...*blanco* ...white
zumo de manzana apple juice
zumo de naranja orange juice

For some useful restaurant vocabulary, see 'Eating Out' in **Language**, p.248.

Beer, Brandy and Other Tipples

Many Spaniards prefer **beer** (*cerveza*), which is also good, though not quite the bargain wine is. The most popular brands vary according to where you are: in Madrid and most of Castile it's Mahou, an excellent light lager; in Catalonia and most of the Mediterranean coast it's Estrella Dorada; in the south it may be Cruzcampo or San Miguel. Beer-drinking habits also vary by place: on the Mediterranean coast beer is usually served in bottles (here called a *mediana*) or on tap in small mugs called *jarras*, while in Madrid beer is predominantly on draught and served in small glasses called *cañas* (and the same-size bottle, if you ask for one, is called a *tercio*), while the Basques have a special drinking culture all of their own, and take beer and wine in incomprehensibly small (considering how much they drink) glasses that are called *txikis* (pronounced cheekies).

Imported whisky and other spirits are pretty inexpensive, although the versions Spain bottles itself are even cheaper. Spanish **brandy** (mostly from Jerez or the Catalan Penedès) is excellent; the two most popular brands, *103* (very light in colour) and *Soberano*, are both drunk extensively by Spanish labourers and postmen about 7am. *Anís* (sweet or dry), a rather Pernod-like aniseed drink, is also quite popular. *Sangría* is the famous summertime punch of red wine, brandy, mineral water, orange and lemon with ice, but beware – it's rarely made very well, even when you can find it. The north of Spain, where apples grow better than vines, produces light **cider**, or *sidra*, which can come as a shock to the tastebuds in the first five minutes, and then goes down just fine, though it may leave you wishing it hadn't the morning after.

Young Spaniards are big on spirit mixes, which in fashionable bars cost the same as beer. **Gin**, believe it or not, is often drunk with Coke. Bacardi and cola, a *Cuba Libre* or *Cubata*, is a popular thirst-quencher but be warned that just asking for a *Cuba Libre* might get you cola with anything, such as gin or vodka. You have to specify a *cubata de ron* to be sure of rum and coke. Then, with a flourish worthy of a *matador*, the barman will zap an ice-filled tumbler in front of you, and heave in a quadruple measure. No wonder the Costa del Sol has a staggering six chapters of Alcoholics Anonymous.

Soft Options

Coffee, tea, all the international soft-drink brands and *Kas*, the locally made orange drink, round out the average café fare. If you want tea with milk, say so when you order, otherwise it may arrive with a piece of lemon. Coffee comes as a big, breakfast cup with milk (*café con leche*), as a small espresso (*café solo*) or as an espresso with just a dash of milk (*cortado*). Spanish coffee is good and strong, and if you want a lot of it order an *Americano*, for a *solo* diluted with twice the normal amount of water. Decaf is *descafeinado*; the really great Spanish winter warmer, on the other hand, is the *carajillo de coñac* (a *café solo* with a shot of brandy).

Look out for *Blanco y negros* (coffee and ice cream treats), and *horchata de chufa*, an unusual non-alcoholic drink made by crushing a kind of nut called a *chufa*, originally from Valencia and Alicante, which can be wonderfully refreshing, not to say addictive, in the summer heat.

Catalonia:
Barcelona and Girona

Catalonia

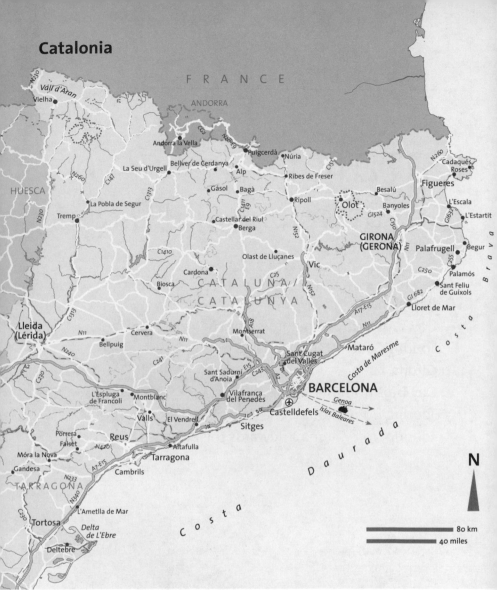

On the map, Catalonia (in Catalan, Catalunya; in Castilian Spanish, Cataluña) occupies a tidy triangle between France, the Mediterranean and the rest of Spain, but that's where tidiness ends. To the north the Pyrenees stretch down to dip their crooked toes in the sea, forming the fabled Costa Brava; to the south the flat sands of the Costa Daurada peter out in the Ebro delta. In between, dead volcanoes and mountains shaped like pipe organs squat over a landscape littered with Iberian, Greek, Roman and Romanesque monuments. Nowhere else in Spain did early 20th-century architecture (*modernista*, as Catalans call it) bloom so furiously, from Gaudí's Barcelona to wine cooperatives in tiny villages. Today, Barcelona is the most exciting and dynamic of all Spain's cities: the capital of an increasingly self-confident Catalan culture, the most cosmopolitan city in the whole of Iberia and a global model for urban planning and design – plus, legendarily, one of Europe's hippest party cities.

Besides Barcelona, Catalonia has other historic cities – like Girona, away to the north, with an evocative medieval quarter. The playful Dalí museum is in Figueres, just off the Costa Brava, Spain's prettiest coast. South of Barcelona, there's Sitges, one of the hottest resorts on the Med. Inland, there are the Pyrenees and more magnificent scenery and rare gems such as the monastery at Montserrat. Besides tripping the *sardana*, in fiestas Catalans love to stack themselves up in towers. Otherwise normal men, women and kids called *castellers* climb on each others' shoulders to the eerie music of the '*gralla*'; the best groups attain eight or nine tiers of bodies.

Barcelona

Barcelona, the treasure house of courtesy, the refuge of strangers... And although the adventures that befell me there occasioned me no great pleasure, but rather much grief, I bore them the better for having seen that city.

Cervantes, Don Quixote, Part II

And so are we all the better for having seen Barcelona, the capital of the Catalans, a city that nowadays fizzes and sizzles like a bottle of *cava* spiked with a red pepper. With its superb legacy of *modernista* architecture, its business acumen, its manic obsession with style and design, Barcelona is a little New York – some say the only really successful modern city in old Europe. Nor is it shy about saying so.

A Little Orientation

Barcelona sits on a plain gently descending to the sea, wrapped in an amphitheatre of hills and mountains, the **Serra de Collserola**. Visible from just about every part of the city is its highest peak, **Tibidabo**, a much-loved spot for its funfair, fine air and priceless views. At the south end of the harbour rises Barcelona's other mountain and oldest landmark, the smooth-humped crag called **Montjuïc**.

Barcelona's lack of prosperity for several centuries left intact its historic centre or **Barri Gòtic**, the greatest concentration of medieval architecture in Europe. It is bounded on the southwest by **Las Ramblas**, Barcelona's showcase promenade; between there and Av. Paral.lel is the piquant **Raval**, with the remnants of the once-notorious red-light district, the **Barri Xinès** or *Chino*. The part of the map that looks as if it was stamped by a giant waffle iron is the **Eixample**, the 19th-century 'extension', the building of which coincided with the era of the *modernista* architects. Ramblas, Barri Gòtic and Eixample meet at an enormous node called **Plaça Catalunya**.

West of the Eixample are once-separate towns like **Gràcia** and **Sarrià**, and other districts spreading up the hills. Post-'80s Barcelona turned its attention seawards: next to the 18th-century dockside district of **Barceloneta**, the **Port Vell** (old port), was transformed into an urban playground, while the **Vila Olímpica**, built for Olympic athletes, became an all-new pleasure port, and the gateway to Barcelona's **beach**.

Getting to Barcelona

Barcelona's international **airport** is **Prat de Llobregat**, 12km to the south. There are three terminals: **A** for international flights, **B** for domestic and some European flights, and **C** for shuttle flights to Spain's major cities. There is a big choice of flights from the UK: **Bmibaby** flies from East Midlands; **easyJet** (including ex-**Go** routes) from Stansted, Bristol, Gatwick, Liverpool and Luton; **British Airways** from Heathrow, Gatwick, Birmingham and Glasgow; and **Iberia** from Heathrow, Gatwick, Birmingham and Manchester.

There are **banks** (*open daily 7am–11pm*) and **tourist offices** (*open daily 9am–11pm*) in terminals A and B, and a **post office**.

Getting from the Airport

The **Aerobús** is usually the quickest way into town (€3.30). It runs from all terminals to Plaça Catalunya (*Mon–Fri 5.30am–11.15pm every 15 mins; Sat and Sun 6am–11.20pm every 30 mins*). **Trains** are slightly cheaper and run from the airport to Barcelona-Sants and Plaça Catalunya (*approx 6am–10pm, every 30 mins*).

A **taxi** to central Barcelona should cost around €15–€18, depending on the traffic.

Useful Numbers

Airport flight information: t 932 98 38 28.
British Airways: t 933 79 44 68.
easyJet: t 902 29 99 92.
Iberia: t 902 40 05 00 .
Train information (RENFE): t 902 24 02 02.
Trasmediterránea: t 902 45 46 45..

Getting Around

The main **train** terminal is **Barcelona-Sants** station, on the south side of the city centre, but many trains also stop at the more central RENFE **Passeig de Gràcia** station. Both connect with the Metro. The **Estació de França** on Av. Marquès de l'Argentera is now used only by a few long-distance and regional lines and some luxury international trains from France.

Ferries to and from the Balearic Islands run from the Estació Marítima, at the foot of the Ramblas. **Trasmediterránea** is now the sole ferry company (*www.trasmediterranea.es*).

Around the City

Barcelona's has a very efficient and cheap transport system, operated by the **TMB**. There are five **Metro** (underground/ subway) lines, each identified by a colour and number. The Metro is generally the most convenient way of getting around town (*trains run Mon–Thurs 5am–midnight Lines 2, 3, 5, 5am–11pm Lines 1, 4; and on all lines Fri–Sat, eves of holidays 5am–2am; Sun, holidays 6am–midnight*). TMB **buses** run on most routes 6.30am–10pm daily, although some run till around midnight. After-hours there are 14 '**Nitbus**' night bus routes, which start from Plaça Catalunya.

There is also an underground rail line that is not officially part of the Metro but is run by Catalan Government Railways (the **FGC**), from Plaça Catalunya (a separate station, linked to the Metro by a tunnel) to Tibidabo, with a fork to Sarrià and Pedralbes. Tickets for trips in Barcelona are the same as for the Metro and buses. The Sarrià line continues into the suburbs, and the FGC has another useful line from Plaça d'Espanya, to Montserrat.
General Transport Information: t 010

Metro and Bus Tickets

Single tickets for the Metro, FGC and buses cost €1 and are bought from ticket windows or machines at all Metro/FGC stations and on board buses. However, unless you make just a very few journeys it is better to get one of the multi-journey tickets (called a *targeta*). You pass them through automatic gates every time you enter the Metro, and on buses, with T-10 tickets, you cancel them in the machines just behind the driver. You can buy them at all Metro/FGC stations, but not on board buses. They are not valid for 'Nitbus' night buses, tickets for which are bought on the spot.

T-10: Ten single rides on bus, Metro or FGC (€5.60). Very convenient, and can be shared.
T-50/30: Fifty single rides within 30 days of buying the pass (€23.40); can also be shared.
T-Dia: Unlimited travel on all three systems for one person for one day (€4.20).
2, 3, 4 or 5-Dies: Unlimited travel for from two (€7.60) to five (€16.50) days on all three systems. Can be bought on the Aerobús.
Aerobús+Bus+Metro: Unlimited travel also including the Aerobús for two (€12) to five (€19.50) days. For sale on the Aerobús.

Taxis

Barcelona's black-and-yellow taxis are ubiquitous, and fares are reasonable: most trips within the city will cost under €5. To call a cab, ring t 933 57 77 55/934 90 22 22/933 00 11 00; for cabs with disabled access, t 933 58 11 11.

Tourist Buses and Special Rides

TMB also runs the **Bus Turístic**, with two routes, both starting at Plaça Catalunya: a red/north loop and a blue/south one, taking in all the best-known sights. With a ticket you can get on and off as many times as you like, on either route (*buses every 20–30 mins daily; one-day ticket €14, two days, consecutive, €18; children 4–12 €8 a day, under-4 free*). Ticket holders get a raft of discounts (for the Sagrada Família, the main museums, etc) which don't have to be used on the same day. Tickets are bought on the bus or from tourist offices.

Barcelona's various **rides** are much-loved parts of the local scene. On Tibidabo there is the **Tramvia Blau**, a pretty 1902 tramcar that runs from the FGC station at Av Tibidabo to Plaça Dr Andreu (*summer daily, winter Sat and Sun only 9am–9.35pm*), to connect with a **Funicular** up to the funfair on top of the mountain, and wonderful views (*€2.10 single; hours vary by season, in summer normally 10am or 12 noon–dark, and till 1am summer weekends*). A less interesting funicular goes from **M** Paral.lel to Montjuïc, where you can continue to Castell de Montjuïc on **Telefèric de Monjuïc** cable cars (*open June–Oct daily; Nov–May Sat and Sun only*). From Montjuïc you can also try the **Transbordador** cable car, a clanking (but restored) metal monster that swings across the harbour to Torre Sebastià in Barceloneta, via the World Trade Centre (*t 934 43 08 59; €4.25 one-way; open daily*).

Lastly, from Moll de la Fusta you can take **Golondrines** 'swallow boats' on a cruise through the harbour, on two routes: a 35 mins trip to the end of the breakwater, or a longer one to the Port Olímpic (*tickets from €3.50; open daily, services less frequent Oct–May*).

Car Hire

For car hire in Spain in general, *see* pp.17–18. To save on trouble and expense in parking in Barcelona, collect your car or have it delivered to your hotel only when you need to use it.

Avis, C/Casanova 209, t 932 09 95 33.
Europcar, Plaça dels Països Catalans, t 934 91 48 22.
Hertz, C/Tuset 10, t 932 17 32 48; airport, t 932 98 36 36; Estació de Sants, t 934 90 86 62.
National-Atesa, C/Muntaner 45, t 932 98 34 33; airport, t 932 98 34 34.
Vanguard, C/Viladomat 297, t 934 39 38 80, *www.vanguardrent.com*. Excellent local company with very good weekend deals.

Tourist Information

Barcelona's tourist offices are very helpful, and the main Plaça Catalunya office has a hotel booking service (for the same night only). Two good **websites** are *www.barcelona-turisme.com* and the city's *www.bcn.es*. In summer there are **kiosks** in Plaça Catalunya, Pg de Gràcia, by Sagrada Família, Vila Olímpica and Port Vell, and '**Red Jacket**' information officers tour streets near the main tourist sites.
Plaça Catalunya: underground on south side of the Plaça, t 906 30 12 82, outside Spain t 933 68 97 30 (*open daily 9–9*). Offices at the **Airport**, **Barcelona-Sants station** and the **Ajuntament** in Plaça Sant Jaume.
Palau Robert: Pg de Gràcia 107, t 932 38 40 00, *www.gencat.es/probert* (*open Mon–Fri 10–7, Sat 10–2.30*). Catalan government office, for information on areas outside Barcelona.
Palau de la Virreina: Ramblas 99, t 933 01 77 75. The City cultural department office: good for information on concerts, theatre and so on, and for buying festival tickets.

Discount Cards and Tickets

Barcelona offers several handy money-saving schemes to help visitors see the city: the **Bus Turístic** ticket (*see left*) is another that cuts cost on entry to a big range of attractions.
Articket: Gives entry to six art centres (MNAC, MACBA, Fundació Miró, Fundació Tàpies, CCCB, La Pedrera) for €15; valid for three months. Sold at participating museums, and through Telentrada (*www.telentrada.com*).
Barcelona Card: Valid for one (€16.25) to five (€26) days, with reductions for children aged 4–12; gives discounts at shops, restaurants and many major attractions, and unlimited Metro and bus travel. Sold at tourist offices.

Guided Tours

The **tourist office** organizes **walking tours** of the Barri Gòtic (very popular, so book early). Tours in English *Sat and Sun at 10am* (€6/€3 for 4–12s). The **Museu d'Història de la Ciutat** (*see* p.52) organizes interesting tours through the Barri Gòtic (information **t** 933 15 11 11).

Useful Numbers

Medical Emergencies: t 061; **Fire service: t** 080. **Police: t** 091/092; **Tourist police: t** 933 01 90 60

The Municipal Police has a special station to assist tourists at Las Ramblas 43, **M** Liceu.

Festivals

Barcelona takes its festivals seriously. Events such as *festes majors* are occasions for a special battery of Catalan folklore and music. By day you'll find processions of *gegants* (tall wood and papier-mâché figures) and *capgrossos* (demonically grinning 'fat heads'), and the daring construction of human towers by *castellers*. At night, the big event is a *correfoc*, or 'fire-running', when terrifying dragons spit fireworks into the crowds, chased by 'devils'. Tourist Ofices (*see* p.45) have full information and precise dates. Some of Barcelona's biggest dates are listed below:

Festival of Sant Jordi, *23 April*. Day of the Book and the Rose (*see* p.22).

Sónar, *June*. Global 'advanced music' festival that has cemented Barcelona's status as a capital of cool. Information on *www.sonar.es*.

Sant Joan, *23 June*. The *Nit del Foc* or 'Night of Fire' on the eve of St John is the maddest night of the year. Only a few small fires are tolerated in the city, but non-stop fireworks shake Barcelona as everyone downs *cava* and sweet cakes called *cocas de Sant Joan*.

Festival del Grec, *late June–mid-Aug*. Summer festival of theatre, music and dance in Teatre Grec, Mercat de les Flors and Plaça del Rei.

Festa Major de Gràcia, *late Aug*. A giant party that draws thousands each summer.

Diada, *11 Sept*. Catalan National Day.

La Mercè, *23 Sept*. The city's week-long *festa major*, with an impressive arts programme, and a huge, frenzied *correfoc*.

Fira de Santa Llúcia, *8–24 Dec*. The Christmas market in front of the cathedral.

Shopping

Barcelona is Spain's fashion and design capital. There are three main shopping areas: the **Old City** (Barri Gòtic, Raval, La Ribera) for trendy streetwear, second-hands, interesting junk or antiques; the central **Eixample** (around Rambla Catalunya and Pg de Gràcia) for high-quality clothes and jewellery; and **Sant Gervasi** (west of Gràcia towards Plaça Macià and Av. Diagonal) for upmarket boutiques.

Serious shoppers hit Barcelona in January, when everything's on sale; look out for the word *rebaixes* (*rebajas* in Castilian).

Where to Stay

Barcelona ✉ 08000

There are good places to stay all over the city, but cheaper choices are clustered in and around the Barri Gòtic. Sentimental travellers often choose to stay on the Ramblas, but note that exterior rooms there may be noisy.

Wherever you stay, it's essential to book in advance: some hotels are fully booked months ahead. If you do arrive without a reservation, there are booking services at the Airport, Sants station and Plaça Catalunya tourist office.

The **price categories** listed here and in Madrid differ from those used for the rest of Spain. *See* **Practical A–Z**, 'Where to Stay', p.27.

Luxury

★★★★★Arts Barcelona, C/Marina 19–21, **t** 932 21 10 00,, *www.ritzcarlton.com*; **M** Ciutadella-Vila Olímpica. Occupies one of the two towers by Port Olímpic; in a class by itself, offering stunning views of the sea and city and with a fantastic seaside pool.

★★★★★Claris, C/de Pau Claris 150, Eixample, **t** 934 87 62 62, *www.derbyhotels.es*; **M** Urquinaona. Gives luxury a twist, blending refined modern design with a connoisseur's collection of art treasures.

★★★★★Husa Palace, Gran Vía de les Corts Catalanes 668, Eixample, **t** 933 18 52 00, *www.ritzbcn.com*; **M** Passeig de Gràcia. Formerly known as the Ritz, this remains Barcelona's classic grand hotel, as it has been since 1919. Snugly plush, it offers luxury in every sense.

Expensive

****Colón, Av. Catedral 7, **t** 933 01 14 04, *www.hotelcolon.es*; **M** Jaume I. The grandest hotel in the middle of the Barri Gòtic, in a historic building with fine views of the cathedral. Parking is available.

****Condes de Barcelona, Passeig de Gràcia 73, **t** 934 84 22 00, *www.hotelcondesde barcelona.com*; **M** Passeig de Gràcia. Designed from twin façades forming an old *modernista* palace. Pool, parking, a/c.

****Regente, Rambla Catalunya 76, **t** 934 87 59 89, **f** 934 87 32 27; **M** Passeig de Gràcia. Behind a *modernista* façade, this has an air of stolid stateliness and lots of oak and gilt. Rooms are traditionally stylish, with fabulous views from the upper floors, and there is an attractive, if small, rooftop pool.

****Rivoli Ramblas, Rambla dels Estudis 128, **t** 933 02 66 43, *www.rivolihotels.com*; **M** Catalunya. Stylishly designed throughout, with a piano bar, a gym and rooftop terrace with great views.

Moderate

España, 9–11 C/Sant Pau, **t 933 18 17 58, **f** 933 17 11 34; **M** Liceu. A *modernista* landmark with a beautiful ground floor by Domènech i Montaner. The functionally furnished rooms are disappointing after all this grandeur, but comfortable, and it's very popular.

Marina Folch, C/del Mar, **t** 933 10 37 09, **f** 933 10 53 27; **M** Barceloneta. A charming choice with only 10 rooms, in the Barceloneta.

Mesón Castilla, C/Valldonzella 5, **t 933 18 21 82, *hmesoncastilla@teleline.es*, *www.hosa.es*; **M** Universitat. In a quiet side street near the Ramblas and the MACBA. It has a lovely interior garden, and spacious air-conditioned rooms; parking.

***Nouvel Hotel, C/de Santa Anna 20, **t** 933 01 82 74, *www.hotelnouvel.com*; **M** Catalunya. Handy for the Ramblas, in a renovated *modernista* building with marble floors and carved wood. Staff are friendly, and rooms (with a/c) are prettily decorated.

***Oriente, Ramblas 45, **t** 933 02 25 58, **f** 934 12 38 19; **M** Liceu. A mouldering classic in one of the street's oldest buildings, from 1670. An ex-monastery cloister serves as the hotel ballroom; come here for faded grandeur, but rooms above the Ramblas can be noisy.

Peninsular, C/Sant Pau 34–6, **t 933 02 31 38, **f** 934 12 36 99; **M** Liceu. Also nestled in the shell of a convent, with rooms set along balconies overlooking a spacious, inner courtyard. It's good value and fills up quickly.

***San Agustín, Plaça Sant Agustí 3, **t** 933 18 16 58, *www.hotelsa.com*; **M** Liceu. A likeable place on a leafy square just off the Ramblas, 200 years old but recently renovated. All rooms have a/c; try for an attic one with beamed ceilings and views of the old city.

Inexpensive

Barcelona House, C/Escudellers 19, **t 933 17 18 16; **M** Drassanes. Comfortable rooms with TV, and central. Best to reserve in advance as it fills up fast, mostly with young travellers.

Hs Eden, C/Balmes 55, 1st and 2nd floors, **t/f** 934 52 66 20, *www.barcelona-on-line.es/hostaleden*; **M** Passeig de Gràcia. A pleasant surprise, up a staircase in an old Eixample building, with 25 spotless and endearingly eccentric rooms. *Closed at Easter and Christmas.*

Hs Gat Raval, C/Joaquín Costa 44, **t** 934 81 66 70, *www.gataccommodation.com*; **M** Universitat. A lovely new *hostal*, perfect for the sophisticated traveller on a moderate budget. Knowledgeable staff are friendly and multilingual; rooms are modern, clean and bright with fans and TV.

Hs Jardí, Plaça Sant Josep Oriol 1, **t 933 01 59 00, **f** 933 18 36 64; **M** Liceu. Book well in advance. The most popular budget hotel in the area, with scrupulously clean rooms with a/c set around a central courtyard; the nicest overlook the tree-filled Plaça del Pi.

Paseo de Gràcia, Passeig de Gràcia 102, **t** 932 15 58 24, **f** 932 15 37 24; **M** Diagonal. Reasonable for this chi-chi district. Some rooms on the eighth floor retain *modernista* fittings.

Cheap

Maldà, C/del Pi 5, **t** 933 17 30 02; **M** Liceu. Small and cheery, up the stairs in Barcelona's oldest shopping arcade; it's sunny, quiet and rooms (none en suite) are very good value.

La Terrassa, C/Junta de Comerç 11, **t** 933 02 51 74, **f** 933 01 21 88; **M** Liceu. Run by the same people as the **Jardí**, but slightly less well equipped and cheaper as a result. Breakfast is served on a pretty patio in summer.

Eating Out

Restaurants

Barcelona's restaurant range is vast: some serve the finest Catalan cuisine, while others feed the masses with more standard fare. Besides the native eateries are restaurants from other regions of Spain and the world. As a rule, book ahead for more expensive restaurants. These also tend to close in August.

The **price categories** listed here differ from those used for the rest of Spain in this guide. See **Practical A–Z**, 'Food and Drink', p.21, for the price ranges. Categories are based on a three-course meal without wine, per person.

Expensive

Agut d'Avignon, C/Trinitat 3, **t** 933 02 60 34; **M** Jaume I. Just off C/de Avinyó, one of Barcelona's swankiest restaurants: classic Catalan cuisine is prepared with the freshest ingredients and imaginative twists. *Open daily 1–3.30 and 9–11.30.*

Bilbao, C/de Perill 33, Gràcia, **t** 934 58 96 24; **M** Diagonal. Specializes in seasonal dishes using the freshest Catalan ingredients. The food is simple yet excellent and beautifully presented. *Open Mon–Sat 1–4 and 9–11.*

Café de l'Acadèmia, C/Lledo 1, **t** 933 19 82 53; **M** Jaume I. In summer you can take in the enchanting Plaça Sant Just from shady tables here, or from grand rooms on the second floor. The emphasis of the menu is Catalan, but international flourishes also abound. *Open Mon–Fri 9–noon, 1.30–4 and 8.45–11.30; closed 2 weeks in Aug.*

Ca l'Isidre, C/de les Flors 12, **t** 934 41 11 39; **M** Paral.lel. A warm, intimate restaurant in an unlikely location, with classic cooking and a renowned wine list. *Open Mon–Sat 1.30–4 and 8.30–11.30; closed 2 weeks in Aug.*

Can Ramonet, C/Maquinista 17, **t** 933 19 30 64; **M** Barceloneta. Barceloneta's oldest tavern (est. 1763), with superb seafood in full meals or *tapas*, and house wine from huge barrels. *Open daily 10–4 and 8–midnight.*

Casa Calvet, C/de Casp 48, **t** 934 13 40 12; **M** Urquinaona. One of the most innovative restaurants, serving imaginative Mediterranean dishes in a house designed by Gaudí. *Open 1.30–4 and 8.30–11.30; closed Sun and last 2 weeks of Aug.*

Gaig, Psg Maragall 402, Horta, **t** 934 29 10 17; **M** Horta. Under the culinary care of the Gaig family for four generations. Its subtle Catalan cooking is superb, with such delicacies as *arròs de colomí amb ceps* (pigeon in rice with wild mushrooms). The wine cellar is out of this world. *Open 1.30–4 and 9–11pm.*

Jean-Luc Figueras, C/Santa Teresa 10, **t** 934 15 28 77; **M** Diagonal. The real deal. To treat yourself to one truly excellent meal during your stay, try this, the lair of a real artist-chef; and don't miss the desserts. *Open Mon–Fri 1.30–3.30 and 8.30–11.30; Sat 8.30–11.30; closed 2 weeks in Aug.*

Passadís d'en Pep, Pla del Palau 2, **t** 933 10 10 21; **M** Barceloneta. Booking essential. Gourmet seafood heaven, if hard to find (down an unmarked corridor). Prices are hefty, but you don't need to scan a menu: food is brought to you. *Open Mon–Sat 1.30–3.30 and 9–11.30.*

Els Pescadors, Pla Prim 1, **t** 932 25 20 18; **M** Poblenou. On a peaceful square, this out-of-the-way place is one of Barcelona's best seafood restaurants. Specialities include *fideuà* (paella made with noodles, not rice) and *arros negre* (seafood with rice cooked in squid ink). *Open daily 1–3.45 and 8–midnight.*

Els Quatre Gats, C/Montsió 3, **t** 933 02 41 40; **M** Catalunya. In the replica of the famous *modernista* taverna, with a smart restaurant specializing in upscale Catalan cuisine. *Open Mon–Sat 9am–2am, Sun 5pm–2am; closed Sun and 3 weeks in Aug.*

Moderate

Agua, Pg Marítim 30, **t** 932 25 12 72; **M** Barceloneta. Elegant beachfront terrace with a wide-ranging menu. *Open Mon–Thurs and Sun 1.30–4 and 8.30–midnight, Fri and Sat 1.30–4 and 8.30–1am.*

Agut, C/d'En Gignàs 16, **t** 933 15 17 09; **M** Jaume I. Warm and traditional. It has been serving up succulent Catalan specialities since 1924. *Open 1.30–4 and 9–midnight; closed Aug.*

Ateneu, Plaça Sant Miquel 2, **t** 933 02 11 98, *www.ateneu.com*; **M** Jaume I. With an adjoining cigar bar, this restaurant serves delicious and creative Catalan cuisine in graceful surroundings, with contemporary art on the walls. The lunchtime *menú del día* is superb value. *Open 1–3 and 8–11.30; closed Sun and first 3 weeks of Aug.*

Can Culleretes, C/d'En Quintana 5, **t** 933 17 31 22; **M** Liceu. Book Sun lunch. In a little side street off C/de la Boqueria is the city's oldest restaurant. Friendly and very popular, it has good-value traditional Catalan dishes. *Open Tues–Sat 1.30–4 and 9–11, Sun 1.30–4.*

Cangrejo Loco, Moll de Gregal 29–30, Port Olímpic, **t** 932 21 05 33; **M** Ciutadella-Vila Olímpica. One of the best among the glut of fish restaurants in the Port Olímpic, with excellent seafood and service, and fine views from its terrace tables. *Open daily 1–1.*

Can Ros, C/Almirall Aixada 7, **t** 932 21 45 79; **M** Barceloneta. One of the best places for seafood in Barceloneta. While waiting for a *paella* or *arrós negre*, sample fresh seafood *tapas*. *Open Thurs–Tues 1–5 and 8–12.*

El Convent, C/Jerusalem 3, **t** 933 17 10 52; **M** Liceu. This spot has been popular a long while (formerly as Egipte). With good reason: it has its ups and downs, but the food is fresh and satisfying. et there early to get a table. *Open 1–4 and 8.30–11.*

La Llotja, Museu Marítim, Av. de les Drassanes, **t** 933 02 64 02; **M** Drassanes. A wonderful location, in the vast, vaulted 13th-century shipyards; it's run by a local food critic, who serves very fine Catalan food. *Open Mon–Fri 8–8, Sat–Sun from 2pm and dinner 9–11pm.*

Mamacafé, C/Doctor Dou 10, **t** 933 01 29 40; **M** Catalunya. The name says it all: buxom, booming and welcoming. A terrific variety of dishes and lively music. *Open Mon 9–5, Tues–Fri 9am–1am, Sat 1–1.*

Plaça, C/Bellafila 5, **t** 934 12 65 52; **M** Jaume I. Delightful, small and chic, with very creative Catalan cuisine. *Open from 2.30pm; dinner Sun–Thurs 9pm–midnight, Fri– Sat 9pm–1am.*

Salero, C/del Rec 60, **t** 933 19 80 22; **M** Jaume I. One of the most fashionable haunts in the Born: a cool white space in which to try an imaginative fusion of Mediterranean and Oriental cuisine. *Open Tues–Thurs 1–4 and 9–midnight, Fri and Sat 1–4 and 9–1, Sun 1–4.*

Silenus, C/dels Àngels 8, **t** 933 02 26 80; **M** Catalunya. Near the MACBA, offering excellent international and Catalan food in a charming, relaxed setting with contemporary art on the walls. Long, light and pretty, it's also a good place to relax over coffee, mornings or afternoons. *Open Mon 1–4pm, Tues–Sat 1–4 and 9–11.30.*

Inexpensive

Compostela, C/Ferran 30 (no phone). **M** Jaume I. Draws crowds for Galician specialities such as *pulpo* and *tetilla* cheese. *Open Wed–Mon 9am–noon, 1–4 and 8–11.*

L'Hostal de Rita, C/Aragó 279, **t** 934 87 23 76; **M** Passeig de Gràcia. Always busy, with long queues, but worth it for a smart operation at unusually low prices; the same owners have the (over-) popular Quinze Nits in Plaça Reial. *Open daily 1–3.30 and 8.30–11.30.*

Jardí de l'Abadessa, Abadessa Olzet 26, Pedralbes, **t** 932 80 37 54. Oasis-like spot for simple, fresh food. *Open winter Mon–Wed 8–6, Thurs and Fri 8–5 and 8–midnight; summer Mon–Fri 8am–midnight.*

Pla dels Angels, C/Ferlandina 23 (opposite MACBA), **t** 934 43 31 03; **M** Universitat. This delightful restaurant feels like an extension of the MACBA. Like the décor, food is imaginative and lively. *Open 1–3 and 8.30–12.30.*

Rodrigo, C/Argenteria 67, **t** 933 10 30 20; **M** Jaume I. By Santa María del Mar, with home cooking at low prices. Full meals only at midday; sandwiches are the fare later on. *Open Fri–Tues 1–4 and 8.30–12, Wed 1–4.*

Restaurante Romesco, C/Sant Pau 28, **t** 933 18 93 81; **M** Liceu. Noisy and cheerful budget favourite off the Ramblas: Cuban *frijoles* (meat, rice, egg and beans) is the speciality. *Open Mon–Sat 1pm–midnight; closed Aug.*

Vegetarian Restaurants

Many restaurants offer vegetarian options.

La Buena Tierra, C/Encarnacio 56, **t** 932 19 82 13; **M** Joanic (*moderate*). Cosy, with imaginative specialities and a garden. *Open Mon and Sun 1.30–4pm, Tues–Sat 1.30–4 and 8.30–12.*

La Flauta Magica, C/Banys Vells 18, **t** 932 68 49 64; **M** Jaume I (*moderate*). One of the most imaginative vegetarian spots, with some organic meat dishes. *Open 9pm–midnight.*

L'Hortet, C/Pintor Fortuny 32, **t** 933 17 61 89; **M** Catalunya (*inexpensive*). A friendly little place for lunch: all-veggie, with fresh juices and bargain set menus. *Open Mon–Thurs and Sun 1.15–4, Fri and Sat 1.15–4 and 9–11.*

Oolong, C/Gignás 25, **t** 933 15 12 59; **M** Jaume I. With an imaginative blend of Asian and Spanish flavours and cool décor, this mostly-vegetarian eatery caters to the groovy. *Open Mon–Sat 8.30am–2.30am, Sun 6pm–2am.*

Cafés, Bars and *Tapas*

There are places that specialize in coffee, or cocktails, or *tapas*, but most serve all three, and a range of sandwiches (*bocadillos*). Many cafés are linked to cake shops, to cater to the Catalan sweet tooth. *Granjas*, or dairy bars, are a Catalan institution, favourite places to indulge in an afternoon pick-me-up of pastries, milkshakes or hot chocolate with cream (*chocolate suizo*). *Orxaterias/horchaterias* specialize in *orxata* (*horchata* in Castilian), a deliciously refreshing summer drink.

Raval, the Old Centre and the Port

Bar Celta, C/de la Mercè 16, t 933 15 00 06; M Drassanes. Essential stop along a Mercè bar crawl, with great Galician seafood. *Open Mon–Sat 10am–1am, Sun 10am–midnight.*

Bodega La Tinaja, C/Esparteria 9, t 933 10 22 50; M Jaume I. Dim corners, candlelight, antiques and superb wines: a romantic spot for *tapas*. *Open daily 6pm–2am.*

Café de la Opera, Ramblas 74, t 933 02 41 89; M Liceu. An institution, the most historic café on the Ramblas, opposite the Liceu. Flouncy nymphs etched in mirrors watch the parade from the four corners of the earth. *Open daily 8.30am–2am.*

Estrella de Plata, Pla del Palau 9, t 933 19 60 07; M Barceloneta. A long-established port bar now serving distinctive gourmet (pricey) *tapas*. *Open Mon–Sat 11–4 and 8–12.*

Euskal Etxea, Plaçeta de Montcada, t 933 10 21 85; M Jaume I. Scrumptious Basque *tapas*, and also a restaurant. *Bar open Tues–Sat 9.30am–11.30pm, Sun 12.45–3.30.*

Granja Dulcinea, C/Petritxol 2, t 933 02 68 24; M Liceu. A classic for atmosphere and frothy, sweet and chocolatey delights. *Open daily 9–1 and 5–9; closed Aug.*

L'Hivernacle, Parc de la Ciutadella, t 933 10 22 91; M Barceloneta. Light-filled café with palms and wicker chairs, in an 1880s greenhouse in the park. *Open daily 10am–1am.*

Horchateria-Turroneria Sirvent, Ronda Sant Pau 3, Montjuïc, t 934 41 76 16; M Sant Antoni. Cool down with delicious ice cream and *horchata*. *Open Mon–Sat 10am–1am.*

La Pineda, C/del Pi 16; M Liceu. A delightful, old-fashioned delicatessen hung with hams, trotters and the like. Try the meats, then pay at the ancient till. *Open daily 9–3 and 5–10.*

Santa María, C/Comerç 17, t 933 15 12 27; M Jaume I. About as sophisticated as *tapas* bars come; a fine wine list, unusual *tapas* and décor make it worth the high-ish prices. *Open Tues–Sat 1.30–3.30 and 8.30–12.30.*

La Soccarena, C/de la Mercè 21; M Drassanes or Jaume I. Popular Asturian bar with *tapas* of goats' cheese and earthy meats, and Asturian cider poured with great ceremony. *Open 1.30–3 and 6pm–3am.*

La Vinya del Senyor, Pla de Santa María 5; M Jaume I. A fantastic selection of 250 wines by the bottle, 20 by the glass, and tidbits (*platillos*) to accompany them. *Open Tues–Sat noon–1.30am, Sun noon–4pm.*

El Xampanyet, C/Montcada 22; M Jaume I. A wonderful old *cava* and cider bar by the Museu Picasso, full of atmosphere and *bonhomie*. *Open Tues–Sat noon–4pm and 5.30–11.30pm, Sun noon–4pm.*

Eixample, Gràcia and elsewhere

Bauma, C/Roger de Llúria 124, t 934 59 05 66; M Diagonal. Slightly old-fashioned, very cosy café. *Open Mon–Thurs 8am–11pm, Fri–Sat 8am–midnight; closed Aug.*

La Bodegueta, Rambla Catalunya 98, t 932 15 48 94; M Passeig de Gràcia. Join the rest of Barcelona in the cellar for *cava* and wines, with fine snacks to soak them up. *Open daily 7am–1.30am; closed Aug mornings.*

Café Zurich, Plaça Catalunya 1, t 933 17 91 53; M Catalunya. Although it's only a shinier clone of the historic Zurich, installed on the same spot in the new Triangle mall, the terrace tables on the square remain one of the city's most popular places. *Open Mon–Fri 8am–1am, Sat 10am–1am, Sun 10am–11pm.*

Laie Llibreria Café, C/Pau Claris 85, t 933 02 73 10; M Passeig de Gràcia. Barcelona's original, very relaxing bookshop-café. *Café open Mon–Fri 9am–1am, Sat 10am–1am; bookshop open Mon–Sat 10.30am–9pm; closed Sun.*

Mora, Av. Diagonal 409, t 934 16 07 26; M Diagonal. Barcelona's most famous cake shop and one of its chicest establishments, a place to linger over tea, or a late breakfast. *Open daily 7.30am–9pm.*

El Roble, C/Lluis Antúnez 7, t 932 18 73 87; FGC Gràcia. A bustling neighbourhood favourite, with big boards listing the Gallego seafood *tapas*. *Open Mon–Sat 7am–1am.*

Nightlife

Barcelona's nightlife cranks up after 11pm and at weekends lasts until breakfast, if you've got the energy (and money) to keep up. Most bars officially close at 2 or 3am, but if the buzz is good the owner will close the door and let the party continue. Favourite spots are the Barri Gòtic, La Ribera and the Born by Santa María del Mar, Gràcia, the Eixample around Passeig de Gràcia, and upscale Sant Gervasi.

Discos and clubs don't gear up for action until after midnight, and stay open until 5am.

Antilla Barcelona, C/Aragó 141–3; **t** 934 51 21 51; FGC Muntaner. The hottest place for salsa, with superb live bands. *Open Mon–Thurs, Sun 11pm–4am, Fri and Sat 11pm–5am.*

Bar Ra, Plaça Gardunya 3, **t** 934 23 18 78; M Liceu. Behind the Boqueria, super-hip staff serve drinks and an array of *tapas* and international fusion dishes, to equally hip music. *Open Mon–Sat 1.30–4 and 9–midnight.*

Bikini, C/Déu i Mata 105; M María Cristina. Giant club that's regularly one of the most popular. *Open Tues–Thurs midnight–4.30am, Fri and Sat midnight–5.30am.*

Espai Barroc, C/Montcada 20; M Jaume I. It's not all techno in BCN: in the historic Palau Dalmases, this fabulous bar is a place to sit and sip amid Baroque luxury, to chamber music. *Open Tues–Sun 4pm–midnight.*

Fonefone, C/Escudellers 24, **t** 933 17 14 24; M Drassanes. Nightly themes range from drum'n'bass to house; the design is modern and retro at the same time. *Open Sun–Thurs 10pm–2.30am, Fri and Sat 10pm–3am.*

KGB, C/Alegre de Dalt 55; M Joanic. A classic neo-Barcelona design creation, with a Cold War spy theme. A traditional late-late last stand. *Open Thurs–Sat 9pm–5am.*

Maremàgnum, Port Vell; M Drassanes. The old port's giant mall has a slew of Latin bars on the first floor, including the Mojito Bar (*open daily noon–4.30am*) and the Tropicana Bar.

Metro, C/Sepúlveda 185, **t** 933 23 5257; M Universitat. Eternally popular (male) gay disco. *Open midnight–5am.*

Mirablau, Pla Dr Andreu, Tibidabo, **t** 934 18 58 79; FGC Tibidabo. A glassed-in bar on Tibidabo with some of the very best views in Barcelona. *Open Mon–Thurs and Sun 11am–4am, Fri and Sat 11am–5am.*

Octopussy, Moll de la Fusta 4, **t** 932 21 40 31; M Drassanes. Very trendy port-side bar-club, with a big gay crowd. *Open Fri and Sat midnight–4am.*

Otto Zutz, C/de Lincoln 15; **t** 932 38 07 22; FGC Gràcia. Dress-code police bristling at the door, this classic club styles itself 'the New York-style disco where the beautiful people go'. *Open Tues–Sat midnight–5.30am.*

La Paloma, C/Tigre 27; M Universitat. Dancers flock to this ornate 1902 dance hall, where a live band plays anything from salsa to tango or bugaloo till 1am, giving way Thurs–Sat to DJ nights. *Open Thurs–Sat 6pm–9.30pm and 11.30pm– 5am, Sun 6pm–9.30pm.*

La Pedrera, C/de Provença 261–5; M Diagonal. The mellow place to be on summer nights, a smooth bar right on Gaudí's roof terrace. *Open July–Sept, Fri–Sat 9pm–midnight.*

Salsitas/Club 22, C/Nou de la Rambla 22, **t** 933 18 08 40; M Liceu. After midnight, Wed–Sat, trendy Salsitas restaurant becomes Club 22. *Open (bar) Tues–Sun 11–5 and 8pm–3am; (restaurant) Tues–Sun 1–4pm and 8–11.*

Torres d'Avila, Poble Espanyol, Montjuïc; M Espanya. The most lavish of all the early-90s design bars, over-the-top postmodern multi-space. *Open Fri–Sat 12.30am–7am.*

Entertainment

Newsstands sell the weekly *Guía del Ocio*, with events listings, and a monthly music calendar *Informatiu Musical* is available free from tourist offices.

L'Auditori, C/Lepant 140; M Marina. New, austere but acoustically pure hall that's now Barcelona's main classical concert venue.

Gran Teatre del Liceu, Ramblas 51–9, *www.liceubarcelona.com*; M Liceu. Rebuilt in the 1990s after a disastrous fire, the city's opera house now has state-of-the-art facilities behind its grand façade.

Mercat de les Flors, C/Lleida 59, **t** 934 26 18 75; M Espanya. Beautiful theatre in an ex-flower market, ideal for big-scale productions.

Palau de la Música Catalana, C/Sant Francesc de Paula 2, **t** 932 68 10 00; M Urquinaona. Irreplaceable: this magnificent 1908 *modernista* concert palace is visually stunning, and has a unique atmosphere.

A compulsive exhibitionist, Barcelona held two great international fairs, in 1888 and 1929, and staged a hell of a show for the 1992 Olympics, bequeathing a festive spirit that colours its incredible complex of buildings.

The Barri Gòtic

Barcelona is designed for walking, through space and time, and there's no better starting point than the ancient heart of the city, the Barri Gòtic or Gothic Quarter, enclosed between Vía Laietana and the Ramblas. At its centre is a gentle hill, the **Mons Tàber**, which was Barcelona's 'acropolis', where the medieval city rose over the ruins of its ancient predecessor, Roman *Barcino*. The Romans enclosed their colony in lofty walls, and when the city gravitated outwards in later centuries it left behind a time capsule on Mons Tàber. One of the best entry points to the Barri Gòtic is Plaça de l'Angel (by *M Jaume I*). Here **Roman walls and towers** make cameo appearances in a mesh of medieval buildings, especially along C/Sots-Tinent Navarro.

Heading into the Barri Gòtic up C/Llibreteria, a first right will take you into **Plaça del Rei**, a magnificent architectural ensemble that once served as the courtyard of the Romanesque-Gothic **Palau Reial Major**, palace of the counts of Barcelona and later the kings of Aragón. The first place to visit is the **Museu d'Història de la Ciutat** (*open Oct–June Tues–Sat 10–2 and 4–8, Sun and hols 10–2; July–Sept Tues–Sat 10–8, Sun and hols 10–2; closed Mon; adm*). The museum occupies a 15th-century Gothic palace; in its basements it offers a fascinating subterranean stroll through Roman *Barcino*, excavated beneath the medieval and modern streets. Also part of the museum are the surviving sections of the Palau Reial, such as the spectacular **Saló de Tinell** or Banqueting Hall (*may be closed for special events*), begun in 1359 and one of the most elegant of all medieval buildings. The hall is linked to the **Capella de Santa Agata**. Begun in 1302, it houses the *Retable del Condestable* (1466) by Catalan Gothic master Jaume Huguet. A narrow, almost hidden staircase leads to the curious 1550s skyscraper that rises over the square, the **Mirador del Rei Martí**, from where you get a great view of the quarter. Just left of the Palau Reial is the **Palau del Lloctinent**. It's now closed, but walk around to C/de les Comtes to peek into the fine courtyard.

Nearby is the **Museu Frederic Marés** (*open Tues and Thurs 10–5, Wed, Fri and Sat 10–7, Sun 10–3; closed Mon; adm*). Incredibly, big as it is, it contains only a fraction of the astonishing collections amassed by sculptor Frederic Marés (1893–1991), Spain's champion hoarder: armies of *ex votos*, a whole array of sweet-faced wooden Virgins and, in the **Museu Sentimental**, every kind of 19th-century flotsam and jetsam.

C/de les Comtes continues beside the huge Gothic **cathedral** (*open Mon–Fri 8–1.30 and 4–7.30, Sat and Sun 8–1.30 and 5–7.30*). It was at least the third church on this site; the first was flattened in a Moorish raid in 985; of the second, Romanesque one only two doorways remain. The earliest bit of the current model is the right transept, built in 1298; carvings on its **Portal de Sant Iu** (by C/dels Comtes) depict St George and Barcelona's first count, Wilfred the Hairy, fighting a dragon and griffon. The cathedral faces **Pla de la Seu**. Its elaborate façade provides a wonderful backdrop to the *sardanes* danced here on Sundays, but sits oddly on this venerable church. This may be because, though based on plans from 1408, it was not actually begun until 1882.

Catalan Gothic is best known for its conquest of space: the cathedral has only three aisles, but its architects made them look like five. In the middle of the nave the elaborate 14th–15th-century **choir stalls** (*open Mon–Sat 9.30–1.30 and 2.30–4; adm; ticket includes lift to the roof*) were emblazoned with arms of the Knights of the Golden Fleece in the 16th century. Below, in the 14th-century **crypt**, Barcelona's co-patroness the 4th-century virgin martyr Santa Eulàlia lies in an alabaster sarcophagus carved with scenes of her martyrdom. Against the wall to the right of the altar, Count Ramon Berenguer I and his wife lie in painted, velvet-covered sarcophagi, while below a door leads to the sacristy and the **treasury** (*not always open*).

The Romanesque **Portal de Sant Sever** leads to a medieval oasis, the **cloister**, begun in 1385, with the **Fountain of Sant Jordi**. At Corpus Christi flowers are wound round the fountain and a hollow egg is set to dance in the jet of water (*l'ou com balla*). There's no need to look for eggs, either, as a flock of white geese natter below. They have been there since anyone can remember, symbolic of Santa Eulàlia's purity or a memory of the geese that saved Rome. The Chapter House holds the **cathedral Museum** (*open daily 10–1; adm*), with superb paintings by medieval masters.

The cloister gives on to C/del Bisbe, which, to the left, passes under a neo-Gothic bridge built only in 1928. To the right, next to Pla de la Seu, a **flea market** takes place every Thursday in **Plaça Nova**, from where C/dels Arcs leads toward Plaça Catalunya.

In the opposite direction, C/del Bisbe leads to **Plaça Sant Jaume**. This grand square has been the heart of civic Barcelona since it served as the Roman forum. It is still something of a forum today, with a dialogue between the Catalan government (the *Generalitat*) and Barcelona's City Hall (the *Ajuntament*) either side of it. Established in 1249, the first Generalitat was one of the most powerful of Spain's medieval parliaments. The **Palau de la Generalitat** (*guided tours 2nd and 4th Sun of month, in English at 11am; adm free, but bring ID and arrive early to sign up*) was begun in the 15th century to give it a permanent seat. When Philip V abolished the Generalitat in 1714 it was occupied by the royal administration, but its original role was never forgotten, and since 1977 it has again been the seat of Catalan government. It turns its fairest face towards C/del Bisbe Irurita, a 1416 façade by Marc Safont peopled by gargoyles and Catalonia's patron, St George, on a medallion over the door. Across Plaça Sant Jaume is the **Ajuntament** (*open Sat and Sun 10–2; bring ID*). The neoclassical façade, added in the 1840s, is unexciting, but the Gothic façade on C/de la Ciutat preserves some of its charm. The oldest part of the building is the 14th-century **Saló de Cent**.

From the plaça, C/Paradís leads to the summit of Mons Tàber, marked by an ancient millstone in the pavement. Inside a Gothic courtyard are four columns from the 1st-century AD Roman **Temple of Augustus**. In the Middle Ages Barcelona's Jewish quarter or *Call* was just west of the Generalitat. On tiny C/Marlet a stone remains, inscribed in Hebrew: 'Sacred foundation of Rabbi Samuel Hassareri, of everlasting life. Year 692.'

From the Gothic side of the Ajuntament, C/Hèrcules leads to **Plaça Sant Just** and two fine medieval palaces: **Moixó**, adorned with *esgrafiados*, and **Palamòs** (*open 3rd Sun of month 10.30–2, or by appt*). Here, too, is the parish church of the count-kings of Aragón, **Sants Just i Pastor**, founded, tradition states, by Charlemagne's son Louis the Pious in 801. In 1893 Joan Miró was born in a Parisian-style arcade called **Passatge de Crédit**, built in 1879 between C/Ferrán and Baixada de Sant Miquel. Several old palaces on nearby C/Avinyó housed brothels by the 1900s; the ladies in one were the subject of Picasso's 1907 *Les Demoiselles d'Avignon*, his unfinished Cubist manifesto.

La Ribera, Carrer Montcada and the Ciutadella

North of Via Laietana is La Ribera, Barcelona's medieval maritime quarter and, nowadays, a decidedly funkier area than the Barri Gòtic. Amid its genteel decrepitude there is one of the great highlights of Barcelona: Carrer Montcada, a street given in 1148 by Ramón Berenguer IV to a rich merchant named Montcada, who sold properties to other gentlemen of the town, creating a medieval Millionaires' Row. It filled up with merchant palaces, forming a narrow gully of solid façades, intimate courtyards and ornate details of immense charm. Today most of these once-secret palaces are museums or galleries, a trend begun in 1963 when the loveliest of them, the 15th-century **Palau Aguilar** and adjacent Castellet and Meca palaces were restored to house the **Museu Picasso** (*open Tues–Sat 10–8, Sun and hols 10–3; closed Mon; adm*). The core of its collection, donated by one of his oldest friends, Jaume Sabartés, is his very early works, beginning with the drawings of an exceptionally gifted 8-year-old in Málaga, followed by Barcelona works like a menu for Els Quatre Gats (1900), his first paid commission. It gives an extraordinary insight into the development of a genius.

A few steps down at C/Montcada 12, the **Museu Tèxtil i de la Indumentària** (*open Tues–Sat 10–6, Sun 10–3; closed Mon; adm; combined ticket with Museu Barbier-Mueller available*) occupies the 16th-century Palau dels Marquesos de Lió, with a café in its pretty courtyard. Dedicated to textiles and fashion, its exhibits run from rare embroideries from Granada to classic '50s frocks by Balenciaga. Alongside it, another Gothic palace holds the **Museu Barbier-Mueller d'Art Precolombí** (*same hours as Textile museum; adm*), an exquisite collection of Pre-Columbian art. Further along at No.20 is the finest Baroque palace in Barcelona, the 17th-century **Palau Dalmases**, complete with a sumptuous café dripping with velvet (*see p.51*). Opposite, **Galerie Maeght**, in the 16th-century Palau dels Cervelló, puts on excellent art shows and has a large shop.

Carrer Montcada ends at Passeig del Born and **Santa María del Mar** (*open daily 9–1.30 and 4.30–8*), the most perfect and pure expression of Catalan Gothic. King Alfons III laid the first stone of this fabulous church in 1329, and for 50 years all the able-bodied men of La Ribera donated their labour to build it. In 1936, Anarchists set it ablaze, destroying the elaborate Baroque fittings added in the 18th century. The current lack of any decoration, though, only enhances its sublime beauty. A great dark mass, the austere façade on Plaça Santa María is only embellished with a rose window. Enter (*from Passeig del Born*), and what was closed and fortress-like from without opens up to a miraculous spaciousness, early evidence of the Catalan vocation for daring architecture. A minimum of interior supports hold up the vaults: the whole converges on a semicircular apse, the raised altar defined by a crescent of slender columns like a glade in a forest. By its southern wall, the fan-shaped **Fossar de les Moreres** marks the mass tomb of Catalan resisters to the troops of Philip V in 1714.

The neighbourhood around Santa María has been gentrifying and trendifying for years. The now bar-lined **Passeig del Born** once hosted medieval tournaments; at its north end, the beautiful 1876 wholesale market the **Mercat del Born** looks set to be reincarnated as a library. Street names recall medieval trades: C/Argenteria, for example, was the silversmiths' street, while C/Corders was home to rope-makers. On **Pla del Palau** stands **La Llotja**, Barcelona's first stock exchange. Though slapped with a neoclassical facelift in 1802, the magnificent 1380s **Sala de Contractacions** inside was left untouched, but sadly, since the exchange moved to a modern building in the 1990s it has been closed up. The grand old **Estació de França** on Av. Marquès de l'Argentera has also lost most of its train passengers to the Estació de Sants, but as one of its new roles now plays host to an annual New Year's bash.

Beyond the Born is Barcelona's most historic park, the **Parc de la Ciutadella** (*open daily, Nov–Feb 10–6; Mar, Oct 10–7; April, Sept 10–8; May–Aug 10–9*). The 'citadel' it is named after was built to keep the populace in check following a bitter date in the annals of Barcelona, 1714, when the city fell to the troops of Philip V after an 11-month siege. In 1869 this hated mastodon was ceded to the city to be made into a park, and in 1888 it was chosen as the site of Barcelona's first Universal Exhibition, a grand stage for architectural innovation, Catalonia's own colourful, eclectic *modernista* style.

The park is well used, as families paddle in little boats around the **Cascada**, a giant rocky fountain by Josep Fontserè, said to have had Gaudí as his assistant. The old citadel's Arsenal is now the seat of the Catalan Parliament. It also houses the **Museu d'Art Modern** (*open Tues–Sat 10–7, Sun 10–2.30; closed Mon; adm*), the MNAC's (*see p.61*) collection of Catalan art from 1850–1920, although at some point it should join the rest of the museum on Montjuïc. It gives a dazzling introduction to *modernisme*.

There are also many relics of the great fair of 1888 the *mudéjar*-style brick **Arc de Triomf** on Pg Lluís Companys, two lovely iron and glass greenhouses, the **Umbracle** and **Hivernacle**, and the **Museu de Geologia** (*open Tues, Wed, Fri, Sat and Sun 10–2, Thurs 10–6.30; closed Mon; adm*), Barcelona's first public museum. Best of all is the **Castell dels Tres Dragons**, designed by Domènech i Montaner as the Exhibition's café and now the **Museu de Zoologia** (*open Tues–Wed and Fri–Sun 10–2, Thurs 10–6.30; closed Mon; adm*). The Ciutadella also contains Barcelona's **Zoo** (*open daily Nov–Feb 10–5; Mar and Oct 10–6; April and Sept 10–7; May–Aug 9.30–7.30; adm exp*).

The Seafront, Barceloneta and the Port Vell

Before the 1980s the seafront north from Barceloneta was filled by industrial sprawl. The need to house 15,000 athletes for the 1992 Olympics, however, linked in with the plans of the reforming Ajuntament as the city embarked upon its biggest-ever urban-renewal scheme. The coast was cleared to create the **Parc de Mar**, behind which a whole new district went up, the **Vila Olímpica**. Converted into housing since the games, the Vila has remained a soulless, un-Barcelona-like area of wide streets, car parks and desolate spaces. The Olympic marina, however, the **Port Olímpic**, is one of the real hits of '92, ringed by restaurants and a hugely popular summer strolling spot, while the kilometres of newly-minted **beaches** – with all-new clean sand, since the old stuff was beyond redemption – are one of 'new Barcelona's' most-loved features.

An older piece of planning, **Barceloneta** or 'Little Barcelona', was created after 61 streets were cleared to make way for the Ciutadella in the 1720s, when a French army engineer designed a *barri* to house the dispossessed on parade-ground lines, in odd, narrow blocks. Famed for fish restaurants, Barceloneta is still vibrantly populated. From there you can cross to Montjuïc on **Transbordador** cable cars (*see p.45*).

Just as important as the reconstruction of the seafront has been the transformation of the city's old harbour, or **Port Vell**, which has also become a leisure zone. The **Palau de Mar**, a giant former warehouse, has been rehabilitated into restaurant space and to house the **Museu d'Història de Catalunya** (*open Tues and Thurs–Sat 10–7, Wed 10–8, Sun and hols 10–2.30; closed Mon; adm*). Nearby, the old Moll d'Espanya quay is crowned by a spectacular shopping mall and all-round leisure complex,

Maremàgnum, with restaurants and bars that draw strollers on Sundays and teen crowds at night, plus cinemas and an **Aquarium** (*open July–Aug daily 9.30am–11pm; June and Sept daily 9.30–9.30; Oct–May Mon–Fri 9.30–9, Sat and Sun 9.30–9.30; adm*).

A handsome footbridge, the **Rambla de Mar**, links the Moll d'Espanya to the foot of the Columbus monument (*see* below) and rotates to let sailing boats through. The final stage of the Port Vell development is I.M Pei's huge **World Trade Centre**, built to spearhead Barcelona's ambition to become the Mediterranean's busiest cruise port.

Back on land, all eyes are drawn to another souvenir of 1888, the **Monument a Colom** or Columbus Monument (*open summer daily 9–8.30; winter Mon–Fri 10–1.30 and 3.30–6.30, Sat–Sun 10–6.30; adm*), a cast-iron column topped by the admiral himself. You can ascend into the crown under his feet in a lift; at the foot of the column you can also catch a *Golondrina* ('swallow boat') across the harbour (*see* p.45). A better memorial to the city's maritime past is the **Drassanes** or royal shipyards, also on Portal de la Pau, built in 1255–1388 and the best-preserved medieval shipyard in the world. It houses the **Museu Marítim** (*open daily 10–7; adm*), and its huge vaults are a superb setting for its ships' models, figureheads, interactive exhibits and a full-size replica of the royal galley used by Don Juan of Austria at the Battle of Lepanto in 1571.

Ramblas, Raval and the Plaça Catalunya

Columbus also marks the beginning of Barcelona's most celebrated street, the **Ramblas**. *Ramla* means 'sand' in Arabic, and long ago this is what it was, the sandy bed of a torrent beside the walls of the medieval city. When dry it was a major thoroughfare, where butchers had their stalls, employers came in search of labourers, and gallows bore their strange fruit. By the 14th century its western side had begun to be built up with a new district, the **Raval**, 'Outside the Walls', site of all sorts of business not allowed inside the old city: slaughterhouses, hospitals, brothels, other kinds of vice. In the 18th century it was decided to make the Ramblas a paved, park avenue.

Day and night the Ramblas – officially five connected streets – are crowded with natives and visitors from every continent, and Elvis impersonators, flamenco buskers and 'human statues'. But, like the rest of post-Olympic Barcelona, it has been tidied up, to the detriment of the sex trade once so prevalent on the lowest *rambla*, **Rambla de Santa Mònica** (now it's squirrelled away in side streets). More visible is the **Museu de Cera** wax museum (*open winter Mon–Fri 10–1.30 and 4–7.30, Sat and Sun 11–2 and 4.30–8.30; summer daily 10–10; adm*). A detour into the Raval down C/Nou de la Rambla leads to the **Palau Güell** (*open Mon–Sat 10.15–1 and 4.15–7; guided tours only, groups of max. 30; tours every 15mins; adm*), an extraordinary 1880s Hispano-Moorish mansion that was Gaudí's first major creation for his patron, financier Eusebi Güell. It has the most complete interior of any Gaudí house, and a truly bizarre roofscape.

The corner of the Ramblas and C/Sant Pau is dominated by Barcelona's opera house, the **Liceu**, hub of an operatic tradition that has produced such fine singers as Caballé, Carreras and Victoria de los Angeles. Devastated by fire in 1994, it has been completely rebuilt. It looks down on **Pla de la Boqueria**, with its colourful mosaic by Miró, the hub of the Ramblas. A bank occupies the 1885 **Casa Bruno Quadros**, a former umbrella-maker's, defended by an oriental dragon holding a brolly. There are two more detours from here into the Raval. C/Sant Pau leads, remarkably, to the city's oldest surviving church, the lovely 12th-century Romanesque **Sant Pau del Camp** (*open Wed–Mon 11.30–1 and 6–7.30, Tues 11.30–12.30*). C/Hospital meanwhile leads to the **Antic Hospital de la Santa Creu**, founded in 1024 and Barcelona's main hospital until 1926, when the doctors relocated to Hospital de Sant Pau (*see* p.60). Today its Gothic halls house Catalonia's national library (*open to card holders only*), but the fine courtyards are open, and the chapel is a gallery, **La Capella** (*open Tues–Sat 12–2 and 4–8, Sun 11–2; adm free*), showcasing young artists. Across Pla de la Boqueria, streets lead towards the Barri Gòtic: C/Cardenal Casañas leads into the **Barri del Pi** (named after a pine tree), and the **Plaça del Pi**, one of old Barcelona's most charming squares.

Rambla de Sant Josep (also known as *Rambla de les Flors*, of flowers) is the most perfumed, lined with flower stalls and kiosks selling birds and rabbits. On the left, a *modernista* arch beckons you into Mercat de Sant Josep, better known as **La Boqueria**, one of the greatest of all food markets. Next to it, the neoclassical **Palau de la Virreina** (*open Tues–Sat 10–8.30, Sun 10–2.30*) now contains an exhibition space and the city's information office for cultural events. Further up, a right on to C/Canuda leads to **Plaça Vila de Madrid**, with excavated 2nd–4th-century AD **Roman tombs**.

A turn left onto C/Bonsuccès in contrast will take you to one of Barcelona's new cultural districts, with the glowing white **Museu d'Art Contemporani de Barcelona** or **MACBA** (*open winter Mon, Wed, Thurs, Fri 11–7.30, Sat 10–8, Sun 10–3; summer Mon, Wed, Fri 11–8, Thurs 11–7.30, Sat 10–8, Sun 10–3; adm*), designed by US architect Richard Meier in 1995 as a contemporary art showcase. Next door and in the same vein, an old orphanage was rebuilt as the **Centre de Cultura Contemporània de Barcelona** or **CCCB** (*open summer Tues–Sat 11–8, Sun 11–3; winter Tues, Thurs and Fri 11–2 and 4–8, Wed and Sat 11–8, Sun 11–7; adm*), the base for a whole raft of exhibitions and cutting-edge arts projects. The last *Rambla*, **Canaletes**, is named after its magical water fountain, which promises that all who drink of it will stay in or return to Barcelona.

Canaletes ends at the **Plaça Catalunya**, the vast, jumbly square that is the hub of human and pigeon life in Barcelona, dividing the medieval city and the 19th-century Eixample; nearly all city buses, Metro and FGC lines converge here, under giant banks and the Corte Inglés department store. Tucked like a pearl off the *plaça* is the simple Romanesque church and Gothic cloister of **Santa Anna** (*open daily 9–1 and 6.30–8.30, hols 10–2*). East of here off Av. Portal de l'Angel, in a *modernista* fantasy building by Josep Puig i Cadafalch, is **Els Quatre Gats**, Barcelona's legendary bohemian-intellectual café-meeting place of the 1900s. Closed for decades, it was reopened in the 1980s with copies of its original décor (*see* p.48).

For *modernista* architecture at its most delightfully extreme, though, continue down C/Montsió and cross Vía Laietana to C/Sant Pere Més Alt, to Lluís Domènech i Montaner's 1908 **Palau de la Música Catalana** (*tours daily 10–3.30; visits by guided tour only, every 30 mins in English, Spanish and Catalan, tours last 50 mins; adm*). This remains Barcelona's most prestigious concert hall, despite the new Auditori (*see* p.51) and its own eccentric acoustics. Undulating and adorned with floral and musical motifs in tiles and mosaics, it's almost too ripe and rich in these narrow streets, like a bouquet stuffed into a cupboard. The interior is, if anything, more colourful.

The Eixample

In the early 19th century, Barcelona was still confined within its medieval limits, hemmed in by the Ciutadella and oppressive city walls. As the population grew and the Industrial Revolution took its first baby steps, the city became ever more claustrophobic, and in the 1850s permission was finally given for the walls to come down. A competition was held for a plan for the development of the new 'extension' or **Eixample**. The winning scheme was that of an engineer called Ildefons Cerdà, for a regular grid with distinctive chamfered corners at the intersections. Hated by many for years, this has since become an inseparable part of Barcelona's identity. Cerdà's great plan had utopian ambitions: he hoped that his rational layout would eliminate social classes, and intended that there should be gardens in the middle of each block (discarded by developers, as buildings were more profitable). Cerdà also hoped to create a new centre for the city at **Plaça de les Glòries Catalanes**, the meeting point of his giant avenues the Gran Via, Diagonal and Meridiana. For decades Glòries was just a giant road junction, but in the 1990s it finally gained more prominence with the building of two of Barcelona's grand new cultural institutions, the Rafael Moneo-designed **Auditori** concert hall and the **Teatre Nacional de Catalunya** by Ricard Bofill.

Also, in spite of Cerdà's egalitarian intentions, social snobbery won out and, just as Paris has its Right and Left Banks, Barcelona has its Right and Left Eixample, divided by the delightful **Rambla de Catalunya**. The Right Eixample is the more prestigious: here, *modernista* architects created visual fireworks to flaunt the status of wealthy clients, producing Europe's greatest treasure trove of Art Nouveau buildings.

The greatest concentration of *modernista* masterpieces is along the Eixample's most elegant boulevard, Passeig de Gràcia. Its most dazzling stretch, between C/Consell de Cent and C/Aragó, is the **Mansana de la Discòrdia** – a pun on *mansana*, which means both 'apple' and 'block' – with three contrasting beauties. The first, at No.35, is the **Casa Lleó Morera** (1905), Lluís Domènech i Montaner's most lavish residential building; three doors down at No.41 stands Josep Puig i Cadafalch's much more Gothick-y **Casa Amatller**; while at No.43 is Gaudí's astonishing **Casa Batlló**. This was a nondescript building when textile magnate Josep Batlló commissioned Gaudí to give it a facelift in 1904. He transformed its flat façade into an allegory of St George and the dragon, a rippling, magical skin of different shades of blue ceramics and tiles, while his collaborator Josep Jujol topped it with an equally sublime coloured roof, the dragon's scaly back. Privately owned, it isn't normally open to visitors, but since the 'Year of Gaudí' for his 150th anniversary in 2002 it has been viewable more frequently.

Around the corner from the Mansana de la Discòrdia, the **Fundació Antoni Tàpies** (*open Tues–Sun 11–8; closed Mon exc on hols; adm*), is housed in Domènech's building for his brother's publishing company, Editorial Montaner i Simón (1880–5). In a classic case of Barcelona's architectural daring, in the 1980s this distinguished brick structure was elegantly transformed into a showcase for the work of Catalonia's most famous living artist, with Tàpies own giant steel-wool sculpture *Núvol i Cadira* ('Cloud and Chair') on the roof. It also presents dynamic shows of other artists.

Casa Batlló created such a sensation that Gaudí was soon given the opportunity to outdo himself a few blocks up Passeig de Gràcia on the corner of C/Provença, with the

Casa Milà, the most extraordinary apartment building ever, nicknamed *La Pedrera*, 'the stone quarry'. The stone façade undulates like a cliff sculpted by waves, rising to a white, foamy crest of a roof, topped by a garden of chimneys. The interior is scarcely less striking. In one of the apartments, **El Pis de la Pedrera** (*open daily 10–8; adm free; guided visits Mon–Fri at 6pm, Sat, Sun at 11am*) the original décor has been re-created, while the **Espai Gaudí** offers an overview of the man's work. In addition, in summer the Pedrera roof becomes the venue for a very special cocktail bar (*see p.51*).

In the streets either side of Passeig de Gràcia are many, many more curving, sensual *modernista* inventions, and enthusiasts can spend happy hours discovering them. Local tourist offices and bookshops offer an excellent range of architectural guides.

The Sagrada Família

George Orwell, writing of the Civil War church burnings in his *Homage to Catalonia*, wondered why there was one that the mobs spared, a peculiar one with spires shaped like bottles. These 350ft bottles belonged to Gaudí's **Sagrada Família** (*open April–Aug daily 9–8; Mar and Sept–Oct daily 9–7; Nov–Feb daily 9–6; adm*). Occupying an entire Cerdà block, the Temple Expiatori de la Sagrada Família is surely the most compelling and controversial building site in the world. It was begun in 1882, on the initiative of a group of conservative Catholic laymen. They first hired Francesc del Villar, who planned a neo-Gothic church, but he only got as far as the crypt before disagreeing with his patrons and being replaced by Gaudí, then 31, in 1883. Gaudí finished the crypt and worked on and off on the project for the next 43 years, as it grew grander with each plan. In his last 15 years he accepted no other commissions, and sold everything he owned to continue the work, living in a hut on the site.

Gaudí intended the Sagrada Família to be 'an immense palace of Christian memory' and wanted every aspect of Catholic doctrine to be expressed in some nook or cranny of the temple; there were to be three façades, dedicated to the Nativity, the Passion and, the main one, to Glory. He started on the **Nativity Façade** and finished one tower, before wandering in front of a tram in 1926. Work came to a halt until 1954, when the Joseph Society, its original sponsors, raised money to carry on, instructing Gaudí's former assistants to draw up plans based on surviving drawings and what they remembered of his ideas. Since 1987, architect Jordi Bonet, sculptor Josep Subirachs and Japanese sculptor Etsuro Sotoo have been in charge. Their work offends purists, who believe the temple is best left as it was when Gaudí died, but another current insists that it must be completed. Subirachs finished the **Passion Façade** in 1998, but there is something depressingly kitsch about the result. You can take a **lift** (*open 10–5.45*) up the Towers, for a truly vertigo-testing ramble above the city. In the crypt is the **Museu de la Sagrada Família**, with photos, diagrams and models, including an astonishing one made of chains and sacks, used by Gaudí to build the Güell crypt.

Avinguda Gaudí, lined with cafés, leads from the Sagrada Família to another giant *modernista* work, one that's both complete and useful. Domènech i Montaner died before finishing his **Hospital de la Santa Creu i Sant Pau**, but his son finished it for him in 1930. Covering nine Eixample blocks, it's a lovely place to visit even if you're well, conceived as a 'garden city' of 26 mosaic-encrusted pavilions with tiled roofs.

Montjuïc, its Museums and the Olympic Ring

Looming up over the port and the old city is the 705ft slope of Montjuïc. For most of Barcelona's history it was reserved for defence, but from 1910 its northern slopes were landscaped to be the site of yet another international fair, finally held in 1929. Many exhibition buildings later became museums. Then, for 1992, Montjuïc's 1930s stadium became the centrepiece of the Olympic Ring. These attractions aside, the mountain is one of Barcelona's favourite green lungs: it's lovely for walking, and the focus of many much-loved rides, with a funicular and two kinds of cable car (*see* p.45).

The show begins in **Plaça d'Espanya**. The entrance to Montjuïc is guarded by tall **Venetian campaniles**, framing the view of the exhibition palaces. In between is the **Font Màgica** (*4 May–4 Oct Thurs–Sun and eves before hols, shows 9.30pm–11.30pm; 4 Oct–4 May Fri–Sat 7pm–8.30pm*), the dancing fountain. Created for the 1929 fair, on weekend nights it performs a dazzling aquatic ballet of colour and light, while search-lights radiate in a peacock's tail from the Palau Nacional; despite all Barcelona's flash new features, this consistently rates as one of its all-time most popular attractions.

From the fountains, a never-ending stair (and escalators) ascend to the **Palau Nacional**, home of the remarkable **Museu Nacional d'Art de Catalunya** or **MNAC** (*open Tues–Sat 10–7, Sun 10–2.30; adm*). Its high point is the world's finest collection of Romanesque murals, rescued in the 1920s from decaying chapels in the Pyrenees, a hypnotic array of bold, expressive images. Gothic art is also well represented, and at some point the Museu d'Art Modern (*see* p.56) is also due to be relocated here.

A short walk west of the Palau Nacional is another relic of 1929, the **Poble Espanyol** (*open July and Aug Mon 9–8, Tues–Thurs 9–2, Fri and Sat 9–4, Sun 9–midnight; Sept–June Mon 9–8, Tues–Sat 9–2, Sun 9–midnight; adm*). Conceived as an anthology of Spanish architecture, it contains replicas of buildings from across the country, arranged with Disneyland deftness. Montjuïc's other attractions lie east (left, from Plaça d'Espanya) of the Palau Nacional. Steps lead down to the oldest gardens of Montjuïc, **La Rosaleda**, and the **Teatre Grec**, used for the summer arts festival. The **Museu Arqueològic** (*open Tues–Sat 9.30–7, Sun 10–2.30; closed Mon; adm, free Sun*) is a 'prequel' to the Palau Nacional, covering Palaeolithic to Visigothic Catalonia.

Av. de l'Estadi leads to the **Anella Olímpica** or Olympic Ring, with the **Piscines Bernat Picornell** pool, the **Estadi Olímpic**, rebuilt within the 1929 shell for 1992, and the spec-tacular **Palau Sant Jordi** indoor arena, by Japanese architect Arata Isozaki. The elegant white needle, death to passing Zeppelins, is the **Torre Telefònica**, a TV relay tower.

Towards the sea, Av. de l'Estadi continues to the **Fundació Joan Miró** (*open Tues, Wed, Fri and Sat 11–7 (July–Sept 10–8), Thurs 10–9.30, Sun and hols 10–2.30; closed Mon exc hols; adm*), in a beautiful white building designed in 1972 by Miró's great friend Josep Lluís Sert. Its core is a fine collection of Miró's own work, but this marvellous space also consistently presents some of Barcelona's most vibrant contemporary art shows.

East of the Fundació, *Telefèric* cable cars swoop up to the **Castell de Montjuïc**. This glowering fortress now hosts the **Museu Militar** (*open Mar–Oct 9.30–7.30; Nov–Mar 9.30–4.30; adm*), and there's a wonderful view from the ramparts. Down below, by the cable-car station at **Miramar**, you can enjoy more fine views over the port.

Other Parts of Town: Parc Güell, Tibidabo and Pedralbes

Gaudí's sublime **Parc Güell** occupies one of Barcelona's balconies, 'Bald Mountain', *Mont Pelat*, between Gràcia and Tibidabo (*M Lesseps, then walk up Travessera de Dalt, left turn up C/Larrard, or bus 24 from Plaça Catalunya; open daily Nov–Feb 10–6; Mar and Oct 10–7; April and Sept 10–8; May–Aug 10–9*). It owes its existence to Eusebi Güell, who hoped to create an 'English-style' garden suburb here. He gave Gaudí free reign to create a grand entrance, central market and terraced drives. As a housing development it was a flop, and after Güell's death was given to the city as a park. It glows like an enchanted mirage: the entrance is flanked by two **pavilions** crowned by Gaudí's signature steeple with a double cross, while the stairway swoops around the most jovial **dragon** imaginable, leading to the covered market, the **Hall of a Hundred Columns**. Its scalloped roof supports the **serpentine bench** on the terrace above, with a fantastic snaking ceramic collage, mostly by Gaudí's assistant Jujol.

Before moving to his hut by the Sagrada Família Gaudí lived for years in a house in the park. Now the **Casa-Museu Gaudí** (*open daily Mar–Sept 10–7; Nov–Feb 10–6; adm*), it has examples of the wonderful furniture Gaudí designed for his houses.

For an incomparable view over Barcelona, ascend the highest peak of Collserola, the 1,804ft **Tibidabo** behind the city, and another favourite place for clearing the head. Getting there is part of the enjoyment: by FGC train to Av Tibidabo, then on the lovely old 1902 *Tramvia Blau* trams to Plaça Dr Andreu (site of some great bars, like the Mirablau, *see* p.51) and then by **Funicular** to the top (for all transport, *see* pp.44–5). On the summit stands an ugly church, restaurants and the **Parc d'Attraccions** (*open Tues–Fri 11–7, Sat and Sun 11–9; adm*) funfair, with one of the most panoramic Ferris-wheel rides imaginable. Just south, another peak is occupied by Norman Foster's 800ft **Torre de Collserola** (*open summer Sat and Sun 11–7, Wed–Fri 11–2.30 and 3.30–7; winter Sat and Sun 11–7; adm*), a high-tech telecommunications tower built for the Olympics, which offers still giddier views. There are lovely walks in the woods nearby.

Now an upscale residential area, **Pedralbes** was until the 20th century just a village, clustered around its monastery. The **Palau de Pedralbes** on Av. Diagonal was built for the Güell family (but not by Gaudí). One wing now houses the **Museu de Cerámica** (*open Tues–Sun 10–3; closed Mon; adm, joint ticket with Museu de les Arts Decoratives*) with a superb collection covering the whole history of ceramics-making in Spain; in another is the **Museu de les Arts Decoratives**, with tapestries, furniture, handicrafts and design. Av. Pedralbes leads from there to the Gothic **Monestir de Pedralbes**, now home to the **Col.lecció Thyssen-Bornemisza** (*bus 22 from Plaça Catalunya or FGC Reina Elisenda; open Tues–Sun 10–2; closed Mon; adm*). Most of the extraordinary art collection deposited in Spain by Baron von Thyssen is in Madrid (*see* p.143), but part of it was placed in Barcelona, mostly early or religious paintings to go with the monastic setting, with early Italian masters such as Fra Angelico (a sublime *Madonna of Humility*), and smaller works by Titian, Tintoretto and Veronese. The **monastery**, founded in 1326, is worth visiting all by itself, a Catalan Gothic time-capsule with a serenely astonishing three-storey **cloister**. On one side is the small **Capella de Sant Miquel**, with the finest Gothic fresco cycle in Catalonia, Ferrer Bassa's *Seven Joys of the Virgin* and *The Passion*, from 1346.

Day Trips and Overnighters from Barcelona

Collserola and Sant Cugat

Some of the most enjoyable escapes from Barcelona can be made very easily just by heading into the Serra de Collserola, the giant ring of mountains that provides the backdrop to the city's stage. Because it rises so steeply behind the city, it's easy to find scarcely built-up woodland just 20 minutes from Plaça Catalunya, along the FGC rail line. **Vallvidrera**, still on the seaward side of the mountain (Baixador de Vallvidrera station), is a tranquil hill suburb with a tremendous view back over Barcelona. It's also the jumping-off point for the **Collserola nature park**, where there are lovely walks and bike tracks amid woods of oak, herbs and pines full of birds (the park **Information Centre** has free maps with well-marked routes). On the other side of the great hill, the main road and train lines emerge from tunnels near **Les Planes**, a small 'plateau' that's been a popular picnic spot for decades, and **La Floresta**, a mellow little village-suburb in the hills with more delightful, very easy walks in the woods.

Since the opening of the Vallvidrera tunnel transformed its road access, **Sant Cugat del Vallès** has been growing fast as a semi-suburb of Barcelona, but it has a charming old town, which grew up around a Visigothic abbey, the **Monestir de Sant Cugat** (*open June–Sept Tues–Sat 10–1 and 3.30–5.30; Oct–May Tues–Sat 10–1; adm*). According to legend founded by Charlemagne or his son Louis the Pious, the Gothic church that now stands is wonderfully austere, with a great rose window and tower; beside it, the 12th-century cloister is a Romanesque masterpiece, with 144 carved capitals depicting scenes from the Testaments by the monk Arnau Cadell. Another masterpiece, the *Retablo of all the Saints* (1395) by Pere Serra, is in the chapterhouse museum, showing the Virgin and Child surrounded by most of the saints on the calendar.

Getting There

All these towns are on the **FGC train** line from Plaça Catalunya to Sabadell or Terrassa. Trains run every 10–20 mins, 5am–midnight daily; journey time to Sant Cugat is around 25mins. Free timetables are available at the FGC information office in Plaça Catalunya, or call t 932 05 15 15 (*see* also p.44).

By **car**, you can choose between the fast Vallvidrera tunnel (toll), a continuation of the Via Augusta in Barcelona (or exit 8 off the Ronda de Dalt ring road), or the much slower but more scenic Carretera de la Rabassada (exit 5 off the Ronda) up and over Collserola.

Tourist Information

Sant Cugat del Vallés: Plaça de Barcelona 17, t 935 89 22 88.

Eating Out

Braseria La Bolera, Baixada de l'Alba 20, Sant Cugat, t 936 74 16 75 (*moderate*). Pretty restaurant in old Sant Cugat with Catalan country classics: meat chargrilled *a la brasa*, with luscious *all i oli* and *pa amb tomàquet*, bread with oil and tomato. *Closed Mon*.

Can Casas, Carretera de la Rabassada Km 6.5, t 935 89 16 68 (*moderate*). In a big, old, plainly-restored farmhouse off the hill road between Tibidabo and Sant Cugat, and naturally serving hearty Catalan country food. *Closed Mon*.

Guiomar, C/Sant Antoni 58, Sant Cugat, t 935 89 31 13 (*inexpensive–moderate*). Modern, eclectic 'Catalan-Mediterranean' cooking, with enjoyable salads and vegetarian and light dishes. The atmosphere is relaxed, and there's a charming garden terrace.

Getting There

The best way to get to Montserrat is by **FGC train** from Plaça d'Espanya (Manresa line, R-5). Trains run every hour, 8.36am–3.36pm. Get off at Aeri de Montserrat station, where you link up with the thrilling *Telefèric* (cable car) to the monastery. A return ticket, cable car included, costs €13; there are also two all-inclusive tickets: the *TransMontserrat*, which includes metro, train, cable car, and Sant Joan funicular (€19.50), and *Tot Montserrat*, which gives you all this plus entrance to the museum and lunch at the self-service café (€34). Trains return to Barcelona hourly 11.35am–6.35pm. For more information, call the **FGC** on **t** 932 05 15 15, *www.fgc.net*.

There's a daily Juliá **bus** to Montserrat (departures at 9am, return 7pm, **t** 934 90 40 00) leaving from the company's depot next to Barcelona-Sants train station.

By **car**, take the A-2 *autopista* to Martorell, exit onto the N-II, and carry on to the turn off at Abrera (60km). The road up to the mountain is slow and winding, and often crowded at weekends, Easter and in holiday seasons.

Tourist Information

Montserrat: Plaça de la Creu, **t** 938 77 77 77.

Where to Stay and Eat

Montserrat is not known as a food destination: places near the monastery tend to be mediocre and overpriced, so many people prefer to take a picnic. The **café** by Sant Joan funicular (*open summer only*) is a bit better than the main self-service café. For a feel for Montserrat stay overnight, but be prepared: it can get cold even in summer. There are two hotels, and there's also a **campsite** near the Sant Joan funicular, **t** 938 35 02 51.

★★★Abat Cisneros, **t** 938 35 02 01 (*expensive–moderate*). A honeymooners' special; bed and breakfast, full- or half-board available; the restaurant is open to non-residents.

Restautant La Pujada, C/Pont 7, Monistrol de Montserrat, **t** 938 35 02 33 (*inexpensive*). Pleasant bar-restaurant in Monistrol (next train stop towards Manresa) with enjoyable Catalan country dishes and *tapas*.

Montserrat, the 'Dream Turned Mountain'

Strange, mystical Montserrat, traditionally the spiritual heart of Catalonia, looms up 40 kilometres northwest of Barcelona. Its name, 'serrated mountain', is apt enough; the fantastical 10-kilometre massif is made up of jagged stone pinnacles rising precipitously over gorges, domes and terraces, all so different from the country below that it seemed heaven itself had dropped it there to prove all things are possible.

Centuries' worth of strange geological phenomena have left a mountain sculpted into a hedgehog of rifts and phallic peaks, with names like Potato, Salamander or Bishop's Belly. Its human history is just as fantastical: St Peter supposedly came here to hide an image of the Virgin carved by St Luke in a cave, and in 880, not long after Christians regained control over the region, a black-faced statue of the Virgin (hidden, it seems, by someone, if not St Peter, before the advance of the Moors) was found on Montserrat. The 'Black Madonna', the *Moreneta*, has been venerated ever since.

The **monastery** created around the Madonna was rebuilt in Baroque style in the 16th century, and hardly competes with the fabulous surroundings. Only one side of the Gothic cloister remains intact. The enthroned Virgin of Montserrat presides over the high altar; the statue dates from the 12th century and is believed to be a copy of the original. The boys' choir or **Escolanía**, founded in the 13th century, still performs daily at 1pm and 6.45pm, except in July. The **museum** (*open Mon–Fri winter 10–6, summer 10–7, Sat, Sun and hols 9.30–6.30; adm*) has gifts donated by the faithful, archaeological finds and a few Old Masters, including an El Greco and a Caravaggio.

Best of all, though, are the walks around the mountain, to its ruined hermitages and caves. An easy walk called **Els Degotalls** takes in a wonderful view of the Pyrenees. A funicular descends from Pla Santa Creu (*10–1 and 3.20–7, every 20 mins*) to the **Santa Cova**, where a 17th-century chapel marks the exact place where the *Moreneta* was found; another (*10–7, every 20 mins*) goes up to the **Hermitage of Sant Joan**, from where there is a spectacular walk up to the **Hermitage of Sant Jeroni**. From here a short path rises to the highest peak in the range (4,110ft). Before leaving, try the monks' *aromas de Montserrat* – a liqueur distilled from the mountain's herbs.

Cava and Wine Land: The Penedès

Just 50 kilometres southwest of Barcelona is Catalonia's première wine region, the Penedès, famed for its white wines and above all the home of *cava*, sparkling wines. **Sant Sadurní d'Anoia** is the Jerez of *cava*, packed with *bodegas* full of the bubbly and sprinkled with *modernista* buildings. All the producers offer tours (with tastings, naturally). The biggest, **Codorniu** – said to be the largest producer of sparkling wines in the world – and **Freixenet**, offer the most complete tours, including, at Codorniu, a mini-train ride through the vast cellars. The Codorniu cellars are also far the grandest establishment in Sant Sadurní, a *modernista* cathedral of parabolic arches by Josep Puig i Cadafalch. The region's capital, **Vilafranca de Penedés**, is known less for *cava* than for wines and brandies, produced above all by Spain's largest family-owned winemaker, **Torres**, north of the town at Pacs del Penedès, which also hosts tours and tastings. A historic town, Vilafranca has a wine museum, the **Museu del Vi**, with exhibits on wine-making history to fascinate any oenophile (plus, a tasting). It's one of six local museums in Plaça Jaume I, all housed in a 12th-century palace (*all open Oct–May 10–2 and 4–7, Sun 10–2; June–Sept Tues–Sat 9–9; closed Mon; adm*).

Getting There

RENFE trains (Cercanías Line 4) run to Sant Sadurní and Vilafranca hourly from Plaça Catalunya or Sants stations, 6am–10pm daily (journey time 45 mins). By **car**, take the A-2 and A-7 *autopistas*, or take the slower but prettier N-340 in Molins de Rei. Barcelona is 44km from Sant Sadurní, 55km from Vilafranca.

Tourist Information

Sant Sadurní d'Anoia:Plaça de l'Ajuntament, t 938 91 12 12.
Vilafranca del Penedés: C/Cort 14, t 938 92 03 58.

Wine and *Cava* Tours

Bodegues Torres, Finca El Maset, Pacs del Penedès, t 938 17 74 87.

Caves Codorniu, Av. Codorniu, Sant Sadurní d'Anoia, t 938 18 32 32.
Caves Freixenet, C/Joan Sala 2, Sant Sadurní d'Anoia, t 938 91 70 00.

Eating Out

Café de la Rambla, Rambla de Nostra Senyora 8, Vilafranca del Penedès, t 938 92 10 52 (*inexpensive*). Pleasant café in the middle of Vilafranca with a good lunch menu.
Cal Ton, C/Casal 8, Vilafranca del Penedès, t 938 90 37 41 (*moderate*). Fine, local cuisine paired with an excellent wine list (of course).
Fonda Neus, C/Marc Mir 14–16, Sant Sadurní d'Anoia, t 938 91 03 65 (*inexpensive*). Very likeable, family-run local restaurant with traditional cooking – especially Catalan canelloni, not the same as the Italian kind – and a few dishes cooked with an opulent touch of *cava*.

A Day at the Beach: Castelldefels and Sitges

Since Barcelona suddenly acquired its own usable, clean beaches as part of its great Olympic makeover the summer-Sunday exodus along the coasts north and south of the city has slackened off a little, but the Poble Nou beaches can get hectic, and for visitors to this Mediterranean city it's only natural to want to explore at least a little. Barcelona's nearest and least-effort traditional Sunday beach is at **Castelldefels**, just 20km south, and increasingly popular as an all-year residential area. It has a fine. broad, open beach, the main disadvantage of which is occasional high winds. Just inland from the town is the much-restored medieval castle that gave it its name, and Castelldefels town has an impressively long, curving seafront lined with enjoyable seafood restaurants, and a smartly-equipped yachting marina at **Port Ginesta**.

Another 20km further on, wedged between the Garraf massif and a lovely long crescent of sand, **Sitges** has been Barcelona's favourite resort ever since the *modernistas* flocked here in the 1890s, led by painter Santiago Rusiñol (1861–1931). Rusiñol's love of jokes anticipated the arch-prankster Dalí, and in his delightful summer home, **Cau Ferrat** (*C/Fonollar 25; open summer Tues–Fri 10–2 and 5–9; winter Tues–Fri 10–1.30 and 3–6.30; adm*), set in the old, original fishing village of Sitges on the rocky promontory above the beach, he hosted his *Festes Modernistes* from 1892 to 1899, scandalous bohemian gatherings featuring theatre, exhibitions, concerts and 'events', such as a performance by an impostor purporting to be the legendary Paris-based American dancer Loïe Fuller – no one was the wiser. Cau Ferrat is now a museum, with two paintings by El Greco (an artist who Rusiñol helped to rescue from historical

Getting There

RENFE trains from Sants and Passeig de Gràcia depart roughly every 20 mins for Castelldefels (Platja de Castelldefels station is a minute from the beach) and Sitges on *Cercanías* line 2; all Regional and many long-distance trains also stop at Sitges, but not all stop at Castelldefels. Sitges is about 30 mins from Barcelona.

By **car**, take the A-16 coastal *autopista* (toll only for the Garraf–Sitges tunnel). Distance to Sitges is 41km. The alternative C-246 old road that winds inland and along the cliff above the motorway can be very slow.

Tourist Information

Castelldefels: Plaça de l'Església, 1, t 936 64 23 61.
Sitges: C/Sínia Morera, t 938 94 42 51, *www.sitges.org*.

Festivals

Sitges: Carnival, *Jan–Feb*. Sitges hosts the most outrageous carnival in Spain; Corpus Christi, *May–June*. Stunning carpets of flowers deck the streets of town.

Where to Stay

Sitges ✉ 08870

Sitges isn't for the staid or economy-minded, nor, often, for those without reservation. Things quieten down off season, when it's much easier to get a room, but many hotels may also close down, so call ahead.
****Gran Sitges, Av. Port d'Aiguadolç, t 938 11 08 11, f 938 94 90 34 (*expensive*). New and huge, with every amenity conceivable, including indoor and outdoor pools.
***La Santa María, Passeig de la Ribera 52, t 938 94 09 99, f 938 94 78 71 (*moderate*). Delightful seafront hotel with bright, pretty rooms and a terrace overflowing with

obscurity), a superb collection of ironwork from the 10th to the 20th centuries gathered together in surreal ways, and drawings and paintings by Rusiñol, his great friend Ramon Casas, Miquel Utrillo and their contemporaries. Next to it, the **Museu Maricel** (*open Tues–Fri 9.30–2 and 4–6, Sat 9.30–2 and 4–8, Sun 9.30–2; adm*), a hospital restored by Utrillo for American millionaire Charles Deering, is adorned with Gothic windows and door, and contains an eclectic collection of medieval to modern art, including a mural on the First World War by Josep María Sert. Another museum, the **Museu Romàntic** (*C/Sant Gaudenci 1; open 15 June–15 Oct Tues–Fri 9.30–2 and 5–9; 16 Oct–14 June Tues–Fri 9.30–2 and 4–6, Sat 9.30–7, Sun 9.30–3; adm*) continues the eccentric Sitges theme. In the centre of town, it conjures up the elegance of the 19th century and its love of gadgets – and so is not to be missed by music-box fans. Also on display inside is a huge doll collection, with over 400 from around the world, dating back to the 17th century. A joint ticket is available for all three museums.

The extravagance of Rusiñol and his friends set the stage for Sitges' role as Barcelona's seaside cockpit of crazy good times, and since the 1960s it has become one of the biggest gay resorts on the Med. In the summer it seems half of Europe's yuppies have washed up here, and many of the quirkier hotels in town have been built or renovated to accommodate them. At the same time, though, Sitges has managed the trick of remaining an un-ghettoized, welcome-to-all resort too, and retains two of its old traditions: an antique car rally to Barcelona on the first Sunday in March, and its Corpus Christi celebrations, when the streets come ablaze with flowers. It also has nude beaches to the south, the first for straights and the second for gays. Consider taking a bike; it's a long walk there in the sun.

geraniums. Downstairs are two enormously popular **restaurants**. Book well ahead.

Hotel Romàntic, C/Sant Isidre 33, **t 938 94 83 75, **f** 938 94 81 67 (*moderate–expensive*). Three atmospheric 19th-century villas very popular with gay couples, with a romantic garden, and furnished with antiques.

El Xalet, C/Isla de Cuba 33–5, **t 938 11 00 70, **f** 938 94 55 79 (*moderate*). Small hotel near the station in one of Sitges' prettiest *modernista* houses; book well in advance.

Parellades, C/Parellades 11, **t** 938 94 08 01 (*inexpensive*). Friendly and popular budget hotel with a small terrace, and large rooms.

Eating Out

Castelldefels

Nàutic, Passeig Marítim 374, **t** 936 65 01 74 (*expensive*). The most distinguished of many seafood restaurants along the seafront in Castelldefels, famed for refined fish dishes.

Sitges

Mare Nostrum, Passeig de la Ribera 60, **t** 938 94 33 93 (*expensive*). Long-established and popular restaurant serving a variety of imaginatively prepared fish and crustaceans (try the fresh cod steamed in *cava*). There's a decent wine list and a pretty seaside backdrop, as well as a good set *menú* (*inexpensive*). *Closed Wed*.

El Velero, Passeig de la Ribera 38, **t** 938 94 20 51 (*expensive*). On a rock overlooking the sea: good fresh seafood and an excellent *menú degustación* (*moderate*). *Closed Sun eve*.

Picnic, Passeig de la Ribera, **t** 938 11 00 40 (*moderate*). Excellent seafood right on the seafront, and a wine list that features lots of regional wines and *cavas* – try the wonderful *fideuà* of noodles with cuttlefish, prawns and other delights.

Los Vikingos, Marqués de Montroig 79, **t** 938 94 96 87 (*inexpensive*). Covering all price ranges and a perennial favourite: fish, burgers, well-prepared chicken and steaks.

Touring South of Barcelona

Day 1: More than Just a Beach Town

Morning: The first three days of this route, along the coast, can be followed relatively easily by train and bus, but to continue inland a car is pretty near essential. To begin, take a leisurely trip by train or by car down the A16 to **Sitges** (*see* p.66). Leave the car at your hotel and wander down seawards through the old town, with its mixture of whitewashed fishermen's cottages and elaborate *modernista* fancies, and similar mix of shops, from hip to camp and old hat. Visit the museum-monument in the old home of artist Santiago Rusiñol, **Cau Ferrat** (*see* p.66), to get a sense of the town's distinctive artistic spirit. Then walk down to the long beachfront promenade beneath the old town, Passeig de la Ribera, for a first drink before lunch.

Lunch: In Sitges, *see* below.

Afternoon: Time to hit the beach. Take a walk along the *passeig*, looking back regularly: the view along Sitges seafront toward the old town, with Cau Ferrat and the 17th-century church of **Sant Bartomeu i Santa Tecla** rising up above the beach, is a classic image that has been painted countless times. Pick your spot on the sands. If you're interested in the nudist beach, save on sweat if you can by driving there, to avoid walking the length of the *passeig* (and then a bit more).

Dinner and Sleeping: In Sitges, *see* below and pp.66–7.

Day 1

Lunch in Sitges
Mare Nostrum, Passeig de la Ribera 60, **t** 938 94 33 93 (*expensive*). The upmarket choice on the *passeig*, with a very high reputation for its carefully prepared versions of classic Catalan and Spanish seafood dishes. The set *menú* is a more economical alternative. *Closed Wed.*

Picnic, Passeig de la Ribera, **t** 938 11 00 40 (*moderate*). If you lunch on the *passeig* it has to be at an outside terrace, and this one is a very enjoyable place to eat while watching the comings and goings along the beach promenade, with high-quality, well-priced traditional seafood dishes – paellas, *fideuàs* – and an interesting wine list to explore.

Dinner in Sitges
Flamboyant, C/Pau Barrabeitg 16, **t** 938 94 58 11 (*moderate*). With tables around a charming garden and modern, eclectic food; very popular on the gay scene.

La Masia, Passeig de Vilanova 164, **t** 938 94 10 76 (*moderate*). Straightforward seafood tends to dominate in Sitges restaurants, but this one varies the mix with fine Catalan country meats – although monkfish with all i oli is still the star choice. Very comfortable, it's in the smart Aiguadolç marina, east of the old town.

La Salseta, C/Sant Pau 35, **t** 938 11 04 19 (*inexpensive*). As darkness falls the crowds move off the beach and into town. This funky little restaurant is very popular, with a good-value mix of traditional and modern dishes.

Sleeping in Sitges
★★Hotel Celimar, Passeig de la Ribera 18, **t** 938 11 01 70 (*moderate*). Likeable alternative to the Santa Maria (*see* p.66), with equally good views over the beach.

★★Hotel Romàntic, C/Sant Isidre 33, **t** 938 94 83 75, **f** 938 94 81 67 (*moderate–expensive*). Romantic by name and nature, between cranky and camp, and now with a mainly (but not exclusively) gay clientèle.

Day 2: Down the Gold Coast to Tarragona

Morning: Head southwest from Sitges on the C246 road (or the parallel rail line), avoiding the A16 as it turns inland. The older road follows the coast through the holiday towns of the Costa Daurada, Catalonia's 'gold coast' – **Calafell** and **Comarruga** have some of the biggest beaches. Past Comarruga, turn on to the N340 to continue along the shore. About 40km beyond Sitges, stop at the remarkably preserved medieval walled town of **Altafulla**. Take a walk around the time-worn little alleys of the old quarter, and up to the imposing, battered castle. The old town is 10 minutes' walk from the sea, where there's one of the *costa*'s prettiest beaches and a still more impressive castle on a rock above the sands, the Castell de Tamarit.

Lunch: In Altafulla, *see* below.

Afternoon: Continue on the N340 for the remaining 10 kilometres into **Tarragona**, and head for the old town (*ciutat antiga*), on a mighty crag high above the sea. Dominating the view is the majestic Gothic cathedral (*open Mon–Sat, Mar–June 10–1 and 4–7; July–mid-Oct 10–7; mid-Oct–Nov 10–12.30 and 3–6; Nov–Mar 10–2; closed Sun; adm, exc. for services*). Nearby begins the Passeig Arqueològic, a path around the Roman walls with fabulous views, from where you can descend to the ruined amphitheatre – only one of the city's many Roman relics – or ponder the view a little more from the Balcó del Mediterrani, 320ft above the beach, before joining the crowds on the Rambla Nova, Tarragona's main boulevard.

Dinner and Sleeping: In Tarragona, *see* below.

Day 2

Lunch in Altafulla

Faristol, C/Sant Martí 5, **t** 977 65 00 77 (*moderate*). Charming, popular restaurant in a distinctive old house with a pretty garden. The owners are Anglo-Catalan, but the menu follows Catalan tradition with great-value country dishes like *fabes a lacatalana* (broad beans and sausage cooked in wine). Excellent wines, too.

Hotel-Restaurant Yola, Via Augusta 50, **t** 977 65 02 83 (*inexpensive*). Pleasant restaurant in a small, modern hotel, with a pool.

Dinner in Tarragona

Sol Ric, Vía Augusta 227, **t** 977 23 20 32 (*expensive*). A celebrated restaurant a 20min walk from the Rambla Nova, specializing in both simple and elaborate seafood; try the spicy *romesco* sauce (a mix of peppers, almonds, garlic and wine). The wine list is comprehensive and you can dine outside in summer. *Closed Sun eve and Mon*.

Barquet, C/Gasòmetre 16, **t** 977 24 00 23 (*moderate*). Enjoyable seafood restaurant near the Roman Amphitheatre, offering well-priced set menus and a discerning wine list. *Closed Sun and Mon eve*.

Bufet el Tiberi, C/Martí d'Ardenya 5, **t** 977 23 54 03 (*inexpensive*). Pleasant, popular neighbourhood local.

Sleeping in Tarragona

★★★★Imperial Tarraco, Passeig Les Palmeres, **t** 977 23 30 40, *imperial@tinet* (*expensive*). Tarragona's finest, modern but beautifully situated on the cliff and handy for the old town; its many amenities include a pool.

★★★Lauria, Rambla Nova 20, **t** 977 23 67 12, *info@hlauria.es, hlauria.es* (*moderate*). Charming hotel with very good service and a pool, but in the centre of town. Prices are very reasonable, especially off-peak.

★★Forum Plaça de la Font 37, **t** 977 23 17 18 (*inexpensive*). Pleasant *pensión*, offering decent rooms (with no ensuite facilities) on an attractive square in the old town.

Day 3: Flatlands: the Ebro Delta

Morning: You may have a tough choice. If you have kids in tow, it may be hard to resist the call of **Universal Mediterrània** theme park (formerly Port Aventura) just south of Tarragona (*open Mar–mid-June, mid-Sept–Nov daily 10–8; mid-June–mid-Sept daily 10am–midnight; adm exp*) and adjacent **Salou**, the Costa Daurada's biggest fun-zone resort. Beware, though once inside either you may not leave in a hurry. Otherwise, continue south on the N340 down an often empty coastline to **L'Ametlla de Mar**. This is one of the most genuine remaining fishing villages on this coast, with a lively little harbour where the day's catch is still auctioned on the quay, and has nice beaches in secluded rocky coves nearby. It's also the last town on the Costa Daurada, or the start of the different world of the *Delta de l'Ebre*, the Ebro Delta wetlands.

Lunch: In L'Ametlla de Mar, *see* below.

Afternoon: Have an early-ish lunch, and continue on the N340 about 30km to **L'Ampolla** before turning left on to one of the minor roads signed for **Deltebre**, the Delta's main (but still small) town. There, find the nature park information centre (*C/Dr Martí Buera 22, t 977 48 96 79, www.ebre.com/delta*). As well as maps of paths, they have bikes for hire (as it is utterly flat, the Delta is wonderful for lazy cycling). The Delta is a strange, different world of immense horizons and damp, misty silences, very far from any resort, and endlessly fascinating to explore. It also hosts over 300 species of birds – flamingos, many birds of prey – and so is a birders' mecca.

Dinner and Sleeping: In Deltebre, *see* below.

Day 3

Lunch in L'Ametlla de Mar

L'Alguer, C/Trafalgar 21, **t** 977 45 61 24 (*moderate*). Traditional local seafood dishes – fish with *romesco* sauce, varied mixes of shellfish and the Delta rice – here always called *arrossejats*, not paella – dominate cooking in this area, and the long-established Alguer is known for some of the best. *Closed Mon*.

Café Xavier, C/Major 17, **t** 977 49 36 49 (*inexpensive*). Enjoyably laidback bar-restaurant near the port, a local favourite with good-quality lunch menus.

Dinner in Deltebre

El Buitre, Carretera de Riumar, **t** 977 48 05 28 (*inexpensive*). Fancy and the Delta don't go together; very plain to look at, this place serves succulent rice *arrossejats* with wonderfully fresh seafood..

Galatxo, Desembocadura Riu Ebre, **t** 977 26 75 03 (*inexpensive*). Another fine rice and seafood specialist, in atmospheric isolation out on the marshes east of the town towards the mouth of the great river.

Sleeping in Deltebre

Facilities here tend to be simple. There are two **campsites** within the Delta reserve; the information office has details.

Hotel-Restaurant Nuri, Pas de l'Illa de Buda, Deltebre, **t** 977 48 01 28 (*inexpensive*). Plain little hotel outside of town towards the river mouth and the campsites; no frills, but rooms are simply comfortable.

L'Illa de Mar, Carretera Marquesa, **t** (mobile) 617 039 867, *victorsorribes@terra.es* (*moderate*). Comfortably converted and modernized farmhouse with four rooms, all with bathrooms, available on a bed and breakfast basis. The owners can also lend bikes and sell their own farm produce, and have information on things to do. Several other farms nearby offer rooms (or whole, *gite*-style annexes; for information, check the Catalan government website (*see* p.45).

Day 4: Wine from the Rocks: Terra Alta and Priorat

Morning: For another radical change of scenery, head out of Deltebre straight along the road beside the river to **Amposta**, cross under the A7 motorway and carry on up the Ebro valley on the C230, passing **Tortosa**. From a dead-flat marsh very soon the landscape becomes dry, rugged, rocky and steep, as the road winds between jagged, craggy hills. About 20km beyond Tortosa at Benifallet, turn left on to the C235 to cross the Serra de Pandols to **Gandesa**. This is the capital of another wine region, the **Terra Alta**. It's an interesting little town, with an impressive medieval church, but its great monument is wine-related, the 1919 Cooperativa Agrícola (wine cooperative) by *Modernista* architect and wine-cellar specialist César Martinell, an extraordinary imbibers' basilica of sweeping brick arches. The local tourist office (*Av Catalunya*, **t** *977 42 06 14*) has information on current vineyard visits and tastings.

Lunch: In Gandesa, *see* below.

Afternoon: Leave Gandesa heading east on the N420, towards Reus, for 36km through more rocky hills to **Falset**. The region of which it is capital, the **Priorat**, is far more celebrated for its wines than Terra Alta, above all for its extraordinarily rich, powerful reds. Falset has another Martinell wine cellar, but not as big as Gandesa's; if you have time, wander out into the Priorat villages north of the town, such as **Bellmunt del Priorat** or **Porrera**. All have small wine cooperatives, where you can sample the brew before heading back to Falset to join the evening stroll.

Dinner and Sleeping: In Falset or Porrera, *see* below.

Day 4

Lunch in Gandesa

Restaurant La Rambla, C/Mola d'irto 9, **t** 977 42 09 29 (*moderate*). Gandesa's smartest eating place, with some more varied and lighter dishes as well as the hearty and meaty local classics.

Fonda Serrés, Via Aragó 8, **t** 977 42 10 25 (*moderate–inexpensive*). Traditional small-town hotel with plenty of strongly-flavoured meats and *all i oli* to go with the local vintage.

Dinner in Falset

Hostal Sport, C/Miquel Barceló 6, **t** 977 83 00 78 (*moderate*). Recently renovated hotel restaurant, run by the same family for 75 years, that's something of a local legend: its menus still have a Catalan country earthiness – roast kid is a speciality – but are prepared with skill and sophistication too. The wine selection is a showcase for the Priorat's best.

Restaurant La Cassola, Carretera de Gratallops a Falset Km 8.5, **t** 977 26 21 46 (*inexpensive*). Farmhouse-style restaurant by the roadside between Falset and the village of Gratallops, an enjoyable stopover.

Sleeping in Falset or Porrera

★★★Hostal Sport, C/Miquel Barceló 6, Falset, **t** 977 83 00 78 (*moderate*). Falset's best restaurant is also, naturally, its best hotel, and its attractively modernised rooms are a burst of luxury in this apparently rustic spot, still at very reasonable prices. Service is charmingly welcoming.

Can Duran, C/Cardesales, 6, Porrera **t** 977 82 80 33 (*inexpensive*). A bed-and-breakfast in the middle of Porrera village, giving you a chance of a quick sampler of Priorat country life very much at first hand. Reservations are essential. There are several more houses offering *turisme rural* rooms in villages in the area; again, the Catalan government tourist office (*see* p.45) is a useful source of information.

Day 5: Royal Monastery: Poblet and Montblanc

Morning: Leave Falset on the Reus road (N420), and after 24km turn left at Les Borges del Camp on to the C242 to wind up into more mountains. Just before Port d'Albarca (27km) turn right onto a minor road to the medieval walled village of **Prades** – one of many sited on top of crags in the Serra de Montsant, an area of much warfare in the Middle Ages. Follow the road signed for L'Espluga de Francolí and the Cistercian Monastery of **Poblet** (*open daily 10–12.30 and 3–6; guided tours only; adm*). An extraordinarily intact medieval complex, it was founded by Count Ramon Berenguer IV in 1151 as a 'royal monastery' with a special link with the crown: part of it is a Gothic royal palace, and in the church are the tombs of most of the Catalan-Aragonese kings. It also once again contains a community of monks, who take tours. Just beyond Poblet is the also-medieval town of **L'Espluga de Francolí**.

Lunch: in L'Espluga de Francolí, *see* below.

Afternoon: After exploring L'Espluga a little, from there it's only a short drive on the N240 to **Montblanc**, one of the most enchanting of Catalonia's medieval towns. It sits within whole stretches of its 14th-century walls (most spectacular seen coming from L'Espluga), and has a Gothic bridge over the River Francolí; inside the town are three very fine medieval churches, a former royal palace, and the remains of a large medieval Jewish quarter. Just outside it are the ruins of another Gothic monastery, Sant Francesc. In the evening, the atmosphere in Montblanc is deliciously peaceful.

Dinner and Sleeping: in Montblanc, *see* below.

Day 5

Lunch in L'Espluga de Francolí

Hostal del Senglar, Plaça Montserrat Canals, t 977 87 01 21, *www.hostalsenglar@worldonline.es* (*moderate*). A local favourite known for satisfying Catalan food, prettily decorated with timber and pottery and with a leafy garden. It's also a pleasant, two-star hotel (*moderate*).

Masia del Cadet, Les Masies de Poblet, t 977 87 08 69 (*moderate–inexpensive*). Very close to Poblet, is this restaurant in a beautifully renovated 15th-century farmhouse, with very friendly owners. Again, it's also a charming country hotel (*moderate*).

Dinner in Montblanc

Hotel Coll de L'Illa, Ctra N240, t 977 86 09 07 (*expensive*). Nearly 30km south of Montblanc at a spectacular crest (*coll*) on the Valls road, this hotel restaurant specializes in game dishes and, from Nov–Mar, *calçotades* (the traditional dish of the Valls region of chargrilled *calçots*, a special kind of spring onion, and lamb).

Fonda Colom, C/Civaderia 5, t 977 86 01 53 (*moderate*). Popular place with fine Catalan dishes and local favourites like Romesco sauce, and Priorat wines. Also has rooms.

El Molí de Mallol, Muralla Santa Anna 2, t 977 86 05 91 (*inexpensive*). Lovely old watermill, serving delicious local specialities accompanied by local wines.

Sleeping in Montblanc

**Hotel Coll de L'Illa, Ctra N240, t 977 86 09 07 (*expensive*). This scenic hotel on the road south with a highly-regarded restaurant (*see* above) has 12 pretty rooms, all with a/c, TV and bath.

**Hostal Ducal, C/Francesc Macià 11, t 977 86 00 25 (*moderate*). Traditional, long-established hotel in the middle of town, with cosy rooms all with ensuite bathrooms.

*Fonda dels Àngels, Plaça Angels 1, t 977 86 01 73 (*inexpensive*). Amiable and very good value little hotel-restaurant right in the centre of town.

Day 6: Santes Creus to the *Cava* Country

Morning: From Montblanc head north, initially on the C240 Tàrrega road, but very shortly turn right on to the C241 (Igualada), and then after another two km on to a minor road through Barberà de la Conca, which will take you in a loop via the impressive **Coll de Cabra** ('goat pass'); then take a left turn in Pla de Santa Maria and right in Pont d'Armentera to **Santes Creus**, another royal monastery founded in the 1150s and just a little smaller than Poblet, and in many ways more beautiful (*open mid-Sept–mid-Jan Tues–Sun 10–1.30, 3–5.30; mid-Jan–mid-Mar 10–1.30, 3–6; mid-Mar– mid-Sept 10–1.30, 3–7; closed Mon; guided tours only, last admission 30mins before closing; adm*). There aren't many places to eat nearby, so continue south and then backtrack a little on the C246 to **Valls**, another fine old town with Gothic churches and two superb market squares, and much celebrated in Catalan folklore.

Lunch: In Valls, *see* below.

Afternoon: Turn back the way you have come on the C246 and then continue along it to turn left onto the N340 near El Vendrell for the Penedès, or cut some time by taking the A2 *autopista* (toll), which joins the A7 and will take you to **Vilafranca del Penedès** very quickly. In Vilafranca, take a wine tour around Bodegues Torres, or if you're more interested in *cava* continue on a little way to **Sant Sadurní d'Anoia**. Vilafranca is overall a more rewarding town to explore than Sant Sadurní, with its fine square and great Museu del Vi wine museum (for both towns, *see also* p.65)

Dinner and Sleeping: In or around Vilafranca del Penedès, *see* below and p.65.

Day 6

Lunch in Valls

Masia Bou, Carretera N240 Km 21.5, t 977 60 04 27 (*expensive*). Valls is home to many Catalan traditions, such as *castells* (human towers) and the *calçotada*, feasts based on chargrilled *calçots*, a specially flavourful kind of spring onion, available only from autumn to spring. This restaurant in a giant old farmhouse outside town is the temple of the *calçotada*, and hosts them all season. At other times it has other Catalan specialities, which can be very varied as well as gutsy.

Can Fèlix, Muralla del Castell 19, t 977 60 11 99 (*inexpensive*). Simpler traditional restaurant in the middle of town, which also has local *calçots* in season.

Dinner in the Penedès

Café de la Rambla, Rambla de Nostra Senyora 8, Vilafranca del Penedès, t 938 92 10 52 (*inexpensive*). Enjoyable set menus, and a pleasant place for a light meal.

Cal Ton, C/Casal 8, Vilafranca del Penedès, t 938 90 37 41 (*moderate*). Fine, local cuisine and a superior local wine list.

Fonda Neus, C/Marc Mir 14–16, Sant Sadurní d'Anoia, t 938 91 03 65 (*inexpensive*). Family-run local favourite with excellent traditional cooking, served in an unfussy atmosphere.

Sleeping in the Penedès

***Hotel Pere III el Gran, Plaça Penedès 2, Vilafranca del Penedès, t 938 90 31 00, (*moderate*). Vilafranca's traditional 'town hotel' has a fine location on the main square, and comfortable rooms.

Fonda Neus, C/Marc Mir 14–16, Sant Sadurní d'Anoia, t 938 91 03 65 (*inexpensive*). The Neus has nine simple, homely rooms, which are very good value.

Masia Can Cardús, Torrelavit, t 938 99 50 18, (*inexpensive*). B &B in a huge old *masia* or traditional Catalan farmhouse (a listed monument), near Torrelavit, 7km north of Sant Sadurní. The location (the farm naturally has a vineyard) is wonderful.

Girona

Spread over a tumble of hills at the confluence of the Onyar and Ter rivers, Girona (in Castilian Spanish *Gerona*, and ancient Roman *Gerunda*) is one of Catalonia's most atmospheric little cities. Its position has brought it a history tormented with sieges, most famously in 1809, when its inhabitants withstood 35,000 French troops for seven months, giving up only when supplies were exhausted. Few of its embattled walls remain; like so many cities in Spain, Girona burst its buttons in the 20th century.

For the last three decades or more, Girona's airport has served as a main entry point to the charms of the Costa Brava, one of the most beautiful stretches of coast anywhere in the Mediterranean, with both big and busy resorts like Lloret or Roses and idyllic secluded corners like Tamariu or Cadaqués. Inland, there is the spectacular scenery of the Pyrenees and its foothills, a magnet for hikers in summer and winter sports fans. Between the coast and the mountains, the centre of the countryside around Girona is surprisingly untouristified, an oasis of rolling green hills and occasional geological oddities often bypassed by visitors on their way to higher-profile locations. It's notably prosperous, thanks to a combination of tourism, rich farmland and a being a prime location for industry and services in the new Europe, and in fact has Spain's highest standard of living. It also has a lot of character, from fine cooking to delicious landscapes and idiosyncratic, marvellously preserved medieval towns.

The Old Town

Fortunately, Girona's **Old Town** (**Barri Vell**) has been lovingly neglected. Its dim, narrow streets and passages, steep stairs, little squares, archways, and solid stone buildings offer any number of elegant perspectives. In recent years, in an attempt to keep the Old Town from falling too deeply asleep, the town approved the placement of various university departments within its quarters, adding a bit of student verve to the area. Across the Onyar from the old town is Girona's **Eixample**, a miniature version of Barcelona's, complete with a handful of minor *modernista* buildings designed by poet Rafael Masó (see the **Casa Teixidor** and **Farinera Teixidor** in C/de Santa Eugénia). Cross between the two on the **Pont de les Peixateries Velles** for the much-photographed view of the colourfully painted houses built up directly over the river.

The main street of medieval Girona, the **Carrer de la Força**, follows the Roman Via Augusta, the road of conquest. Narrow and winding, it seems to have changed little since the day when Girona's famous Jewish quarter, **El Call**, was defined by its southernmost reaches, around the steep alleys of Sant Llorenç and Cúndaro. Like the *calls* of Barcelona and Tarragona, the quarter came under the direct authority of the king, enjoying total autonomy from the municipal council, the *Jurats* – a situation designed to exacerbate tension, for the kings not only regarded the Jewish communities as a national resource and favoured them at the expense of others, but made use of these enclaves to meddle in city affairs. But before the decline into the 15th century, when the *Jurats*, egged on by a fanatical clergy and jealous debtors, managed to isolate the *Call* into a ghetto with one sole entrance, Girona's Jews had founded an important school of Jewish mysticism, the Cabalistes de Girona. Its most celebrated member,

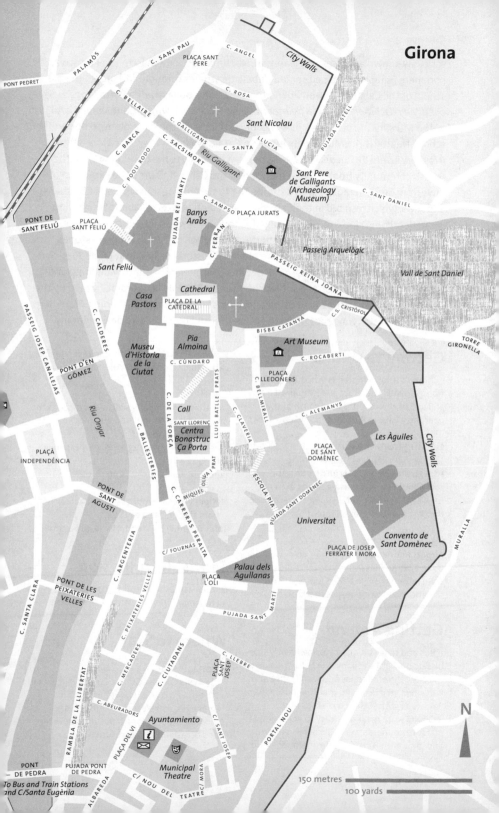

Girona

City Walls

PONT PEDRET

PALAMÓS

C. SANT PAU

PLAÇA SANT PERE

C. ANGEL

C. ROSA

C. BELLAIRE

C. GALLIGANS

Sant Nicolau

C. SANTA

LLUCIA

PUJADA CASTELL

C. BARCA

C. POOU RODO

C. SACSIMORT

Riu Galligant

Sant Pere de Galligants (Archaeology Museum)

C. SANT DANIEL

PONT DE SANT FELIÚ

PLAÇA SANT FELIÚ

PUJADA REI MARTÍ

C. SAMPSO PLAÇA JURATS

Banys Arabs

C. FERRAN

Passeig Arqueòlogic

PASSEIG REINA JOANA

Vall de Sant Daniel

Sant Feliú

PASSEIG JOSEP CANALEJAS

C. CALDERES

PONT D'EN GÓMEZ

Casa Pastors

Cathedral

PLAÇA DE LA CATEDRAL

BISBE CATANYA

CRISTÒFOL

TORRE GIRONELLA

Museu d'Historia de la Ciutat

Pia Almoina

C. CÚNDARO

Art Museum

C. ROCABERTI

PLAÇA LLEDONERS

Riu Onyar

C. DE LA FORÇA

C. BALLESTERIES

Call

SANT LLORENÇ

Centra Bonastruc Ça Porta

LLUÍS BATLLE I PRATS

C. BELLMIRALL

C. CLAVERIA

C. ALEMANYS

Les Àguiles

City Walls

MURALLA

PLAÇÀ INDEPENDÉNCIA

PONT DE SANT AGUSTI

MIQUEL

OLIVA I PRAT

ESCOLA PIA

PUJADA SANT DOMÈNEC

PLAÇA DE SANT DOMÈNEC

Universitat

Convento de Sant Domènec

C/ FOURNÁS

C. CARRERAS PERALTA

PLAÇA DE JOSEP FERRATER I MORA

PONT DE LES PEIXATERIES VELLES

C. ARGENTERIA

C. PEIXATERIES VELLES

Palau dels Agullanas

PLAÇA L'OLI

PUJADA SANT MARTI

C. SANTA CLARA

C. MERCADERS

C. CIUTADANS

C. LLEBRE

PLAÇA SANT JOSEP

C. ABEURADORS

RAMBLA DE LA LLIBERTAT

Ayuntamiento

PORTAL NOU

PONT DE PEDRA

PUJADA PONT DE PEDRA

PLAÇA DEL VI

Municipal Theatre

C/ NOU DEL TEATRE

C/ SANT JOSEP

C/ MORA

ALBAREDA

To Bus and Train Stations and C/Santa Eugènia

N

150 metres

100 yards

variously known as Moses Ben Nahman, Nachmanides or Bonastruc da Porta, was born here in 1194 and helped spread Cabalistic studies throughout Europe. The old school of the Cabala has been opened as the **Centre Bonastruc da Porta** (*t 972 21 67 61; open May–Oct Mon–Sat 10–8 (winter until 6), hols 10–2; adm*) on Sant Llorenç, and just as the Muslims are building a new mosque in Granada, there are plans to refound the school. Nearby is the **Museu dels Jueus en Catalunya** (*open May–Oct Mon–Sat 10–8 (Nov–April until 6), Sun and hols 10–3; adm*), which charts the development of the Jewish community from the first mention of the Call in 898 until the expulsion of Jews from Spain in 1492. Charts describe the tense relationship between Christians and Jews, which resulted in the Call being sealed off and its inhabitants forced to wear identifying clothing; periodically this tension blew up into pogroms. There's a section on Nachmanides, and an important collection of Jewish funerary stones.

Carrer de la Força continues past the **Museu d'Historia de la Ciutat** (*open Tues–Sat 10–2 and 5–7, Sun and hols 10–2; adm*) set in a charming 18th-century building and with changing exhibits on the subject of cities, to **Plaça de la Catedral**, framed by the 18th-century **Casa Pastors** (law courts) and the stately Gothic **Pia Almoina**. From here a spectacular stairway leads up to the cathedral and its lofty **Torre de Carlemany**.

Getting to Girona

Girona's small **airport** has scheduled flights from Stansted with **Buzz** and **Ryanair** (*see* p.11) and lots of charters. It is 11km south of town, near the village of Riudellots de la Selva.

Getting from the Airport

There is no regular transport link to the city, so **taxis** are the only way into Girona; this will cost about €12–15. There are nearly always taxis at the airport, but if you need to call one the best number is Taxi Girona, **t** 972 22 23 23.

Useful Numbers

Airport information: **t** 972 18 66 00.
Buzz: **t** 917 49 66 33.
Train information (RENFE): **t** (national information) 902 24 02 02; (local) 972 20 70 93.

Getting Around

Bus and **train** stations are conveniently side by side on Plaça d'Espanya, on the west side of the city centre. All trains between France and Barcelona stop here, and there are buses from Barcelona with TEISA (**t** 972 20 48 68).

Girona's size means it's easy to get around on foot, but there's a good local **bus** system, and **taxis** are easy to find. The main ranks are at the train station and Plaça Independència; a cab within Girona rarely costs over €10.

Car Hire

The bigger companies all have offices at the airport and in Plaça d'Espanya, in or near the train station. Also *see* p.17.
Avis, airport, **t** 972 47 43 33; Plaça d'Espanya, **t** 972 22 46 64.
Europcar, airport, **t** 972 18 66 18; train station, **t** 972 20 99 46.
National-Atesa, airport, **t** 972 47 42 16; train station, **t** 972 22 13 64.
Totautorent, train station, **t** 972 44 64 06.

Tourist Information

Girona: Rambla Llibertat 1, **t** 972 22 65 75, *www.ajuntament.gi*. Also at the station.

Where to Stay

Girona ✉ **17000**
★★★★**Melià Confort Girona**, Ctra de Barcelona 112, **t** 972 40 05 00 (*luxury*). Part of an upmarket, reliable if unexciting chain: mostly attracts Spanish business travellers and occasional choosy tourists.

The Cathedral

One of the masterpieces of Catalonia, Girona's cathedral (*open Tues–Sat 10–2 and 4–7; adm*) surpasses the grandeur of the stairway with the widest single nave in all Christendom: 72ft across. It was first planned as a typical three-aisled nave, and work began early in the 14th century. A century later the master architect Guillem Bofill suggested an aesthetic and money-saving improvement: to add a single great nave to the already completed apse. His proposal was so radical that all the leading architects of Catalonia were summoned to a council to solicit their opinions as to whether or not such a thing would stand. Most said no, but Girona let Bofill do it anyway.

Inside there are plenty of fine details, but it's the colossal Gothic vault, supported by its interior buttresses, that steals the show. The stained glass is recent, the heads of all the saints reduced to simple black ovals – a haunting effect. The *retable* over the high altar is a 14th-century masterpiece of silverwork, surmounted by an equally remarkable silver-plated canopy, or baldachin. A ticket will get you into a small but exceptional **museum** (*open summer daily 10–2 and 4–7; winter Mon–Fri 10–2 and 4–6; adm*), featuring the unique Tapestry of Creation, an 11th-century view of Genesis, with the Creator surrounded by sea monsters, the seasons, and Eve popping out of Adam's

****Hotel Carlemany**, Plaça Miquel Santaló 1, **t** 972 21 12 12, *www.carlemany.es* (*expensive*). A few minutes from the Barri Vell, Girona's première hotel is mainly geared towards business travellers, and offers immaculate if conventional rooms and smooth service. The **restaurant** is excellent too.

***Costabella**, Av. de França 61, **t** 972 20 25 24 (*moderate*). Functional, modern hotel with pool in the north of the city.

** **Hotel Peninsular**, C/Nou 3, **t** 972 20 38 00 (*inexpensive*). This hotel has been newly renovated, with bright, attractive rooms and a good location just five minutes from the centre – with wonderful views from the roof.

Pensió Bellmirall, C/Bellmirall 3, **t** 972 20 40 09 (*inexpensive*) A pleasant, diminutive charmer in the old town, near the cathedral, with the best breakfasts in Girona.

*Pensió Viladomat**, C/Ciutadans 5, **t** 972 20 31 76 (*inexpensive*). Popular, good-value hostel.

Eating Out

Celler de Can Roca, Ctra Taialà 40, **t** 972 22 21 57 (*expensive*). A local institution: a rather grim exterior conceals one of the finest restaurants in the region, run by three charming brothers, and with a Michelin star to boot.

Try the *velouté de crustáceos*, a silkily special fish soup. *Closed Sun and Mon.*

La Penyora, C/Nou del Teatre 3, **t** 972 21 89 48 (*expensive–moderate*). Much recommended by locals: a first-class meal here will verge on *expensive*, but there's also a satisfying budget *menú del dia* (*inexpensive*). It offers good choice for vegetarians, too. *Closed Sun eve and Tues.*

Albereda, Albereda 9, **t** 972 22 60 02 (*expensive–moderate*). In the basement of Girona's historic casino: it's elegantly furnished and the food is beautifully prepared, especially any dishes with *bacalao* and the delicious carpaccios. *Closed Mon eve.*

Cipresaia,C/General Fournas 2, **t** 972 22 24 49 (*moderate*). Comfortable place near the Museu d'Art, with an elegant interior and quiet atmosphere.

El Pou del Call, C/de la Força 14, **t** 972 22 37 74 (*moderate*). Another much-loved local haunt serving reasonably priced, hearty Catalan dishes at very decent prices.

Casa Marieta, Plaça Independència 5, **t** 972 20 10 16 (*inexpensive*). Across the Onyar from the cathedral, and very popular: generous helpings of hearty Catalan country fare such as *botifarra amb mongetes* (pork sausage with white beans) are a mainstay, with good wines to wash them down.

side. Then there's the *Còdi del Beatus*, an illuminated commentary on the Apocalypse from the year 974, with richly coloured Mozarabic miniatures. The ticket also admits you to the trapezoidal Romanesque **cloister**, with exquisitely carved capitals, including one of a giant rabbit menacing a man.

More medieval delights await in the **Museu d'Art** (*open Tues–Sat 10–7 (winter until 6), Sun 10–2; closed Mon; adm*) next to the cathedral in the old Episcopal Palace. Among the exhibits there's a beam from 1200, carved with funny-faced monks lined up like a chorus line, a beautiful 15th-century catalogue of martyrs and a *Calvary* by Mestre Bartomeu (13th century), portraying a serenely smiling Christ with a face like Shiva, ready to dance off the Cross. Upstairs, there are rooms of 19th- and 20th-century Catalan paintings, with a selection by the 'Olot School' of landscape painters.

Portal de Sobreportas

Head back down the 90 steps to Plaça de la Catedral, turn right to pass through the **Portal de Sobreportas** and its two round towers. The stones of their bases predated the Romans, and there's a niche hollowed out on a statue of 'Our Lady of Good Death', invoked by unfortunates who were led through the gate on their way to execution.

To the left stands the 13th-century **Sant Feliú**, at the head of its own flight of stairs. It has a curious spire, amputated by lightning, and is believed to have been built over an early Christian cemetery, where the city's patron saint Narcís suffered martyrdom. Inside the church are two Roman and six Palaeochristian sarcophagi with fine carvings. On the right after Portal de Sobreportas, a door leads to the 13th-century **Banys Arabs** (*open April–Sept Tues–Sat 10–7, Sun 10–2; Oct–Mar Tues–Sun 10–2; closed Mon; adm*), a 13th-century version of ancient Roman *hammams*, built by Moslem craftsmen and illuminated within by an elegant eight-sided oculus on white columns.

Down the Pujada del Rei Marti and across the Galligans river stand two attractive 12th-century works: tiny **Sant Nicolau** with its three apses, and the former **Monestir de Sant Pere Galligants**, now the **Archaeology Museum** (*open summer Tues–Sat 10.30–1.30 and 4–7, Sun 10–2; winter Tues–Sat 10–2 and 4–6, Sun 10–2; closed Mon; adm*), with an extensive collection of medieval Jewish headstones and a cloister that's interesting to compare with the cathedral. From here the **Passeig Arqueològic** (*open daily 10–8*) offers a garden-like stroll along the walls, with fine views over the pretty Vall de Sant Daniel from the ruins of the Roman **Torre Gironella**. Once through the Portal de Sant Cristòfol you can return to the cathedral or take C/dels Alemanys to the Plaça de Sant Domènec, with Girona's best-preserved ancient walls and the remains of the city's old university, the Renaissance **Les Àguiles**. Down the steps from this square is the beautiful **Palau dels Agullanes**, with its low arch spanning the junction of two stairs. From here, C/Ciutadans returns to the Plaça del Vi, with the 19th-century **Municipal Theatre**, where two Catalan fiesta *gegants* (giants) stand vigil in the courtyard. Nearby, **Rambla de la Llibertat** is Girona's main café promenade. If you cross over the Ter on the Pont de Pedra and take a right turn you will also find a recently-opened attraction, Girona's **Museu del Cinema** on C/Sèquia (*open May–Sept Tue–Sun 10–8; Oct–April Tue–Fri 10–6, Sat 10–8, Sun 11–3; closed Mon; adm*), a charming, intriguing collection on the entire history of cinema, very well presented in several languages.

Day Trips from Girona

Banyoles

No one thinks of lakes when they think of Spain, but there's a lovely one north of Girona called Banyoles, filling a very long-extinct volcanic crater. For years it slumbered peacefully, until it hosted the rowing events in the 1992 Olympics, and more developments sprang up. The town has a 13th-century porticoed square, and a copy of a Neanderthal jawbone found here in its **Museu Arqueològic** (*open July and Aug Tues–Sat 11–1.30 and 4–8, Sun 10.30–2; Sept–June Tues–Sat 10.30–1.30 and 4–6.30, Sun 10.30–2; closed Mon; adm*), housed in the Gothic **Pía Almoina**. The mouldering Benedictine **Monastir de Sant Esteve**, founded in 812, is rarely open but, if it is, you can admire a 15th-century *retable* by Joan Antigo. On the other side of the lake, the tiny village of **Porqueres** has a gem of a Romanesque church, **Santa María** (1182), and there are prehistoric cave paintings nearby in **Serinyà** (*ask in Girona about opening hours*).

Besalú

On up the Fluvià (14km north of Banyoles) is one of Catalonia's purest, least commercialized medieval gems, Besalú. For one brief, shining hour, after its reconquest by Louis the Fair in 800, it ruled an independent county, before being absorbed by the House of Barcelona in 1020. From the main road, you can see the old 12th-century **fortified bridge**, built at an unusual angle, with a tower at the bend, and eight arches of irregular shape and size.

Getting There

The TEISA company (t 972 20 48 68) runs frequent **buses** to Banyoles (journey time 30mins) and Besalú from the bus station on Plaça d'Espanya. By **car**, follow the N-II north out of Girona, then turn left onto the C150.

Tourist Information

Banyoles: Passeig Indústria 25, t 972 57 55 73.
Besalú: Plaça Llibertat 1, t 972 59 12 40, *besalu@ddgi.es*.

Eating Out

Banyoles

Hostal de L'Ast, Passeig Dalmau 63, t 972 57 04 14 (*moderate*). A pleasant lakeside hotel with good views from its restaurant, and a pool.
Quatre Estacions, Passeig de la Farga s/n, t 972 57 33 00 (*moderate*). The best place to eat in town; traditional cuisine based on whatever is in season. Try the mouthwatering seafood *croquetas*, and finish up with a local liqueur.
Fonda Comas, C/Canal 19, t 972 57 01 27 (*inexpensive*). Down-to-earth little *pensión* in town with a decent restaurant serving a filling daily menu.

Besalú

Pont Vell, C/Pont Vell 28, t 972 59 10 27 (*moderate*). Right next to Besalú's historic bridge, with wonderful views from its outdoor tables. On the menu are modern, strong-flavoured Catalan dishes. *Closed Tues*.
Fonda Siqués, Av. President Companys 6–8, t 972 59 01 10 (*inexpensive*). Old-fashioned stone guesthouse at the entrance to the town with a pool and a very popular restaurant serving classic local dishes.
Cúria Reial, Plaça de la Llibertat 15, t 972 59 02 63 (*inexpensive*). Very lovely café and restaurant wonderfully located in an old convent refectory in the heart of Besalú. Great-value menus feature Catalan country favourites and lighter, modern touches.

Across the bridge, where the Jewish **Call** once stood, there's a Romanesque **Mikwah** (a ritual bathhouse connected to a synagogue), the only one in Spain, and one of only three in Europe. Besalú has two 12th-century churches: **Sant Pere**, decorated by stone lions obviously carved from hearsay rather than an authentic model, and **Sant Vicenç**, its entrance prettily decorated with floral motifs. A medieval domestic building, **Casa Cornellà** (*open for hourly tours July–Sept Mon–Sat*) has been furnished with antique tools and household items, but the whole, ancient town is the greatest sight of all.

Figueres

Figueres is the capital of Alt Empordà, transport hub for the northern Costa Brava, and a wind sock; the town has erected a statue of a woman about to be blown away and called it the **Monument to the Tramontana**, the name of the most notorious high wind that sometimes blasts for weeks on end in winter. It's near to Pujada Castell and Figueres' star attraction, nothing less than the 'spiritual centre of Europe' as its creator proclaimed: everyone else calls it the **Museu Dalí** (*www.salvador-dali.org; open July–Sept daily 9–7.45; Oct–June daily 10.30–5.45; adm exp*). Salvador Dalí, born in Figueres in 1904, created this dream museum in 1974 in a merrily crazy reconstruction of his home town's old municipal theatre. The result is the most visited museum in Spain after the Prado. Expect the outrageous: the former stage has a set by Dalí, accompanied by an orchestra of mannequins. Dalí himself, who died here in 1989, is entombed nearby, his mortal remains the final exhibit. Elsewhere, Figueres is a pleasant town (despite ugly outskirts), with an attractive *Rambla* for strolling.

Getting There

All **trains** from Barcelona and Girona to France, long-distance or *Regional*, stop in Figueres, and Barcelona Bus (**t** 932 32 04 59) runs regular services from Barcelona. Figueres is also the centre of the **bus** network for the upper Costa Brava, with the SARFA company.

By **car**, take the A7 *autopista* (toll) from Girona, or follow the cheaper and slightly more restful N-II, parallel to it. Figueres is 27km north of Girona.

Tourist Information

Figueres: Plaça del Sol, **t** 972 50 31 55.

Eating Out

Hotel Durán, C/Lasauca 5, **t** 972 50 12 50, *www.hotelduran.com* (*expensive*). In the centre of town, right on the Rambla, this attractive traditional hotel has one of the oldest and most prestigious restaurants in Catalonia; people drive in from miles around to enjoy the succulent classic dishes such as *zarzuela con langosta* (fish stew with lobster) served up in a huge and bustling dining room. *Open all year.*

Hotel Empordà, Ctra N11, Km763, **t** 972 50 05 62 (*expensive*). This modern hotel, with slightly dated décor, is 3km north of Figueres; its restaurant has been described as 'a cathedral to Empurdan cuisine' and is one of the finest in Catalonia, acclaimed for its imaginative adaptations of regional specialities. Game dishes are a high point, as are mint salads and *taps de Cadaqués* – an incendiary rum cake. If you don't want the whole hog, there are fine lunch menus (*moderate*).

Presidente, Ronda Firal 33, **t** 972 50 17 00 (*moderate–inexpensive*). Around the centre of Figueres are any number of outdoor-terrace restaurants. The Presidente is reliably enjoyable, with pleasant service, an attractive wine selection and good-value menus of Catalan dishes. *Closed Mon.*

Touring from Girona 1: The Costa Brava

Day 1: Cork-towns to Resorts: Girona to Palamós

Morning: The Costa Brava – the coast east of Girona, from Blanes to the French border – is a very easy area to explore at leisure (be aware that some of its tourist facilities may close up from November to March). Begin by heading southeast from Girona on the C250 road, through the pretty old town of Cassà de la Selva, and then turn left in Llagostera for **Sant Feliu de Guíxols**. Before tourism was invented, this coast's main cash-business was exporting cork, and due to its cork-port past Sant Feliu has more character than many beach towns, and fine *modernista* buildings. Take a look too at its 11th-century gate, the Porta Ferrada, before a walk along the lovely seafront Passeig Marítim. The best beaches are just north of town, at **Sant Pol**.

Lunch: In Sant Feliu de Guíxols, *see* below.

Afternoon: Heading north along the coast, don't fail to call in at **S'Agaró**. This very neat, beautifully landscaped development of luxury villas was the first-ever such 'urbanization' in Spain in the 1940s, a very grand model for later projects. Further up, you can call in at **Platja d'Aro**, this area's biggest resort, or there is a quieter, prettier beach at **Sant Antoni de Calonge**, just before **Palamós**. Stroll around the harbour; also built for the cork boom, it's still a lively, charming sailing and fishing port.

Dinner and Sleeping: In Palamós, *see* below.

Day 1

Lunch in Sant Feliu de Guíxols

Nàutic, Passeig Marítim, t 972 32 06 63 (*moderate*). The restaurant in Sant Feliu's sailing club (the Club Nàutic) is open to non-members, and has a superb location (naturally) right on the seafront, and delicious, classic Catalan seafood dishes.

Hotel Sant Pol, Platja de Sant Pol 125, t 972 32 10 70 (*inexpensive*). Friendly, family-run hotel restaurant with an outside terrace right on the beach, with varied fare from light lunches to seafood feasts. The rooms above are also attractive, with fine sea views.

Dinner in Palamós

Maria de Cadaqués, C/Notaries 36, t 972 31 40 09 (*expensive*). Highly regarded, long-running restaurant known for opulent versions of local seafood dishes like *suquet* (a rich, mixed fish and seafood stew), and Empordà specialities combining meat and fish, plus very moreish, fruity desserts. The wine list covers the range of the best Catalan wines. *Closed mid-Dec–mid-Jan, and Sun evenings and Mon.*

Can Blau, C/Vapor 3, t (mobile) 630 52 39 18 (*inexpensive*). A much simpler alternative, a bright, bustling café-restaurant with all the local favourites – especially rice dishes, and prawns and other seafood – and friendly service.

Sleeping in Palamós

★★★Hostal Guillermo, Passeig Josep Mundet 68, Sant Antoni de Calonge, t 972 65 05 64, *www.capitanes.com/guillermo* (*moderate*). Recently-renovated beachfront hotel in Sant Antoni de Calonge, just outside Palamós. It's run with some style, and the rooms and restaurant are very attractive.

★★Hostal Vostra Llar, Av. President Macià 12, t 972 31 54 00, *www.vostrallar.com* (*inexpensive*). Great value hotel-restaurant in Palamós that has been redecorated in an attractive, traditional style, with very welcoming owners. *Closed Oct–Mar.*

Day 2: Via Gala's Castle to Palafrugell

Morning: Backtrack a little from Palamós through Calonge, and turn inland on the road signposted for La Bisbal. From there, carry on up the C255 for about 8km to a left turn for **Púbol**, site of the Castell de Púbol, the 12th-century castle that Salvador Dalí bought for his wife and muse Gala (*open mid-Mar–mid-June and mid-Sept–Oct Tues–Sun 10.30–6; mid-June–mid-Sept Tues–Sun 10.30–8; closed Mon and Nov–mid-Mar; adm*). He himself was not allowed to visit; like everything associated with the couple, it has a deeply bizarre feel. From there, head back to **La Bisbal**, a lovely medieval town with an arcaded main street that shelters some excellent cafés. A brief detour to the east will also take you to **Peratallada**, a fascinatingly well-preserved medieval walled village.

Lunch: In or around La Bisbal, *see* below.

Afternoon: With no hurry, head down the 12km to **Palafrugell**. The pine-clad coves and cliffs immediately to the west were the original 'rugged coast' for which the label Costa Brava was thought up in the 1900s, and Palafrugell is the jumping-off point for all of them. Intimate, green-walled bays like **Tamariu**, **Llafranc** and **Calella de Palafrugell** are spectacularly beautiful, and remarkably untouched by big development; pick one and settle in, or carry on exploring. So steep are the bay-sides that each one has its own narrow, winding entry road, so you find yourself continually going up and down the hills through Palafrugell.

Dinner and Sleeping: In Palafrugell, *see* below.

Day 2

Lunch around La Bisbal

Hostal La Riera, Plaça de les Voltes 3, Peratallada, t 972 63 41 42 (*moderate*). Delightful restaurant in a giant 15th-century *masia* or traditional farmhouse in the heart of the ancient village of Peratallada. Chef-owner Felip Quadra has won a high reputation for his skilful cooking, based in the traditions of the Empordà, with subtle use of seafood and herbs.

La Cantonada, C/Bisbe 6, La Bisbal, t 972 64 34 13 (*inexpensive*). Popular, homely local restaurant in the middle of La Bisbal, with very generous, well-prepared set lunches.

Dinner around Palafrugell

Terramar, Passeig Cipsela 1, Llafranc, t 972 30 02 00 (*moderate*). Right on the seafront in the lovely bay of Llafranc, serving excellent regional dishes such as *arròs a la cassola*, the local equivalent of paella and a speciality of Palafrugell.

La Xicra, C/Estret 17, t 972 30 56 30 (*moderate*). Chef Pere Bahí is widely praised for his creative, regional cuisine, with the emphasis on seafood. Prices are very reasonable.

La Casona, Passatge la Sauleda 4, Palafrugell, t 972 30 36 61 (*moderate*). Good food at moderate prices; try the *arròs negre*.

Sleeping in Palafrugell

★★★Hotel Hostalillo, C/Bellavista 22, Tamariu, t 972 62 02 28, f 972 62 01 84 (*expensive –moderate*). White, modern hotel set on the cliffs above the beach, with a lovely, geranium-filled sun terrace. *Open June–Sept.*

★★★Hotel Sant Roc, Pla Atlàntic 2, Calella de Palafrugell, t 972 614 250, f 972 61 40 68 (*moderate*). Pleasantly 'lived-in', family-run hotel surrounded by gardens and a terrace with fine views of the bay. This is popular with return visitors, so do to book ahead. Prices jump in August. *Closed Nov–Mar.*

★★Sol d'Or, C/Riera 18, Tamariu, t 972 30 04 24 (*inexpensive*). Simple, seaside hotel with very accessible prices. *Open all year.*

Day 3: Blue Water and Anchovies: Begur to L'Escala

Morning: If you haven't managed to see them the day before, don't leave Palafrugell without looking in at **Begur**, the entry point for more ravishingly lovely bays, with fabulous, deep-blue water – most beautiful of all are **Aiguablava** and **Aiguafreda**, while **Sa Riera** has the best beach. If you can tear yourself away, turn inland from Begur and north through **Pals**, another near-unnaturally intact medieval village that is, in its entirety, a national monument (and now mostly bought up as second homes). A few kilometres further up, turn seawards to **L'Estartit**. A busy fishing port, this is also Catalonia's biggest centre for scuba diving, around the **Illes Medes**, the small islands visible in the distance, which have some of the best coral in the Mediterranean. If you're not a diver, you can take a glass-bottomed boat trip.

Lunch: In L'Estartit, *see* below.

Afternoon: Heading inland, stop at **Torroella de Montgrí**, a quiet town with a remark-able mixture of medieval and Renaissance buildings, a lovely main square and an imposing 12th-century castle. Then head coastwards again to **L'Escala**, another town that's both a resort and a busy little fishing port. The Empordà region, from Palamós to France, is known for many things in Catalonia: high winds in winter, cranks like Salvador Dalí, and refined cooking – often, unusually, mixing meat and seafood in *mar i muntanya* (sea and mountain) dishes. L'Escala has an added attraction in that it's known especially for its anchovies, a highlight in local restaurants.

Dinner and Sleeping: In L'Escala, *see* below.

Day 3

Lunch in L'Estartit

Restaurant La Gaviota, Passeig Marítim 92, t 972 75 20 19 (*moderate*). Classic harbourfront restaurant, with, of course, plenty of local rice and seafood cooking, and enjoyable meats. *Closed midday Mon April–Oct, all day Mon Nov–Mar.*

Santa Anna, C/del Port 46–48, t 972 75 13 26 (*inexpensive*). Relaxed and homely restau-rant with less sophisticated versions of the local seafood dishes. Set menus are very good value.

Dinner in L'Escala

El Molí de L'Escala, Camp dels Pinars, Camí de les Corts, t 972 77 47 27 (*expensive*). Opulent restaurant in a lavishly restored old mill on the road towards Empúries, on the north side of the town. The food matches the setting: sophisticated Catalan cooking making use of the freshest ingredients, with French touches.

Hostal El Roser, Plaça de l'Església 7, t 972 77 02 19, *www.elroser.com* (*inexpensive–moderate*). This family-run hotel also has a very popular restaurant, with excellent seafood dishes – making especially good use of the local lobsters and anchovies – in generous portions. They also have a less-traditional-looking offshoot by the harbour, **Roser 2**, with similar cooking plus a sea view. *Closed Nov.*

Sleeping in L'Escala

★★★Nieves-Mar, Passeig Marítim 8, t 972 77 03 00 (*expensive–moderate*). This has tennis, children's activities, and a seawater pool in modern surroundings. Rooms have recently been renovated. *Closed Nov–Mar.*

★★Hostal El Roser, Plaça de l'Església 7, t 972 77 02 19, *www.elroser.com* (*moderate*). Charming hotel with welcoming owners who take great pride in their establishment – a likeably old-fashioned seaside-y place that can seem like a surprising find among Spain's modern resorts.

Day 4: Ancient Stones and Surrealist Figueres

Morning: From L'Escala, head just two km north to the ruins of the ancient Greek city of **Empúries**, founded in 600 BC (*open June–21 Sept daily 10–8; 22 Sept– May Tues–Sun 10–8; adm*). As attractive as the ruins themselves is the location, right beside a beach, where the bay that served as the ancient port is still clearly visible. Take a look too at the small museum, which gives a good idea of what the whole town was like. Continue on through winding, minor roads along the coast to **Sant Pere Pescador**, a very pretty sandstone village on the edge of the Empordà marshes, the *Aiguamolls*. If you still feel like hitting the beach, or want to see birds, you may wish to stay there, but otherwise head west on the C252 road to **Figueres**.

Lunch: In Sant Pere Pescador or Figueres, *see below*.

Afternoon: The natural first stop in Salvador Dalí's home town is the Museu Dalí (*see* p.80), created to his own design as a theatrical production, monument and eventual tomb, with rooms of deliberately incomprehensible 'tableaux'. To see that Figueres does not begin and end with Dalí, visit also the Museu de l'Empordà, on the Rambla (*open Tue–Sat 11–7; Sun 11–2; closed Mon; adm*), an attractively-run museum with some exquisite relics of the Greek, Roman and Visigothic inhabitants of the area, and records of later figures of this region known, as with Dalí, for cranky eccentricity. Since the museum is right on the Rambla, as you leave you can join in the evening stroll, and also wander up the attractive streets nearby like Carrer de La Jonquera.

Dinner and Sleeping: In Figueres, *see below*.

Day 4

Lunch in Sant Pere or Figueres

Restaurant-Grill Can Trona, Plaça Major 9, Sant Pere Pescador, t 972 52 00 34 (*inexpensive*). Sant Pere's village restaurant serves no-nonsense Catalan food, with plenty of chargrilled meat served with powerful *all i oli*, and great red wines to go with them.

Presidente, Ronda Firal 33, Figueres, t 972 50 17 00 (*moderate–inexpensive*). One of several outdoor-terrace restaurants in central Figueres, near the Rambla. This one is consis-tently enjoyable, and a fine place for watching the town go by. *Closed Mon.*

Dinner in Figueres

See also p.80.

Mas Pau, Avinyonet de Puigventós, t 972 54 61 54 (*expensive*). A place of culinary pilgrimage in a *masia* in a village northwest of town. Ferran Adrià worked here before opening El Bullí in Roses (*see* p.85), and it continues to serve some of the finest Catalan food.

Hotel Bon Retorn, Carretera N–IIA, Km3, t 972 50 46 23 (*moderate*). Also outside central Figueres, this hotel-restaurant is worth the trip, for fine traditional dishes, prepared and served with warmth.

Sleeping in Figueres

See also p.80.

★★Hotel Bon Retorn, Carretera N–IIA, Km3, t 972 50 46 23 (*moderate*). Oddly located by the highway south of town, this little hotel is very well looked-after, and the owners are very welcoming. It also has an excellent restaurant (*see* above).

★España, La Jonquera 26, t 972 50 08 69 (*inexpensive*). A modest *pensión* with straightforward, adequate doubles.

El Molí, Siurana d'Empordà, t 972 52 51 39 (*inexpensive*). Another alternative to one of the bigger Figueres hotels: bed and break-fast rooms in a lovely old farmhouse and mill in Siurana, 7km southeast of town. The friendly owners also provide meals on request, using farm produce.

Day 5: Luxury and Bohemia: Roses and Cadaqués

Morning: Follow the C260 road east just 16km across the flattest part of the Empordà to **Roses**. The biggest all-out resort on the northern Costa Brava, it has a lovely long, curving sandy beach, backed by any number of restaurants, bars, shops and other attractions. When you've had enough beach-sitting for a while, wander along to the west end of the beach and take a look at the ruins of a 16th-century citadel, built to defend this coast against the French. Roses also has its luxurious, fashionable side, which you can find if you head eastwards along the winding little road to **Cala Montjoi**, site of the legendary restaurant **El Bulli** (*see* below).

Lunch: In Roses, *see* below.

Afternoon: Have lunch early: the mountain road over the rocky crags to **Cadaqués** is one of the most spectacular parts of this trip, best appreciated slowly. In splendid isolation at the end of **Cap de Creus** (there used to be no road at all), the white-washed village of Cadaqués has stayed untouched by large-scale developments. It has been a refuge for many artists and writers, but is best-known as the third point in the Empordà's 'triangle' of Dalí-sites, with his own house unmistakable on the little cove of **Port Lligat** (*open 14 Mar–14 June and 16 Sept–6 Oct Tues–Sun 10.30–6; 15 June–15 Sept 10.30–9; adm*). Follow the same road also to the tip of Cap de Creus, past the weird rock formations that so inspired Dalí. Apart from that, Cadaqués is always a delicious place to spend some time, with an atmosphere all of its own.

Dinner and Sleeping: In Cadaqués, *see* below.

Day 5

Lunch in Roses

El Bulli, Cala Montjoi, 6km from Roses, **t** 972 15 04 57, *www.elbulli.com* (*very expensive*). Included here as an obligatory reference: being voted by critics the best restaurant in the *entire world* has done a lot for the name of chef Ferran Adrià, but for other mortals has made it very difficult to get in (the waiting list is about a year). However, if you plan your trip with time... *Closed Mon and Tues in April, May and June; closed Oct–Mar.*

Restaurant-Bar Cacharón, Av. Platja 8, **t** 972 25 40 04 (*moderate*). Classic seafront cooking.

Can Ramon, C/Sant Elm 8, **t** 972 25 69 18 (*inexpensive*).If you can't get into El Bulli, try this homely place, with fine seafood and meats.

Dinner in Cadaqués

La Galiota, C/Narcis Monturiol 9, **t** 972 25 81 87 (*moderate*). The most fashionable restaurant in Cadaqués, with good seafood and soufflés. Crowded in summer, so book.

Casa Anita, C/Miguel Roset, **t** 972 25 84 71 (*inexpensive*). A long-established, family-run café-restaurant with doodles by Picasso and Dalí. Wonderful mixed seafood platters.

Cap de Creus, Cap de Creus, **t** 972 19 90 05 (*inexpensive*). In the heart of the Natural Park of Cap de Creus, by from the lighthouse, with eclectic menus that even includes a vindaloo among local rice dishes. Book ahead to get tables with stunning views.

Sleeping in Cadaqués

★★★Llane Petit, Dr Bartomeus 37, **t** 972 25 80 50, **f** 972 25 87 78 (*expensive*). Smallish, modern and very comfortable hotel with a garden, on the beach of the same name.

★★Port Lligat, Platja de Port Lligat, **t** 972 25 81 62, *portlligat@intercom.es* (*moderate*). Long established, right next to Dalí's house, with fine views over the bay and a children's playground and pool. *Open all year.*

★Pensió Vehi, C/Església 5, **t** 972 25 84 70 (*inexpensive*). The most economical place to stay; four little rooms, without baths.

Touring from Girona 2: Towards the Pyrenees

Day 1: Volcanic Catalonia: Besalú and Olot

Morning: Heading north from Girona, turn left very soon on to the C150 for Banyoles. Pass the lake by this time, and go on to the wonderfully peaceful medieval town of **Besalú**, apparently lost in time. From the south you have a wonderful view of the fortified bridge, one of the most graceful products of Catalan Gothic architecture. Wander around the old town and the remains of the Jewish Call, before settling into one of Besalú's restaurants, which conspire not to break the spell (*see also* p.79).
Lunch: In Besalú, *see* below.
Afternoon: Take the N260 west from Besalú, passing the extraordinary village of **Castellfollit de la Roca**, perched almost death-defyingly on top of the huge rock that gives it its name. Beyond there you descend towards **Olot**. The stubby hills around you are the remains of over 30 long-extinct volcanoes, the Garrotxa region's most unusual feature. There are lovely walks among them; carry on through Olot to the minor road for Banyoles to find one of the most beautiful, in the beechwood called the **Fageda d'en Jordà**. Back in Olot, visit the Museu de la Garrotxa (*open Wed–Sat and Mon 11–2 and 4–7, Sun 11–2; closed Tues*) to see the work of a local school of painters who were inspired by these distinctive, lush landscapes.
Dinner and Sleeping: In Olot, *see* below.

Day 1

Lunch in Besalú
Pont Vell, C/Pont Vell 28, **t** 972 59 10 27 (*moderate*). Have your lunch admiring the graceful curves of Besalú's historic bridge from one of this restaurant's terrace tables. The rich Catalan dishes on the menu are enjoyable too. *Closed Tues*.
Cúria Reial, Plaça de la Llibertat 15, **t** 972 59 02 63 (*inexpensive*). Not quite the same view, but this café-restaurant in a former convent refectory still has a very special feel. Its lunch menus are excellent value.

Dinner in Olot
Les Cols, Mas Les Cols, Ctra de la Canya, **t** 972 26 92 09 (*moderate*). Market-fresh, imaginative local cuisine – one of the most renowned restaurants in the area. It's just north of Olot, near the road towards Camprodon. *Closed Sun and Mon eves*.
Ramón, Plaça Clarà 10, **t** 972 26 10 01 (*moderate*). Unfussy local restaurant with rich Catalan country food – grilled botifarra sausage and white beans, grilled lamb or rabbit, excellent soups, rich wines – at very decent prices.

Sleeping in Olot
★★★Hotel Cal Sastre, C/Cases Noves 1, Santa Pau, **t** 972 68 00 49, **f** 972 68 04 81, *sastre@aftot.es* (*moderate*). Delightful, small hotel in the centre of the historic town of Santa Pau, just east of Olot; each room is individually decorated with antiques, including beautifully hand-painted bedsteads. There's a charming **restaurant**, well known for its preparation of *fèsols* (local green beans). You can even get them as a dessert if you choose the *menú degustación*.
★★★Perla d'Olot, Av. Santa Coloma 97, **t** 972 26 23 26, **f** 972 27 07 74, *hperla@agtat.es*, *www.agtat.es* (*moderate*). Friendly, very reasonable, modern hotel in Olot with gardens and a children's play area.
Stop, C/Sant Pere Màrtir 29, **t** 972 26 10 48 (*inexpensive*). For those on a tighter budget.

Day 2: Up to the High Peaks: Ripoll to Núria

Morning: From Olot take the road north, towards Camprodon (C153), but after a few
kilometres of mountain bends take a left fork towards **Sant Joan de les Abadesses**.
The Romanesque abbey around which it was built and which gave it its name was
founded in 887, and mostly built in the 12th century (*open mid-Mar–June and
Sept–Oct daily 10–2 and 4–7; July–Aug daily 10–7; Nov–mid-Mar Mon–Fri 10–2, Sat
and Sun 10–2 and 4–6; adm*). Nearby is a remarkable bridge, begun in 1140. Another
10km on is a still greater medieval jewel at **Ripoll**, the monastery of Santa Maria de
Ripoll (*open daily 8–1 and 3–8*), one of the greatest masterpieces of early medieval
architecture. Around it, Ripoll is a close-packed, engaging mountain town.

Lunch: In Ripoll, *see* below.

Afternoon: The N152 road follows the Freser valley from Ripoll to **Ribes de Freser**,
departure point for the *cremallera* or 'zipper train' light railway up to the **Sanctuary
of Núria**, on a majestic alpine plateau over 2,000 metres (6,500ft) up (*trains run
daily approx 7am–9.30pm; closed Nov*). Núria is, with Montserrat (*see* p.64), one of
two great shrines to the Virgin Mary in Catalonia (both are popular girls' names).
The great, grey Sanctuary is actually pretty ugly, and Núria is as popular with hikers
and climbers as it is with pilgrims. There are wonderful walks all around it, and
tourist offices have maps (or check *www.valldenuria.com*). You can stay at the top, or
in Ribes; in between, the village of **Queralbs** is a favourite stop-off for walkers.

Dinner and Sleeping: In Núria or Ribes de Freser, *see* below.

Day 2

Lunch in Ripoll

Hostal Rama, Carretera de Sant Joan Km4.5,
t 972 70 38 02 (*moderate*). Housed in a fine
old stone *masia* on the Sant Joan road north
of Ripoll, this atmospheric restaurant has
excellent traditional dishes and a charmingly tranquil feel.

Bar El Punt, Plaça Civica 10, t 972 70 29 84
(*inexpensive*). Sandwiches, *tapas* and very
tasty crêpes out on the terrace.

Dinner in Núria or Ribes de Freser

Racó de la Vall, Estació de Montanya Vall de
Núria, t 972 73 20 00 (*moderate*). The Núria
hotel offers a choice of restaurants: this one
is the most intimate, and has the most
sophisticated menu. **La Cabana dels Pastors**
is bigger, simpler and cheaper (*inexpensive*).

La Plaça, Plaça de la Vila, Queralbs, t 972 72 70
37 (*inexpensive*). The only place to rest up
and eat in Queralbs village is also very enjoyable, and much appreciated by hikers.

Sleeping in Núria or Ribes de Freser

★★★Vall de Núria, Estació de Montanya Vall de
Núria, t 972 73 20 00, *www.valldenuria.com*
(*expensive–moderate*). Set in the grim-
looking sanctuary, but with nicely furnished
rooms, fine views, and restaurants (*see* left).

★★★Catalunya Park, Passeig Salvador Maurí 9,
Ribes de Freser, t 972 72 71 98 (*moderate*).
This mountain-resort style hotel is big and
modern, but has many attractions: a
pleasant **restaurant**, and very comfortable
rooms, the best with balconies with fabulous views. *Closed Nov–Mar*.

★★Hotel Prats, C/Sant Quintí 30, Ribes de
Freser, t 972 72 70 01 (*inexpensive*). A very
likeable little hotel with extras unexpected
at this price – a pool – and an excellent
restaurant with imaginative Catalan
cooking – try the trout or duck. *Closed Jan*.

★Hotel Porta de Núria, C/Nostra Senyora de
Gràcia 3, Ribes de Freser, t 972 72 71 37 (*inexpensive*). In the middle of Ribes town very
near the *cremallera* station, this small hotel
has snug, comfortable rooms. *Closed May*.

Day 3: Mountain Air in the Cerdanya

Morning: If you've stayed the night up in Núria, you'll be slower to get off the next morning, or may want to try some early walks on the plateau. However, when ready, continue west from Ribes on the N152. Be ready to stop after about 18 km of ever-more winding bends at the crest of **Coll de Toses**, where you see below you a giant, green bowl in the mountains. This plateau, the **Cerdanya**, is visibly one place, but since France and Spain settled on their frontier in 1659 half has been on one side and half on the other. Self-contained, almost like a Pyrenean Shangri-La, the Cerdanya has a special climate, balmy in summer and with winter snow that makes it a major skiing destination. In warmer weather, slow-moving villages like **Alp** or **Bellver de Cerdanya** are lovely places just for meandering around, with fine walks.

Lunch: In the Cerdanya, *see* below.

Afternoon: After lunch, having seen enough of the villages, wander into the capital of the Cerdanya (on the Spanish side), **Puigcerdà**. For an eccentric experience continue through it to the village of **Lliviá**, which is Spanish, but by an anomaly of the 1659 treaty was left as an 'island' surrounded by French territory. It also has what is believed to be Europe's oldest pharmacy, from 1415 (*open April–Sept Tues–Sat 10–1 and 3–7, Sun and hols 10–2; Oct–Mar Tues–Sat 10–1 and 3–6, Sun and hols 10–2; adm*). Puigcerdà itself is a likeable town, with invigorating mountain air, that fills up with skiers in winter; just outside it, there's a delightful lake where you can hire boats.

Dinner and Sleeping: In Puigcerdá, *see* below.

Day 3

Lunch around the Cerdanya

Fonda Ca L'Eudald, Passeig Agnès Fabra 4, Alp, t 972 89 00 33 (*moderate*). Country inn in a lovely village, making great use of duck and wild mushrooms. Also a **hotel** (*moderate*).

Fonda Cobadana, Camí de la Rota, Urús, t 972 89 01 29 (*moderate*). The Cerdanya's popularity as a winter sports location means that in its villages you can find surprisingly sophisticated restaurants – as in this chalet-style inn at the foot of the Serra del Cadí. Also has five **rooms** (*moderate*).

Fonda Biayna, C/Sant Roc, Bellver de Cerdanya, t 973 51 04 75 (*inexpensive*). An unusually grand house in the middle of Bellver houses this hotel-restaurant, with a pretty terrace. Set menus and **rooms** are amazing value.

Dinner in Puigcerdà

Torre del Remei, Camí Reial s/n, t 972 14 01 82, This renowned hotel's restaurant is easily the finest in the region, with refined local cuisine; the *menú degustación* has a heady price, but the setting alone is worth it.

Restaurant El Caliu, C/Alfons 1, t 972 14 08 25 (*inexpensive*). Comfortable little restaurant with a warm feel, run by a young couple who serve up varied menus, with lighter choices and good salads.

Sleeping in Puigcerdà

★★★★**Torre del Remei**, Camí Reial s/n, t 972 14 01 82, *www.relaischateaux.fr/torremei* (*luxury*). For a real treat, head for this stunning, lemony *modernista* palace, 4km outside town in Bolvir de Cerdanya. With extensive gardens, a pool, a big, elegant terrace and plenty of activities including golf, hiking and skiing close by, plus its famed restaurant (*see* left).

★★★**Avet Blau**, Plaça Santa María 14, t 972 88 25 52 (*moderate*). Small and very charming; just six rooms, so book well ahead.

★**Internacional**, C/La Baronia s/n, t 972 88 01 58 (*inexpensive*). One of the many budget *hostals*: mid-sized and well priced.

Day 4: Picasso's Retreat: the Berguedà

Morning: Leave Puigcerdà on the N260, Seu d'Urgell road, and near Bellver look for signs left (south) for the C1411 and the *Túnel del Cadí*. This giant project of the Catalan government, cutting beneath the massive ridge of the **Serra del Cadí**, has opened up an all-new route between the Cerdanya and the Berguedà, the next region to the south. You emerge from it north of **Bagà**, a lovely medieval village. Behind you, the Cadí is a giant wall of rock, one of the most impressive parts of the whole Pyrenees, and now a nature park. A short way on below Guardiola, turn right onto a narrow road for the 27km to **Gósol**. This very remote village in the heart of the Cadí was where Picasso came with his lover Fernande Olivier in 1906, and spent a summer painting some of the most important works of his rose period. The charming if rarely open Museu de Gósol on the main square (*open Sept–July Sat 11–2, Sun noon–2; Aug 11–2 daily; adm*) has copies of the pictures painted here.

Lunch: In Bagà or Gósol, *see* below.

Afternoon: Head back to the C1411 road and turn south for **Berga**, one of the most attractively atmospheric of Catalan towns. Its streets and squares wind up and down over many hills, and it has a medieval castle, and the remains of a Jewish quarter. If you're nearby in May, do not miss the Patum on Corpus Cristi, one of the most frenzied, firework-heavy fiestas in Catalonia. It's also a great base for walking, and known for wild mushrooms, which are a high note in local cooking.

Dinner and Sleeping: In Berga, *see* below.

Day 4

Lunch in Bagá or Gósol

Fonda Ca l'Amagat, C/Clota 4, Bagá, **t** 938 24 40 32 (*moderate–inexpensive*). The Catalan countryside is full of surprises: this inn in Bagá, run by the Balderic family for four generations, offers very skilful cooking at country prices – anything with trout, game or wild mushrooms is wonderful. The hotel's 18 rooms are also pleasant (*moderate*).

Cal Púxica, C/Pintor Picasso 7, Gósol, **t** 973 37 02 61 (*inexpensive*). Easygoing little café-restaurant in the middle of the village: a place to see all Gósol go by.

Dinner in Berga

Restaurant La Sala, Passeig de la Pau 27, **t** 938 21 11 85 (*moderate*). Berga's favourite restaurant, in the middle of town: again, there are delicious dishes with local wild mushrooms throughout the main autumn-to-spring season, and some are even on the menu at other times.

Fonda Cal Nen, Drecera de Queralt, **t** 938 24 40 32 (*moderate–inexpensive*). A quiet, long-running hotel-restaurant just outside town, on the road up to Queralt. Its menus feature great fresh local fare – game, sausages, river fish – and the owners are very charming.

Sleeping in Berga

★★★Hotel Estel, C/Sant Fruitós 39, **t** 938 21 34 63 (*moderate*). Comfortable and popular mid-range hotel with a good range of facilities in the centre of town.

★★Fonda Cal Nen, Drecera de Queralt, **t** 938 24 40 32 (*moderate*). Cal Nen also has very cosy, old-fashioned rooms, with a very peaceful atmosphere.

Cobert de Vilaformiu, Carretera Antiga de Gironella, **t** 938 21 21 21 (*inexpensive*). In splendid isolation on a hillside 5km north of Berga, this is a centuries-old farmhouse that has been restored and turned into bed-and-breakfast rooms. Horses can be hired at a riding centre nearby for mountain treks.

Day 5: Through the Lluçanés to Vic

Morning: From Berga head south on the C1411, but in Gironella (seven km), look for a turn left on to the C154, signposted to Vic. This will take you through more dramatic, constantly changing mountain scenery in one of the least-known parts of Catalonia, the valleys and plateaux known as the **Lluçanés**. The road winds back and forth between giant banks of rock, and occasional lush, forested dells. Some areas are like moorland and contain small, stocky horses, for which the area is known. Along the way are very placid stone villages, often with ancient Romanesque churches. Maybe surprisingly, they also contain some very good restaurants. This is another popular area for walking: the Catalan Government tourist office in Barcelona is a good source of information (*see* p.49).

Lunch: In the Lluçanés, *see* below.

Afternoon: Leave the Lluçanés on the C154 and drop down into the Plana de Vic, around its capital-town. In **Vic**, head first of all for the Plaça Major, one of the most impressive market squares in Catalonia, which still holds a vibrant market every Saturday, and livestock markets before each Easter. In one corner is the 14th-century Casa de la Ciutat or town hall. Nearby is a surviving part of a Roman Temple, and the cathedral, which has an 11th-century tower but was mostly rebuilt in a totally different style in the 1780s. One of the big sights of Vic, though, happens every evening, when the arcades around the Plaça Major fill with shoppers and strollers.

Dinner and Sleeping: In Vic, *see* below.

Day 5

Lunch in the Lluçanés

Els Casals, Carretera de Sagás, t 938 25 1200 (*moderate*). Another rustic surprise, although here the owners are creative, city-trained chefs who have moved to this remote spot for fresh air. It's up the turning to the tiny village of Sagás off the C-154 road, and very worth finding.

Fonda Sala, Plaça Major 17, Olost de Lluçanés, t 938 88 01 06 (*moderate-inexpensive*). The family who own this country inn lag behind no one in the care they take with their fine traditional cooking. It's also a **hotel**, with just six rooms (*inexpensive*). An excellent place to get a real feel of a mountain village.

Dinner in Vic

Jordi Parramón, C/Cardona 7, t 938 86 38 15 (*expensive*). In an attractive old town house around the corner from the Roman temple and much praised for its fresh and creative cuisine. *Closed Sun eve and Mon.*

La Taula, Plaça Don Miquel de Clariana 4, t 938 86 32 29 (*moderate*). Classic, old-fashioned restaurant in the heart of Vic serving traditional local dishes.

Sleeping in Vic

★★★★Parador de Vic-Sau, t 938 12 23 23, vic@parador.es (*expensive*). Some 14km from Vic on the road to Roda de Tera, this is a bit like a giant idealization of a Catalan *masia*, or traditional farmhouse, in a spectacular location in a pine grove above the gorges of the River Ter. Its many comforts include a lovely pool, and a good restaurant.

★★★Hotel Ciutat de Vic, C/Jaume el Conqueridor, t 938 89 25 51 (*expensive–moderate*). Vic's biggest and best hotel: recently comprehensively renovated, its rooms are very comfortable, and some have great views of the old town and the market square.

★★Ausa, Plaça Major 4, t 938 85 53 11 (*inexpensive*). Overlooking Vic's central square – a feast for the eyes and ears on market days.

The Basque Lands and Cantabria:
Bilbao and Santander

06

The Basque Lands and Cantabria

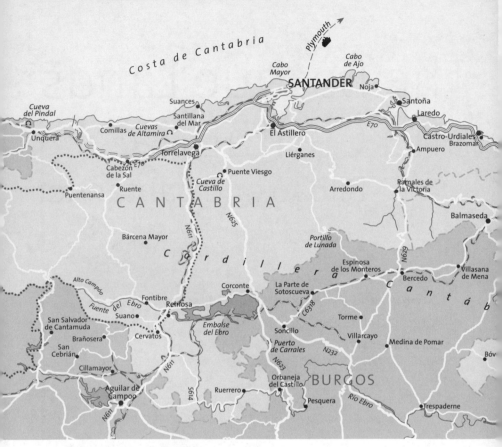

Spain in the last 25 years has been the land of dramatic urban transformations, a place where whole cities reinvent themselves – Barcelona is the benchmark – but nowhere has done such a spectacular hey-presto act as Bilbao in the 1990s. Spain's traditional capital of heavy, iron-and-grit industry, known not so long ago for being covered in soot and having a river that looked as if it contained anything else but water, has suddenly become an essential destination on the international art trail, and an elegant, vibrant city to be enjoyed at leisure. This great change is often put down to just one museum, the irresistible, dazzling Guggenheim, but it also reflects a huge effort made across the city to renovate old factory areas, clean the place up and bring out qualities that, often unnoticed under the murk, it had always possessed: a strong, earthy character, fine architecture, superb food, an unstoppable, very special bar and street life and a remarkable location, in a giant strip along the steep-sided, narrow *ría* or fjord of the Nervión. And most recently even this much-abused river has been taken in hand, so that it can now look as gracious as the rest of the city.

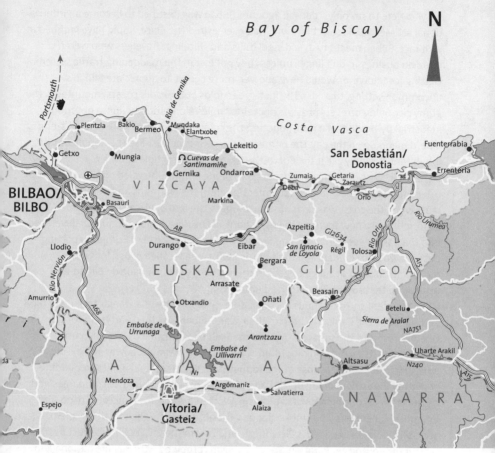

Bilbao is also the largest city of the Basque Country, in Basque *Euskadi*, consisting, officially, of the provinces of Vizcaya, Guipúzcoa and Álava, although to most Basques it also includes most of Navarra and large parts of France. When it isn't raining, this is one of the most charming corners of Spain, lush and green, even if its people are a tad self-obsessed, and every bridge has been painted with the Basque flag and slogans of ETA (*Euskadi Ta Askatsuna*, 'Freedom for Basques'), the violent nationalist minority that has given this ancient people a bad press. East of Bilbao is San Sebastián (or Donostia, to Basques), simultaneously a centre of Basque culture and cuisine and a grand seaside resort from the 19th century, with a superb beach.

West of Bilbao is Santander, capital of non-Basque but also green and mountainous Cantabria, and linked to Britain by ferry. Like San Sebastián, Santander grew into an elegant resort in the 1860s, patronised by royalty. Nowadays the big crowds head for the Mediterranean, but Santander, with its long promenade along Sardinero beach, still combines its Belle Epoque charm with a very Spanish feel of the seaside.

Bilbao (Bilbo)

If you were to say only a decade ago that Bilbao was destined to become an international art Mecca, the select few who had ever visited the place would have laughed in your face. Bilbao meant rusty old steel mills and shipping. Travellers who weren't there on business didn't linger, unless they got lost in the maddening traffic system. Getting lost, however, would have allowed more people to appreciate Bilbao's uncommon setting, tucked in the lush green folds of Euskadi's coastal mountains, the grimy city filling up every possible pocket for miles along the Nervión, a notorious industrial by-product of a river, adopting the colour of chocolate milk or robin's-egg blue, depending on the day. The name is Bilbo in Basque, just like the hobbit, but its inhabitants lovingly call it the *Botxo*, the Basque word for hole or orifice.

The orifice was originally a scattering of fishing hamlets huddled on the left bank of a deep *ría*, where the hills offered protection from the Normans and other pirates. In 1300, when the coast was clear of such dangers, the lord of Vizcaya, Diego López de Haro, founded a new town on the right bank of the Ría de Bilbao. It quickly developed into the Basques' leading port and Spain's main link to northern Europe, exporting Castile's wool to Flanders and the swords Shakespeare called *bilbos*. In 1511 the merchants formed a council to govern their affairs, the Consulado de Bilbao, an institution that survived and thrived until 1829.

The 19th century had various tricks in store: the indignity of a French sacking in 1808 and sieges by the Carlists in both of their wars; Bilbao was the 'martyr city' of the Liberal cause. But the 19th century also made Bilbao into an industrial dynamo. Blessed with its fabled iron mountain, forests, cheap hydraulic power and excellent port, Bilbao got a double dose of the Industrial Revolution. Steel mills, shipbuilding and other industries sprang up, quickly followed by banks, insurance companies and all the other accoutrements of capitalism. Workers from across the country poured into gritty tenements, and smoke clogged the air. It became the fourth city of Spain, and still is; it looks like Spain's Pittsburgh, and before the Civil War it was just as full of worker misery and exploitation. Social activism combined with Basque nationalism created a sturdy anti-fascist cocktail; during the Civil War, Bilbao was besieged again and Franco punished it crushingly. Then, in the late 1950s, Bilbao was whipped forward to become once more the industrial powerhouse of Spain, but on an artificial life-support system that was unplugged in the new Spain of the EU. The iron mines gave out. In the 1980s, unemployment soared from six per cent to 20 per cent.

Something had to be done to save the *Botxo* from becoming a real hole, and the Basques found the political will to do it. Thanks to banking, insurance and such less obviously dirty business, the economy was doing pretty well in spite of all the lay-offs, and this has allowed the city to embark on an ambitious redevelopment programme, reclaiming vast areas of the centre formerly devoted to heavy industry. The rusting machinery has been removed and the once-seedy dock area gentrified. The hugely popular Guggenheim Museum, which opened in October 1997, has by itself significantly boosted the city's prestige, attracting almost four million visitors to date. Other new projects include cleaning up the Nervión (it even has a few fish now), a concert hall and convention centre and a library, a park, hotels, offices and residential build-ings, all to be constructed on the site of the old shipyards. A 'passenger interchange', which will put local and international bus and train services under one enormous roof, is planned, and the metro, with sleek, modern stations designed by Norman Foster, was completed in 1995. The airport got an elegant new terminal designed by Santiago Calatrava in December 2000, and the port is being given a boost as part of a vast harbour expansion project. The ongoing political problems of the Basques aside, Bilbao is shaping up to become one of the cities of Europe's future.

The Casco Viejo

The Casco Viejo, or old centre, hub of the city from the 15th–19th centuries, is a snug little knot of streets on the east bank of the Nervión; tucked away from the modern centre, it remains the city's heart. From near the train stations, Puente del Arenal leaves you in **Plaza de Arriaga**, known as *El Arenal* for the sand flats that stood here. Befitting Basque tradition, its monuments are both musical: the opera house, or **Teatro Arriaga**, and a glorious Art Nouveau pavilion in steel and glass that holds Sunday concerts. Adjacent is the arcaded **Plaza Nueva**, in its day a symbol of Bilbao's growth and prosperity, only recently covered in grime, but now spectacularly cleaned up so that its elegant architecture can be appreciated. Around the plaza there are plenty of fine examples of one of Bilbao's greatest institutions, its bars.

Philosopher Miguel de Unamuno was born on nearby C/La Ronda, not far from the **Museo Vasco** (*La Cruz 4; open Tues–Sat 10.30–1.30 and 4–7, Sun 10.30–1.30; closed Mon; adm*). Located in an old Jesuit cloister, it displays a scale-model of Vizcaya, a recon-struction of the rooms of the Consulate, tools, ship-models and Basque gravestones. In the middle is the ancient *Idolo de Mikeldi*, the museum's treasure; like a primitive depiction of the cow that jumped over the moon. Behind the museum, the **Catedral de Santiago** sends its graceful spire up over the old quarter. Begun in the 1200s, most of the elegant grey stone church is 14th–15th-century Gothic, though the façade was added in the 1880s.

To the south of the cathedral is the most characterful part of the old city, in the **Siete Calles** ('Seven Streets'), the core of the original village, a calm grey world by day but packed with bar-hopping crowds nearly every night. The neighbourhood's daytime colour and animation is concentrated in the 1929 **Mercado de la Ribera** on the riverfront, the largest covered market in Spain. Nearby, the **Diocesan Museum of Sacred Art** (*open Tues–Sat 10.30–1.30 and 4–7, Sun 10.30–1.30*) displays over eight centuries' worth of religious art and finery; vestments of gold brocade, glittering silverware and numerous sculptures and paintings by Basque artists.

As the 'Seven Streets' are hemmed in by cliffs, Bilbao's centre migrated over the bridge as the city grew, while garden suburbs grew up on the cliffs. Behind the church of **San Nicolás**, an elevator ascends to the upper town, from where it's a short walk to the Vizcayans' holy shrine, the **Basílica de Begoña** with its unusual spire stuck on an early 16th-century church. Inside, a venerated statue of the Virgin holds court with some huge paintings by the slapdash Neapolitan Luca Giordano, probably the most popular painter of his day. There are fine views of the old town below.

Getting to Bilbao

Bilbao's **airport**, usually known as **Sondika** but now often officially referred to as **Loiu** (since a shiny new terminal edged the airport closer to the village of the same name) is 10km northeast of the city. From the UK, **easyJet** flies from Stansted (and ex-**Go** route) and **British Airways** and **Iberia** from Gatwick.

The dock for the P&O Portsmouth–Bilbao **ferry** is in **Santurtzi**, 13km from the centre of town at the mouth of Bilbao's *ría* or fjord, on the west bank. There is an information and sales office in Bilbao (C/Cosme Echevarrieta 1).

Getting from the Airport

The main transport into town is Bizkaibus **bus** A-3247, which runs every 30mins between the airport and the central Plaza Moyúa, with stops on the way (*Mon–Fri 6am–11pm, Sat and Sun 6.30am–11pm*). Tickets cost €1 and the full trip takes 45 mins. A **taxi** from the airport will take about 20–30 mins, and cost €16–20.

Getting from the Ferry Dock

With a **car**, follow the N-644 road out of the harbour and turn left, onto the A-8 motorway or the N-634 highway, for the 13km to Bilbao – but *see* below, for the problems of parking.

Trains run from Santurtzi to Abando station in Bilbao, on a RENFE local line. There are one or two each hour around the clock (more during the day); the trip takes 20 mins and costs €1. Santurtzi station is about 10 mins walk from the ferry; head out of the dock, and turn left (south) on Paseo Reina Victoria.

Useful Numbers

Airport flight information: t 944 53 23 06.
easyJet/Go: t 902 29 99 92.
Iberia: t 902 40 05 00.
P&O Portsmouth: t (Bilbao Office) 944 23 44 77; (Santurtzi Dock) 944 83 87 67.

Getting Around

Bilbao has several different **train** lines. The main Spanish Railways (RENFE) station is the **Estación de Abando**, in the city centre on Plaza Circular, and is the station to use for long-distance services and RENFE local (*Cercanías*) lines, especially up and down the *ría*. Next to

Abando at C/Bailén 2, but facing the river, with a colourful tiled front, is the **Estación de Santander** (also known as La Concordia) from where narrow-gauge **FEVE** trains run to Santander and Oviedo. The little **Estación de Atxuri**, at C/Atxuri 6 in the Casco Viejo, is used by the Basque regional line **Eusko Tren**, which has a line to San Sebastián by way of Durango, Zarautz and Zumaya, and another to Gernika and Bermeo. Most FEVE and Eusko Tren destinations are also served by buses: between the two, trains are usually more scenic, but slower.

Inter-urban **bus** lines run from **Termibus**, a modern terminal near San Mamés stadium on the west side of the Ensanche, C/Guturbay 1. There are frequent services to San Sebastián and other Basque Country destinations, and several daily to other parts of Spain. **BizkaiBus** serves destinations within Vizcaya, including Gernika and the coastal villages. Routes have different starting points in Bilbao: many begin from a terminal on **Paseo del Arenal**, near the Casco Viejo, or from by **Abando** train station.

Around the City

Bilbao's complex topography makes it a beast to negotiate the city by **car**; miss a turn, and you may have to circle around 40km (no exaggeration). If you make it to the centre, parking is equally frustrating; there are city car parks at Plaza Nueva, Instituto Correos, Plaza del Ensanche and Plaza de Indautxu. If the car you parked vanishes, it may have been towed away: call the Grúa Municipal, **t** 944 20 50 98.

And, in any case, all of Bilbao's attractions are within walking distance in the centre, and when you do need to travel further, or quickly, an efficient bus service (**Bilbobus**) and **Metro** are on hand to take you. Bilbao is very proud of its metro, designed by Norman Foster and opened in 1995 – so proud, in fact, that the glass and chrome tubes like great larvae that lead down to it have become one of the city's sights, dubbed '*Fosteritos*'. Its layout is conditioned by the unusual layout of Bilbao and its suburbs themselves: at present it consists of a single line running all the way along the east side of the valley out to Plentzia. In the city centre, handy stations are **Casco Viejo**, **Abando** (for RENFE trains), **Plaza Moyúa** (closest to the Guggenheim) and **San Mamés** (for Termibus). Services run about every 5mins in the centre, and every 20mins to Plentzia, with a less frequent service on Sundays; in the city centre the metro is open Mon–Fri 6am–11pm, and from Sat 6am to Sun 11pm, with two trains an hour during the night (*Sat 11pm–Sun 6am*).

Bilbao also has a recently built **tram** line, which runs more or less beside the river, connecting Atxuri and the Casco Viejo with San Mamés via Abando and the Guggenheim.

A special trip is the **Funicular de Artxanda**, which runs every 15 mins from Plaza Funicular, and climbs to the summit of Artxanda (*Mon–Sat 7.15am–10pm, Sun 8.15am–10pm, until 11pm in summer on Sat, Sun and hols*).

Useful Numbers

Train information (RENFE): t 902 24 02 02.
Train information (FEVE): t 944 23 22 66.
Train information (Eusko Tren): t 944 33 80 08.
Termibus: t 944 39 52 05.
Metro information: t 944 25 40 25, *www.metrobilbao.net*.
Bilbobus: t 944 75 82 00.

Fares and Tickets

Each system has its own fares, but there is some coordination between them. Metro and bus fares vary by zones, but Zone A on both covers the whole of the city centre. Single metro and bus tickets currently cost €1. For the metro you can buy a **Bono Plus** ticket (€2.15), valid for 10 rides, or a **Bono Día**, giving unlimited travel for a day (€3). Also available are **Creditrans** tickets, valid on nearly all the local systems, which can be bought to the value of €5, €10 or €15. They are sold at metro stations, tobacco shops and several other outlets.

Taxis

Bilbao taxis are white with a red stripe, and a green light on the roof means they're free. Most trips in town cost around €3–€5. For a **radio taxi**, call **t** 944 16 23 00/**t** 944 44 88 88..

Car Hire

For car hire in Spain in general, *see* pp.17–18. Many companies have offices at the airport.
Alquibilbo, C/General Eguía 20, **t** 944 41 20 12.
A.Rental, C/Pérez Galdós 22, **t** 944 27 07 81.
Europcar, Plaza Circular 2, **t** 944 23 93 90.
National-Atesa, Av Sabino Arana 9, **t** 944 42 32 90.

Tourist Information

Bilbao's city tourist offices provide a wide range of information, free arts guides and very good maps. The **airport** office is in the arrivals hall, near the luggage carousel; you have to visit it before you head through customs. The city website is at *www.bilbao.net*.
Main Office: Paseo del Arenal 1, **t** 944 79 57 60 Across the river from Abando station.
Av Abandoibarra 2. By the Guggenheim.
Airport: t 944 53 23 06.

Tours

Bus tours: Bilbao Bus Vision, t 944 15 36 06, make a circuit from the Guggenheim to the Funicular de Artxanda; buses leave every two hours from 10am to 6pm, from Plaza del Sagrado Corazón, near San Mamés (€6).
River tours: El Barco Pil-Pil, t 94 424 59 21, offers one-hour sightseeing tours (€11 approx.) and dinner cruises. Tickets are sold at a stand in the Guggenheim car park.
Walking tours: walks around the Casco Viejo leave from the tourist office (Paseo del Arenal) every Tues, Thurs and Sat at 10.30am (€3 approx; be there 30mins before start).

Festivals

16 July A marine procession navigates the Río de Nervión in honour of the Virgin Mary.
Semana Grande This begins on the Saturday after 15 August and is a huge city-wide party with balls, parades of huge papier-mâché giants, and bullfights. The tourist office has information on the different events.

Shopping

The **Siete Calles** are a good place to start, particularly **C/Bidebarrieta** and **C/Correo**, with plenty of upmarket clothing and shoe shops, and tacky souvenir places knocking out Jeff Koons-style ceramic 'Puppys'. For something funkier try **C/Somera**, where youthful fashions dominate. The trendiest fashion boutiques and big international labels are concentrated in the **Ensanche**, mostly south of the Gran Vía around Pla Indautxu; **C/Ercilla** is a good place to start window-browsing.

Where to Stay

Bilbao ✉ 48000

The 'Guggenheim Effect' has filled Bilbao's hotels with the kind of culture-seeking tourist other cities dream of, so book in advance.

Luxury–Expensive

Catering mainly for businessmen, these hotels often offer big discounts at weekends.

***Barceló Hotel Nervión, C/Campo Volantin 11, t 944 45 55 66 (*expensive*). One of the newest hotels, this has a sleek glass façade overlooking the river, near the town hall.

*****Lopez de Haro, C/Obispo Orueta 2, t 944 23 55 00, *www.hotellopezdeharo.com* (*luxury*). Currently the most fashionable option, with an elegant restaurant, Club Náutico. It doesn't look much from the outside, but the interior is opulent.

****NH Villa de Bilbao, Gran Vía 87, t 944 41 60 00, *www.nh-hoteles.es* (*luxury*). On the city's grandest street, near Plaza del Sagrado Corazón, this sleek modern hotel with marble and iron façade offers every amenity. Weekend rates are excellent value.

****Hotel Indautxu, Plaza Bombero Etxaniz, t 944 21 11 98 (*luxury*). This giant glass cube has every comfort in a quiet location; the house **restaurant** Etxaniz (*expensive*), does delicious things with fish and lobster. *Restaurant closed Sun and early Aug.*

Moderate

**Hostal Mardones, C/Jardines 4, t 944 15 31 05. A spotless little hostal overlooking one of the old quarter's most animated streets. It's at the lower end of this price category.

**Hotel Iturrienea Ostatua, C/Santa Maria 14, t 944 16 15 00. The choice option in the Casco Viejo; great care and attention have gone into equipping the rooms with a mix of antique and new furniture, while hosts of flowering plants trail from the balconies.

**Hotel Zabalburu, C/P.M. Artola 8, t 944 43 71 00. Pleasant rooms in a modern setting, with parking. It's family run, friendly and in a quiet neighbourhood just down from the Plaza de Zabálburu.

**Hotel Ripa, C/Ripa 3, t 944 23 96 77. On the riverfront opposite the Casco Viejo, with nicely renovated rooms with good views.

Inexpensive–Cheap

Most of these are found in the Casco Viejo.

**Hs Arana, C/Bidebarrieta 2, t 944 15 64 11. An old-fashioned hotel in a 19th-century building, with comfortable, modern rooms.

**Hs Gurea, C/Bidebarrieta 14, t 944 16 32 99. From the outside this may look shabby and tumbledown, but inside are clean, simple rooms (with bath) and friendly owners.

**Roquefer, C/Lotería 2, t 944 15 07 55. In an old building with high ceilings, and nice showers down the hall. Some rooms have sunny little balconies overlooking Plaza Santiago and the cathedral – pretty by day, but bring earplugs if you want to lie in.

Eating Out

Restaurants

For the purest Basque cuisine, look for the strangest names.

Expensive

Bermeo, C/Ercilla 37, t 944 70 57 00. Traditional and sumptuous; if it's on the menu, try the special Basque *cocochas*: 'cheek and throat' of hake in a garlic and parsley sauce. *Closed Sat lunch, Sun eve and first fortnight in Aug.*

Goizeko-Kabi, C/Particular de Estraunza 4–6, t 944 42 11 29. Has the right-sounding name and, indeed, excellent cooking to match.

GVictor, Plaza Nueva 2, t 944 15 16 78. Has been around for over 40 years, to build up its enviable reputation as one of the Casco Viejo's best restaurants; the *bodega* boasts over 1,500 different wines. *Closed Sun and Aug.*

El Perro Chico (Perrotxico), C/Arechaga 2, t 944 15 05 19. Close to Ribera market is one of Bilbao's most talked-about restaurants. Deep blue walls, tiles and lots of paintings give it a chic atmosphere in which to dine on succulent fish or a delicious *pato asado* (roasted duck). *Closed Mon eve and Sun.*

Zortziko, Alameda de Mazzarredo 17 (near Pza de España), t 944 23 97 43. The city's finest restaurant, where quirky décor and fine service prepare you for innovative and immaculately presented treats from the kitchen: green almond soup and *estofado* of wild pigeon, washed down with fine Rioja wines. *Closed Sun and first fortnight in Sept.*

Expensive–Moderate

Bola Biga, C/Enrique Eguren 4, **t** 944 43 50 26. This friendly little place specializes in three things the Basques do best: *merluza* (hake), *bacalao* (cod) and *rabo de toro* (oxtail).

Guggenheim, Guggenheim Museum Bilbao, **t** 944 23 93 33 (*expensive–moderate*). Full of light, organic lines, and furniture designed by Frank Gehry; the food is a snapshot of some of the best of Basque cooking.

La Granja, Plaza de España (*moderate*). An attractive old place right on the plaza.

Serantes, C/Licenciado Poza 16, **t** 944 21 21 29, and **Serantes II**, C/Alameda de Urquijo 51, **t** 944 21 10 45 (*moderate*). Famous local favourites that are always busy. They specialize in superbly fresh fish, but have a good selection for carnivores too.

Inexpensive

Amboto, C/Jardines. A seafood place off Plaza Arriaga that specializes in *merluza* (hake) in a delicious crab sauce.

Metro Moyúa, Gran Vía 40, **t** 944 24 92 73. A good *menú* of modern Basque cuisine.

Guggen, Alameda de Rekalde 5. Perhaps the best of those cashing in on their proximity to the Guggenheim, with a solid *menú*.

Vegetariano, C/Urquijo 33, **t** 944 44 55 98. Has great value *menús* of innovative vegetable-based dishes. *Open Mon–Fri lunch only*.

Café Boulevard, C/Arenal 3. First opened in 1871, providing cultured society with a pre-opera meeting place, and revamped 50 years later, the café retains its elegant interior.

Tapas/Pinchos/Pintxos

One of the city's greatest pleasures is the *txikiteo*, the ritual bar crawl, selecting a titbit from the groaning bar tops. There are three main areas to enjoy this: in the **Casco Viejo**, in the streets around **Calle Ledesma** in the Ensanche, and the central area around **Calle Licenciado Poza** and the **Plaza Indautxu**.

Café Iruña, Jardines de Albia. Across in the Ensanche the later-evening crowd gather around C/Ledesma, centred around this legendary and beautiful *mudéjar*-style café.

Los Fueros, C/Los Fueros 6. This bar's reputation rests on one thing: *gambas a la plancha* – fresh, simply cooked prawns. Try them with a glass of chilled *amontillado* sherry.

María Mani, C/Henao 3. Across the road from the Jardines de Albia, this bar serves an imaginative range of *pintxos*: *morros* (pig's cheeks) *a la vinagreta*, *salpicón* (a kind of salad with meat or fish) and a very refreshing *gazpacho* soup in summer.

Saibigain, C/Barrencalle Barrena 16. Curing hocks of ham dangle above a lovely, tiled wooden bar in this lively favourite.

Victor Montes, Plaza Nueva. Boasts a vast array of delectable *pinxtos*, and plenty of *crianzas* and *reservas* to wash them down. The arcaded Plaza Nueva has numerous great old *taperías*, with tables outside and elegant dining rooms for full-blown meals.

Ziripot, C/Licenciado Poza 40. All manner of beers on tap and sturdy *pintxos* to help them down. A young, lively crowd enjoys the *croquetas de jamón* (ham croquettes) and *tortilla* served with a hunk of bread.

Nightlife

C/Barrenkale is a busy place with a number of clubs, while **C/Somera** has friendly, funky bars, very popular with the Basque Nationalist set; in the Ensanche, there are many more bars on **C/Pérez Galdós** and **C/Licenciado Poza**. The **Cotton Club**, C/Gregorio de la Revilla 25, has occasional live jazz and blues, as does the **Palladium**, C/Iparraguire 11. The big techno-disco in town is **Distrito 9**, on C/Ajuriaguerra.

Entertainment

One cultural form of which the city is particularly enamoured is **opera**, hosting regular performances throughout the year. Fans of Bertolt Brecht and Kurt Weill, though, will be disappointed to learn that 'Bill's Ballhaus in Bilbao' was only a figment of their imagination. For current programmes, check the back pages of *El Correo* newspaper, and the *Bilbao Guide*, free from tourist offices.

Teatro Arriaga, Pza de Arriaga 1, **t** 944 16 33 33. Regular operatic performances take place here, alongside theatre and comedy.

Palacio de la Música y de Congresos Euskalduna, Abandoibarra 4, **t** 944 03 50 00. This puts on opera, plays and musicals, and sometimes big-name foreign acts.

The Ensanche

Nobody in the 19th century had a sharper sense of urban design than Spaniards, and wherever a town had money to do something big, the results were impressive. Bilbao in its boom years had to face exponential population growth, and its mayors chose to plan for it; in the 1870s they annexed the '**Anteiglesia de Abando**', an area of farmland across the river, and commissioned a trio of planners, Severino de Achúcarro, Pablo de Alzola and Ernest Hoffmeyer, to lay out what came to be known as the **Ensanche** ('extension'). They came up with a simple-looking but pretty ingenious plan, with diagonal boulevards dividing up the broad loop of the river like orange segments. The Ensanche begins across from El Arenal; just over the bridge from the old town, a statue of Bilbao's founder, Diego López de Haro, looks benignly over the massive banks and circling traffic in the **Plaza Circular**. This has become the business district, with the big grey skyscraper of the BBV bank, built in the 1960s, to remind us who is the leading force in the city's destiny today. The RENFE station occupies one corner of the square; behind it, on the riverfront, is one of the city's industrial-age landmarks, the Bilbao–Santander **station** of the FEVE company, a charming Art Nouveau work with a wrought-iron and tile façade by Severino de Achúcarro. The vast desolation of tracks and sidings behind the stations is about to be reclaimed as the centrepiece of Bilbao's facelift: the **Intermodal**, a huge commercial project to be built in the air right over the tracks. A brand new station under an elliptical glass dome is also envisaged. South of the stations, **Plaza Zabálburu** marks the beginning of Bilbao's less salubrious quarters. On the cusp lie the Vista Alegre **bullring** and the **Museo Taurino** (*open Mon–Fri 10.30–1 and 4–6; adm*), with mementoes from over 250 years of bullfighting history, including a magnificent embroidered cape by Goya.

Westwards from Plaza de España extends the **Gran Vía de Don Diego López de Haro**, the Ensanche's main boulevard. The great hub and centrepiece of the Ensanche is **Plaza Moyúa**, also known as *La Elíptica*. Here is the Hotel Carlton, still one of the city's posh establishments, which served as the seat of the Basque government under the Republic and during the Civil War. From Plaza Moyúa, wide streets lead off in all directions: the Alameda de Recalde will take you in a few minutes' walk up to the Guggenheim, while C/Elcano leads to the **Museo de Bellas Artes** (*open Tues–Sat 10.30–1.30 and 4–7.30, Sun 10–2; adm*), on the edge of the lovely Parque de Doña Casilda Iturriza. Its worthy collection ranges from Flemish paintings (Metsys' *The Money Changers* is one of the best) to Spanish masters such as Velázquez, El Greco, Zurbarán and Goya, as well as modern art by Picasso, Gauguin, Léger and Mary Cassatt, and 19th- and 20th-century Basques. Overflow from the Guggenheim has brought in more visitors, and the museum is being enlarged to accommodate them. The park itself is a very agreeable place, with exotic trees, a lagoon, and a new light-and-colour bauble called the 'Cybernetic Fountain'.

Since the 1980s, major developments have taken place along the Nervión, and evenings see the Bilbaínos stream in to stroll along its banks in a new riverfront park. Halfway along, the billowing, glass-floored **Zubi Zuri** ('white bridge') sails over the river, from where a **funicular** glides up to the hilltop park on **Monte Artxanda** (*see* p.99), with its several restaurants and extensive views.

The Guggenheim Museum

Avenida Abandoibarra 2; t 944 35 90 80 (groups t 944 35 90 23); www. guggenheim-bilbao.es; open Tues–Sun 10–8 (last adm 30mins before closing); adm. Long queues (up to an hour) are frequent, especially at weekends. Free audioguides are available at the information desk; free guided tours (in English) take place several times daily; you can register up to 30mins ahead.

Downstream from Zubi Zuri a 60ft tower of steel and golden limestone heralds the presence of Frank Gehry's Museo Guggenheim. This titanium clipper ship occupies the **Abandoibarra flats**, until 1987 home to Bilbao's biggest shipyard; it fits in perfectly, at once utterly futuristic and yet in keeping with the city's industrial past. The museum's innovative design attracts universal curiosity: most visitors spend as much time wandering around the exterior as they do looking at artwork inside. Depending on the angle from which you see it, ships' hulls, truncated fish bodies and palm trees all protrude from the bulging mass, the juxtaposition of natural forms and 21st-century technology suggesting a new genre of 'bio-architecture'. Interior spaces are no less remarkable, with galleries radiating out from a 150ft-high atrium of white light and swooping curves, a sculptural work of art in its own right. Outside the atrium, the Nervión is incorporated into the design by way of an ingenious raised walkway, rising and curving and creating a union between river and water garden.

After Gehry's architectural fireworks, the **collection** has a hard act to follow; whether or not it succeeds will depend on when you go, for the museum displays not so much a collection of its own as the holdings of the Guggenheim Foundation, which are rotated around its museums in New York, Venice, Berlin and here. The Guggenheim also has links with major galleries worldwide and so excellent access to the masterworks of 20th-century art, yet the shifting nature of the exhibits means there's no guarantee what will be on show, so it's worth calling ahead to check.

Some works are normally resident in Bilbao, and if the **permanent collection** is up, look out for a good selection of European avant-garde art: a pivotal Miró, Kandinskys, some Modiglianis and scattered works by Picasso and Klee. Underpinning these is a distinguished collection of Abstract Expressionism, with Robert Motherwell, Pollock and De Kooning; the polychromatic chaos is balanced by a tranquil Rothko and Yves Klein's *Large Blue Anthropometry* (1960). A patchy collection of Pop Art includes a subdued Lichtenstein, and there are fine pieces by Schnabel and Basquiat. Elsewhere, there's a small collection of work by Basque and Spanish artists, which the museum's directors have pledged to augment with future purchases. And one artwork that never moves, and is literally unmissable, is Jeff Koons' *Puppy*, a giant dog covered in flowers, in the street outside, to contrast with the sleekness of the architecture.

The Guggenheim Effect

The Guggenheim's success has spawned restoration projects throughout Bilbao, most notably alongside the museum on the Abandoibarra flats, where an immense development is sprouting up designed by Cesar Pelli. A park is planned, completing the 'green corridor' between Parque Doña Casilda Iturriza and Paseo del Arenal.

Day Trips and Overnighters from Bilbao

Gernika (Guernica)

The ancient sacred city of the Basques is rebuilt now, and most of its inhabitants too young to remember the horror that occurred one market day in 1937, when 1,645 people were killed in concentrated bombardment by German aircraft. Other than the beautiful setting in the Mundaka valley near the sea, and the oak tree by the 19th-century Basque parliament building, there's not much to see, but it's a town with a lot of atmosphere. The **Tree of Gernika**, the seedling of an ancient oak, is the symbol of Basque democracy; under it Basque representatives assembled from the early Middle Ages, and after 1300 the kings of Castile came here to swear to uphold Basque *fueros* or ancient laws. When the tree died in 1860, it was replanted with a sapling from one of its acorns. Nearby are the **Museo de la Paz**, covering the bombing and wider world conflicts (*open mid-June–Aug Mon–Sat 10–7, Sun 10–2; Sept–mid-June Mon–Sat 10–2, 4–7, Sun 1–2; adm*), and two memorials, by Eduardo Chillida and Henry Moore.

Surrounding Gernika is the 220 sq km **Urdaibai Biosphere Reserve**. It's hardly a pristine wilderness – besides Gernika it counts 18 towns within its boundaries – but the sympathetic interaction between the inhabitants and their environment has led it to be considered an embodiment of that elusive ideal, sustainable development. Farms and factories share Urdaibai with wetlands and lush oak forests; greenshank and bar-tailed godwit stalk the mud flats, while lucky observers may get a glimpse of the nocturnal genet, an odd mixture of raccoon and tabby cat with enormous eyes.

Getting There

Bizkaiabus **bus** A3523 runs to Gernika from beside Abando train station in Bilbao. There are five daily on weekdays, and four on Sundays (*Mon–Sat 6.15am–8.15pm, Sun 8.15am–8.15pm; returns run at approx. the same times*). The journey takes about 45mins.

Trains on the Eusko Tren local **railway** run from the Estación de Atxuri (Bermeo line), and are more frequent, but slower (*about 1 hour*).

To get there by **car** you can choose between the A8 motorway, turning on to the BI-635 at exit 18, or a quieter country route through Mungía. To get to this road, follow signs for *Aeropuerto* out of town then fork right onto the BI-631 for Mungía, where you turn right onto the BI-2121 for Gernika (about 40km).

Tourist Information

Gernika: C/Artekale 8, t 946 25 58 92.
Market Days: on Monday, Gernika hosts the biggest country market in Euskadi.

Eating Out

Zimelea Etxea, C/Carlos Cangoiti 57, t 946 25 10 12. The best choice in town (*expensive*).
Boliña, C/Barrenkalle 3, t 946 25 03 00 (*moderate*). In the heart of the pedestrian area in the middle of Gernika, this charming hotel-restaurant offers an excellent *menú de degustación* of Basque delights for very reasonable prices.
Zallo Berri, C/Juan Calzada 79, t 946 25 18 00 (*moderate*). A delightful, simple restaurant serving traditional food (excellent value *menú del día*), although the young chef likes to throw out a few surprises.
Baserri Maitea, Ctra. BI-635 (Bermeo road), Km2, t 946 35 34 08 (*moderate*). A wonderful restaurant in a 300-year-old farmhouse just outside the town to the north, with wooden beams; the fish here is wonderful.
Lezika, near Gernika's Santimamiñe caves. This fine restaurant (*moderate*) is located in an 18th-century Basque chalet in a charming woody grove.

About 5km northeast of Gernika, the **Cueva de Santimamiñe** (*guided tours Mon–Fri 10, 11.15, 12.30, 4.30, 5.30; only 15 people at a time are allowed in*) has fine Palaeolithic engravings. A path leads from it to the **Forest of Oma**, where artist Agustín Ibarrola has fused art with nature by painting multicoloured bands and symbols on the trees.

Castro Urdiales

Just an hour west of Bilbao, Castro Urdiales is one of Cantabria's most scenic fishing ports, with a beach and seafood restaurants that draw hordes of *bilbaínos* every summer weekend. Ancient graffiti, discovered in a cave in the 1960s, date its first inhabitants to 12,000 BC; later, the Romans founded *Flavióbriga*, where the castle stands today. A stronghold of the Templars in the Middle Ages, it declined later, and suffered grievously in 1813 when the French punished it for its resistance to them by burning most of it to the ground. Only a few streets near the harbour escaped the flames, beyond the 18th-century **Ayuntamiento**, at the top of the Paseo Marítimo.

From here, walk up to the fortress-like church of **Santa María de la Asunción**, a magnificent Gothic temple. Built almost entirely in the 13th century, it has Templar touches in the unusual symbolism of the figures in the frieze around the top – rabbits kissing oxen, dragons devouring serpents devouring birds and more, although to see them properly you'll need binoculars. A Roman milestone remains in place in front of the church, while over the striking Roman/medieval bridge, most of the walls of Castro's pentagonal **Templar castle** have survived, and now shelter a lighthouse.

Castro Urdiales' beach, **Playa Brazomar**, is at the other end of town; if you're feeling like peeling, there's also a naturist beach just outside town at **El Pocillo**. The best beach, however, is 8km west at **Islares**, a small village with a magnificent strand of sand under the cliffs, interspersed with shallow lagoons ideal for young children. Just west of there at **Oriñón** there's another beach worth stopping off at, and a camp site.

Getting There

Bizkaibus A3346 runs every 30mins to Castro Urdiales from C/Lutxana, on the Ensanche side of Abando station (*Mon–Fri am–10.30pm, Sat and Sun 8.30am–10.30pm; from Castro Mon–Fri 9.30am–10.30pm, Sat and Sun 8.30am–10pm*). This takes the motorway for much of the way; another bus (A3345) goes by smaller roads, stopping all the way en route, and so is much slower.

By **car**, head west out of Bilbao, and take the A8 motorway or N634 Santander road to Castro (27km).

Tourist Information

Castro Urdiales: Avda de la Constitución 1, t 942 87 15 12.
Market Day: Thursday.

Eating Out

Miramar, Avda de la Playa 1, t 942 86 02 04, (*expensive*). A stylish hotel that has excellent views of the cathedral from its second-floor restaurant, and is also near the beach. To go with the view there's high-quality local seafood, and service is pleasantly attentive.

El Segoviano, La Correría 19, t 942 86 18 59 (*expensive*). A culinary shrine in the area, even if the style of some of the specialities is not strictly 'local'. Make your way here for Castilian roast suckling-pig, or a more Cantabrian seafood grill.

Mesón El Marinero, La Correría 23 (in the Casa de los Chelines, by the fishing port), t 942 86 00 05 (*moderate*). The place to go for heaped plates of delicious, fresh seafood at reasonable prices, or a big, equally impressive selection of *tapas* at the bar.

San Sebastián (Donostia)

At the beginning of the 21st century it's hard to imagine a place like San Sebastián (Donostia, in Basque) could ever exist. The Belle Epoque may be a hundred years away, but in San Sebastián the buildings still seem to be made of ice cream, with trimmings in Impressionist colours and brass streetlights; people still dress up instinctively for the evening *paseo*. This confection embraces one of Spain's most enchanting bays, the oyster-shaped **Bahía de La Concha**, protected from the bad moods of the Atlantic by a wooded islet, the **Isla de Santa Clara**, and **Monte Urgull**, the hump-backed sentinel on the easternmost tip of the bay. It looks a bit like Rio de Janeiro, and is a movie set when the sun's shining, which even on this Atlantic coast happens a lot of the time.

San Sebastián has probably been around as long as the Basques, but the earliest mention of it is as a Roman port called *Easo*. It resurfaced in the Middle Ages; in the 12th century the Navarrese built the first fortress on Monte Urgull, which has been rebuilt many times since. The first recorded tourist came against his will – François I, king of France, was locked up here for a time by Charles V after being captured at the Battle of Pavia in 1527. In the 19th century, the city found a new role as the cynosure of fashion; long before there were '*costas*', wealthy Spaniards came here to spend their summers. In the 1850s it was blessed by the presence of Queen Isabel II, who brought the government and court with her in summer. Shortly afterwards the Paris–Madrid railway was laid through here, making the city easy to reach from both capitals.

It's still a classy place to go today, a lovely, relaxed resort in a spectacular setting. And the *Donostiarrak*, as its inhabitants are known, know how to throw a party. The wild 24-hour non-stop *Tamborrada,* beginning at midnight on 19 January, honours the town's patron saint with a mad tattoo of drums and barrels, recalling how the town's laundresses mocked Napoleonic troops by following their drummers about, banging away on their washtubs; now the roles are played by the *txokos*, gastronomic societies, who dress up as soldiers and chefs. A big jazz festival takes place in July, followed by a week of partying for the *Semana Grande* (8–15 August), with an International Fireworks Festival. The International Film Festival is in September, along with ocean-going rowing races, the *Regatas de Traineras de La Concha* (on the two first Sundays), one of the most closely followed events on the Basque sports calendar.

Playa de la Concha and the Comb of the Winds

Sheltered within the bay is the magnificent golden crescent of the **Playa de la Concha**, San Sebastián's centrepiece and its largest beach, beautifully hemmed by the Paseo de la Concha, an elegant promenade with flouncy balustrades, and dotted with creamy Belle Epoque cafés and the matronly bathhouse. On its western end stands a promontory topped by the mock-Tudor **Palacio de Miramar de María Cristina**, built as a summerhouse for the royal family. It is now owned by the city and used for receptions and special exhibitions, but you can sit in the gardens. A tunnel under Miramar leads to the **Playa de Ondarreta**, a traditional society retreat, with a smart tennis club and graceful old houses. Ondarreta beach itself comes to a dead end at **Monte Igueldo**, crowned by a **Parque de Atracciones**. You can get to the top by road or by the

Getting There

There are two options on public transport for getting from Bilbao to San Sebastián. The recently modernised Basque railway Eusko Tren has at least 15 **trains** daily, 6am–8pm (from San Sebastián 5.47am–19.47pm), leaving from Estación de Atxuri and arriving at the little Estación de Amara, in the new town, in San Sebastián. The journey takes 2½ hours and tickets cost €5.50 single, €9.65 return.

Buses are run by Transportes Pesa from Termibus in Bilbao to Plaza Pío XII in San Sebastián, on the south side of town. There are around 24 each day, usually 6.30am–10pm in each direction, and the trip usually takes about 2 hours. Tickets are €7.45 each way.

San Sebastián is 119km from Bilbao. By **car** you can get there in under two hours on the A8 *autopista* (toll). To get to it, head west from the city centre, and follow signs for San Sebastián/Donostia or Madrid. At this point the A8 is combined with the A68 for Vitoria and Madrid; they separate south of Bilbao. The coast road, through Gernika and Lekeitio, offers a longer, more leisurely ride (*see* p.112). **Eusko Tren**, t 902 54 32 10, *www.euskotren.es*. **Transportes Pesa**, t 902 10 12 10.

Tourist Information

Tourist offices: The municipal office is on the river, C/Reina Regente, t 943 48 11 66. The Basque government office as at Paseo de los Fueros 1, t 943 42 62 82.

Tours

Walking tours: Every Thurs, Fri and Sat in July and August with Guitour, t 943 43 09 09 (€12, not including admission fees).

Bus tour: A guided tour bus, t (mobile) 696 42 98 47, departs from the city tourist office every hour, picking up and dropping off at all the major sights (€9).

Shopping

Along with the tourist shops in the Parte Vieja, there are a number of more original places that sell a range of items from surf-punk paraphernalia to exquisite home-made chocolates. The **Centro Romántico** has a wide range of fashionable boutiques, from chains like Zara and Mango to individual establishments selling Spanish designers.

San Sebastián has wonderful **markets**. The central **Mercado de la Brecha** has been given a glass roof and a string of fast-food outlets, but underneath you'll find immaculate stalls with all kinds of fresh produce. The **Mercado de San Martín** in the Centro Romanticó is more traditional and devoted entirely to local produce.

Where to Stay

San Sebastián ✉ 20000

In general, the further back from the sea, the less expensive accommodation will be.

Luxury–Expensive

*****María Cristina, C/Okendo 1, t 943 42 49 00, *hmc@sheraton.com* (*luxury*). For a touch of Belle Epoque elegance, this grande dame is one of Spain's best hotels; it looks onto the Río Urumea's promenade, a short walk from La Concha.

****Hotel Londres y Inglaterra, C/Zubieta 2 (on La Concha beach), t 943 44 07 70, *h.londres@paisvasco.com* (*luxury*). The city's other most luxurious address, with splendid views, first-class service, and plenty of charm, as well as one of the city's best restaurants (*moderate*).

****Mercure Monte Igueldo, on the top of the mountain, t 943 21 02 11, (*expensive*). Peace and quiet and absolutely stunning views over the bay.

***La Galeria, C/Infanta Cristina 1–3, t 943 21 60 77, *www.hotellagaleria.com* (*expensive*). A couple of minutes from Playa Ondarreta on a lovely quiet street, this French-inspired turn-of-the-last-century *palacete* has rooms full of antiques and individuality.

Moderate

San Sebastián being the posh resort it is, most *hostales* here fall into this price band.

**Pensión Bikain, C/Triunfo 8, t 94 345 43 33, f 94 346 80 74. Has four-star facilities at a very good price, close to the beach and the Parte Vieja, as well as spotless rooms, parking facilities and a very helpful owner.

**Pensión Donostiarra, C/San Martin 6, t 943 42 61 67, f 94 343 00 71. Light, airy rooms with either a little balcony of flowers or a glassed-in *solana* full of pot plants.

**La Estrella, Plaza de Sarriegi 1, t 943 42 09 97. On the edge of the Parte Vieja, a short walk from the bay.

Inexpensive

The best you'll find will be at the higher end of the *inexpensive* slot, and there are several in the Parte Vieja and the centre.

**Hs Eder II, Alameda del Boulevard, t 943 42 64 49. A well-run place at the edge of the Parte Vieja, right in the centre.

**Pensión La Perla, C/Loiola 10, t 943 42 81 23. An old-fashioned budget choice, handily located between the cathedral and market.

*Pensión Urgull, C/Esterlines 10, t 943 43 00 47. A delightful low-cost choice; there are only four immaculate rooms with two shared bathrooms. The charming owners are kind, friendly and more than happy to help out with local information.

*Pensión Easo, C/San Bartolomé 24, t 943 45 39 12. A good bargain choice.

*Hotel Record, Calzada Vieja de Ategorrieta, t 943 27 12 55, f 943 27 85 21. A little family-run hotel in a villa by the beach at Gros.

Eating Out

Eating is the local obsession, so it's not surprising the city can claim several of Spain's most renowned restaurants – cathedrals of Basque cuisine. For something cheaper, follow the crowds to the *tapas* bars of the Parte Vieja.

Restaurants

Expensive

Arzak, Alto de Miracruz 21, t 943 27 84 65. Often described as the finest restaurant in Spain, offering a constantly changing menu of delights (the *menú de degustación* is the real thing to choose for a gourmet splurge). Chef Juan Mari Arzak is often at hand to make suggestions, as dishes change with the seasons and market availability. Among specialities that you might see is *cola de rape enveulta de hierbes* (monkfish encrusted with herbs). Book weeks in advance. *Closed Sun eve and Mon, most of June, and the first fortnight in Nov.*

Akelarre, in the Barrio de Igueldo, t 943 21 20 52. Celebrated for its mixture of some of the most innovative New Basque cuisine with a delicious array of traditional local dishes – wonderfully prepared langoustines. A place to see and be seen during the city's film festival – and there's a beautiful mountain-side setting with views over the sea to boot. *Closed Sun eve and Mon.*

Casa Nicolasa, Aldaman 4, t 943 42 17 62. Another culinary shrine, founded in 1912, it specializes in classic Basque cookery and offers a big choice of dishes, among them *almejas gratinadas* (gratinéed clams). *Closed Sun eve and Mon.*

Urepel, Paseo de Salamanca 3, t 943 42 40 40. Another of San Sebastián's most eminent restaurants, serving classic Basque cuisine with original touches. The house speciality is the *sopa de pescados* (fish soup), a rich, flavoursome dish that won't leave much room for dessert. *Closed Sun, Tues, Christmas, Easter and three weeks in July.*

Rekondo, Paseo de Igueldo 57, t 943 21 29 07. A superb, elegant choice, specializing in grilled fish and meat and with a huge wine cellar.

Moderate

Beti Jai, C/Fermín Calbetón 22, t 943 42 77 37. Bang in the middle of 'Restaurant Walk', this is one of the city's finest and liveliest seafood restaurants, although there are plenty of other things on the menu and a hectic bar if you don't want to sit down. The *salpicón de mariscos* (seafood salad) is excellent. *Closed Mon, Tues, Christmas and end June–early July.*

Salduba, C/Arrandegui 6, t 943 42 56 27. At this wooden-beamed retreat from the crowds in the heart of the Parte Vieja, you'll find traditional dishes and attentive service.

Casa Urola, C/Fermín Calbetón 22, t 943 42 11 75. A wonderful old favourite, this refined restaurant offers a very decently priced, high-quality *menú del día*, and also has a less expensive bar area packed with locals. The wine list is particularly good.

Bodegón Alejandro, C/Fermin Calbetón 4, t 943 47 77 37. This delightful establishment offers popular, traditional cooking based on the freshest produce and accompanied by an excellent selection of wines.

Cheap and Vegetarian

Casa Tiburcio, C/Fermin Calbeton, t 943 42 31 30. A popular choice in the Parte Vieja for a varied *menú* and excellent *pintxos*.

Makrobiotika, C/Intxaurrondo 52. The best vegetarian restaurant, serving a variety of cereal-based dishes. Take bus nos.13 or 24 from the centre, as it's a bit of a trek.

Ttun Ttun Taberna, C/San Jeronimo 25, t 943 42 68 82. This unassuming tavern is an enclave of Basquedom, serving a wonderful soul-satisfying bargain *menú*.

Sagardotegiak Plaza Berri, C/Nueva 18, t 943 29 30 00. A rare *sidreria* in the city limits.

Tapas/Pinchos/Pintxos

The **Parte Vieja** is proud of its reputation for having more bars per square metre than anywhere else in the world; every street is lined with them. Perhaps the gastronomic heart of the Parte Vieja are Calle Mayor and C/31 de Agosto, both filled with the most traditional bars, restaurants and the famous gastronomic societies that feast in secret.

The **Plaza de la Constitución**, with its freshly painted balconies and cool arcades, is a lovely place to while away an hour or two, and **C/Fermín Calbetón** is sometimes known as 'Restaurant Walk', thanks to its virtually unbroken string of busy locales.

Clery, Plaza de la Trinidad 1, t 943 42 34 01. Tucked away near the Santa María Basilica, this is one of San Sebastián's most well-loved bars, with a great terrace where you can sample tasty *pintxos*. A great place to eat during the spring jazz festival, when concerts take place in the Plaza.

Martinéz, C/31 de Agosto 13, t 943 42 49 65. A classic old town bar with a broad counter piled staggeringly high with delicious *pintxos*. Try the *champis*, wild mushrooms which are sometimes stuffed with a pungent slice of cured sausage.

Ormazabel, C/31 de Agosto 22, t 943 42 99 07. A little, family-run *bodega* with an excellent selection of local wines to accompany the unusual spinach *croquetas*, or the *chiperones*, baby squid, which have been everyone's favourite for more than 40 years.

Gambara, C/San Jeronimo 21. A tiny bar with a big reputation for its wide array of *pintxos*: excellent prawns, fresh asparagus in season, good cured meats, all washed down with some of the best *txakoli* local wine.

Aselena, C/Iñigo 1 (just off Plaza de la Constitucíon), t 943 42 62 75. The city's hot spot on the feast of St Tomás in December, when the Plaza fills up with revellers.

Tamboril, C/Pescadería 2, t 943 42 35 07. All kinds of *banderillas* (mini *tapas* skewered on toothpicks) are on offer here, but the house speciality is stuffed mushrooms (*champis*), served on a slice of crusty bread.

Borda Berri, C/Fermin Calbetón 12, t 943 42 56 38. An elegant, historic bar with a range of innovative *raciones* – stuffed peppers with tuna and a light red capsicum mousse among them – and, unusually for this part of town, a refined cocktail list.

Casa Alcade, C/Mayor 19, t 94 342 62 16. Walls of bullfighting memorabilia and hanging hams are the backdrop for the food at this bar, virtually unchanged for 80 years. Wafer-thin slices of *serrano* ham make a fine accompaniment to the excellent Riojas.

Aloña Berri, C/Berminghan 24, t 94 329 08 18. Not in the Parte Vieja but across the river int the Gros district, this has some of the most imaginative *banderillas* in the city, all beautifully arranged; the cod is exceptionally good.

Joxean, C/Secundino Esnaola 39–41, t 943 27 85 15. A lively bar in Gros with a young crowd and small restaurant. *Pintxos* give a twist to old favourites, as in *hojaldre de pimientos rellenos*, pastry with stuffed peppers.

Entertainment and Nightlife

The centre of the serious party action is the Parte Vieja. Late-night bars and clubs are also found around the end of Ondarreta beach. For listings, check the back pages of *El Diario Vasco*, the local newspaper.

Akerbeltz, C/Mari. A tiny bar with a popularity that far exceeds its size, so everyone just congregates outside to enjoy the view of the bay with their beer.

Etxekalte, C/Mari 1. Has two floors of dance music and is almost always chock-full.

delightful, rickety old **funicular** from the end of the beach, and the reward is a spectacular view over San Sebastián, the Bay of Biscay and the Cantabrian mountains. Back on the shore, beyond the beach and the funicular, stands one of the most talked-about monuments of modern Spanish sculpture, Eduardo Chillida's **Peine de los Vientos**, the *Comb of the Winds*. It's a series of terraces, built into the rocks that guard the entrance to the bay, decorated with cast-iron constructions, the 'teeth' of the comb that smooths the winds coming from the sea towards the city. Chillida was a native of San Sebastián, and his house is on the cliffs above the monument.

The Centro Romanticó

Nearly all the city behind the beaches of La Concha and Ondarreta dates from the 19th century; San Sebastián is an ancient place, but it has been burned to the ground 12 times in its history, lastly by Wellington's drunken soldiers. It was rebuilt and expanded a few decades later, in a neat neoclassical grid now called the Centro Romanticó, with the **Catedral del Buen Pastor** at its centre. The **Mercado de San Martín** squats nearby, with stalls packed with fresh produce from the sea and the surrounding mountains. In the north of the district is the arcaded **Plaza de Gipuzkoa**, overlooked by the neoclassical **Palacio Foral**. Heading towards the river, **Plaza de Okendo** is flanked by the grand María Cristina hotel, with swathes of colourful tiles, and the prim 1912 **Victoria Eugenia Theatre**. This trim neighbourhood is the main shopping district, with swanky designer stores and a swathe of classy teashops.

A promenade-lined river, the **Urumea**, divides 19th-century *Sanse* (as the city is affectionately known) from the newer quarter of **Gros**, once a workingmen-student-bohemian enclave, a lively place full of bars and restaurants and with its own beach, the **Playa de la Zurriola**, which is always less crowded but lies outside the sheltered bay, so is subject to wind, waves and debris. Still, it's great for surfers, who come in droves. The beachfront landscape here has lately received a new adornment: a rather fearsome convention centre called the **Kursaal**. Of the three charming bridges that span the Urumea, the María Cristina (by the station) most resembles a cream pastry.

The Parte Vieja and Monte Urgull

Most of the action in town takes place under Monte Urgull in the narrow streets of The Parte Vieja, or old town. From La Concha beach, its entrance is guarded by a well-manicured square, **Parque Alderdi Eder**, and the enormous **Ayuntamiento**, or town hall, formerly the casino that María Cristina built (the new one is in the Hotel de Londres). Behind it, the swanky yacht club, in a white rationalist building from the 1930s, looks like something from an Agatha Christie novel. What remains of the city's fishing fleet may be seen in the harbour behind the Ayuntamiento, a picturesque tumble of whitewashed cottages rimmed by souvenir shops, mostly pricey restaurants, and a pair of salty museums: the **Museo Naval** (*open summer Tues–Sat 10–1.30 and 5–8.30, Sun 11–2; otherwise 10–1.30 and 4–7.30, Sun 11–2; adm*), devoted to the Basques' naval history, and, at the far end of the port, the **Aquarium** (*open July–Sept 10–10, rest of the year 10–8; adm*), stuffed with model ships, the skeleton of a whale that went belly-up in San Sebastián's port and tanks of fish and other sea creatures.

From here you can stroll along the outer edge of **Monte Urgull** on the Paseo Nuevo, a splendid little walk between turf and surf. In the late afternoon, when the light is best, stroll up one of the paths to the summit of the rock; Monte Urgull is really the city's park, closed to traffic and including surprises along the way such as a peaceful British cemetery from Wellington's campaign, and some of the old bastions and cannons of the city's defences. At the top is the half-ruined **Castillo de Santa Cruz de la Mota** (16th century), with a small but excellent museum of local history. It's topped with an ungainly kitsch statue of Christ from the Franco era called the **Sagrado Corazón**, which keeps an eye on the holiday-makers on La Concha beach below.

The centre of the Parte Vieja is the arcaded **Plaza de la Constitución**, which once did double duty as the local bullring. Within a few blocks stand San Sebastián's three best monuments. From Calle Mayor, the distant spires of the Catedral del Buen Pastor outstare the hyper-ornate façade of **Santa María del Coro** (18th century), on Vía Coro, topped with a writhing statue of St Sebastian full of arrows. It's gloomy inside, with *retablos* half-hidden in shadows, but the main altarpiece is well lit and surmounted by the church's treasure, a statue of the Virgin said to have been found up the sleeve of a priest who was trying to smuggle it out and placed in its present position to discourage further attempts. Don't miss, at the back, an alabaster Greek cross by Eduardo Chillida in a pale arc of light. Next to the church is **Plaza de la Trinidad**, focus of the city's jazz festival in July and popular with skateboarders the rest of the year.

At the other end of C/31 de Agosto is the solid Gothic church of **San Vicente** (16th century), the oldest building in the city. The *Pietá* (1999) by Oteiza and José Ramon Anda on the outside walls is extremely moving. Nearby, an old monastery is now the fascinating **Museum of San Telmo** (*open summer Tues–Sat 10.30–1.30 and 5–8.30, Sun 10–2; winter Tues–Sat 10.30–1.30 and 4–8, Sun 10–2; adm*). Basque discoidal tombstones, adorned with geometric patterns and solar symbols, are lined up in the cloister; upstairs, the museum has three El Grecos, two bear skeletons, Basque lucky charms and amulets, sports paraphernalia, the interior of a Basque cottage and more.

The great attraction of the Parte Vieja, though, is as a social centre. It has countless bars, where the evening crowds hasten to devour delectable seafood *tapas* and Basque goodies. Here in the homeland of the Basque gastronomic societies, eating is an obsession; at the same time, the Parte Vieja is also a hotbed of radical, belligerent Basque nationalism, so demonstrations may appear among all the busy socializing.

Around San Sebastián

A fun excursion is to gather up some of the city's fine food and row it out to **Isla de Santa Clara** for a picnic (*in summer there's also a regular ferry to the island from El Muelle, the dock behind the Ayuntamiento; boats run from 10am to 8pm*). There are also lovely parks in the hills around the city. **Parque Monte Ullia**, east of Gros, once had its own funfair and funicular, but these have long disappeared. Nowadays, you have to clamber up under your own steam from Sagües station on the edge of Gros for dramatic views of the Cantabrian Sea. A mile inland from La Concha is the graceful **Aiete Palace**, built in the late 19th century for the duke and duchess of Bailén, and surrounded by breezy woods and pretty landscaped gardens with a lake.

Touring the Basque Country

Day 1: Along the Green Sea Cliffs to Lekeitio

Morning: From central Bilbao, head west, turn north on the A8, and take the giant bridge to the east side of the Nervión and the coast road. (From Santander, it's an 80km drive east along the E80 to Bilbao first). A first stop is **Getxo**, a mix of Sunday beach and wealthy residential suburb, with a waterfront lined with fine villas. Next, **Plentzia** (last stop on Bilbao metro) has a medieval core, and quite a clean beach. Turn on to a minor road to stay close to the sea, along an exquisite coast of deep green hills and sheer cliffs. **Bakio** (15km on) is a village known for *txakoli*, the crisp Basque white wine. Roll on round **Cape Matxitxako** to **Bermeo**, a colourful, working fishing town, and **Mundaka**, a labyrinth of alleys with a lovely bay-side promenade.

Lunch: In Mundaka, *see* below.

Afternoon: Carry on south along the west bank of the Ría de Mundaka down to **Gernika** (*see* p.104). Then, turn back up the east bank and again stay on the minor, coast-hugging road round to **Elantxobe**, an immaculate fishing village at the foot of an utterly steep cliff. From there it's a winding 11km to **Lekeitio**, another town that became a fashionable summer haunt in the days when everyone who could avoided the heat, and so has ornate mansions as well as fine beaches and a lively harbour.

Dinner and Sleeping: In Lekeitio, *see* below.

Day 1

Lunch in Mundaka

Asador Zaldua, Sabino Arana 10, **t** 945 87 08 71 (*moderate*). A classic traditional Basque restaurant that serves a wonderful array of fresh fish and succulent steaks grilled to perfection. *Lunch only Nov–Jun.*

Casino, José Mari, C/Mayor, **t** 946 87 60 05 (*moderate*). A very distinctively Basque institution: once the local fishermen's guild auction house, this is now a local eating club that, unusually, has opened its doors to the public. The seafood is superb, and has usually been caught recently by a club member.

Dinner in Lekeitio

Méson Arropain, Ctra. Marquina Ispaster, **t** 946 84 03 13 (*expensive*) . Five kilometres from Lekeitio, this friendly restaurant cooks up excellent fish dishes smothered with bubbling *salsas*, and has good *txakoli* to wash it all down with.

Zapirain, Igualdegui 3, **t** 946 84 02 55 (*moderate*). A homely, straightforward restaurant that serves excellent fish dinners, in very ample portions .

Sleeping in Lekeitio

★★★Emperatriz Zita, C/Santa Elena Etorbidea s/n, **t** 946 84 26 55, *rlekeitio@usa.net* (*moderate*). A recently opened modern palace of a place, complete with a thalas-sotherapy centre. It was built over the ruins of the home of the last Austro-Hungarian empress, who spent her final years in Lekeitio, hence the name.

★★★Zubieta, Portal de Atea, **t** 946 84 30 30, *hzubieta@line-pro.es* (*moderate*). Charming hotel in the grounds of a castle, in the former gatehouse, with lovely rooms and lovely owners.

Hosteria Señorio de Bizcaya, José María Cirarda 4, **t/f** 946 19 47 25 (*moderate*). A noble old palace, lovingly restored and surrounded by gardens with beautifully restored rooms.

Day 2: Sybaritic Seaside: Getaria to San Sebastián

Morning: Staying with the coast road – bigger and busier here than before – you twist and turn on through more green-clad cliffs and tangy fishing towns. One to stop at is **Deba** (22km from Lekeitio), another place where Spain's wealthy chose to build some grand villas above the long beach in the 1880s. It also has a fine Gothic church, Santa María la Real. **Zumaya**, another 13km on along the N634, has both 12th- and 15th-century churches, and a spectacular beach at **San Telmo**, known for its crashing surf. From there, it's only 6–7km to **Getaria**, one of the loveliest village in Euskadi, hugging a steep slope down to its harbour, on a narrow inlet known as 'the mouse'. It was the home of Juan Sebastián de Elcano, first man to sail around the world (his commander Magellan having died on the way), who is buried in the great 13th-century church of San Salvador. It's also a great centre of *txacolí* production.

Lunch: In Getaria, *see* below.

Afternoon: If you still want more beaches, stop at **Zarautz**, Euskadi's longest, and a big magnet for surfers. Otherwise, continue on the short way into **San Sebastián**. Leave the car at a hotel and stroll along the Concha, one of Europe's most archetypal, incorribly genteel seaside proms, and around Monte Urgull for some great views. Then, as evening comes up, head into the Parte Vieja to join in one of the essential local rituals, *tapas*-hunting in its many, many bars, to prepare properly for dinner in the city considered the Basque (and often Spain's) culinary capital.

Dinner and Sleeping: In San Sebastián, *see* below and pp.106–11.

Day 2

Lunch in Getaria

Kaia Kaipe, Gral. Arnao 10 (upstairs), t 943 14 05 00 (*expensive*). With good Basque seafood and views, this is one of many restaurants crowding the harbour, with *txakoli* wine grown in the nearby hills .

Elkano, Herrerieta 2, t 943 14 06 14 (*expensive*). Boasts the best grilled fish on the harbour.

Iribar Jatexea, Kale Nagusia 38, t 943 14 04 06 (*inexpensive*). A excellent *asador* (grillhouse) with good-value fresh local meat and fish.

Talaipe, Puerto Viejo, t 94 314 06 13 (*inexpensive*). Right on the tip of the old port, this place has wonderful views and nautical décor to go with the delicious fresh fish.

Dinner in San Sebastián

Akelarre, in the Barrio de Igueldo, t 943 21 20 52 (*expensive*). Celebrated for its mixture of some of the most innovative New Basque cuisine with a delicious array of traditional local dishes – wonderfully prepared langoustines. A place to see and be seen during the city's film festival – and there's a beautiful mountain-side setting with views over the sea to boot. *Closed Sun eve and Mon.*

Beti Jai, C/Fermín Calbetón 22, t 943 42 77 37 (*moderate*). A less opulent but also impresive choice: one of the city's finest and liveliest seafood restaurants, with a hectic bar. *Closed Mon, Tues, Christmas and end June–early July.*

Sleeping in San Sebastián

★★★★★**María Cristina**, C/Okendo 1, t 943 42 49 00, hmc@sheraton.com (*luxury*). For a touch of Belle Epoque elegance, this grande dame is one of Spain's best hotels; it looks onto the Río Urumea's promenade, a short walk from La Concha.

★**Pensión Urgull**, C/Esterlines 10, t 943 43 00 47 (*inexpensive*). A delightful low-cost choice; just only four immaculate rooms with two shared bathrooms. The charming owners are kind, friendly and more than happy to help out with local information.

Day 3: Pilgrimages: Tolosa, Azpeitia and Loyola

Morning: Take a bracing morning stroll along the Concha before setting off. The road out of San Sebastián, the N1, is easy to find and rapidly takes you out of the city into the mixture of small industrial towns and areas of rural calm characteristic of the province of Guipúzkoa. **Tolosa**, 25km south, is both in one. It's ringed by paper mills, but in the Basque way it's also celebrated for food, especially biscuits and sweets, and special beans, *alubias de Tolosa*, for which there's a denominación de orígen. It also has an atmospheric old town (in C/Arbol de Gernika is Pastelería Gorrochategui, the temple of local sweets) and a superior choice of restaurants.

Lunch: In Tolosa, *see below*.

Afternoon: After lunch head south and very soon turn right on to the little GI-2634 road to climb up and over through superb scenery for the 18km to **Azpeitia**. The importance of this spot varies depending on whether you had a Catholic education. Just south is **Loyola**, birthplace in 1491 of St Ignatius of Loyola, founder of the Jesuits, and in this tiny village is the Santuario de San Ignacio, with his house and a basilica that is one of the most extravagant High Baroque churches in Spain, designed by Carlo Fontana in 1689 (*open daily 10–12.30, 3.30–7; the basilica is often open at other times*). The façade is ornate enough, but nothing prepares you for the interior of the dome, a blaze of carving by the Spanish Churriguera brothers. Below, Azpeitia, despite its many pilgrims, remains a quiet, very ancient Basque country town.

Dinner and Sleeping: In Azpeitia and Loyola, *see below*.

Day 3

Lunch in Tolosa

Frontón, C/San Francisco Ibiltokia 4, **t** 943 65 29 41 (*expensive*). Longstanding classic from the 30s with an Art Deco interior and New Basque cuisine – try *lomo de merluza alvapor sobre salsa de piquillos*. Also likely to have the town's famous beans on the menu.

Casa Julián, C/Santa Clara 6, **t** 943 67 14 17 (*moderate*). Tolosa's oldest restaurant and still one of the best, specializing in steaks, *pimientos del piquillo* and local desserts, with a good list of Riojas. *Closed Sun*.

Sausta, Paso Belate 78, **t** 943 65 54 53 (*moderate*). The young chef here has trained with some of the region's most formidable cooks, and for some of the most innovative New Basque cuisine at very decent prices, this attractive restaurant is a must. Try the *mero a la planch sobre salsa de marisco* (sea bass with shellfish sauce) and top it all off with a wonderful chocolate soufflé with passion fruit.

Dinner in Azpeitia

Juantxo, Loiola Blde 3, **t** 943 81 43 15 (*moderate*). That Azpeitia is still only a very small, homely little place is summed up by this welcoming, old-fashioned restaurant, which has an excellent reputation for its fine traditional Basque cuisine all made with market-fresh local produce, and washed down with a pungent, equally local *txakoli* wine. The home-made desserts featuring *tejas de Tolosa* – almond biscuits – are especially good.

Sleeping in Loyola

*Izarra, Avda de Loyola s/n, Loyola (near the basilica), **t** 943 81 07 50 (*moderate*). A fairly new hotel with a swimming pool, but still very reasonable prices.

*Hs Uranga, Plaza de Loyola 7, **t** 943 81 25 43 (*inexpensive*). Nearby, this is a more auster option, but its old-style bathless rooms are quite pleasant, and there's a decent, simple local restaurant.

Day 4: Mountain Renaissance: Bergara to Oñati

Morning: Go south from Azpeitia on the GI-631 Zumárraga road, but after 7km look for a minor road off to the right, for Elosu and Bergara. This is another wild, steep, winding road, where from industry you suddenly find yourself amid nothing but green crags and lonely stone farmhouses. It rejoins a slightly busier world at **Bergara**, which nevertheless still offers a step back in time. Its streets are lined with palaces, churches and other monuments from the 16th and 17th centuries. A very aristocratic town in its heyday, it's a delightful place to wander around, with ornate coats-of-arms over everyday shop doorways. Especially impressive is the Palacio Arrese, with its cut-out corner windows in best Spanish Renaissance style.

Lunch: In Bergara, *see* below.

Afternoon: Leave Bergara on the GI-632 Mondragón road, but after 7km turn left on to the GI-2630 for **Oñati**, another Renaissance gem lost in the country, in a rich, rolling valley beneath massive mountains. It once had the only Basque University, founded in 1540 and now its greatest landmark, with an august Plateresque façade. Nearby, the 15th-century church of San Miguel has many treasures. Around them and the also distinguished Ayuntamiento are well-preserved medieval palaces, one of them the birthplace in 1511 of the mad conquistador Lope de Aguirre, who tried to find El Dorado and then carve out a kingdom of his own in Peru. To the south, a 9km road winds to **Aránzazu**, lofty shrine of the Madonna who is the patroness of Guipúzcoa.

Dinner and Sleeping: In Oñati, *see* below.

Day 4

Lunch in Bergara

Restaurante Lasa,Palacio Otaeza Zubiaurre, t 943 76 10 55 (*expensive*). A special place for a special meal; just south of the town off the Mondragón road, this occupies a magnificent 1565 palace built for a relative of St Ignatius. Inside, its stone chambers have been beautifully restored and are deliciously comfortable, a fit setting for the work of chef-owner Koldo Lasa, who has a very high reputation for his dedication to his craft. Fish dishes are especially sublime. *Closed Mon.*

Zumelaga Jatetxea, C/San Antonio 5, (*inexpensive*). A much more basic option, a straightforward local place that still offers good versions of strongly-flavoured local Basque cooking.

Dinner in Oñati

Txopekua, Barrio Uribarri, t 943 78 05 71 (*moderate*). A good restaurant in Oñati, in a Basque homestead on the road to Aránzazu .

Iturritxo, Atzeko Kale 32, t 943 71 60 78 (*inexpensive*). A well-loved local establishment inside Oñati village which is always full; its secret is the excellent regional cooking – grilled meats are the highlight, but fish is impressive too – and the very reasonable prices. Service is briskly charming.

Sleeping in Oñati

*Etxe Aundi, Torre Auzo 10, t 943 78 19 56, *cu37993@cempresard* (*inexpensive*). This likeable small hotel has all the modern comforts and a good restaurant, in a lovely old stone building.

*Etxeberria, C/R. M. Zuazola 14, t 943 78 04 60 (*inexpensive*). A pleasant small *hostal* with straightforward rooms in the middle of the village.

Soraluze Ostatua, Carretera Aranzazu, Barrio Uribarri s/n, t 943 71 61 79 (*inexpensive*). Seven kilometres up the road towards Aránzazu, this hotel offers 12 comfortable rooms, fine views and also a babysitting service, but still at very amenable prices.

Day 5: A Small Capital: Vitoria

Morning: Retrace your route out of Oñati along the GI-2630, and at the GI-632 turn south to go through the town known as **Arrasate** (Basque) or **Mondragón** (Spanish). A very busy small town, it is famous for its industrial cooperatives. From there it's 40km down to **Vitoria** (Gasteiz, in Basque), since 1980 the capital of the Basque autonomous government. Though small, it's a city with style, and a slight air of a Ruritanian capital. Leave your car and find the Plaza de la Virgen Blanca, a delightful piece of medieval town design that's the hub of the Casco Viejo (old city); next to it, the neoclassical Plaza de España provides a perfect contrast. To the north, the medieval streets are ideal for strolling, with dignified stone façades leading to the Gothic cathedral of Santa María. Two streets away on C/Correría is El Portalón, a rambling 16th-century brick and timber structure that's one of the oldest in the city.

Lunch: In Vitoria, *see* below.

Afternoon: After lunch, walk south to Parque de la Florida, site of the 20th-century new cathedral and the Basque parliament. From the elegant 19th-century park, Paseo de la Senda leads to the small but impressive Museo de Bellas Artes (*open Tues–Fri 10–2 and 4–6.30, Sat 10–2, Sun 11–2; adm*), with works by Picasso, Miró and Spanish Baroque masters. For some last sightseeing, follow the *paseo* and the streets that follow on from it for 20 minutes to the 12th-century church of San Prudencio. From Vitoria, a fast road leads to Bilbao and on to Santander.

Dinner and Sleeping: In Vitoria, see below.

Day 5

Lunch in Vitoria

Dos Hermanas, C/Madre Vedruna 10, t 945 13 29 34 (*moderate*). A local institution for more than a century, where you'll find excellent Basque dishes like *lomo de merluza al vino blanco* (hake with white wine) and *rabo de buey estofado* (stuffed oxtail).

Mesa, C/Chile 1, t 945 22 84 94 (*moderate*). A very popular place (it's worth booking during festivals) serving flavoursome, down-to-earth local dishes. *Closed Wed.*

Dinner in Vitoria

Elkea, C/Castilla 27, t 945 14 47 47 (*expensive*). One of the most renowned restaurants in Euskadi, this is where to find truly original cuisine that incorporates international elements from Japanese to French but still manages one of the best versions of *patatas alavesa*, a rustic local potato dish, around.

I Portalón, C/Correría 151, t 945 14 27 55 (*moderate*). Enjoyable, with tables on three floors of an august old building (*see* above) and traditional Basque food, like *lautada itzaso*, combining meat and fish.

Sleeping in Vitoria

★★★★**Hotel Ciudad de Vitoria**, Portal de Castilla 8, t 845 14 11 00 (*expensive*). A place with more character than many city hotels of this grade in Spain, with friendly staff and an indoor garden; good discounts are available at weekends and in summer.

★★★**Almoneda**, C/Florida 7, t 945 15 40 84, *information@hotelalmoneda.com* (*moderate*). This newly renovated little hotel has simple, tasteful rooms and a pleasant lounge furnished with an eclectic, engaging collection of antiques.

★★**Dato 28**, C/Eduardo Dato 28 (near the train station), t 94 514 72 30 (*inexpensive*). Convenient, modern and imaginatively furnished; cheaper than the others, and a good bargain too. Reserve in advance or you will be sent to the slightly less attractive Residencia Dato 2.

Santander

The capital of Cantabria, Santander has a lot in common with San Sebastián – a large city beautifully situated on a protected bay, popularized by 19th-century royalty and aristocracy as a summer resort. The story has it that Queen Isabel II first came down in the 1860s in the hope that the sea air would help with a bad dose of the clap (which she may well have got from General O'Donnell, the prime minister, or another up and coming politician). In the 1900s and 1920s it was *the* fashionable place to go for Madrileños, especially with the founding of an international summer university (named after Ramón Menéndez Pelayo, Santander's favourite son and Spain's greatest antiquarian), offering holiday-makers highbrow culture to complement its wide beaches. Still, despite this and its widely acclaimed International Festival in August, Santander generally lacks the excitement and *joie de vivre* of San Sebastián.

On the other hand, Santander has been a great town for disasters. Two of the most recent were the explosion of a ship full of dynamite in 1893, killing 500 and clearing most of the harbour area, and the fire of 1941, which started in the Archbishop's Palace and destroyed most of the old centre. No city in northern Spain shows a more striking split personality. At the centre it's a gritty, workaday town rather like Bilbao, but stray a few streets to the other side of the peninsula and you'll be in what seems to be a Belle Epoque dream resort, casino and all. The Santander of the festivals shows a bright modern face to the world, but – to some extent in bloody-minded reaction against its Basque neighbours – it's also a notably conservative town, and part of the real atmosphere of the place is still best represented by the pigeon-spattered statue of Franco in the centre, and the grey streets – unlike those in many other parts of Spain – still named after Nationalist hoodlums of the Civil War.

The Cathedral and Museums

In the centre, Santander's much-altered and rebuilt **cathedral** is interesting mostly for its early Gothic crypt; this now forms the separate church of **Santísimo Cristo**, where a glass floor has been installed over the remains of a Roman building. The **Museo de Prehistoria y Arqueología**, next to the Provincial Council on C/Juan de la Cosa (*open Tues–Sat 10–1 and 4–7, Sun 11–2; adm*), has exhibits devoted to Cantabria's prehistoric cave-dwellers, including tools, reproductions of their art, and two disc-shaped star tombstones the size of tractor tyres made just before the Roman conquest, discovered in the valley of the Buelna.

The best parts of old Santander lie to the north, across the main Avda Calvo Sotelo. Near the Ayuntamiento, the **Museo de Bellas Artes** (*Mon–Fri 10.30–1 and 5.30–8, Sat 10.30–1, closed Sun; adm*) has, besides a contemporary art collection of dubious merit, a Zurbarán and several Goyas, including a portrait of Ferdinand VII, which the city commissioned to flatter the king. Nearby, the **Casa Museo de Menéndez Pelayo** (*open weekdays only 9.30–11.30; guided tours every half-hour*) has an extensive collection of books, many of them by great Catalan writers, donated to the city by the scholar himself. Behind the Ayuntamiento, the iron and glass **market** is the most colourful sight in Santander, especially the pride of the town, the glorious fish market.

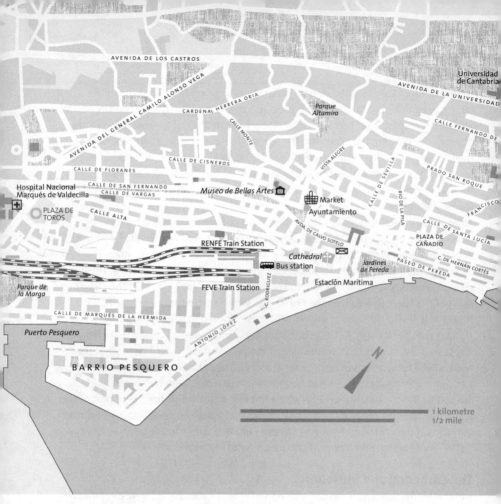

On the way out to the beaches, Avenida Reina Victoria passes Santander's new **Museo Marítimo del Cantábrico** (*open summer Tues–Sat 11–1 and 4–7, Sun 11–2; winter Tues–Sat 10–1 and 4–6, Sun 11–2; adm*), in a suitably nautical setting overlooking the harbour, with an array of model ships, exhibits on great sailors, voyages and all the local maritime traditions, and an aquarium.

El Sardinero

The 1941 fire destroyed most of Santander's character but it spared the beach suburb of **El Sardinero**, with its long, classic promenade and fine twin beaches, imaginatively named **Primera** (First) and **Segunda** (Second), backed by the enormous Belle Epoque **casino**, which has recently been refurbished in an effort to revive some of the city's former panache. The centre of grand-dame resort Santander, El Sardinero is separated from the working end of the city by the beautiful **Peninsula de la Magdalena**, a city park fringed by two more splendid beaches, the **Playa de la Magdalena** and the **Playa del Promontorio**. The Tudor-style **Palacio de la Magdalena** at the end of the peninsula was a gift from the city to King Alfonso XIII in 1912. When

Santander

Estadio Municipal del Sardinero

Segunda Playa

Universidad Internacional Menéndez Pelayo

EL SARDINERO

CALLE PALENCIA

AVENIDA DE LOS CASTROS

AVENIDA DE CASTAÑEDA

Primera Playa

LOS RÍOS

PALAZUELOS

PASEO DE GENERAL DAVILA

AVDA. DE LOS HOTELES

Gran Casino

JOAQUIN COSTA

PASEO MENÉNDEZ DE PELAYO

CALLE DE TETUÁN

Museo de Prehistoia y Arqueologia

PASEO DE CANALEJAS

REINA VICTORIA

Peninsula de la Magdalena

CASTELAR

PASEO DE PEREZ GALDOS

AVENIDA DE LA REINA VICTORIA

Playa de la Magdalena

Museo Marítimo

Playa del Promontorio

Palacio Real

the king accepted it, and virtually made Santander Spain's 'summer capital' for the next 20 years, the city's fashionable status as a summer resort was guaranteed. Today it is part of the university, and also hosts events during the August festival (*see* p.121).

In addition to the Sardinero, one of the glories of Santander is its location, on a broad and lovely green bay that forms a superb natural harbour. Besides the beaches in the city, there are several miles of golden dunes on the opposite side of the Bahía de Santander around the attractive villages of **Somo**, **El Puntal** and **Pedrena**, linked every 15 minutes by boat from the centre of town; **Playa las Atenas** nearby is a naturist beach. About 10km west of Santander along the coast at **Liencres** there is another beautiful and very popular beach, **Valdearenas**, a huge, curving expanse of dunes bordered by pine woods that's partly a nature reserve. And if you have children in tow you will probably want to visit the **Parque de la Naturaleza de Cabárceno** (*opening hours change regularly; call* **t** *942 56 37 36 for information; adm exp*), 10km south of the city at **Obregón**, where a piece of land that had been wasted by strip mining has been recycled into an attractive and enormous zoo with all the zoo favourites from apes to zebra.

Getting to Santander

Brittany Ferries's twice-weekly **ferries** from Plymouth (*see* p.15) dock right in the middle of the harbourfront at the Estación Marítima. It's only a short walk to the town centre.

Santander also has an **airport**, Parayas, 7km to the south at Maliaño (no buses), with Spanish domestic flights to Barcelona and Madrid with Iberia.

Getting Around

The two **train** stations are next to each other on Plaza de las Estaciones: the main Spanish railways (**RENFE**) station for all long-distance routes, and the narrow-gauge **FEVE** which runs to Oviedo and Bilbao, but only partly along the coast.

The central **bus** station is also very handily located, opposite the train stations. Buses to the coastal towns, the Picos de Europa and other parts of Spain all depart from here. **Turytrans** is the main company for the coast; **Palomera** for the Picos.

The whole of central Santander is within easy walking distance of the ferry and train stations, and when you need them there are frequent **buses** and **trolleys** (nos.1, 2 and 7) from the centre to El Sardinero, 20mins away. There's also a **boat** service with **Lanchas Regina**s to the beaches across the bay, with departures every 15mins from 10.30am to 8.30pm from next to the ferry dock. They also offer tours of the bay and excursions around the Río Cubas.

Taxis are cheap; for a radio taxi call **t** 942 33 33 33, or **t** 942 36 91 91.
Bus information:t 942 21 19 95.
Train information (RENFE): t (national) 902 24 02 02, (local) 942 28 02 02.
Train information (FEVE):t 942 321 16 87.

Car Hire

For car hire in Spain in general, *see* pp.17–18. All companies also have offices at the airport.
Avis, C/Nicolás Salmerón, **t** 842 25 10 14. The office is just south of the FEVE station.
Europcar, Plaza de las Estaciones, **t** 942 21 78 17. At the RENFE station.
National-Atesa, Plaza de las Estaciones, **t** 942 22 29 26. At the RENFE station.

Tourist Information

Regional: Plaza. de Velarde 5, **t** 942 31 07 08.
Municipal: Jardines de Pereda (in the city centre facing the port), **t** 942 21 61 20; at the centre of the beach strip near the casino, **t** 942 74 04 14; and in the bus station.

Shopping

Santander is a fine shopping city, where it's easy to while away an afternoon strolling such streets as **C/San Francisco** in the city centre. On the pedestrian-only streets, **C/Arrabal** and **C/del Medio** have some good clothing shops, as well as local arts and crafts galleries.

There are **markets** in Plaza de la Esperanza behind the **Ayuntamiento** (Tues, Wed, Fri and Sat for food; Mon and Thurs for clothes) and in **Plaza de México** (Mon, Wed, Fri and Sat for food; Tues and Fri for clothes), by the bull ring at the end of C/San Fernando.

Where to Stay

Santander ✉ 39000

July, August and September are the busy (and expensive) months here, especially the first two, when the music festival and International University are in full swing. Prices are quite high, but there are plenty of *casas particulares* to preserve your budget. Show your face at the bus or train stations and someone will probably lead you to one.

Luxury

Santander's most elegant places to stay are all on the north side of town by the beaches.
★★★★★Hotel Real, Pso de Pérez Galdós 28, **t** 942 27 25 50, *www.realsantander.husa.es*. A lovely *modernista* hotel near the Playa de la Magdalena, offering marvellous views over the bay, fine rooms and a fine garden.
★★★★Rhin, **t** 942 27 43 00, *www.gruporhin.com*. Enjoys a smart location on Avda Reina Victoria, the main street facing the beaches.

Expensive

★★★Hotel Sardinero, Pza de Italia 1, **t** 942 27 11 00. Popular and conveniently located near the beaches of Sardinero and the casino.

****Castelar**, C/Castelar 25, **t** 942 22 52 00, *www.grupocastelar.com*. A recent addition to the city centre, with fine sea views.

***Piñamar**, C/Ruiz de Alda 15, **t** 942 36 18 66. Modern, functional and near the stations.

Moderate

****Paris**, Avda de los Hoteles 6, **t** 942 27 23 50. Elegantly furnished rooms in a rambling, palatial old queen of a building.

***Hotel Residencia Carlos III**, Avda Reina Victoria 135, **t** 942 27 16 16. Comfortable, near the sea, and a good bargain.

Inexpensive

Cheaper hotels here have a certain notoriety for being either dreary or rip-offs. A common sting is to include a 'secret' breakfast for which you will be charged whether or not you ever see it; an official room-only price list should be posted somewhere near the front door.

****Hs La Mexicana**, C/Juan de Herrera 3, **t** 942 22 23 50. Good value and central, with friendly management and pleasant rooms.

***Pensión La Porticada**, C/Méndez Núñez 6, **t** 942 22 75 17. Sparkling rooms in a building speaking of vanished glory, with balconies. Cheaper rooms share bathrooms.

****Hs Rocamar**, Avda de los Castros 41, **t** 942 27 72 68. On a street in El Sardinero that has several more budget places to choose from.

Eating Out

Santander is not known for its cuisine. Seafood, however, is always good here, and the traditional place to get it is the **Barrio Pesquero**, south of the train stations. Near the beaches, restaurants are more elaborate.

La Sardina, C/Dr Fleming 3 (in El Sardinero), **t** 942 27 10 35 (*expensive*). A fashionable place in a very pretty setting, offering imaginative renderings of traditional dishes such as *bacalao* (cod) with red peppers.

Bodega del Riojano, Río de la Pila 5 (north of Jardines de Pereda), **t** 942 21 67 50 (*moderate*). One of the typical *bodegas* in the old quarter, offering healthy servings of *tapas*. Specialities are *rabo de buey* (oxtail), *morcilla estofada* (a blood sausage stew), and stuffed peppers. *Closed Sun eve.*

La Casona, C/Cuesta 6 (near the Ayuntamiento), **t** 942 21 26 88 (*moderate*). An old favourite that over decades has accumulated over a hundred paintings on its walls; seafood and grilled meats are specialities.

Iris, C/Castelar 5, **t** 942 21 52 25 (*moderate*). One of numerous eateries in the Puerto Chico, between the centre and the beaches, with sumptuous displays of seafood.

Zacarías, C/Hernán Cortés 38, **t** 942 21 06 88 (*moderate*). Offers a total '*mar y montaña*' Cantabrian culinary experience, including a great selection of the region's excellent, powerful cheeses.

Casa José, C/Mocejón 2 (*inexpensive*). One of the best straightforward bar-restaurants in the *barrio*, with a great *menú del día*.

Bodega Cigaleña, C/Daoiz y Velarde 19, **t** 942 21 30 62 (*inexpensive*). A typical, dark *bodega* which harbours a wine museum; come here to get a feel for traditional fare.

Entertainment and Nightlife

Nightlife in Santander is concentrated in two places: the proper *marcha* grounds are in the old town, with a vast number of bars and clubs around C/de la Pila and Plaza de Cañadío – this is where you're most likely to find live music and a raucous good time. Somewhat more staid entertainment can be had around El Sardinero; the Plaza de Italia attracts the older set, while the overdressed young head for the bars and discos in Calle Panamá.

Festival Internacional de Santander. Since 1951 this festival, running for the whole of August, has showcased a huge range of music and dance. Along with big-league culture, popular concerts, dance, magic and fireworks take place every night at the Auditorium and Finca Altamira. For information contact **Oficina del Festival**, **t** 942 21 05 08, *www.festival-int-santander.org*.

La Conveniente, C/Gómez Oreña. An old, pleasant bar with occasional live music.

Malaespina, C/Santa Lucía 4. One of the flashier discos in town.

Rockambole, C/Hernán Cortés 10. An especially popular venue, with plenty of space to party until the rosy-fingered aurora appears.

Day Trips from Santander

Laredo and Santoña

Cantabria's biggest resort has little in common with its namesake on the Río Grande. The scenery isn't too different, but on its streets there is hardly a cowboy alive or dead. This Laredo does have an old town, hidden among *urbanizaciones*, but you'll remember it mostly as a somewhat brash modern holiday town, a bit of the Costa dropped on Cantabria by mistake. Lots of people love it, and it has its charms.

Laredo was the Roman *Portus Luliobrigensium*, the place where the Romans finally subdued the last diehard Celtiberians in a great sea battle. The medieval Puebla Vieja over the harbour was walled in by Alfonso VIII of Castile to safeguard the region from pirates; its 13th-century church **Santa María de la Asunción** has five naves, and curiously carved capitals. The late-Renaissance **Ayuntamiento** in Plaza Cachupín is said to mark the location of the harbour quay where the Emperor Charles V landed on his way to retirement at Yuste. Not really glossy or chic, Laredo attracts families, who cover its splendid beach and fill the scores of cafés, bars and discos in the Puebla Vieja. *Urbanizaciones* meanwhile have marched nearly to the tip of Laredo's wide, sheltered pride and joy: **Playa de Salvé**, a gentle 3-mile-long crescent of sand.

West of Laredo the parade of beaches continues: **Santoña** is another fishing-port resort and home town of Juan de la Cosa (b. 1460), the great cartographer who accompanied Columbus on his second voyage to America, and is remembered with a suitably large monument. Another lovely village five km to the west, **Noja**, has another stretch of fine sandy beaches. According to local legend it takes its name from Noah; the Ark, so they say, washed up on one of the mountains nearby. The rest of the way to Santander there are plenty of fine and unexploited beaches, reachable on back roads off the main coastal route (S-430): the **Playas de Arnuero**, near the lighthouse at Cape Ajo, and the **Playas de Barayo**, west of Ajo, are among the best.

Getting There

For **Laredo** and **Santoña**, there are four FEVE **trains** daily on the Santander–Bilbao line that stop at **Treto** and **Cicero** stations, about 5km away, from where taxis are available. Trains run 9.25am–8pm and the journey takes one hour. There are eight **Turytrans buses** daily from Santander bus station (four on Sundays) direct to both towns. By **car**, take the A8 (here an *autovía*, so toll-free) to Laredo (42km), or turn left off it up the east side of the Bahía de Santander onto the slower S430 coast road.

Tourist Information

Laredo: Alameda Miramar, **t** 94 261 10 96.
Santoña: C/Santander 5, **t** 94 266 00 66.

Eating Out

Risco, C/La Arenosa 2, **t** 942 60 50 30, (*moderate*). This hotel restaurant is generally rated as Laredo's top seafood palace, featuring elaborately delicious creations such as a *capricho* of lobster, chicken breasts and figs.

El Rincón del Puerto (*inexpensive*). This place consists of just a few long tables under an awning next to a grill at the far end of Laredo's fishing port, where you can feast on fresh sardines, prawns, striped tuna, paella, fish soup and other maritime delicacies.

Asador Orio, Avd. José Antonio 10, **t** 942 60 70 93 (*inexpensive*). A pleasant local restaurant supplying good-value meals; roast meats (*asados*) are a speciality.

Getting There

The **bus** company for Puente Viesgo is **Continental Auto**; look for buses going to Ontaneda, on the Burgos road. By **car**, head west from the city and then south on to the N623, signposted for Burgos. Puente Viesgo is 24km south.

Eating Out

Méson El Cazador, Ctra N623, **t** 942 59 42 50 (*moderate*). An enjoyable, real country restaurant in San Vicente de Toranzo, 16km south of Puente Viesgo along the highway; it offers hearty and rich boar, pheasant and other game dishes.

The Caves of Puente Viesgo

Sadly, Cantabria and Spain's most famous prehistoric cave paintings at Altamira, near Santillana (*see* p.124) are now very hard to see. However, even without an appointment you can get into the region's second most spectacular set of prehistoric grottoes at **Puente Viesgo**, 24km south of Santander. There are five caves altogether, but the only one open to the public is the **Cueva de Castillo** (*Tues–Sun 9–12 and 3.30–6.30, closed Mon; adm, EU passport holders get in free; children under 12 strictly not admitted*). Decorated with graceful line drawings of stags, horses and other animals, this ensemble is believed to predate the even more eloquent art at Altamira.

Santillana del Mar

Jean-Paul Sartre, who had always wanted to be a guidebook writer but couldn't get a break, practised on Santillana del Mar, pronouncing it 'the most beautiful village in Spain'. Sooner or later someone in town will remind you of this, and it's best not to argue. The tour buses disgorge hundreds daily upon this tiny village (which despite the 'del Mar' is not on the sea), and in summer it can be an inferno. If you come here, do so out of season, or spend the night after the day-trips have all left.

Santillana is at once an evocative medieval town of grand palaces and a country village of dairy farmers, whose pastures lie on the hills just beyond the stone and half-timbered houses that line its one street. Its past distinctions come from great wealth in medieval times, earned from wool and linen. By 1600 nearly every man in town was a noble, or *hidalgo* (from *hijo de algo*, 'son of somebody'). So they stopped doing any work, and Santillana has changed little since. It is famous as the birthplace of a fictional rogue, Gil Blas, and home of the real Marqués de Santillana, Íñigo López de Mendoza, a warrior, poet and courtly lover whose house still stands on C/Cantón. Other houses have equally noble pedigrees; an archduchess of Austria owned the one across from the **Colegiata**. The latter is a 12th-century masterpiece, dedicated to St Juliana (or Iliana), a Christian martyr whose remains have lain here since the 6th century, and who gave her name to the town. The beautiful **cloister** has capitals carved with biblical and hunting scenes (*open 10–1 and 4–6; adm*).

The ticket to the cloister also admits you to the **Museo Diocesano** (*open 10–1 and 4–6*), in the 17th-century Convento de Regina Coeli, an exceptional collection of ecclesiastical artefacts. In Plaza Ramón Pelayo is the **Ayuntamiento**, rebuilt in 1770, and from the same century, the **Palacio de Barreda-Bracho**, now the Parador Gil Blas. If you're in a hurry to get to the promised Mar, the closest beaches are at **Suances**, 5km away; it's a fishing village and a small resort, though the sea here isn't the cleanest.

As well as for its historic houses Santillana is celebrated for the **Caves of Altamira**, with perhaps the greatest prehistoric cave paintings in the world. You can walk up to the caves, south of the town, in 20 minutes, but don't expect to get in unless you've written three years ahead, and are one of the 20 chosen ones permitted a 15-minute glimpse at these sublime masterpieces of Palaeolithic art, undulating caverns covered with stunningly exuberant and vivid paintings of bison, horses, boars and stags.

The story of the discovery of Altamira is a parable of perceptions. An ancient landslide sealed the entrance of the caves (and more or less vacuum-packed the paintings) until it was rediscovered by a hunter and his dog in 1868. In 1875, Don Marcelino de Sautuola, an amateur prehistorian, was intrigued by the drawings in the outer rooms, and began to explore them, taking his nine-year-old daughter María along. The child wandered a little deeper into the caves, and lifted her eyes to the superb polychrome paintings. Although no one had ever seen the like, Sautuola at once recognized the ceiling for what it was: a ravishing work of genius from the Stone Age. Excited, he published a description of Altamira but, rather than receiving the expected response of awe from the 'experts' in the field, he was mocked, ridiculed and even accused of forging the paintings; scholars simply refused to believe that people who used stone axes were capable of painting, one of the 'civilized arts'. Undaunted, the Marquis held his ground, insisting Altamira was for real, and died heartbroken in 1888, vilified and as forgotten as the caves themselves. Not until 15 years later did the discovery of a dozen painted caves in the Dordogne lead to a general change of mind.

Although the 'white disease' caused by visitors' breath has restricted admission to the caves, you can now do the next best thing: visit a replica, in a new **museum** (*open Mon–Sat 9.30–2.30, closed Sun; adm*). You can also explore a small stalactite cave that is prettily lit to emphasize nature's wonders, as compensation for the inaccessibility of the more fragile works of man.

Getting There

La **Cantábrica bus** company usually has six buses daily to Santillana from Santander bus station (journey time around 45 mins). By **car**, follow the N611 Oviedo road out of Santander, and after about 20km look for a right turn onto the S6316 for Santillana (28km).

Tourist Information

Santillana del Mar: Pza de Ramón Menéndez Pelayo s/n, **t** 94 281 82 51, *www.santillana-del-mar.com*

Eating Out

Excellent *tapas* and reasonably priced meals can be had in the **bar** nearest the Colegiata.

Parador Gil Blas, Pza Pelayo 11, **t** 942 81 80 00, **f** 94 281 83 91, *santillana@parador.es* (*expensive*). Santillana's top hotel, a wonderfully atmospheric *parador* with a very elegant dining room.

Hotel Altamira, C/Cantón 1, **t** 942 81 80 25 (*expensive*). Another hotel in a palace, with a patio and garden, and a seductively comfortable restaurant offering big plates of roast meats (and some seafood) – possibly the best restaurant in town.

Los Blasones, Plaza de la Gándara 8, **t** 942 81 80 70 (*inexpensive*). If you happen to be in Santillana at the weekend you can feast on local and mountain specialities here – everything from *fabada* to grilled *langostinos* (crawfish).

La Robleda, C/Revolgo, **t** 942 81 83 36 (*inexpensive*). You pay even less for *fabada* and *langostinos* here.

Madrid

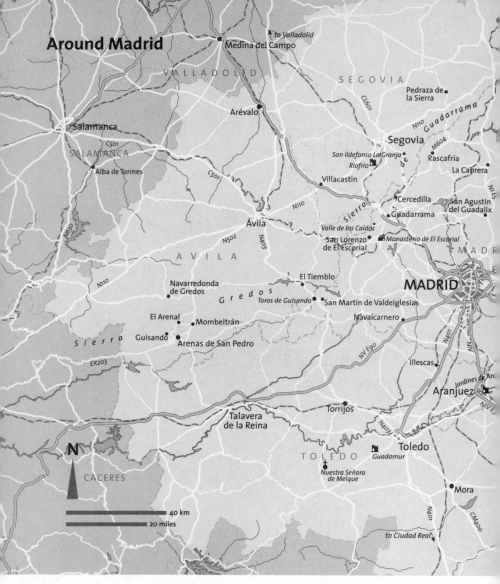

Around Madrid

to Valladolid
Medina del Campo

VALLADOLID

SEGOVIA

Pedraza de
la Sierra

CL601

Arévalo

N110 Guadarrama
Segovia
M604
San Ildefonso La Granja
Riofrío
Rascafría

La Cabrera

Salamanca
CS01
SALAMANCA
CS01
Villacastin

Sierra de

Alba de Tormes

Cercedilla
San Agustín
del Guadalix
Guadarrama

N630

N502
Ávila
Valle de los Caídos
San Lorenzo
de El Escorial
Monasterio de El Escorial
MADR

N403

AVILA
El Tiemblo
MADRID
N110
Navarredonda
de Gredos
Gredos
Toros de Guisando
San Martín de Valdeiglesias

El Arenal
Mombeltrán
Navalcarnero
N401
N501
Sierra
Guisando
Arenas de San Pedro
NV E90

EX203
Illescas
N IV

NV E90
Jardines de Arc
Aranjuez
N IV E

Torrijos
Talavera
de la Reina
N401

N401
TOLEDO
Guadamur
Toledo

N
Nuestra Señora
de Melque

CACERES

Mora

N401
CM400

40 km
20 miles

to Ciudad Real

Sifting through all the books that have been written about Spain, opinion on its unlikely capital seems about evenly divided. Some writers are sure it's the heart and soul of the nation, but dissent has been coming in ever since it's been on the map; some despise it. Like Bonn or Washington, it's an artificial capital, created on the whim of the Habsburg kings. The city has great museums, wide boulevards and a cosmopolitan air. It doesn't have a beautiful setting, or world-famous monuments, and the climate can be a shock to the uninitiated.

So why come here? Art is one reason; the city of Velázquez, Goya and connoisseur Habsburg kings has one of this planet's greatest hoards of paintings. Old Madrid, the area around the Plaza Mayor that has changed little since the 17th century, is another.

The biggest reason for many, though, is that Madrid is just better equipped than any city in Spain to give you a good time, with an infinite variety of street- and nightlife and human attractions to make you forget all about Velázquez and Goya.

And around Madrid is a garland of lovely, much older towns, each with something different to offer. Everyone goes to **Toledo**, and romantically beautiful **Segovia**. But Madrid also serves as a base for visiting medieval **Ávila**, the old university town of **Alcalá de Henares**, the royal palaces at **Aranjuez**, or **El Escorial**. Whenever Madrid's traffic, nightclubs, and museum corridors become too much, any of these towns can provide a little peace and quiet. And if Madrid is the kind of metropolis you're trying to get away from, you can always stay in one of them – and make day trips to Madrid.

Madrid

One of the foremost features that make Madrid such an enjoyable, vibrant city is its compactness, the way so much of its life still goes on within the old, Habsburg city, the irregular shape roughly between the Retiro park in the east and Palacio Real in the west, and the Glorieta de Bilbao to the north and Puerta de Toledo in the south. It was founded in the 860s around a Moorish *Alcázar* or fortress, on the site of which the Palacio Real now stands, and after it was captured by the Christians in 1086 grew only modestly in the next few centuries, so that by the 1450s it had only spread as far as the Puerta del Sol, its modern centre, which began life as its easternmost gate. It was one of many Castilian small towns with a royal residence attached, in the rebuilt *Alcázar*, and was generally visited by the kings of Castile only when they felt like hunting in the woods to the northwest. Then, in 1561 King Philip II suddenly decided to make it the centre of his worldwide empire, and it became the boom town of the 16th century, doubling and trebling in size and expanding still more to occupy the whole area now known as 'Old Madrid' by the 1650s, until the decline of the empire brought this growth to an almost equally abrupt stop. Madrid stayed within its tight, narrow knot of 17th-century streets, where life developed a special intimacy. It did not finally break out of its Habsburg limits until the 1860s, and then grew massively through the 20th century, into new suburbs sprawling across the Castilian plain.

Even so, a huge proportion of its people still home in on the old city for work, culture, to see a film or to meet up and have fun, because they've never lost the habit, or are just addicted to its shoulder-rubbing, very Spanish human intensity. The majority of its attractions for the visitor – from the great museums to charming squares or the best bars and restaurants – are within this same area too. Consequently, there are few cities in the world where you can find so many pleasures in the space of a short walk.

Puerta del Sol

Ten streets radiate from this, the hub of the old city, as well as three metro lines and dozens of bus lines; however you're travelling, you're likely to cross the 'Gate of the Sun' – so-called because it was once Madrid's east-facing, outer gate – and everyone agrees that it remains the centre of all things in Madrid. The medieval gate is long

Orientation

Madrid goes on and on – today it's home to over 4 million people – but almost everything of major interest is within one mile of the Puerta del Sol between **Parque del Retiro** in the east and **Plaza de Oriente** in the west, with the Palacio Real. Near the Retiro and the broad boulevard called the **Paseo del Prado**, you'll find the '*triángulo de arte*', Madrid's triple crown of art museums, the **Prado, Thyssen**, and **Reina Sofía**. The **Puerta del Sol** sits squarely in the centre, and the oldest quarter of the city, around the **Plaza Mayor**, is just west of it. Keep these landmarks in mind, and learn a few of the main streets, and you'll not get lost – Madrid isn't nearly as complicated as it looks on the map. Because the centre is so compact, Madrid is easy to get about on foot, but the Metro and buses are on hand for reaching the more outlying sights.

gone, and the plaza is chaotic, dirty and crowded, but it endears itself to *madrileños* in a way no formal postcard plaza ever could. Here, at the mouth of a shopping street (C/Carmen), stands a sculpture of the city's emblem, the **Oso y Madroño** (bear and strawberry tree). It's a small, unshowy bronze, upstaged by an equestrian **statue of Charles III**. Little that is *auténtico* in Madrid strays far from Sol; jammed into this tight-knit district of narrow streets are scores of curious shops and family businesses, while the *tascas* south of the plaza, their windows piled high with shellfish and other delicacies, are some of the oldest and best-known bars in town. In the 19th century, Sol's fashionable cafés made it the liveliest place in Madrid, a centre not only for gossip but for revolts and demonstrations. From Sol, you can choose to head either west to the old town and Palacio Real, north to funky Malasaña and Chueca, or east to the Retiro and the museums.

The Paseo del Arte: Madrid's 'Golden Triangle'

A joint **Paseo de Arte** *voucher allows you to visit each of the big three museums for €8; but don't even think about trying to 'do' all three in a single day. The ticket can be used any time in the same year.*

If the Prado wasn't enough to make Madrid a major art destination, the re-opening of the Reina Sofía Centre in 1990 and the acquisition of the Thyssen-Bornemisza collection in 1992 removed all doubt. Madrid is rightly proud of its 'golden triangle' of art treasures – three superb museums within strolling distance of each other, linked by the leafy Paseo del Prado. They complement each other neatly. The **Museo del Prado** is best known for its hoard of masterpieces of Spanish painting from the 12th to the 19th centuries, and rich collections of 15th–17th-century Flemish and Italian painting. The **Centro de Arte Reina Sofía** picks up the thread with its permanent collection of 20th-century art (including Picasso's *Guernica*), while the **Museo Thyssen-Bornemisza** is a remarkable gathering of European and American art spanning eight centuries, which fortuitously manages to fill in gaps left by the other two, with Impressionism, Post-Impressionism, German Expressionists, Pop Art and more.

Museo del Prado

Paseo del Prado, t 913 30 29 00; M Banco de España; open Tues–Sat 9–7, Sun and hols 9–2; closed Mon, 1 Jan, Good Friday, 1 May and 25 Dec; adm; adm free Sat after 2.30pm, Sun, and 18 May, 12 Oct and 6 Dec.

King Charles III intended this to be a natural history museum when it was begun in 1785, but the building lay empty until Ferdinand VII, realizing that his predecessors had accumulated one of Europe's greatest art hoards, decided it should be relocated under one roof, and that this roof should that of the Prado. It opened to the public in 1819, and while the building has been altered and reworked the collections have not changed much since. For the masterpieces of the Prado we can thank the practised eyes of Charles V, Philip II and Philip IV; not only did they know good painting when they saw it, but it was Philip IV who, in his will of 1665, made all the paintings Crown property and prohibited the dispersion of a single one.

Getting to Madrid

There are plenty of flights from Britain: **easyJet** flies from Luton and Liverpool, **British Midland** from Heathrow, and the Spanish airline **Air Europa** from Gatwick. **British Airways** has three flights daily from Heathrow and others from Birmingham, Edinburgh, Gatwick, Glasgow and Manchester;while **Iberia** has three or more daily from Heathrow and flies from Birmingham, Edinburgh and Gatwick. From Ireland, **Aer Lingus** and **Iberia** have flights from Dublin.

Madris-Barajas has three terminals. Nearly all flights from Britain, Ireland, the USA and most long-haul destinations use **T1**; Iberia flights from many other parts of Europe and most Spanish domestic flights use **T2**; while **T3** is mainly used for the Madrid–Barcelona air shuttle and other domestic routes. There's a longish walk (over 5mins) between terminals.

In T1 there are **currency exchange offices** (*open 24 hours*), **cash machines**, a **post office**, a **RENFE train ticket office**, and a free **accommodation service** (*open daily 8am–midnight*). In all the terminals there are **car hire** desks, and **tourist information** stands (*open 24 hours*).

Getting from the Airport

Madrid's **Barajas** airport is 15km northeast of the city, off the N-II/A2 Barcelona highway.

The **Metro** (underground/subway) is generally the most convenient and certainly the cheapest way into town, and gets you to the city centre in about 45 mins. One hitch is that Barajas Metro is between Terminals T2 and T3, so that from T1 you first have a 10-mins walk. For Puerta del Sol, the centre of Madrid, you must change twice: take Line 8 to Nuevos Ministerios, then change to Line 10 to Tribunal, and change there onto Line 1 for Sol. For more on the Metro, tickets and fares, *see* p.133.

Buses also run between all the Barajas terminals and Plaza de Colón, every 15 mins daily 4.45am–2am, taking 25 mins–1 hr depending on traffic. They stop en route at Av de América, C/María de Molina, C/Velázquez and C/Serrano. The fare is €2.40 one way.

A **taxi** to central Madrid can cost anything from €13–€20, depending on where you're going and the state of the traffic. The fare will include a special airport supplement.

Useful Numbers

Airport flight information: t 902 35 35 70.
Air Europa: t 902 40 15 01.
British Airways: t 902 11 13 33.
British Midland: t 913 05 83 43.
easyJet: t 902 29 99 92.
Iberia: t 902 40 05 00.

Getting Around

Madrid has two main RENFE (Spanish railways) **train** stations, **Atocha** and **Chamartín**. Atocha, in the city centre at the southern end of Paseo del Prado, handles trains to southern and eastern Spain, including the high-speed AVE to Córdoba and Seville. **Chamartín**, in the north Madrid at the top of Paseo de la Castellana, is the main station for anywhere north and northwest, including Barcelona and France. There are Metro stops at Atocha and Chamartín, and also exchange offices and a tourist information desk at Chamartín.

RENFE also has an extensive *cercanías* local rail network in the Madrid area, which is very handy for day trips. All *cercanías* trains pass through the mainline stations of Atocha, Recoletos, Nuevos Ministerios and Chamartín.

Most long-distance **buses** operate from the **Estación Sur de Autobuses**, at C/Méndez Alvaro (**M** Méndez Alvaro). However, some companies do not use the bus station but their own depots, so check before going there; for buses to towns featured in this guide, see the relevant 'Getting There' sections.
Train information (RENFE): t 902 24 02 02.
Estación Sur de Autobuses: t 914 68 42 00.

Around the City

Madrid's **Metro** is the most popular means of getting around. It's safe, clean and well-used: trains run **6am–1.30am**. There are 11 lines, identified by a colour and a number. Study the Metro map a little before setting out: there are so many lines that in the centre it's easy to make a Metro trip with a change of lines for a distance that would be a 10-mins walk. To find the right platform, you need to know the line number, and the name of the station at the end of the line in the direction you're travelling (ie, northbound platforms on Line 1 are signed *Dirección Plaza Castilla*).

The city transport authority (EMT) also runs a full **bus** network. Visitors tend to use them less than the Metro, but they're very handy for filling in 'gaps' in the Metro network; there is, for example, no Metro line along Paseo de la Castellana, so for getting up and down this great avenue buses 14 and 27 are more useful. On city buses, you enter at the front, and pay the driver or, if you have a *metrobús*, validate your ticket in the machine behind the cab, and leave by the doors in the middle. Most routes run **6am–midnight**, and are marked at each stop. During the night 20 **night bus** routes operate, all of which start at the Plaza Cibeles and fan out to different parts of the city.

Metro information: t 915 52 59 09, *www.metromadrid.es*

EMT bus information: t 914 06 38 10.

Metro and Bus Tickets

Single tickets for the Metro, bought at stations, and buses, bought on board, cost the same, currently €0.95. However, since you'll almost certainly make more than a couple of journeys it's much better to get a *metrobús* ticket, which is valid for 10 trips on Metro and buses and can be shared between two or more people, and currently costs €5. You pass them through automatic gates every time you enter the Metro, and on buses must cancel them in machines behind the driver. *Metrobús* tickets can be bought at all Metro stations from ticket windows or automatic machines, but note that you cannot buy them on buses, so you must get one before boarding a bus.

Taxis

Madrid has thousands of taxis, so finding one is rarely a problem. They are white, with a red diagonal stripe on each front door. There are supplements to the basic fare for luggage, for journeys at night (11pm–6am) and on Sundays, for trips from the airports and bus and main rail stations, and for leaving the city limits. Even so, an average ride costs under €4. For a radio cab, call **Radio Taxi:** t 914 47 51 80, or **Radio Taxi Independiente:** t 914 03 75 11.

Tourist Buses

The companies listed provide similar hop-on, hop-off sightseeing tours, with which you can get on and off the buses of each company as many times as you like the same day. All pass through Sol and the Gran Vía, on a circuit round all the major sights. Fares are also similar: a one-day ticket costs approx. €9.60, 7–16s and over-65s €4.80, and under-7s travel for free, and two-day tickets are also available.

Madrid Vision, t 913 02 03 68, *www.trapsa.com/madridvision*. Tours run daily mid-June–Sept 9.30am–Midnight, mid-Mar–mid-June, late-Sept–late Dec 10am–9pm, Dec–mid-Mar 10am–7pm.

Sol Open Tours: t 902 30 39 03, *www.solopentours.com*. Runs daily 9am–7pm.

Car Hire

For car hire in Spain in general, *see* pp.17–18. All the big companies have several offices in Madrid; those listed here are the most central, clustered especially near Plaza de España. Having a car is a great asset for going where you please outside Madrid, but a near-liability within the city – parking is a nightmare. When you hire a car, collect it or have it delivered to your hotel only when you need to use it.

Avis, Gran Vía 60, t 915 48 42 04.

Econocar, C/Félix Boix 2, t 913 59 14 03. Local company with very good weekend rates.

Europcar, C/San Leonardo 8, t 915 41 88 92.

Hertz, Edificio España, Plaza de España, t 915 42 58 05.

National-Atesa, Plaza de España, t 915 42 50 15.

Tourist Information

Madrid's tourist offices are a little limited in the information they offer, providing maps, brochures, and a free booklet called *En Madrid*. For entertainment listings it's worth buying the *Guía del Ocio*, on sale at newsstands. Offices help with accommodation, but when they are busy will direct you to the accommodation desks in the train stations and at Barajas airport.

General tourist information: t 902 10 00 07.

Main tourist office: C/Duque de Medinaceli 2, t 914 29 37 05, M Banco de España (*open Mon–Fri 9–7, Sat 9–1; closed Sun*). There are branch offices at the **Airport**, **Chamartín** station, and **Mercado Puerta de Toledo**.

City of Madrid office: Plaza Mayor 3, t 913 66 54 77, *www.munimadrid.es*, M Sol (*open Mon–Fri 10–8, Sat 10–3; closed Sun*).

Guided Tours

For city **walking tours**, contact the **Patronato Municipal de Turismo**, C/Mayor 69, **t** 915 88 29 06, *www.munimadrid.es*. Currently three routes are available, one on *The Madrid of Velázquez*, usually on Fri or Sat mornings.

Useful Numbers

General emergency number (fire, police, ambulance): **t** 112; **Police: t** 091/092.

Festivals

Madrid puts on excellent fiestas, ranging from modern arts events to old-fashioned neighbourhood *verbenas*, or street festivals. The city tourist office website (*see* p.133) lists events on a monthly basis. Some of the city's main dates are listed below.

Noche Vieja, *New Year's Eve*. Gather in the Puerta del Sol to see the year in, and try to eat a grape on each one of the 12 chimes – for good luck.

Carnaval, *Jan–late Feb*. Marked with parades, dressing up, gigs and parties.

Dos de Mayo, *2 May*. A city holiday celebrating Madrid's rising against Napoleon's forces in 1808. The main events take place around Plaza Dos de Mayo in Malasaña.

San Isidro, *15 May*. Madrid's patron saint's feast day is on the 15th, but merits a whole week of festivities, in the Plaza Mayor and many other venues. Coinciding with it is Spain's première bullfighting *feria* at Las Ventas.

Verbena de la Paloma, *14–15 Aug*. The biggest summer *fiesta*, centred in the heart of old Madrid, La Latina, south of the Plaza Mayor.

Festival de Otoño, *late Oct–Dec*. Madrid's big theatre, music and general arts festival.

Shopping

Madrid has several fashion centres. For designer labels and anything upmarket head for the **Salamanca** district, and Calles Serrano, Goya, Claudio Coello, Velázquez and Ortega y Gasset (**M** Serrano, Velázquez or Núñez de Balboa). **Chueca**, centre of the gay scene, also has funky shops for women's clothing, and Calles **Hortaleza** and **Fuencarral** are the avenues for young, alternative, club fashion.

El Rastro, Plaza Cascorro and C/Ribera de Curtidores; **M** La Latina. One of Europe's greatest flea markets, held every Sunday morning. As well as antiques and curios the Rastro has loads of junk too, and is addictive for browsers. Be aware it's also staked out by pickpockets, so watch your bags.

Where to Stay

Madrid ✉ 20080

With 50,000 hotel rooms in Madrid, there are always enough to go around. Upper-range hotels are mostly on or near Paseo del Prado and Paseo de la Castellana; Madrid's many budget hotels cluster in the old centre, near Plaza Santa Ana or Puerta del Sol. One problem with lower-range hotels in these bar-filled streets is that they can be noisy, so for peace and quiet think of staying elsewhere.

There are **accommodation desks** at the **airport** and main **train stations**. **Price categories** listed here differ from those used for the rest of Spain. *See* 'Where to Stay', p.27.

Luxury

*******Hotel Orfila**, C/Orfila 6, **t** 917 02 77 70, *www.hotelorfila.com*; **M** Colón. Arguably Madrid's most beautiful hotel, a sensitively converted 19th-century *palacete*. There's an idyllic garden, tearoom and **restaurant**, and the décor is restrained luxury.

*******Hotel Westin Palace**, Plaza de las Cortes 7, **t** 913 60 80 00, *www.palacemadrid.com*; **M** Banco de España. The movers' and shakers' hotel, between Prado and Sol and opposite the Spanish parliament, with 1900s architecture and luxury facilities. Public areas, and the **restaurants** and bars, are stunning.

*******Hotel Ritz**, Plaza de la Lealtad 5, **t** 915 21 28 57, *www.ritz.es*; **M** Banco de España. Consistently rated among the best hotels worldwide. To stay here is to be pampered – from its sumptuous rooms to the **restaurants** and 'place-to-be-seen' garden terrace.

*******Hotel Santo Mauro**, C/Zurbano 36, **t** 913 19 69 00, *www.ac-hoteles.com*; **M** Rubén Darío. Built as a palace in the 19th century, this small-but-perfectly-formed hotel has been strikingly converted with classical-style public areas and contemporary rooms.

Expensive

★★★★Hotel NH Alcalá, C/de Alcalá 66, **t** 914 35 10 60, *nhalcala@nh-hoteles.es*; **M** Príncipe de Vergara. Friendly staff provide a warm welcome at this popular hotel, and many longtime visitors to Madrid wouldn't stay anywhere else. Interior rooms look onto a courtyard garden, and so are quieter.

★★★★Hotel Emperador, Gran Vía 53, **t** 915 47 28 00, *www.emperadorhotel.es*; **M** Callao. Home to the only remaining roof-top hotel pool in Madrid, with stunning views, and at the heart of the city's traditional shopping centre. Its large, well-decorated rooms are much in demand all year round.

★★★★★Hotel Villa Real, Plaza de las Cortes 10, **t** 914 20 37 67, *www.slh.com/villareal*; **M** Banco de España. Although built in 1990, the Villa Real has captured the historic feel of the area, and is ideally situated for the main museums and the Puerta del Sol.

Moderate

★★★Hotel Atlántico, Gran Vía 38, **t** 915 22 64 80, *hotel-atlantico.com*; **M** Callao. Of the Gran Vía hotel line-up this is one of the nicer options, an historic building with decent facilities, and in the centre of everything.

★★★★Hotel Bauza, C/de Goya 79, **t** 914 35 75 45, *www.hotelbauza.com*; **M** Goya. Refurbished in the Philippe Starck mould, this well-appointed hotel has earned itself an extra star in the process, and is excellent value.

★★★Hotel Inglés, C/de Echegaray 8, **t** 914 29 65 51; **M** Sevilla or Sol. With 150 years of history under its belt, this venerable hotel has more character than many, and an utterly central location near Santa Ana. Exterior rooms are noisy and the staff could be more on the ball, but it's still good value.

★★Hotel Paris, C/Alcalá 2, **t** 915 21 64 91; **M** Sol. The chandeliered hotel lobby is packed with character and china bric-a-brac, and friendly staff make visitors feel right at home. Two steps away from Puerta del Sol; the best of the wooden-floored rooms look onto a courtyard garden.

★★Hotel Plaza Mayor, C/Atocha 2, **t** 913 60 06 06, *www.h-plazamayor.com*; **M** Tirso de Molina or Sol. Beautifully renovated rooms in an old building across the street from one of the quieter edges of the Plaza Mayor.

★★★La Residencia de El Viso, C/Nervión 8, **t** 915 64 03 70; **M** República Argentina. A charming hotel in one of the most picturesque residential areas, north of Salamanca. A refreshing antidote to central hotels, it has 12 rooms and a garden, and is very peaceful.

Inexpensive

★Hs Don Juan, Plaza Vázquez de Mella 1, 2°, **t** 915 22 31 01; **M** Chueca or Gran Vía. Here you'll find a funky zebra-tiled floor, velvet couch and big old armoire filled with books, and light, airy rooms with new bathrooms.

Hs Las Fuentes, C/las Fuentes 10, 1°D, **t** 915 42 18 53, *www.hostallasfuentes.com*; **M** Opera. A classically *castizo* building in a quiet street, with Plaza de Oriente a stone's throw away. Spacious rooms with bath, a/c and phone.

Hs Prim, C/Prim 15, 2°, **t** 915 21 54 95; **M** Chueca. On a quiet street close to Recoletos, the Prim is ideal if you want budget lodgings in a buzzy neighbourhood. Funky retro chairs in the lounge, and all rooms have a/c and TV.

★★★Hotel Reyes Católicos, C/Angel 18, **t** 913 65 86 00, *www.reyescatolicos.com*; **M** Puerta de Toledo. In a nice old area near San Francisco el Grande; small, personal, and a good bargain for the services offered.

★★Hotel Santander, C/Echegaray 1, **t** 914 29 95 51; **M** Sevilla or Sol. High ceilings, a jumble of furniture and light, if sometimes noisy, exterior rooms make this a favourite of many travellers. All rooms have TV, phone and a/c.

★★Hs Sil, C/Fuencarral 95, **t** 914 48 89 72; **M** Bilbao. At the north end of Fuencarral, this *hostal* is kept spick and span by the pleasant couple who run it. With private baths, a/c, TV and phones, rooms are very good value.

★★HSR La Torre, C/de Espoz y Mina 8, 3°, **t** 915 32 43 03; **M** Sol. Probably the best-value option in this area, a bright *hostal* with big twin rooms with fabulous balconies.

Cheap

★Hs Almirante, C/del Almirante 4, 2°, **t** 915 32 48 71; **M** Chueca. Slightly 1970s-style rooms, but this place is cute, the owner nice, and the price is unbeatable. Book ahead.

Hs Madrazo, C/de los Madrazo 10, 1°, **t** 914 29 45 75; **M** Banco de España. In a tranquil, elegant neighbourhood, this is bare-bones, but the quality–price ratio is astounding.

Eating Out

Restaurants

Scarcely anywhere in Spain can offer such a wide choice, with gourmet restaurants, places offering the cuisine of every region of Spain and others from many far-off lands within a short radius of the Puerta del Sol. The city's own traditional *madrileño* cuisine is a reflection of the cooking of Castile: roast meats and stews. The pinnacle of Madrid's culinary arts is *cocido*: part soup, part meat and two veg. Meat, chickpeas and vegetables are cooked in broth, then removed and set aside; the broth, sometimes with added *fideos* (noodles), is then served as the first course of a *cocido completo*. Another local standard is *callos a la madrileña*, which might convince you to give tripe a go, cooked in a rich spicy sauce. Also, despite its land-locked location Madrid is one of the world's biggest consumers of seafood and fish, which are shipped here completely fresh, and are great favourites in city bars.

The **price categories** listed here differ from those used for the rest of Spain in this guide. *See* **Practical A–Z**, 'Food and Drink', p.21, for the price ranges. Categories are based on a three-course meal without wine, per person.

Expensive

Botín, C/Cuchilleros 17, t 913 66 42 17; M Sol. Hemingway called it 'the best restaurant in the world' no less, and it's officially the world's oldest, founded 1725. It's renowned for its original interior and Castilian roasts; pricy, but meals here rarely fail to deliver. *Open daily 1–4 and 8–midnight.*

Casa Santa Cruz, C/de la Bolsa 12, t 915 21 86 23; M Sol. Originally the parish church of Santa Cruz, this restaurant is an exquisite throwback to another age, from its stunning dining room to the menu of classic Spanish cuisine. *Open daily 1–4 and 8.30–midnight.*

El Cenador del Prado, Paseo del Prado 4, t 914 29 15 61; M Antón Martín. Mediterranean cuisine served in luxurious surroundings. *Open Mon–Fri 1.30–4 and 9.30–midnight, Sat and Sun 9.30pm–midnight; closed Aug.*

Lhardy, Carrera de San Jerónimo 8, t 915 22 22 07; M Sol or Sevilla. A Madrid institution founded in 1839, and almost unchanged. The dining rooms upstairs offers French and a high-class version of *madrileño* cuisine. Downstairs in the bar, clients help themselves to sweet or savoury delicacies. *Open Mon–Sat 1–3.30 and 8.30–11, Sun 1–3.30pm.*

El Olivo, C/General Gallegos 1, t 913 59 15 35; M Cuzco. French chef Jean Pierre Vandelle's cooking makes special use of Spain's olive oil, in Mediterranean cuisine at its best. *Open Tues–Sat 1–4 and 9–midnight.*

Posada de la Villa, C/de la Cava Baja 9, t 913 66 18 80; M La Latina. *Muy auténtico*, in décor and in the kitchen, with a wood-fired oven producing succulent suckling pig. Popular, and always enjoyable. *Open Mon–Sat 1–4 and 8–midnight, Sun 1–4pm; closed Aug.*

Thai Gardens, C/Jorge Juan 5, t 915 77 88 84; M Serrano. Palm fronds, waterfalls and East Asian décor make this one of the sexiest restaurants in Madrid. *Open Sun–Thurs 2–4 and 9–midnight, Fri and Sat 2–4 and 9–1.*

La Vendimia, Plaza Conde del Valle de Suchil 7, t 914 45 73 77; M San Bernardo. On one of Madrid's loveliest squares, this celebration of modern Basque cooking is a treat. *Open Mon–Sat 1–4 and 9–midnight, Sun 1–4pm.*

Viridiana, C/de Juan de Mena 14, t 915 23 44 78; M Banco de España or Retiro. An exceptional wine cellar, plus faultless service and delicious, imaginative dishes. *Open Mon–Sat 1.30–4 and 9.30–midnight; closed Aug.*

Moderate

La Ancha, C/Zorrilla 7, t 914 29 81 86; M Banco de España. The formula is simple: impeccable service, fine ingredients and wines, and dishes based on traditional cuisine. *Open Mon–Sat 1.30–4 and 8.30–11.30.*

La Barraca, C/de la Reina 29, t 915 32 71 54; M Gran Vía. An *arrocería* with Valencian delicacies – paellas, 'black' rice – and a refined wine list. *Open daily 1–4 and 8.30–11.30.*

Café Gijón, Paseo de Recoletos 21, t 915 21 54 25; M Banco de España. A legendary haunt of Madrid's intellectuals, the Gijón has been in business since 1888; it's good for breakfast, a set lunch, or afternoon tea or coffee. *Open Sun–Fri 9am–1.30am, Sat 9am–2am.*

Casa Ciriaco, C/Mayor 84, t 915 48 06 20; M Opera. Founded in 1917, with a beautiful old tiled bar for *tapas* grazing, and tasty traditional food in the restaurant. *Open Thurs–Tues 1–4 and 8–midnight; closed Aug.*

Casa Gallega, Plaza San Miguel 8, **t** 915 47 30 55; **M** Sol. Just off Plaza Mayor is this traditional Galician restaurant. Fresh seafood is brought straight from Galicia; the terrace gets crowded in summer, so it's worth booking. *Open daily 1–4 and 8–midnight*.

Casa de Vacas, C/Jorge Juan 12, **t** 915 77 16 07; **M** Serrano. An imposing bull's head greets you at this Salamanca haunt. Excellent meat and grilled fish, and tasty *pinchos* if you have to wait for a dining-room table. *Open Mon–Sat 1–4 and 9–midnight, Sun 1–4pm*.

Cornucopia, C/de la Flora 1, **t** 915 47 64 65; **M** Opera. In a 19th-century palace, this is a gem of a restaurant, offering European cuisine with a slight American flavour. *Open Tues–Sun 1.30–4.30 and 8.30–midnight*.

Currito, Pabellón de Vizcaya, Casa de Campo, **t** 914 64 57 07; **M** Lago. In summer, this is the best open-air place to eat in Madrid, on the edge of Casa de Campo park. *Open Mon–Sat 1.30–4 and 8–11.30, Sun 1.30–4pm*.

El Espejo, Paseo de Recoletos 31, **t** 913 08 23 47; **M** Banco de España. Despite its location and elaborate (but fake) 1900s décor, El Espejo offers excellent food at good prices. The big draw, though, is the outdoor terrace on Paseo Recoletos. *Open daily 1–3 and 9–midnight; café open throughout the day*.

Malacatín, C/de la Ruda 5, **t** 913 65 52 41; **M** La Latina. A genuine Madrid experience; book for their renowned *cocido* (€13) for lunch and ask what time to show up. *Open Mon–Sat 1–3.30pm; closed 15 July–15 Aug*.

La Recoba, C/Magdalena 27, **t** 913 69 39 88; **M** Antón Martín. A legend, this smoky little Argentinian spot is possibly the only place in Madrid where you can eat a pizza (and salads) at 4am. *Open daily 9.30pm–6am*.

Sarrasín, C/Libertad 8, **t** 915 32 73 48; **M** Chueca. With only a set *menú*, this is one of the most enjoyable of the many (mainly) gay restaurants in Chueca. *Open Mon–Sat 1–4 and 9–midnight*.

Viuda de Vacas, C/Cava Alta 23, **t** 913 66 58 47; **M** La Latina. One of the more modestly priced of the *tabernas* with stout *madrileño*-Castilian cooking, and a mecca for the unpretentious foody – *cocidos* and roasts are excellent. No reservations, so queues at busy times. *Open Mon–Wed, Fri and Sat 1.30–4.30 and 9–midnight, Sun 1.30–4.30pm*.

Inexpensive

Círculo de Bellas Artes, C/Marqués de Casa Riera 2, **t** 915 21 69 42; **M** Banco de España. The Círculo is one of Madrid's grandest buildings, with an exquisite grand salon, where a wonderful-value lunch menu is served – a great find. *Open daily 1.30–4pm*.

Fausto el Paladar, C/Aguila 1, **t** 913 64 56 40; **M** La Latina. This friendly Cuban enclave on the fringes of La Latina is a fun place to try some tasty Caribbean specialities. *Open Mon–Thurs 12.30–5 and 8.30–11, Fri and Sat 12.30–5 and 8.30–1, Sun 12.30–midnight*.

Ribeira do Miño, C/Santa Brígida 1, **t** 915 21 98 54; **M** Tribunal. A classic Galician *marisquería* with bustling waiters and fish nets on the walls. Giant *mariscadas*, mixed shellfish platters, are the thing to go for, and wonderful value. *Open Tues–Sun 1–4 and 8–midnight*.

Terraza 'El Ventorillo', C/Bailén 14, **t** 913 66 35 70; **M** Opera. A *terraza* with good *tapas* and views over Casa de Campo. *Open Sun–Thurs 11am–2am, Fri and Sat 11am–2.30am*.

El Viajero, Plaza de la Cebada 11, **t** 913 66 90 64; **M** La Latina. A rooftop terrace serving delicious pasta and grilled meats. *Open Tues–Thurs 1pm–12.30am, Fri and Sat 1pm–1am, Sun 1–7pm*.

Vegetarian Restaurants

Madrid used to be a veggie's nightmare, but the city now offers a decent range of options.

La Biotika, C/Amor de Dios 3, **t** 914 29 07 80; **M** Antón Martín (*inexpensive*). This wholefood eatery has an ultra-low-price *menú* (with vegan options), and a shop. *Open daily 1.30–4.30 and 8–11.30*.

Chez Pomme, C/Pelayo 4, **t** 915 32 16 46; **M** Chueca (*inexpensive*). A mod-vegetarian spot in Chueca, with inventive *menús del día* that are another great bargain.

El Estragón Vegetariano, Plaza de la Paja 10, **t** 913 65 89 82; **M** La Latina (*moderate*). On the recently restored Plaza de la Paja, El Estragón has a young clientele and a relaxed feel. *Open daily 1–4.30 and 8–midnight*.

La Sastrería, C/Hortaleza 74, **t** 915 32 77 71; **M** Alonso Martínez (*inexpensive*). Dressmakers' dummies complete the 'tailor' theme in the name. It has Spanish food with a twist, with many veggie options. *Open Mon–Fri 10am–2am, Sat and Sun 11am–3am*.

Cafés, Bars and *Tapas*

Old Madrid: Austrias to Huertas

Las Bravas, C/de Alvarez Gato 3, **t** 915 32 26 20; **M** Sol. The name comes from the hot sauce poured on deep-fried potato chunks, a favourite in every Spanish bar, but which they claim to have invented. An institution. *Open daily 11–3.30 and 7.30–2.*

Café Barbieri, C/Ave María 45, **t** 915 27 36 58; **M** Lavapiés. A beautiful old café, with huge mirrors and a civilized atmosphere. Soothing by day and quietly sociable by night. *Open Sun–Thurs 3pm–2am, Fri–Sat 3pm–3am.*

Café de la Esquina, C/Príncipe del Anglona 1, **t** 913 66 91 13; **M** La Latina. Just up from C/Segovia, this little café is a dream in summer, with outdoor tables and, inside, soft lighting and red velvet chairs. *Open Mon–Sat 6pm–2.30am, Sun 6pm–2am.*

Café del Nuncio, C/de Segovia 9, **t** 913 66 08 53; **M** La Latina. A classic Madrid haunt, which spreads out onto the little plaza outside in summertime. *Open daily 12.30pm–2.30am.*

La Carpanta, C/Almendro 22, **t** 913 66 57 83; **M** La Latina. At the epicentre of the weekend wine-and-*pinchos* scene, this lively bar offers a dizzying selection of wines and sophisticated *tapas*. *Open Sun–Wed 11am–1.30am, Thurs 11am–2am, Fri and Sat 11am–3am.*

Casa Paco, Plaza Puerta Cerrada 11, **t** 913 66 31 66; **M** Sol. A classic *taberna*, covered with colourful tiles, a good stop for *tapas*. *Open Mon–Sat 1.30–4 and 8.30–midnight.*

La Casa de las Torrijas, C/de la Paz 4, **t** 915 32 14 73; **M** Sol. An atmospheric blast from the past, serving a fine selection of wines and a rarity – *torrijas*, sweet bread fritters, soaked in wine and spices, dipped in sugar and fried. *Open Mon–Sat 10–4 and 6–10.30; closed Aug.*

Cervecería Cervantes, Plaza Jesús 7, **t** 914 29 60 93; **M** Banco de España or Antón Martín. Beer steins hanging on the walls give the place a vaguely German feel, despite its eminently Spanish name, splendid *tapas* and line-up of hams behind the counter. *Open Mon–Sat noon–1am, Sun noon–4pm.*

La Moderna, Plaza Santa Ana, **t** 914 20 15 82; **M** Sevilla. The best of the *tapas* bars that line Plaza Santa Ana, with an above-average range of wines and *tapas*. *Open Sun–Thurs 11am–12.15am, Fri and Sat 11am–1.15am.*

Taberna de Antonio Sánchez, C/Mesón de Paredes 13, **t** 915 39 78 26; **M** Tirso de Molina. A landmark of Lavapiés, a friendly *taberna* founded by a bullfighter in 1830 and full of bullfight memorabilia. *Open Mon–Sat noon–4 and 8–midnight, Sun noon–4pm.*

Taberna de Los Austrias, C/del Nuncio 17; **M** La Latina. Dark exposed beams, brick walls, tables fashioned from wine barrels, and refined *tapas*. *Open Sun–Thurs noon–4 and 8–midnight, Fri and Sat noon–4 and 8–12.30.*

Taberna Dolores, Pza de Jesús 4, **t** 914 29 22 43; **M** Antón Martín. Tucked away behind the Palace Hotel, this 1930s relic owes its fame to the sublime canapés it serves. *Open Sun–Thurs 11am–1am, Fri and Sat 11am–2am.*

La Torre de Oro, Plaza Mayor 26, **t** 913 66 50 16; **M** Sol. Hectic Andaluz bar with great *pescaditos fritos* (whitebait) and other delights, and cheerful waiters. *Open daily 10am–1am.*

Malasaña, Chueca and Elsewhere

Café Comercial, Glorieta de Bilbao 7, **t** 915 21 56 55; **M** Bilbao. A great institution: an old-fashioned grand café where you can sit and talk for as long as it takes, with old leather seats for relaxing and reading. *Open Sun–Thurs 7.30am–1am, Fri and Sat 7.30am–2am.*

Café Figueroa, C/Augusto Figueroa 17, **t** 915 21 16 73; **M** Chueca. Chueca's gay crowd favour this chatty, relaxed attractive café. *Open Sun–Thurs 2.30pm–midnight, Fri and Sat 2.30pm–2.30am.*

Café Manuela, C/San Vicente Ferrer 29, **t** 915 21 70 73; **M** Tribunal. Pretty, bohemian Art Nouveau café. *Open daily 3.30pm–3am.*

Café Ruiz, C/Ruiz 11, **t** 914 46 12 32; **M** Bilbao. Another wonderful venue, with dark wood, mirrors and banquettes. Deliciously peaceful by day, crowded and noisy at night.

Mallorca, C/Serrano 6, **t** 915 77 18 59; **M** Retiro. A pastry shop and gourmet food store extraordinaire, with excellent coffee, fresh orange juice, and refined cakes and snacks at the little bar. *Open daily 9.30am–10pm.*

Mendocino Café, C/Limón 11, **t** 915 42 91 30; **M** Noviciado. A San Francisco café transported to Madrid: paintings on the walls, readings and even Sunday brunch with pancakes and maple syrup. *Open Mon–Thurs 9am–midnight, Fri 9am–2am, Sat noon–2am, Sun noon–midnight.*

Nightlife

Madrid has one bar for every 96 inhabitants, so there's always somewhere to go. Don't, whatever you do, expect to start early: first-time visitors to Madrid are often surprised at just how late *madrileños* stay out. In general, people go to *tapas* bars after work, have dinner, and then move on to *bares de copas* (bars that only serve drinks) as the night wears on. The rule generally is to head for an area and then wander from bar to bar. **Clubs** are the next port of call, and often don't even begin to get started until 1am.

La Boca del Lobo, C/Echegaray 11; **M** Sevilla. An old-time cellar bar playing old-time music from the 30s up to the 60s, attracting a nice mixed crowd. *Open daily 11pm–5am.*

Champañería-Librería María Pandora, Plaza Gabriel Miró 1; **M** La Latina. In leafy Las Vistillas, with a snug, intimate feel and *cava* cocktails. A nice end to a romantic evening. *Open Mon–Thurs 7pm–2am, Fri and Sat 7pm–3am, Sun 4pm–2am.*

Flamingo, C/Mesonero Romanos 13, **t** 915 31 48 27; **M** Gran Vía. This venue hosts a range of sessions: Thursdays it's 'Cream' for house, 'Ocho y Medio' Fridays are for techno pop, and Sunday nights are for the gay Shangay Tea Dance. *Open Wed–Sun midnight–5am.*

Los Gabrieles, C/Echegaray 17; **M** Sevilla. A handsome old bar with tiles that are almost world-famous, and now full of loud music and lively company. *Open daily 2pm–2am.*

Joy Eslava, C/Arenal 11, **t** 913 66 37 33; **M** Sol. Madrid's best-loved classic disco, attracting all sorts of urban fauna from businessmen and hen nights to drag queens. *Open daily 11.30pm–6am.*

Kapital, C/Atocha 125, **t** 914 20 29 06; **M** Atocha. Seven floors of fun, including cinema, karaoke bar and chill-out areas. The rooftop bar has fantastic views. *Open Thurs–Sat midnight–6am.*

Ohm, Plaza Callao 4; **M** Callao. A fun dance scene for people of all stripes – gay, lesbian, straight. *Open Fri and Sat midnight–6am.*

Palacio de Gaviria, C/Arenal 9, **t** 915 26 60 69; **M** Sol or Opera. In a former palace, with a labyrinthine, ornate interior that offers a range of ambiences, drawing a mixed crowd. *Open daily 10.30pm–dawn.*

Star's Café, C/Marqués de Valdeiglesias 5; **M** Banco de España. Loungy by day, this gay-friendly spot comes alive at night with dance sessions. *Open Mon–Wed 9am–2am, Thurs 9am–3am, Fri and Sat 9am–4am.*

Teatríz, C/Hermosilla 15; **M** Serrano. Its Philippe Starck '80s design still draws the Salamanca smart set. Restaurant, disco and bar, in an old theatre. *Open daily 1.30–4 and 9–1.*

La Vieja Estación, Av Ciudad de Barcelona; **M** Atocha. The city's biggest open-air summer *terraza* is in a concrete chasm next to Atocha station. With bars, dance floors and a restaurant, this is one of the best places in the city for dancing beneath the stars. *Open May–Sept daily till 6am.*

Villa Rosa, Plaza Santa Ana 15; **M** Sevilla. A classic stop on any nocturnal Madrid tour, featured in Almodóvar's *High Heels*. More great tiles. *Open Mon–Sat 11pm–5am.*

Viva Madrid, C/Manuel Fernández y González 7; **M** Antón Martín. A classic, historic bar that retains its gorgeous tiled façade, and now welcomes a young, international crowd. *Open daily 1pm–2am.*

Entertainment

For listings information, the *Guía del Ocio* is the most complete guide, covering all aspects of entertainment and nightlife.

Auditorio Nacional de Música, C/Príncipe de Vergara 146, **t** (information) 913 37 01 39, **t** (advance sales) 902 33 22 11, *www.auditorio nacional.mcu.es*; **M** Prosperidad. Home to the Orquesta Nacional de España symphony orchestra, the *auditorio* also stages some jazz events. The concert season is Oct–June.

Casa Patas, C/Cañizares 10, **t** 913 69 04 96; **M** Antón Martín. The most important flamenco venue in the city, with the biggest programme. All the best names in flamenco music and dance can be caught here.

Suristán, C/de la Cruz 7, **t** 915 32 39 09; **M** Sol. The only club dedicated to world music. *Open daily 10pm–5.30am.*

Teatro Real, Plaza de Oriente, **t** 915 16 06 60, *www.teatro-real.com*; **M** Opera. Finally open after years of renovation, Madrid's opera house has state of the art facilities within its 150-year-old shell. It also hosts ballet and orchestral concerts.

Finding Your Way Around the Prado

Expect crowds, but don't be dismayed by huge mobs at the entrances: they're likely to be tour groups counting heads, and you should be able to pass right through. The earlier you go, the fewer you'll have to contend with. The best place to begin a comprehensive visit is to enter at ground level by the Puerta de Goya at the north end. The museum is laid out chronologically: the **ground floor** is mostly medieval and Renaissance, covering 14th–16th-century Spanish, Flemish, German and Italian works. The **first floor** covers Baroque, with Velázquez, and some of the Goyas. The rest of these are on the **second floor**. Free floor plans are available at the entrances.

Argument has gone on for many years over the Prado's dire space problem, since its exhibition areas were only large enough to display one-seventh of the vast collection. Now in progress is a giant expansion plan, which includes the takeover of the church of **Los Jerónimos**, behind the museum, for temporary exhibitions, the comprehensive renovation of the **Casón del Buen Retiro**, which houses the Prado's stock of 19th-century Spanish art, and the takeover of the building that now houses the **Museo del Ejército** (Army Museum), which is also the only surviving part of Philip IV's **Palacio del Buen Retiro**. While all this work goes on some rooms may be closed.

Although, in such a huge museum, there's a natural tendency to head for the highlights, to get a full taste it's best to start with the ground floor by the Puerta de Goya, and take your time. The first rooms are devoted to **Spanish medieval religious works**: some of the best art in the Prado is here, including stunning 14th- and 15th-century *retablos* such as *Archbishop Don Sancho de Rojas* by Rodríguez de Toledo. After that comes **Flemish art**: even before Philip II, who valued Flemish painters above all others, the Low Countries' close ties with Spain ensured that many works would turn up here. They are arranged roughly chronologically, beginning with 15th-century paintings such as **Rogier van der Weyden**'s breathtaking *Descent from the Cross* (c. 1435). The biggest crowds will be around the works of **Hieronymous Bosch** (known in Spain as 'El Bosco'), whose eerie fantasies like *The Garden of Earthly Delights* were avidly collected by Philip II. If you like Bosch, get to know his countryman Joachim Patinir, some of whose best work is here. Probably no other museum has such a large dose of terror to balance its beauty; between Goya, Bosch, other northern painters and the religious hacks, a trip to the Prado can seem like a ride in a carnival funhouse. A climax comes in *The Triumph of Death* by **Pieter Brueghel the Elder** (1525–69), with phalanxes of leering skeletons turned loose upon a doomed, terrified world.

German paintings are few but choice. **Albrecht Dürer**'s *Self-portrait* (1498) seems a masterpiece of narcissism, painted at a time when self-portraits were uncommon. Also of interest are his twin paintings of *Adam and Eve*, Hans Baldung Grien's *Teutonic Three Graces* and *Three Ages of Man and Death*, and works by **Cranach** and **Mengs**.

Next comes the Prado's main **Italian** collection, with several paintings by Raphael and **Fra Angelico** – an intensely spiritual *Annunciation* – and an unusual trio of scenes by **Botticelli** from Boccaccio's *Decameron*, *The Story of Nastagio degli Onesti*. Andrea del Sarto, Mantegna, Veronese, Caravaggio, Tintoretto and Correggio are all well represented, and there are rooms full of works by **Titian**, who was a favourite painter of

Charles V and Philip II, producing powerful portraits of both kings. Nearby is an artist of no fixed abode: to appreciate the genius of Domenikos Theotocopoulos, or **El Greco**, there is no substitute for a visit to Toledo, but the Prado houses fine examples of his 'vertical pictures' – biblical figures with elongated limbs and faces – including *The Annunciation* and *The Adoration of the Shepherds*. Beyond them are **17th century Flemish**, **Dutch** and **Spanish** painters. **Rubens**, another Habsburg favourite, is well represented here, with his epic *Adoration of the Magi* and chubby *Three Graces*, and his famous collaboration with **Brueghel the Younger**, the *Allegory of the Five Senses*. Rubens' works are followed by those of later Flemish masters, such as delicate portraits by **Anthony van Dyck**. The small Dutch collection consists mostly of hunting scenes, but there is one good **Rembrandt**, a dignified portrait, *Artemisia*. A dozen rooms are filled with Spanish Baroque religious painting by masters such as **Francisco Ribalta**, **Alonso Cano**, the Caravaggio-influenced **Ribera**, **Zurbarán** and **Murillo**.

For all the great range of the Prado's holdings, though, to a huge extent people come to this museum to see the work of two, very local artists, **Velázquez** and Goya. Many Spaniards and more than a few foreigners consider Diego de Silva y Velázquez (1599–1660) to be the greatest painter of all time. Almost all his major paintings are in the Prado: *Los Borrachos* (*The Drunkards*), *Las Hilanderas* (*The Tapestry Weavers*) and *The Surrender of Breda*, which in Spain is called *Las Lanzas* (*The Lances*). His portraits of court dwarves, such as *Francisco Lezcano*, give his sitters a dignity denied them in daily life. Also present are royal portraits: lumpy, bewildered Philip IV appears in various poses, and his daughter, the doll-like Infanta Margarita, appears by herself and in the most celebrated of all Velázquez's works, *Las Meninas* (*The Maids-of-Honour*, 1656), a composition of such inexhaustible complexity and beauty that the Prado gives it pride of place. Picasso was obsessed with this picture, and painted variations on it countless times (many now in Barcelona's **Museu Picasso**, *see* p.55).

The **Goya** collection is spread over the first and second floors. Like Velázquez, Francisco de Goya y Lucientes (1746–1828) had the office of court painter, but, also like Velázquez, was not inclined to flattery. The job he did on Queen Maria Luisa is legendary: in every portrait and family scene, she comes out looking half-fairy-tale witch, half-washerwoman. Among the famous Goyas here are the *Maja Desnuda* (*Nude Maja*) and *Maja Vestida* (*Clothed Maja*), and *Los Fusilamentos del Dos de Mayo* (*The Executions of the Second of May*) and *Fusilamentos de Moncloa* (*The Executions of Moncloa*), the pair commemorating the 1808 uprising against the French and its aftermath. Nothing like this had ever been painted before, an unforgettable image and a prophetic prelude to the era of total war. Goya's early works on the second floor, his remarkable 'cartoons' or designs for tapestries to be made by the Royal tapestry factory, provide a dose of joy and sweetness, with vivid colours bathed in clear Castilian sunshine. In stark contrast are some of the Prado's greatest treasures, his **Pinturas Negras** ('Black Paintings'), the late works separated from the others by a stairway, as if it were feared they would contaminate the sunnier paintings upstairs. All the well-known images of dark fantasy and terror are here: *Saturn Devouring One of his Sons, Duel with Cudgels, The Colossus* (*Panic*), and even a nightmarish vision of the same San Isidro festivities Goya painted so happily when he was healthy.

Museo Nacional Centro de Arte Reina Sofía

*C/Santa Isabel 52, **t** 914 67 50 62; **M** Atocha; open Mon and Wed–Sat 10–9, Sun 10–2.30; closed Tues; free **guided tours** Mon and Wed at 5pm, Sat at 11am; adm; adm free Sat after 2.30pm, Sun, and 18 May, 12 Oct and 6 Dec.*

In the early 1980s, amid the first flowering of cultural excitement that followed the restoration of Spanish democracy, it was decided to give Madrid a world-class 20th-century art museum, to replace the tired old Museo Español de Arte Contemporáneo. Conversion of Madrid's defunct General Hospital began in 1980, and the Centro de Arte Reina Sofía was inaugurated by the queen in 1986. Cynics claimed this was just a vote-catching ploy by the Socialist government in an election year, since the building wasn't actually ready. Four years later, a second, 'real' opening was held. The building, graced by its three landmark glass lifts by British architect Ian Ritchie, was by then fully equipped to house temporary shows and a permanent collection. It was two more years, however, before the Reina Sofía really made its début, with the arrival in 1992 of Picasso's *Guernica*, arguably the 20th century's most famous painting.

This masterpiece aside, the permanent collection has often been criticised: the core of it came from the old Museo de Arte Contemporáneo, and has works by every signif-icant Spanish 20th-century artist – Picasso, Dalí, Miró, Juan Gris, Julio González, Antoni Tàpies and Antonio Saura are all represented – but few masterworks. However, it has been added to by later acquisitions, and a growing slate of non-Spanish artists. It begins on the **Second Floor** in the 1900s, with the Catalans **Anglada-Camarasa** and **Casas**. Shortly after them come the curvy, colourful works of **Sonia Delaunay**, and mature paintings by **Juan Gris**, while a tiny room displays the superb skin-skeletons of **Pablo Gargallo**, who introduced Picasso to metal sculpture. Nearby, a hefty knot of people is usually gathered around *Guernica*, alone on one wall. Picasso's stern *Woman in Blue* (1901) presides over an adjacent gallery of his early work. **Dalí** also has a room to himself, and his film collaborations with **Luis Buñuel** are screened in Room 12.

On the **Fourth Floor** the museum picks up the story in the 1940s, post-Civil War and under Francoism, with boxy sculptures by Jorge de Oteiza and bristling pieces by Pablo Serrano. These currents are put into a European context with **Francis Bacon**'s bleak figures, the minimalism of **Yves Klein**, or **Henry Moore** sculptures. This varied series culminates in a room devoted to texture-obsessed **Antoni Tàpies**. Politicised art is here in the Equipo Crónica group's jibe at American mass culture in the Pop Art *Painting is like Hitting* (1964), but Minimalism strikes back with the bright canvases of **Ellsworth Kelly** and **Soto**'s staggering *Yellow and White Extension* before **Schnabel**'s vast *Buen Retiro Ducks* series. Take a look too at whatever is in place on the Third Floor; the Reina Sofía is one of Europe's foremost centres for big-scale exhibitions.

Finding Your Way Around the Reina Sofía

The permanent collections occupy the **second** and **fourth floors** and are grouped chronologically and according to stylistic affinity. **Temporary exhibitions** – often spectacular – are in Espacio UNO on the ground floor and on the third floor. There is also an excellent bookshop, a café-restaurant and an oasis of a courtyard garden.

Museo Colección Thyssen-Bornemisza

Palacio de Villahermosa, Paseo del Prado 8, t 914 20 39 44;
M Banco de España; open Tues–Sun 10–7; adm.

The directors of the Reina Sofía were glad when attention switched up the road to the Palacio de Villahermosa in 1993. Thanks to the persuasiveness of his Spanish wife, Carmen 'La Tita' Cervera, Baron Hans-Heinrich Thyssen-Bornemisza decided on Madrid as the home for his unique collection of art, and the Spanish government agreed to convert the palace into a suitable showcase to house it. The Thyssen collection, begun in the 1920s by the present baron's father, is considered the finest private art collection in the world. It's also idiosyncratic, eclectic and fun, and gives a fascinating insight into the personal taste of two men with a magpie-like compulsion. Like a prized stamp collection, it contains a bit of everything – there's an entry on practically every page of art history, with some favourites (portraits) in larger quantities. To create the gallery spaces, architect Rafael Moneo was given a shell of a building, and his finished work has a beautiful balance of natural and artificial light.

From the top (the **Second Floor**), the collection opens with one of its highlights, a treasure-trove of **Medieval Italian religious art**, followed by **15th-century Flemish** works, among them Van Eyck's brilliantly executed *Annunciation Diptych* (*c.* 1435–41). **Early Renaissance portraits** are another high point: there are familiar faces here, such as **Holbein**'s *Henry VIII* (*c.* 1534–6) and Memling's *Young Man at Prayer* (1485), as well as the exquisite *Portrait of Giovanna Tornabuoni* (1488) by **Domenico Ghirlandaio**. Moneo designed the long and windowed **Villahermosa Gallery** to recall *gallerias* in Italian palaces, and it mainly contains **Italian paintings**, including a Raphael portrait and the rare *Young Knight in a Landscape* (1510) by **Vittore Carpaccio**, remarkable for its richly detailed allegorical backdrop. Among the **16th-century German works** is **Dürer**'s oppressively compact *Jesus among the Doctors* (1506). The **Baroque** collection kicks off with a fabulous early **Caravaggio**, *St Catherine of Alexandria* (1597).

Below on the **First Floor** are **17th-century Dutch paintings**, followed by **Rococo and neoclassical works**, including a Watteau and portraits by Reynolds and Gainsborough. Next comes one of the Thyssens' special enthusiasms, a collection of paintings by **19th-century American artists** that's virtually unique in Europe, a mixed bag from chocolate-boxy sunsets by Frederic Edwin Church to an innovative still life by John Frederick Peto, *Tom's River* (1905). Among the many **19th-century European works** are three late Goyas, including the delightful *El Tio Paquete*, a fine, shimmery Corot, and, very surprising to find in Madrid, **Constable**'s *The Lock* (1824). The selection of **Impressionists** is slim, but **Post-Impressionists** and **Fauves** are better represented: gloriously lurid Van Goghs; a Cézanne; Degas' snapshot-like *Swaying Dancer*. **German Expressionism** – almost unseen in Spain before the Thyssen opened – is another of the museum's great strengths, with powerful paintings by Ernst Ludwig Kirchner, Max Beckmann, Egon Schiele, Otto Dix and the **Blaue Reiter** painters.

On the **Ground Floor** comes a change in atmosphere with a collection clumped together as the **Experimental Avant-gardes**. **Cubism** is represented by its brightest stars, Braque, Picasso and Juan Gris, followed by the **Russian avant-garde**, and there is

> **Finding Your Way Around the Thyssen-Bornemisza**
> The chronological sequence begins on the top floor and works its way downwards,
> so that the modern works benefit from being hung in the high-ceilinged ground-
> floor rooms. In the basement is a café and a space for temporary exhibitions.

plenty of space to appreciate the scale of the Mondrians and Filonov's astounding untitled canvas. A section titled '**The Synthesis of Modernism**' contains **Chagall**'s dreamlike *The Rooster* (1929) plus glittering works by Ernst, Klee, Kandinsky and Miró, leading up to **American Modernists**: Mark Rothko, Jackson Pollock, emigré Surrealist Arshile Gorky and a magnificent **Georgia O'Keeffe**, *New York with Moon*. The very last section is perhaps the most striking of all: **Edward Hopper**'s *Hotel Room* (1931); a char-acteristically disturbing Francis Bacon; an unforgettable **Lichtenstein** (*Woman in the Bath*; 1963); a Hockney and **Richard Estes**' multilayered slices of New York (*Telephone Booths*; 1967), one of the very best works in this dazzling diverse storehouse of art.

The Retiro and the Paseo del Prado

Behind the Prado museum is Madrid's great central park, properly known as the **Parque del Buen Retiro**. The 'Good Retreat' began life as a royal preserve surrounding a giant palace (the *Palacio del Buen Retiro*), both created in the 1630s by Philip IV's great minister the Conde-Duque de Olivares in order to exalt the stature of his shy, hesitant, art-loving monarch. Most of the palace was destroyed in the Napoleonic wars, but otherwise much of the Retiro has changed little, an elegant, formal garden, perfect for the pageants and dalliances of the Baroque era. Among its 400-odd acres are foun-tains, a Japanese garden and a seemingly endless expanse of quiet paths among shady trees. A favourite thing to do is rent boats on the **Estanque**, the broad lagoon at the park's centre. The Retiro is also dotted with an assortment of buildings, used for free exhibitions, such as the **Palacio de Velázquez** and the enchanting glass and iron **Palacio de Cristal** by the lake. At the southern end of the park, seek out the *Angel Caído* ('Fallen Angel', 1878), a statue to the devil, and the 1790 **Observatorio Astronómico Nacional** (*open Mon–Fri 9–2; adm free*). Between the park's southwest corner and **Paseo del Prado** is an especially lush urban oasis, the **Real Jardín Botánico** or botanical garden (*open June–Aug daily 10–9; Sept–May daily 10–dusk; adm*). Just to the south, Paseo del Prado ends at the massive traffic interchange next to **Atocha** train station, an 1880s wrought-iron giant renovated – with a 'tropical garden' in the centre – by Rafael Moneo in 1992. If you walk southeast along the busy Paseo Infanta Isabel you can visit a handicrafts workshop fit for kings: the **Real Fábrica de Tapices** (*open Mon–Fri 10–2; closed Aug; adm*) or Royal Tapestry Factory, for which Goya produced his 'cartoons', as tapestry designs. The guided tours are charming, and allow you to get close to the master weavers still working with strictly traditional methods.

There are several more museums in the district around the Prado. Pride of place must go to the **Museo del Ejército** or Army Museum (*open Tues–Sun 10–2; closed Mon; adm; adm free Sat*), since it occupies the largest surviving part of the Retiro palace (although not for much longer, as the Prado intends to take it over, *see* p.140). Within its grand chambers the museum recounts Spain's military history in massive detail, and allows the country's more elderly military men to indulge their ideological preferences (glorification of General Franco). Just as butch is the **Museo Naval** (*open Tues–Sun 10.30–1.30; closed Mon and Aug; adm free*), which also has relics of the Age of Exploration such as Juan de la Cosa's *Mapa Mundi* of 1500, the earliest Spanish map to show the American coast. Around the corner on C/Montalbán is the **Museo de Artes Decorativas** (*open Tues–Fri 10–5, Sat, Sun and hols 10–2; closed Mon; adm, adm free Sat after 2pm and Sun*), with furniture, ceramics, textiles, gold and silver from the 15th to the 20th century. And a walk across Paseo del Prado and up C/Cervantes will take you to the **Casa-Museo de Lope de Vega** (*open Tues–Fri 9.30–2, Sat 10–1.30; closed Sun, Mon, hols and Aug; adm, adm free Sat*), where Spain's greatest dramatist lived for the last 25 years of his life. House and garden were restored with an inventory of his possessions left when he died, a fascinating insight into 17th-century life. Tours are usually in Spanish, but if you call by a little in advance can be arranged in English.

Going northwards, the Paseo del Prado comes to an end at **Plaza de Cibeles**, where streams of traffic swirl around Ventura Rodríguez' fountain of the goddess Cybele in a carriage drawn by lions. The extravagant pile on the southeast side of the plaza is only the main post office, the 1904 **Palacio de Comunicaciones**. East of here, C/Alcalá runs to Pza de la Independencia and its centrepiece, the stately **Puerta de Alcalá** (1778), once the actual gate on the road to Alcalá de Henares. Above Cibeles the paseo changes name to **Paseo de Recoletos**, along the shady flanks of which are some of Madrid's best traditional-style cafés, such as the **Café Gijón** (*see* p.136). Recoletos in turn ends at **Plaza Colón**, north of which begins the **Paseo de la Castellana**, Madrid's endless north-south artery. Colón is Spanish for Columbus, and accordingly the plaza has a monument to the great explorer, incorporating a fantastic urban waterfall. Dominating the square, though, is the vast and florid pile on its eastern side, the **Biblioteca Nacional**, Spain's national library. In the same building, but entered from the other side (C/Serrano) is the **Museo Arqueológico Nacional** (*open Tues–Sat 9.30–8.30, Sun 9.30–2.30; adm, adm free Sat after 2.30pm, Sun, 18 May, 12 Oct and 6 Dec*), a massive compendium of the country's pre- and early history, from relics of the Palaeolithic, Neolithic, Bronze and Iron Ages in Iberia, through Greek vases and Egyptian mummies – all found in Spain – mosaics and jewellery from Roman Seville and Tarragona, to early Christian and Visigothic art and Islamic ceramics. Its greatest treasure is the 5th-century BC Iberian image known as *La Dama de Elche*, found at Elche (see p.182), one of the finest sculptures of antiquity. Outside the museum, by the gate, a 'cave' houses replicas of the Palaeolithic paintings of **Altamira** in Cantabria, not a bad alternative since it's now difficult to see the originals (*see* p.124).

Old Madrid

Shoehorned into a half-kilometre between Puerta del Sol and the Palacio Real is a solid, enduring Castilian town, often known as 'El Madrid de las Austrias' because most of it was built under the Habsburgs, and as evocative in its own way as Segovia or Toledo. At its heart is the **Plaza Mayor**, the grand ceremonial square of Golden Age Madrid. It was begun for Philip II in the 1560s, but only completed for Philip III in 1619. Few squares in Spain are lovelier, and none is better used. Between concerts, festivals, political rallies and the popular Sunday market peddling stamps and coins, something is likely to be on when you visit. If there isn't, someone will be strumming a guitar at the hoofs of the **equestrian statue of Philip III**, while the tourists look on from the cafés. Kings traditionally took their places for ceremonies in the building with twin spires on the north side of the plaza, the **Casa de la Panadería** (1590). Its façade was redecorated in 1992 by Carlos Franco in a groovy neo-hippie celebration of Madrid.

A short walk west of Plaza Mayor some of Madrid's oldest buildings can be seen around **Plaza de la Villa**. City Hall, the distinguished **Casa de la Villa**, is one of Madrid's finest buildings, built by Juan Gómez de Mora in the 1630s. Across the square is the 15th-century **Torre de los Lujanes**, which, according to legend, once imprisoned no less a personage than King François I of France. The area to the south and down to **Plaza del Humilladero** and **La Latina** makes up the oldest, most characterful corner of old Madrid, with streets that still follow those of the early medieval town, a slightly run-down but pleasant place for a stroll. **Calle Ribera de Curtidores**, south of **Plaza Cascorro**, is home to Madrid's flea market, the **Rastro** (*see* p.134). To the east is sharp-edged **Lavapiés**, historically Madrid's most distinctively *castizo* district (*castizos* being the 'true born' *madrileños*, similar to London's Cockneys), and nowadays home to a diverse population including recent migrants from China, Pakistan and North Africa.

Old Madrid naturally has plenty of churches, although oddly enough by Spanish standards they're not especially distinguished. Madrid didn't even have a proper **cathedral** until the opening of **Nuestra Señora de la Almudena** in 1993. It took 110 years to complete, but the result is drab. Before 1992, Madrid had used a stand-in cathedral in the shape of the huge, twin-towered **Colegiata de San Isidro** on C/Toledo, which had actually been built for Madrid's Jesuit community in the 1620s, in a Baroque style typical of the order. It is dedicated to Madrid's patron saint San Isidro, who, it is said, liked to pray a few streets away in the **Iglesia de San Andrés**, more typical of the blank, severe style of Madrid's older parishes. Behind the church on Costanilla San Andrés is the splendid **Capilla del Obispo**, designed in the 1540s for the aristocratic Vargas family, and the finest Renaissance building in Madrid. The city's largest church, the **Basílica de San Francisco el Grande**, does live up to its big name, with a dome 108ft in diameter, but there's little more to say for it, except that it has a Goya, *San Bernardino of Siena*. A more fascinating religious building is north of C/Mayor, off C/Arenal, the **Real Monasterio de las Descalzas Reales** (*open Tues–Thurs and Sat 10.30–12.45 and 4–5.45, Fri 10.30–12.45, Sun and hols 11–1.30; visits by* **guided tour** *only, in Spanish; adm, free to EU passport-holders on Wed*). Still home to a closed community of nuns, just alongside the fashion stores of central Madrid, this 16th-century convent contains several centuries' accumulation of rich tapestries, furniture, art and holy relics, all displayed in its ornate, entirely unchanged original corridors.

The western boundary of Old Madrid is really the oldest part of it – since it stands on top of the remains of the Moorish fort – the **Palacio Real** or **Palacio de Oriente** (Royal Palace; *open April–Sept Mon–Sat 9–6, Sun and hols 9–3; Oct–Mar Mon–Sat 9.30–5, Sun and hols 9–12; closed frequently for official functions; adm, free to EU passport-holders on Wed*). It has some 2,800 rooms, and when King Philip V first commissioned it after Philip II's *Alcázar* had burnt down in 1734 he actually had to be talked out of an even grander version by his wife. Today, King Juan Carlos, with a more modest approach, does not live here, but only uses it for occasional ceremonies.

The exterior is very imposing, the effect heightened by its setting on a bluff above the Manzanares. The entrance is by way of the **Plaza de la Armería**, a courtyard big enough to hold the entire Plaza Mayor. Not all 2,800 rooms are open, but even so expect a mild delirium after the first three dozen or so. Some stand out, with frescoes by Giambattista Tiepolo, Francisco Bayeu and Antonio Velázquez, Stradivarius violins or paintings by El Greco and Goya. Off the courtyard are two special sections: the **Farmacia Real**, one of the world's oldest farmacies, and the **Armería Real** (Armoury), a stunning collection of weapons and suits of armour, many of them made for Charles V and Philip II. Around the Palacio Real are formal gardens: the **Campo del Moro**, below the bluff towards the river, has lovely views back and upwards to the palace.

Gran Vía to Plaza de España and the Casa de Campo

Cut through the old city in the 1900s, the **Gran Vía** is the Madrid of the bright lights, replete with skyscrapers, banks, shops and cinemas with enormous hand-painted billboards, and swarming with traffic and people into the night. Marking the western end of the Gran Vía is the broad but unlovely **Plaza de España**. Northwest from here is the beautifully landscaped **Parque del Oeste**, with **La Rosaleda**, a rose garden, at its centre. There is also an unexpected ornament: an Egyptian 4th-century BC temple, the **Templo de Debod** (*open April–Sept Tues–Fri 10–2 and 6–8, Sat and Sun 10–2; Oct–Mar Tues–Fri 9.45–1.45 and 4.15–6.15, Sat and Sun 10–2; closed Mon and hols; adm, adm free Wed*). It's genuine, sent as an act of friendship by the Egyptian government in 1968. From Parque del Oeste you can also take the *Teleférico* cable car (*operates April–Sept Mon–Fri 11–3 and 5–8.30, Sat, Sun and hols 11–3 and 4.30–9.30; Oct–Mar Sat, Sun 12–3 and 4–8*), one of Madrid's favourite rides, across to the Casa de Campo.

By the *Teleférico* a path leads down to Paseo de la Florida (or you can walk from Plaza Príncipe Pío and Campo del Moro) and the **Ermita de San Antonio de la Florida**, burial-place of Goya and a milestone of Spanish art (*open Tues–Fri 10–2 and 4–8, Sat and Sun 10–2; closed Mon and hols; adm, adm free Wed and Sun*). There are two identical neoclassical chapels: the one you want is on the right. It was built in 1798, and Goya was commissioned to paint frescoes on its walls, ceiling and dome. He did so in a way never seen before in any church. The figures covering the ceiling have the same faces as the people in his cartoons, only instead of angelic *madrileños* they have become angels in fact. Restored in 1996, the frescoes are more beautiful than ever.

West of La Florida and the Manzanares is a huge area that was kept by Spain's monarchs as a hunting estate. Hence, it was preserved as an almost entirely unbuilt-up woodland when, in 1931, the city took it over as a park. The **Casa de Campo** was the happy result: a stretch of quiet countryside for picnics and outings, in spite of a certain reputation for illicit goings-on. In summer, the **outdoor pool** and **boating lake** are packed with sizzling *madrileños*. Also here are two big draws: the **Parque de Atracciones** funfair (*open winter Sun–Fri noon–11pm, Sat noon–1am; summer Sun–Thurs noon–11pm, Fri and Sat noon–3am; adm*) and Madrid's **Zoo-Acuario** (*open Mon–Fri 10.30–8, Sat and Sun 10.30–9.30; adm exp*).

North of the Puerta del Sol

The area immediately north of Puerta del Sol is central Madrid's main middle-of-the-road shopping district. On the broad C/de Alcalá is the **Real Academia de Bellas Artes de San Fernando** (*open Tues–Fri 9–7, Sat–Mon and hols 10–2; adm, adm free Wed*), Spain's most august art school. Its rooms display a fascinating selection from five centuries of Spanish painting; alongside quirky works there are works by El Greco and Velázquez and several Goyas. It also houses the national print collection (**Calcografía Nacional**), which holds Goya's original plates for his staggering series of engravings.

North of Gran Vía are the *barrios* of Malasaña and Chueca. A jumble of narrow streets, **Malasaña** is the heart of Madrid's grunge-leaning teen scene. Its heart is the **Plaza de Dos de Mayo**, scene of the bloody battle of 2 May 1808 immortalized by Goya; around it, the streets are full of great bars and cafés. Just east across C/Fuencarral, **Chueca** can seem very similar, but instead of grunge it has become the city's unquestioned gay centre, which has led to an injection of prosperity, shops and restaurants and made this the hippest part of town, for gays and non-gays alike. These barrios provide a perfect setting for the **Museo Municipal** (*open Tues–Fri 9.30–8, Sat and Sun 10–2; closed Mon and hols; adm*), the city's own museum, housed in the 18th-century Hospicio de San Fernando, with an exuberant Baroque portal by Pedro de Ribera.

Moncloa and the Museo de América

North of the Parque del Oeste is Madrid's enormous **Ciudad Universitaria** (**M** Moncloa). Its main visitor attraction is at the southern end, the **Museo de América** on Av Reyes Católicos (*open Tues–Sat 10–3, Sun and hols 10–2.30; closed Mon; adm, adm free Sat after 2pm and Sun*). Oddly unknown to *madrileños*, this is the greatest collection of Pre-Columbian American artefacts outside the Americas, with, among other treasures, one of only four **Mayan illustrated manuscripts** in existence.

The Barrio de Salamanca and Chamberí

The area of neat, straight avenues east of Recoletos and the Castellana is the Barrio de Salamanca, laid out after Madrid finally spread outside its walls in the 1860s. Ever since then its grand apartment blocks have been the favourite residence of the well-heeled of Madrid, so this is the best area for luxury and fashion shopping. Salamanca also has one of Madrid's best museums, the recently restored **Museo Lázaro Galdiano** at C/Serrano 122 (*open Tues–Sun 10–2; closed hols, Aug, 1, 3 and 10 Nov, 6, 24 and 31 Dec; adm, adm free Wed*). It's the former home of financier Lázaro Galdiano, an extraordinary collector: around its walls are works by nearly every important Spanish painter, Bosch, Rembrandt, Gainsborough, Turner and Reynolds, and several Goyas. His eclectic tastes also extended to medieval armour, fine metalwork and early clocks.

West of the Castellana is the less plush district of **Chamberí**. In it on Paseo General Martínez Campos is the **Museo Sorolla** (*open Tues–Sat 10–3, Sun and hols 10–2; adm, adm free Sat after 2pm, Sun*), another home, that of the hugely popular painter of sunlit scenes Joaquín Sorolla (1863–1923). His house, studio, garden and some paintings remain much as he left them, giving a charming feel of the man and his art.

Day Trips and Overnighters from Madrid

El Escorial

Some Spaniards of a conservative persuasion refer to Philip II's palace-secretariat-monastery-mausoleum as 'the eighth wonder of the world'. Any building with a 528ft façade, 2,673 windows, 16 patios and 15 cloisters is entitled to some consideration, but it's not so much the glass and stone of El Escorial that make it remarkable but the neurotic will of the king who created this folly on an imperial scale. An *escorial* is a slag heap – there once was some sort of mine on this site – and so the proper title of Philip's dream-house translates as the Royal Seat of the Royal Saint Lawrence of the Slag Heap. The reason usually given for the dedication to San Lorenzo is that Philip won a victory over the French on the saint's day in 1557, at St Quentin in Flanders, and vowed to build him something in return. Work began in 1563, but the original architect Juan Bautista de Toledo died four years later, and El Escorial was entrusted to his pupil Juan de Herrera, who completed it in 1584. By stripping Renaissance building to its barest essentials, he captured perfectly the Spanish empire's mood of austere militancy, and Philip's taste. The king was more than pleased, as he contemplated work in progress from the spot in the hills above called *La Silla de Felipe II* (Philip II's Seat).

You can sign up for guided tours of the **Monasterio de San Lorenzo El Real de El Escorial** (*open April–Sept Tues–Sun 10–6; Oct–Mar Tues–Sun 10–5; closed Mon and hols; adm; adm free for EU nationals Wed*) at the north entrance, or can explore independently, but note that some areas (the Palacio de los Borbones, Casita del Príncipe) are only visitable with a tour; also, this is one place where without any guidance you can miss out on intriguing details, as well as getting lost. The official tours begin in the

Getting There

Buses are the most convenient means of public transport, since they run direct to the Monastery and San Lorenzo de El Escorial. The Herranz company's buses **661** and **664** run about every 30mins from the bus terminal next to **M** Moncloa in Madrid, and the journey takes about 1hr. There are frequent **trains** on *Cercanías* line C-8a, which stops at Atocha and Chamartín, but note that these run to the town of El Escorial, from where local buses make the short trip to San Lorenzo and the Monastery. The alternative is a gentle 2km-walk uphill from the station.

By **car**, take the N-VI (Carretera de La Coruña) road northwest out of Madrid, then turn off onto the well-marked M505 (50km).

Herranz also runs an infrequent bus service (usually once a day) from San Lorenzo to the **Valle de los Caídos**, but otherwise the only way to get there is by car.

Tourist Information

San Lorenzo de El Escorial: C/Floridablanca 10, **t** 918 90 15 54, near the bus station.

Eating Out

Charolés, C/Floridablanca 24, **t** 918 90 59 75 (*expensive*). Steeped in tradition, this is one of the town's best eateries: its weekly Wednesday *cocido* is an event in itself.

El Croché, C/San Lorenzo 6 (*inexpensive*). An old-world café connected to Charolés and the perfect place for a mid-afternoon snack.

Fonda Génara, Plaza San Lorenzo 2 (*moderate*). On the pretty Plaza de la Constitución, with a terrific midday *menú* (*inexpensive*).

Parrilla Príncipe, C/Floridablanca 6, **t** 918 90 16 11 (*moderate*). An intimate, restful haven in an 18th century *palacete*, with lovely views of the monastery, and excellent meat and fish. *Open Wed–Mon 1–4 and 8.30–midnight.*

northeastern section, a part never used by Philip II, but converted by the Bourbons Charles III and Charles IV into a royal residence, the **Palacio de los Borbones**. These two do not seem to have had any interest in Philip's idea of El Escorial, but used it as a glorified hunting-lodge. Consequently, they furnished their apartments in light, comfortable 18th-century style, with tapestries after works by Goya and others. One of the most interesting rooms is the **Hall of the Battles**, with a huge fresco showing every detail of the 1431 Battle of Higuerela, fought with the Moors of Granada. Upstairs, the **Nuevos Museos** (New Museums) occupy a corridor along the eastern walls. Much of Philip's painting collection is here, including works by Bosch (*The Crown of Thorns* and *The Seven Deadly Sins*), Titian, Veronese, El Greco and Dürer.

Such is the reputation Philip earned for himself – the evil genius of the Inquisition – that the little palace he tacked on to the back of El Escorial for himself, the **Palacio de Felipe II**, comes as a real surprise: simple rooms reminiscent of interiors by Vermeer, with white walls, Delft-blue tiles, and windows opening on to gardens and forests. It was here that Philip was brought the news of the Armada disaster, the national bankruptcies, the independence of the Netherlands. Here he endured the diseases that killed him. He made sure his bed was situated above the High Altar of his Basilica, and had a spyhole cut in the bedchamber wall so that he could observe Mass down below. In the throne room, be sure to see the marvellous inlaid wood **doors**, decorated with *trompe l'œil* scenes and architectural fantasies by an anonymous German artist.

An opulent but narrow staircase leads down to the **Panteón Real**, beneath the Basilica's High Altar, with the tombs of Spain's kings. All manner of stories have grown up around it: Charles II, it is said, spent days down here, ordering that the gilded marble tombs be opened so that he could gaze on his mummified ancestors. Royal relations fill a maze of corridors off the Pantheon, guarded by enormous white heralds with golden maces. Beyond are the **Sacristía** (sacristy) and **Salas Capitulares** (chapterhouses), with collections of religious art. Another section is the **Biblioteca** (library), measuring 180ft by 30ft and entered by a stair near the main gate. Philip's books meant as much to him as his paintings, and he built up one of the largest collections of Latin, Greek, Hebrew and Arabic books of his time. The large globe in the centre of the library was used by King Philip in making astronomical calculations.

In many ways, the **Basilica** is the *raison d'être* of the entire complex. Three tremendous naves and four enormous pillars form the shape of the cross and sustain the sky-high cupola, in the image and likeness of St Peter's in Rome, only in grey instead of gold. No church in Spain is colder inside. Just inside the entrance, in the **lower choir**, note the unusual ceiling and its 'flat vaulting', an architectural trick that creates the illusion of flatness. From here, the eye is drawn to the bright *retablo*, by several then-fashionable Italian artists, including Pellegrino Tibaldi, and above them a golden figure of Christ on the Cross. Notable too are the gilded bronze ensembles to the sides of the altar, the families of Charles V and Philip II (with all three of his wives) at prayer. In all, there are over 40 chapels; one that stands out houses Benvenuto Cellini's stunning *Crucifixion*, a seminal piece of 16th-century Italian sculpture. The west doors of the Basilica open onto the **Patio de los Reyes**, El Escorial's main courtyard. It is named after sculptures by Monegro of six mighty Kings of Judea, on the church's western façade. On the far side of the courtyard is the **west gate**, the ceremonial entrance to El Escorial. The two statues in the centre represent David and Solomon.

Two little country houses within walking distance are included in the ticket. The **Casita del Príncipe** and **Casita de Arriba** (also known as the Casita del Infante), built in 1772 and 1767 for Charles IV, are tasteful, cosy and full of pretty pictures, and the Príncipe has neat, well-tended gardens, **Los Jardines del Príncipe**, so that they provide a refreshing contrast to all that dark Habsburg religiosity. It's worth taking a field guide to European trees on the walk down to the Casita del Príncipe: the **bosquecillo** has magnificent examples, many over 100 years old. Since the building of El Escorial a pleasant little town has also grown up around it: **San Lorenzo** has held onto its village atmosphere, with pretty small squares, and boasts a tiny, exquisite theatre, the **Real Coliseo**, founded by Charles III, on C/Floridablanca a short walk from the monastery.

El Valle de los Caídos

If you came to El Escorial expecting freakishness and gloom, you needn't be disappointed. A few kilometres north, atop a high peak in the Guadarrama, is Francisco Franco's own idea of building for the ages. The 'Valley of the Fallen' (*open April–Sept Tues–Sun 9.30–7; Oct–Mar Tues–Sun 10–6; closed Mon; adm*) was supposedly meant as a memorial to the dead on the Francoist side (not the others) from the Civil War, but commemorates above all the *Generalísimo* himself (prisoners from the Republican side, meanwhile, were used as slave labour to build it, and many died in the process). The **cross**, 410ft tall, is claimed to be the largest in the world; below, the cave-church **basilica** is impressive, as the palace of a troll-king might be. The nave goes on and on, past Fascist angels with big swords, ending in a plain, circular altar. Although the *Valle* is supposed to be a collective monument there are just two names, on the tombs of José Antonio Primo de Rivera, founder of the Falange, and Franco, beside the altar.

Segovia

Three distinct cultures have endowed this once-prominent town with three famous monuments. The Romans left Segovia a great aqueduct, and the age of Emperor Charles V (Carlos I of Spain) contributed a cathedral. The third, the *Alcázar*, should be as well known. Begun by the Moors and rebuilt in the Middle Ages, its present incarnation is pure 19th-century fantasy, a lost stage set from a Wagnerian opera. Segovia has other monuments but the memory the visitor tends to take away is a first, visual impression. The delicate skyline silhouetted on a high, narrow promontory between two green valleys gives the city the appearance of a great ship among the rolling hills of Castile. To enter it is to climb into a lost, medieval dream-Spain of unusually quiet streets (rampaging tourists apart), making all old Segovia seem a single work of art.

When the Roman Emperor Trajan built the aqueduct in the 2nd century AD, Segovia was already a venerable city. It was of little importance to the Moors, but after it fell to the Christians in the 11th century, Segovia blossomed amid the expansion of medieval Castile, and by the time of the Catholic kings it was one of its leading cities. Like most of Europe's medieval cities that have survived intact, Segovia's present-day serenity hides a dark secret. The economic policies and wars of Charles V and his successors ruined Segovia as thoroughly as the rest of Old Castile, and it is only the centuries of stagnation that followed that allow us to see old Segovia as it was.

The **Plaza Mayor** remains the centre of the old town, with its arcades and cafés. From here, the **cathedral** (*open Mar–Oct daily 9–6.30; Nov–Feb daily 9–5.30; adm*) is just a stone's throw away. This has been called the 'last Gothic cathedral' of Spain; most of the work was done between 1525 and 1590, though parts were not completed until the 18th century. The best parts of this cathedral are the semi-circular eastern end, where an exuberant ascent of pinnacles and buttresses (which surely inspired Gaudí in his Sagrada Família) covers the chapels behind the main altar, the unique squarish belltower and an elegant dome over the choir. There's little to see inside – a comment on the hard times 16th-century Segovia had come into. See the **cloister**, though, if it's open; this is part of the town's original cathedral, burnt down in the Comunero revolt in 1521. Built in the Isabelline Gothic style by Juan Guas, the cloister was moved here and reassembled after it survived the fire.

The **Alcázar** (*open summer 10–7; winter 10–6; adm*) jutting out on its cliffs over the confluence of the Río Eresma and smaller Clamores, was one of the royal residences

Getting There

The best way to get to Segovia on public transport is by **bus**. La Sepulvedana runs 20 or more each day (fewer at weekends) from its depot at Paseo de la Florida 11 (**t** 915 30 48 00) in Madrid. Journey time is about 1¼ hours. The bus is a great deal quicker than the **train**, which takes about two hours, from Atocha or Chamartín. There are nine trains every weekday and seven a day at weekends

By **car**, follow the N-VI (Carretera de La Coruña) road northwest out of Madrid to a little beyond Guadarrama, and then turn off right onto the N-603 (90km).

Tourist Information

Segovia: Plaza Mayor 10, **t** 921 46 03 34. Also an office by the viaduct at Plaza del Azoguejo 1, **t** 921 46 22 914.

Where to Stay

Segovia ✉ 40000

***Los Linajes**, C/Doctor Velasco 9, **t** 921 46 04 75 (*expensive*). One of the most serenely pretty locations of any hotel in Castile: on the northern walls with a terrace overlooking the valley of the Eresma, and only a short walk from the cathedral.

Las Sirenas, C/Juan Bravo 30, **t** 921 46 26 63 (*moderate*). Stately establishment with a/c and TV in all rooms.

Hs El Hidalgo, C/José Canalejas 5, **t** 921 46 3 5 29 (*inexpensive*). Good quality *hostal* in a characterful 18th-century building close to Plaza Mayor, with an attractive **restaurant**.

Eating Out

Segovia is the capital of traditional Castilian cuisine, and the streets around Plaza Mayor are packed with dimly lit *típico* restaurants. Roast meats are the great speciality: here master *asadores* serve up Spain's best *cochinillo* (suckling pig), milk-fed lamb and other formidable Castilian favourites.

The most attractive cafés are under the portals of the Plaza Mayor: **La Concha** is the best, with tables and chairs outside.

Restaurante José María, C/Cronista Lecea 11, **t** 921 46 11 11 (*moderate*). First-rate in every department, and with decent prices. Master-roaster José María is also passionate about Castilian wines, and owns his own vineyard.

La Cocina de Segovia, Pso Ezequiel González 26, **t** 921 43 74 62 (*moderate*). More elaborate, creative cooking.

Restaurante Lazaró, C/Infanta Isabel, **t** 921 46 03 16 (*inexpensive*). Centrally located, with a good cheap *menú*, as well as *cochinillo*.

of Castile when Segovia was at the height of its prominence, and Alfonso the Wise spent much of his reign here. By the 19th century, though, the old castle was just a military school, and in 1862 some cadets managed to set fire to it. No one, it seems, recorded the names of the architects who oversaw its restoration in the 1880s, who are thus fated to be forgotten heroes of the picturesque, for they turned the Alcázar into a flight of fancy worthy of Mad King Ludwig of Bavaria, with pointed turrets and curving, crenellated walks. As if displayed for effect, ravens perch on the turrets and walls. The people of Segovia have joined in the fun, fitting out the interior in a fashion that would make the characters of any Sir Walter Scott novel feel at home, with 14th-century cannons, an arquebus or two and dusty paintings of Visigothic kings.

Between the cathedral and Alcázar lies the oldest district of Segovia. The *esgrafiado* work on some of the houses is a local speciality; a coat of stucco is applied, then scraped away around stencils to make decorative patterns. In a small plaza west of the cathedral stands the finest of the city's Romanesque churches, the 13th-century **San Esteban**, with an arcaded porch typical of Segovia's Romanesque architecture. Across the plaza is the **Palacio Episcopal** (*open Fri–Sat 10–2 and 5–7*) or Archbishop's Palace, its plain façade enlivened by the reliefs of a serpent-woman over the entrance. Within Segovia's walls, streets meander languidly; to wander along them is a treat, and fortunately the town is small enough that you never get utterly lost. Medieval churches are everywhere: **San Andrés**, a solid, simple 12th-century work on Plaza Merced; **La Trinidad** on Plaza Doctor Laguna (off C/Trinidad), **San Martín** on C/Juan Bravo and **San Juan de los Caballeros** on Plaza de Colmenares. Nearby, the **Casa de los Picos** is another landmark, a 15th-century mansion with a façade like a waffle-iron, a style copied in many buildings in Spain and even a famous church in Naples.

A few steps away a gap in the wall will give you a fine view of Segovia's most cele-brated feature, its **Aqueduct**. Little else remains from Roman *Segóbriga*, but for the city to have merited such a water supply it must have had nearly as many inhabitants in the 2nd century AD as it has now, 50,000. Its two-storey arcade rises 97ft over Plaza Azoguejo, making it the tallest surviving Roman aqueduct. And the Romans, antiq-uity's master plumbers, did not build it there just to show off: it brought water from a distant source, the Río Frío, 15km away. What you see here is only a small part of the system; there was also an underground watercourse from here to the Alcázar, and from the other end you can follow the channel, ever shallower as the ground rises, up C/Fernán García from Plaza Azoguejo and right out of the city.

On no account should you leave Segovia without a walk through the valley of the Eresma. Through either of the old *mudéjar* gates in the city's northern walls, the road leads down to the river through woods dotted with wild flowers. Across the river you arrive at the church of **La Vera Cruz** (*open summer Tues–Sun 10.30–1.30 and 3.30–7; winter Tues–Sun 10.30–1.30 and 3.30–6; closed Mon and Nov; adm*), one of the most interesting surviving Templar foundations, built in 1208. Considered a 'holy valley', the Eresma was the site of many chapels and convents in the Middle Ages. Gregorian chants are still sung each noon at the most interesting of the monasteries, **El Parral** (*open Mon–Sat 10–12.30 and 4–6, Sun 10–11.30*), a little to the east of La Vera Cruz along the river.

More Bourbon Palaces: La Granja de San Ildefonso and Ríofrío

South of Segovia towards the *sierra* are two more 18th-century royal palaces.
La Granja ('the farm') **de San Ildefonso** (*open summer Tues–Sat 10–6, Sun 10–2; winter Tues–Sat 10–1.30 and 3–5, Sun 10–2; closed Mon; adm, adm free for EU nationals Wed; gardens open summer daily 10–8; winter daily 10–6*), 11km from town on the C601, is another work of Spain's first Bourbon King Philip V, he of an insatiable appetite for palaces. It has a certain Rococo elegance, but its fame is due to its **gardens**. French Philip originally conceived of La Granja as a scaled-down version of Versailles, where he had grown up, and the gardens completed the picture. There are 70 acres of them, with remarkable fountains everywhere (26 in all). There is only one day of the year when they all work, on 25 August, and it's worth watching them come alive.

Ten kilometres south in another direction, towards Madrid, is a closely related palace at **Riofrío** (*same hours as La Granja*). Here Isabella Farnese, Philip V's second wife, let her taste for things Italian run riot after his death. It's a very feminine building, with pink walls and wooded parkland, even though part of it is now a hunting museum.

Alcalá de Henares

Anyone from the Arab world would recognize the name's origin – *al-qalat*, a fortress – and it was the Moors who built this town, on the site of Roman *Complutum*. In the 12th century it was captured for Christianity, and in 1508 Cardinal Cisneros, Queen Isabella's foremost spiritual adviser, founded his 'Complutensian University' here, an institution that quickly rivalled Salamanca as the foremost centre of learning in Spain. For a brief, brilliant period it was one of the intellectual lights of Europe; its great achievement was the creation of the Complutensian Polyglot Bible, the first authoritative edition in modern Europe, with Latin, Greek, Hebrew and Aramaic originals in parallel columns. Then, in the 17th and 18th centuries the university fell into a long, sorry decline, and by 1837 half its buildings lay in ruins, at which point the remnants were moved to Madrid. In 1977, though, a university reopened in Alcalá, which in a few years has returned to the town and its old colleges a good deal of academic brio. Alcalá's centre is the **Plaza de Cervantes**, with flower stands at one end

Getting There

Alcalá is on the C2 and C7a *Cercanías* local train lines from Atocha, Chamartín and several other stations in Madrid (*see* p.132). There are at least five trains each hour, 5.10am–11.30pm daily. Alcalá station is about a 10min walk from the centre (walk down Paseo de la Estación). By **car**, just follow the NII/A2 Barcelona highway past the airport (31km).

Tourist Information

Alcalá de Henares: Callejón Santa María 1, just off Pza Cervantes, **t** 918 89 26 94.

Eating Out

Hostería del Estudiante, C/Colegios 3, **t** 918 88 03 30 (*expensive*). The highly regarded restaurant of Alcalá's *parador*, in an annexe of the Colegio Mayor: traditional, but pricey, Castilian cuisine. *Open Mon–Sat 1–4 and 9–11.30, Sun 1–4 and 9–10.*

La Cúpola, C/Santiago 18, **t** 918 80 73 91 (*moderate*). Inspired meals served in a 17th-century convent. Book at weekends. *Open daily 12–5 and 8–11.30.*

Mesón del Paso, C/Diego de Torres 2, **t** 918 78 76 95 (*inexpensive*). A local restaurant with a high-value lunchtime *menú*. *Open Mon–Sat 11am–midnight, Sun and hols 12–3.*

and gossipy cafés at the other. Touching its edge is the arcaded **Calle Mayor**, the lovely main street, which comes alive with yet more café tables on summer evenings.

University buildings are spread all over town, but the best is the **Colegio Mayor de San Ildefonso** on Plaza San Diego, with a wonderful Plateresque façade by Rodrigo Gil de Hontañón (who also worked on the cathedral of Segovia), adorned with the arms of Cisneros. Inside are the **Capilla Universitaria**, a Plateresque chapel, and the great hall or **Paraninfo** with a dazzling carved wooden ceiling. The building can only be fully visited with a guided tour, from the tourist office. Other noteworthy buildings are the **Colegio de la Palma** on C/de los Colegios and the **Casa de los Lizana**, with its brave stone lions, on C/Postigo. On C/Mayor is a small museum devoted to Alcalá's most famous son, Miguel de Cervantes: the **Museo Casa Natal de Cervantes** (*open Tues–Fri 10.15–2 and 4–6.25, Sat and Sun 10–1.30 and 4–6.25; closed Mon; adm*), a lovingly-kept reconstruction of the house in which the author was born, furnished to look like a 16th-century family dwelling, and with a display of rare editions of *Don Quixote*.

Aranjuez and Chinchón

There has been a royal residence in Aranjuez since the days of Philip II, but most of his palace, built by Bautista and Herrera, burned down in the 17th century. Philip V began the replacement **Real Palacio de Aranjuez** (*open summer Tues–Sun 10–6.15; winter Tues–Sun 10–5.15; closed Mon; adm exp, adm free for EU nationals Wed; gardens open summer Tues–Sun 8–8.30; winter Tues–Sun 8–6.30; closed Mon*) at the same time as he was building La Granja (*see* p.154), and in the same way, it's an attempt to emulate some of the grandeur of Versailles. Aranjuez is a natural location for a palace; the waters of the Río Tajo make it an oasis among the brown hills, and centuries of royal attention have given the area more trees than any other corner of Castile. Even today it is famous in Spain for its strawberries and asparagus.

As at La Granja, the biggest attractions are the lushly romantic **gardens** – which inspired Rodrigo's *Concierto de Aranjuez* – full of sculptural allegory and fountains, shady avenues and riverside walks. Visitors are guided through the **Palacio Real**,

Getting There

Cercanías line C3 **trains** from Atocha run to Aranjuez at least twice an hour, 5am–11.50pm, with a less frequent service at weekends. From the station, a local bus runs to the palace, but it's a pleasant walk: right out of the station, and left down the avenue. For **Chinchón**, La Veloz **buses** run direct from **M** Conde de Casal.

By car, follow the N-IV (Granada road) south out of Madrid (47km).

Tourist Information

Aranjuez: Plaza San Antonio 9, t 918 91 04 27.
Chinchón: Plaza Mayor, t 918 93 53 23.

Eating Out

La Mina, C/Príncipe 71, Aranjuez, t 918 91 11 46 (*expensive*). In an ancient palace: great fresh seafood as well as wood-fired roasts.

Casa José, C/Abastos 32, Aranjuez, t 918 91 14 88 (*expensive*). A welcome change from the usual fare: inventive, international cuisine.

La Rana Verde, C/Reina 1, Aranjuez, t 918 91 32 38 (*inexpensive*). On the riverfront: better to pay a little extra for one of the fish or game specialities than opt for the simple *menú*.

Mesón de la Virreina, Plaza Mayor 28, Chinchón, t 918 94 00 15 (*inexpensive*). One of the best on the plaza: good local specialities such as roast lamb, *sopa castellana* or *pisto manchego* (the local ratatouille).

packed full of chandeliers and mirrors, with porcelain, fancy clocks and court costume. Within the gardens is another charming small palace, the **Casa del Labrador**, and a **museum of boats**, royal pleasure craft used for cruising along the river.

About 20km northeast of Aranjuez is **Chinchón**, a little town of faded terracotta roofs and steep streets. After the noise of Madrid, it feels rustic in the extreme. Chinchón is celebrated for its *anís*, a powerful aniseed-flavoured liqueur. It's famous above all, though, for its amphitheatre-like **Plaza Mayor**, ringed by three-tier balconies, a classic image of Spain that has been a location for any number of movies.

Toledo

No city in Spain has seen more, or learned more, or stayed true to itself for so long through the shifting fortunes of history. Under the rule of Madrid for the last 400 years, its talents and achievements have dried up, and today this city is pretty much at the mercy of the tourists. It isn't Toledo's fault that it has become a museum city, but it carries out the role with considerable grace. No matter how you come to Toledo, you'll be glad when you finally arrive. The surrounding countryside is a desolate desert with a tinge of green, but Toledo has a beautiful setting on a plateau above the Río Tajo, and its plazas and narrow streets are like an oasis in brick and stone.

Toledo was a capital of sorts when the Romans found it, a centre for Celtiberian tribes called the Carpetani. Roman *Toletum* did not gain much distinction, but the Visigoths made it their capital in the 6th century, although they were not great builders. In 716, Toledo fell to the Moslem Moors, and under its new masters Toledo embarked on a career that would be the stuff of legends. Here the Christian, Islamic and Jewish worlds first met in a city renowned throughout the Mediterranean for learning. Toledo, conveniently close to a mercury mine at Almadén, became a centre for the study of alchemy, and schools of occult philosophy and mathematics proliferated. In 1085, though, following the collapse of Córdoba's caliphate, it was taken by the Christians of the north under Alfonso VI of Castile. For a long time Toledo under Castilian rule continued its role as a city of tolerance and scholarship, and its Moorish and Jewish populations easily accommodated new Christian settlers. By the 15th century and the accession of Ferdinand and Isabella, however, this atmosphere of coexistence was at an end. The expulsion of the Jews, and later the Moors, put an end to the city's long-established culture, and the establishment of the capital at Madrid put an end to its former political importance. By the 18th century, it had become a historic backwater, and even now, if you stay the night, you'll find that after museum hours the old town becomes surprisingly tranquil.

The centre of Toledo is the **Plaza de Zocodover**, a name that, like the *souk* of a Moroccan city, comes from the Arabic for market. Despite bearing the brunt of Toledo's role as a tourist destination, the triangular plaza endures as a place for residents to meet up and exchange gossip, and a market is still held here on Tuesdays. On the eastern edge of the triangle, the stately building with the clock is the seat of the provincial government. From the archway under the clock, stairs lead down to C/Cervantes and the fascinating museum within the 1544 **Hospital de Santa Cruz**

Getting There

There are at least 10 **trains** to Toledo from Atocha every weekday, about every two hours 7am–8.25pm (last return 8.56pm), with a more restricted service at weekends. The trip takes about an hour. Note that the charming neo-*mudéjar* station is over 1km from the old city down a steep hill; if you don't want to walk up it, take local bus 6 to the Puerta de Bisagra. The Galeano Continental company's **buses** provide a less attractive ride but leave you closer to the centre, at Toledo's bus station only a 5-min walk from the city walls. They leave from Estación Sur in Madrid about every half-hour, roughly 6.30am–10pm.

By **car**, take the N401 off the M30 (70km).

Tourist Information

Toledo: outside the Puerta de Bisagra (Bisagra Gate), **t** 925 22 08 43. Stop on your way up to avoid making the trip down again.

Where to Stay

Toledo ✉ 45000
★★★★**Parador Conde de Orgaz**, Cerro del Emperador, **t** 925 22 18 50, *www.parador.es* (*expensive*). South of town, the *parador* is inconvenient for sightseeing (no.7 bus runs

you to the centre), but the El Greco-esque view from the terrace is superb. It has a very fine **restaurant**; ideal for a picturesque drink.
★★★**Hs del Cardenal**, Paseo Recaredo 24, **t** 925 22 49 00, *www.cardenal.asernet.es* (*moderate*). Less expensive than others; just outside the city walls by Puerta de Bisagra, in an old palace with a terraced garden and **restaurant**; a tranquil haven.
★**P. Lumbreras**, C/Juan Labrador 9, **t** 925 22 15 71 (*inexpensive*). A very central old building, in the street beside Hotel Carlos V; rooms are around a tiled patio.

Eating Out

One of the prettiest places for a drink is the tiny square off C/Santo Tomé; **Cafetería Nano** sets tables out under the trees.

Asador Adolfo, Hombre de Palo 6 and De la Granala 6, **t** 925 22 73 21 (*expensive*). Considered Toledo's best restaurant and the place to go for truly flamboyant dining.

La Judería, C/San Juan de Dios 7, **t** 925 25 65 12 (*moderate*) In the Judería, and with a menu full of traditional Castilian cuisine.

Hierbabuena, C/Cristo de la Luz 9, **t** 925 22 34 63 (*moderate*). Light, imaginative cooking with a hint of vegetarian.

Maravilla, Pza de Barrio Rey 5, **t** 925 22 23 30 (*inexpensive*). Good, basic cooking: one of a clutch of budget options on C/Barrio Rey.

(*open Tues–Sat 10–2 and 4–6.30, Sun 10–2; closed Mon*). A little bit of everything is here: archaeological finds from *Toletum*, paintings and tapestries, Toledo swords and daggers, paintings by El Greco.

North from Plaza Zocodover is the Cuesta de Armas, the old road to Madrid. It descends past the **Mirador** to the **Puerta del Sol**, a pretty gatehouse from the 12th century. Further down, in the old quarter called the **Arrabal** because it was outside the Moorish walls, is the 11th-century **Santiago del Arrabal**, a joyous excess of pointed arches and brick towers. A detour to one side up typically steep, narrow C/Cristo de la Luz will take you to the **Mezquita del Cristo de la Luz**, a church that in reality is a mosque, built around 980 and incorporating elements of an earlier Visigothic church. One of the oldest surviving Moorish buildings in the country, it is an exceptional example of the craftsmanship of Moslem Spain. Further down the modern road curves around the **Puerta de Bisagra** (where you will probably have entered Toledo, from the train or bus stations), more like a palace than a gate, with pointed spires and courtyard. Outside the gate, the tourist office is on the edge of a park, the **Paseo de**

Merchán, on the other side of which is another 16th-century hospital made into a museum, the **Hospital de Tavera** (*open daily 10.30–1.30 and 3.30–6*). Cardinal Tavera was a member of the Mendoza family, a grandee of Spain. His art collection, including works by El Greco, shares space with objects and furnishings from the era.

A walk just south of the Zocodover, meanwhile, will take you to the **Alcázar**, Toledo's unmistakable fortress (*open Sun 10–2 and 4–6; adm*). Romans, Visigoths and Moors all had some sort of fortress on this spot, at the highest point of the city; the present big, square palace-fortress was constructed for Charles V, but rebuilt after destructions in the Napoleonic Wars and again in the Civil War. It's now a military museum; the defence of the Alcázar by Francoist forces against the Republicans in 1936 became a propaganda legend in Franco's Spain, and is still adoringly recounted in the exhibits.

The Cathedral

From another side of the Zocodover, C/Comercio winds off to the **cathedral** (*open daily 10.30–2 and 4–6.30; museum open Tues–Sat 10.30–1 and 3.30–6, Sun 10.30–1; closed Mon*).This isn't a building that can be approached directly; most of its bulk is hidden behind walls and old buildings, with corners peeking out where you least expect them. Circumnavigating the great building will take you all through the neighbourhood, until finally, arriving at the **Plaza Ayuntamiento**, you enjoy the final revelation of the west front. It's a little disappointing. Too many cooks have been at work, and the great rose windows are hidden behind superfluous arches. Turn your glance across the square instead, and you'll see one of Spain's most beautiful city halls, the 1618 **Ayuntamiento**, by El Greco's son, Jorge Theotocópoulos. Don't give up on the cathedral yet, though; few Gothic churches in Spain can match its **interior**, unusually light and airy, and with memorable artworks in every corner. Some 800 stained-glass windows dispel the gloom. Some of the best work is in the Old Testament scenes around the *coro*: its stalls are decorated with detailed scenes of the conquest of Granada, done just three years after the event. The **Capilla Mayor**, around the main altar, also has superb sculpture, but all eyes tend to turn here towards the *Transparente*. Even in a cathedral where so much is unusual, this takes the biscuit. In the 18th century, someone decided Mass here would seem even more transcendent if somehow a shaft of light could be directed over the altar. To do this holes were chopped in the wall of the Capilla Mayor; the difficult question of how to reconcile this intrusion was given to the sculptor Narciso Tomé and his four sons, and in several years' work they transformed the ungainly openings into a Baroque spectacular, a cloud of saints, angels and men that grow magically out of the cathedral's stones. In the southwest corner of the cathedral is a rare, living relic of medieval Toledo, the **Mozarabic Chapel**. The *Mozárabes* were Christians who lived in Moslem Spain, with their own liturgy. After the Christian conquest they clashed with many in the official Catholic church, who regarded them as tainted by Islam. Some Castilian kings and churchmen, however, protected the *Mozárabes*, and places were set aside for them to worship, as in this chapel. Mozárabic rituals are still celebrated here, but it's often kept locked. Other sections of the cathedral open by separate admission include the **Sacristy**, with frescoes and an altarpiece by El Greco, and a *Holy Family* by Van Dyck.

West of the Cathedral: El Greco and the Judería

Here the streets become even narrower and more winding. Just three intractable blocks northwest of the cathedral, the 13th-century church of San Román has been converted into the **Museo de los Concilios y de la Cultura Visigótica** (*open Tues–Sat 10–2 and 4–6.30, Sun 10–2; closed Mon; adm*), the only one of its kind in Spain. 'Councils' refers to the several General Councils of the Western Church that were held in Toledo in the days of Visigothic rule, but the majority of the exhibits are Visigothic relics, jewellery and religious artworks. Some show an idiosyncratic talent, but much is unimpressive. The building itself is more interesting, half-Christian and half-Moorish, with naïve frescoes of the Last Judgement and the 12 Apostles in a garden, and painted angels and saints peering out from the ceilings and horseshoe arches. A small **Museo de Arte Contemporánea** (*open Tues–Sat 10–2 and 4–6.30, Sun 10–2; closed Mon; adm*) is two blocks west of here.

As long as the streets continue to slope downwards from there, you'll know you're going in the right direction for the **Judería**, Toledo's Jewish quarter before 1492, a narrow strip of land overlooking the Tajo in the southwestern corner of the city. El Greco too lived here, and the back streets of the Judería have some of old Toledo's most intriguing and interesting monuments. The church of **Santo Tomé**, on the street of the same name, is unremarkable in itself, but in a little chamber to the side is El Greco's *El Entierro del Conde de Orgaz* (The Burial of the Count of Orgaz), Toledo's most visited relic of all. More nonsense has been written about this work, perhaps, than any other Spanish painting. A miracle was recorded at this obscure count's burial in 1323: Saints Stephen and Augustine came down from heaven to assist with the obsequies, and this is the scene El Greco portrays. A group of the Count's friends and descendants had petitioned Rome for his beatification, and it was perhaps in support of this that El Greco received the commission, over 200 years later. The portrayal of the burial has for a background a row of gravely serious men, each one a portrait in itself; above, the earthly scene is paralleled by the Count's reception into heaven. This painting is perhaps the ultimate expression of the intense and slightly twisted spirituality of 16th-century Castile. Its heaven, packed with grim, staring faces, seems more of an inferno, and nowhere is there any sense of joy or release. The longer you look at it, the more disturbing it becomes.

The **Casa-Museo de El Greco** (*open Tues–Sat 10–2 and 4–6, Sun 10–2; closed Mon; adm*), not far away, is where the painter lodged for most of the years he lived in Toledo. Domenico Theotocópoulos, a Cretan who had studied art in Venice, came to Spain hoping to find work in the building of El Escorial. Philip II didn't care for him, but 'the Greek' found Spanish life and religion amenable, and spent the rest of his life in Toledo. The city itself, seen from across the Tajo, was a favourite subject (his most famous *View of Toledo* is now in the Metropolitan Museum of Art, New York). The best parts of the restored house are the courtyard and tiled kitchen; only a few of his paintings here are of merit – notably a portrait of St Peter, another frequent subject.

The **Taller del Moro** or Moor's Workshop (*open Tues–Sat 10–2 and 4–6.30, Sun 10–2; closed Mon; adm*), just around the corner from Santo Tomé church, owes its name to the days when it was a workshop for the cathedral craftsmen. The building itself is an interesting work of *mudéjar* architecture; inside is a collection of the sort of things the craftsmen made. Next door is the restored 15th-century **Palacio de Fuensalida** (*visits possible in small private groups; contact the custodian at the palace*), now used by the head of the Castilla-La Mancha regional government.

Not surprisingly, in a city where Jews played such a prominent and constructive role for so long, two of Toledo's best buildings are synagogues, saved only by good luck after centuries of neglect. The 12th-century **Sinagoga de Santa María la Blanca** (*open Sat–Thurs 10–2 and 3.30–6, Fri 10–2 and 3.30–7*), so called from its days as a church, is stunning and small, a glistening white confection of horseshoe arches, elaborately carved capitals and geometric medallions rightly considered a masterpiece of *mudéjar* (Hispano-Moorish) architecture. Just as good, though in an entirely different style, is the **Sinagoga del Tránsito** (*open Tues–Sat 10–1.45 and 4–5.45, Sun 10–1.45; closed Mon*), built by Samuel Leví, treasurer to King Pedro I (the Cruel) before that whimsical monarch had him executed. It is much later than Santa María la Blanca, and shows the influence of the Granada Moors: the interior could be a room in the Alhambra, with its ornate ceiling and carved arabesques, except that the calligraphic inscriptions are in Hebrew instead of Arabic, and the Star of David is interspersed with the arms of Castile and León. It now houses the **Museo Sefardí** (Sephardic Museum), an enormously impressive museum of Jewish life in Spain.

Nearby is a building that meant a great deal to the Spanish Jews' greatest persecutors Ferdinand and Isabella, the **Monasterio de San Juan de los Reyes** (*open daily 10–2 and 3.30–7; adm*). The 'Catholic Kings' built a church here before the conquest of Granada, with the intention of making it their last resting place. The architect was Juan Guas, who worked the perpendicular elegance of Isabelline Gothic perfectly in every detail. The exterior of the church is famous, its western wall covered with the chains of prisoners released from the Moors in the Granada campaigns. The **cloister**, surrounding a peaceful courtyard where a lone orange tree keeps meditative company with a solitary pine, is another of Toledo's architectural treasures, with elegant windows and vaultings. A merry band of restorers was let loose on this building in the 1880s, and if you go to the second floor and gaze up from the arches you will see the hilarious collection of gargoyles they added: all manner of monsters, and a frog riding a fish; see if you can find the cat.

The **Plaza de San Juan de los Reyes Católicos**, in front of the church, has a wide prospect over the valley of the Tajo; from here you can see another of Toledo's fancy 16th-century gateways, the **Puerta del Cambrón**, and the fortified, medieval **Puente de San Martín**. The **Carretera Circunvalación**, on the other side of the Tajo, will give you more views of Toledo than El Greco ever did. On its way it passes a goodly number of country houses called *cigarrales*, the *parador*, and the 14th-century **Castillo de San Servando**, rebuilt from an older Templar foundation. Beneath the castle, the old **Puente de Alcántara**, even better than the Puente de San Martín, will take you back across the Tajo in the neighbourhood of Plaza de Zocodover. There's a fine walk beside the walls between the puertas of Bisagra and Cambrón, along the **Paseo de Recaredo**, and for a bankside stroll around Toledo, make for the water by **El Baño de la Cava**, just west of San Juan de los Reyes.

Touring from Madrid 1:
North: The Sierras and Old Castile

Day 1: Mountain Greenery: the Sierra de Gredos

Morning: First, get out of Madrid: get on to the M30 ring road, work out roughly
where you are, and make your way round to the N-V, the Carretera de Extremadura.
After 12km, exit right on the M501 (signed Villaviciosa de Odón) for the **Gredos**, most
beautiful of the mountain *sierras* around Madrid. Traffic thins, and after 55km, at
San Martín de Valdeiglesias, you turn right up the N403. A detour left leads to the
Toros de Guisandó, mysterious giant stone bulls, of pre-Roman, Iberian origin.
Around **El Tiemblo** there are delicious pine woods, and a lovely reservoir, **El Burguillo**.
Head back to El Tiemblo for lunch or go on to **Burgohondo** (via a left turn, AV902).

Lunch: In El Tiemblo or Burgohondo, *see* below.

Afternoon: Continue west to **Navarredonda**, check in wherever you're staying, and
then drive 2km further west and turn left directly into the *sierra*. From the end of
this road (13km) there are superb walks up to the **Circo de Gredos**, a stupendous ring
of peaks around an exquisite lake, the **Laguna Grande**. The full walk there and back
takes about five hours, but you can try part of it (watch the mountain weather,
though, which can change very fast). After that, you'll need a rest and a good dinner.

Dinner and Sleeping: In Navarredonda de Gredos, *see* below.

Day 1

Lunch in El Tiemblo or Burgohondo
Alternatively, take water and make up some
sandwiches to have on the way, especially if
you aim to try any walks.

La Bodega, C/Mártires 10, El Tiemblo, t 920 62
53 85, (*inexpensive*). A simple village bar-
restaurant with a generous *menú del día* of
local classics: lots of beans and steaks.

Hostal Mirasierra, Carretera de Avila,
Burgohondo, t 920 28 30 67 (*inexpensive*).
Burgohondo's village eating-spot, with
another very generous menú, or simple
tapas and satisfying *bocadillos*.

Dinner in the Sierra de Gredos
Venta Rasquilla, N-502 near junction with the
C-500, t 920 34 82 21 (*inexpensive*). A very
traditional, family-run roadside inn at one of
the Gredos' historic crossroads. Don't expect
much variety in the cooking, but Avila's celebrated steaks are at their best here, at very
low prices. It also has **rooms** (*inexpensive*).

Hostal Alburquerque, Plaza de la Soledad 2,
Mombeltrán, t 920 38 60 32 (*inexpensive*). A
little hostal on the southern side of the
sierra with pleasant **rooms** and a **restaurant**
serving good, simple meals, of more hearty,
meaty mountain cooking.

Sleeping in Navarredonda
★★★El Parador de Gredos, Ctra Barraco-Béjar,
3.2km from Navarredonda de Gredos, t 920
34 80 48, (*expensive–moderate*). Spain's first
ever *parador*: it occupies an old stone
hunting lodge once used by King Alfonso XIII
set in a beautiful pine forest on the north
edge of the mountains, not far from
Almanzor, the range's highest peak at
8,502ft. It's not as plush as some *paradores*,
but rates are lower, and it has a charming,
country-house feel, as well as a good **restaurant**. Excellent as a base for walking.

★Hostal El Refugio de Gredos, C/Pajizo, Barajas
de Gredos, t 920 34 80 47 (*inexpensive*). This
makes a fine, simple retreat, in a tiny hamlet
just west of the *parador*.

Day 2: Saints, Ancient Walls and Red Meat: Avila

Morning: Retrace your way east from Navarredonda and at the N502 turn north for the 55km to **Avila**. Slow up as you approach to appreciate its extraordinary feature: its walls. This is the most intact walled city in Spain, with an old town still ringed by 12th-century fortifications with 88 towers. From the west, you get the best view. Find a way in through one of the nine gates, and leave the car. Wander through the tangled streets of the old town: you can climb the walls at Puerta del Alcázar, south of the cathedral, and Puerta San Vicente, to the north (*open Tues–Sun 10–6; closed Mon; adm*). Stroll back to Plaza de la Victoria, centre of the old town, for a drink and *tapas* at a café (light lunch is advisable, to keep the big deal for the evening).

Lunch: In Avila, *see* below.

Afternoon: As well as for its walls, Avila is known above all for St Teresa of Avila, and has even more churches and convents than most old Castilian towns. Pay your respects to the saint at the Convento de Santa Teresa, on the spot where she was born (*open daily 9.30–1.30 and 3.30–7.30*). The severe cathedral is half-church and half-fortress (*open summer daily 10.30–1 and 3.30–6; winter daily 3–5*). Having soaked up the atmosphere, you're ready for the local fare. If Segovia is known for pork and lamb, Avila is famed for beef, from Iberian black cattle (the same breed as fighting bulls). Most restaurants here offer steak and more steak: for vegetarians it's hell, but for meat-eaters it's heaven. Just don't expect anything fashionably light.

Dinner and Sleeping: In Avila, *see* below.

Day 2

Lunch in Avila

Bodeguita de San Segundo, C/San Segundo 19, t 920 21 42 47. An excellent, if pricey, place for a midday tipple, accompanied by a delicious variety of *tapas*.

Doña Guiomar, C/Tomás Luis de Victoria 3, t 920 25 37 09 (*moderate*). Inventive cooking and friendly service.

Dinner in Avila

El Almacén, Ctra de Salamanca 6, t 920 25 44 55 (*expensive*). Outside the walls on the river: its menus feature regional favourites and cleverly conceived variations on traditional themes.

La Casona, Plaza Pedro Dávila 6, t 920 25 61 39 (*inexpensive*). Small, with the perfect *patrón* and huge portions.

Mesón del Rastro, Plaza del Rastro 1, t 920 21 12 18 (*inexpensive*). Classic Castilian: veal, pickled trout, roast lamb and *judias de Barco* (bean casserole with *chorizo*).

Sleeping in Avila

★★★★**Parador Raimundo de Borgoña**, C/Marqués Canales de Chozas 2, t 920 21 13 40 (*expensive*). Avila has an exceptional choice of hotels, set in historic buildings: this is the *crème de la crème* of *paradores*, in a stupendously converted Renaissance palace, with an excellent **restaurant** and beautifully decorated with antiques. A delight.

★★★★**Hotel Palacio de los Velada**, Plaza de la Catedral 10, t 920 25 51 00 (*expensive*). A very classy, pricey palace by the cathedral, with blue rooms and huge bathrooms.

★★★**Hostería Bracamonte**, C/Bracamonte 6, t 920 25 12 80, (*moderate*). In a palatial building steeped in history, with a spectacular interior full of 18th-century tapestries; an excellent choice and good value.

★★**Hs El Rastro**, Pza del Rastro 1, t 920 21 12 18, (*inexpensive*). The best budget choice: in the shadow of the walls, with plain-looking rooms, a garden and a popular **restaurant**, the 'Mesón del Rastro' (*see* left). Book in advance, especially in July and Aug.

Day 3: The Gleaming Spires of Salamanca

Morning: Head northwest on the N501 road through typically empty, brown Castilian countryside to **Salamanca** (97km). It is as historic as Avila, but, as the home of Spain's oldest university, founded 1218, has a more sophisticated style. Approaching from the southeast, you first cross the **River Tormes**, passing (but not using) a 1st-century AD **Roman Bridge**. Again, inside the old city leave the car and walk. A natural place to start is the magnificent 1729–55 Plaza Mayor, finest work of the Churriguera brothers, the master architects of Spanish Baroque. This giant square and its delightful arcades (with plenty of fine cafés) have been a natural meeting place ever since they were built, with a constant movement of people.

Lunch: In Salamanca, *see* below.

Afternoon: After lunch try some more concentrated sightseeing, although this city has more historic sights than can fit into one day. Head south from the plaza down Rúa Mayor to the unique 'dual cathedral', with a 16th-century Gothic Catedral Nueva and 12th-century Catedral Vieja alongside each other (*New open daily 9–2 and 4–8; Old open daily 10–1.30 and 4–7.30; adm*). Nearby is the main entrance to the University, the Patio de las Escuelas, with its hugely ornate Renaissance façade, and another must-see is just west, the Convento de las Dueñas (*open daily 10.30–1 and 4.30–7; adm*) with a superb 16th-century cloister. By then it may be time to join in another of studenty Salamanca's sights, its notably lively bar life.

Dinner and Sleeping: In Salamanca, *see* below.

Day 3

Lunch in Salamanca

La Montaraza, C/José Jáuregui 9, **t** 923 26 00 21 (*moderate*). A traditional Salamanca favourite that serves up a heaving board of *tapas*, or well-priced full meals with oven-baked soup, cod, and crumbly Castilian cakes. *Closed Mon and Aug.*

Roma, C/Ventura Ruiz Aguilera 10, near Plaza Mayor, **t** 923 21 72 67 (*inexpensive*). Thanks to the student population, you can easily eat for less in spots like this with meals around the €6 mark; there are many others like it.

Dinner in Salamanca

Chez Victor, C/Espoz y Mina 26, **t** 923 21 31 23 (*expensive*). Just off Plaza Mayor, this is one of Spain's best French restaurants, with imaginative, creative cuisine, especially duck and game dishes. Top it all off with the 20-year-old port. *Closed Mon, Sun eve, and Aug.*

Rio de la Plata, Plaza Peso 1, **t** 923 21 90 05 (*inexpensive*). Arrive early if you want a table at this great-value, buzzy little restaurant with excellent *turbot a la plancha*. *Closed Mon and July.*

Sleeping in Salamanca

****Parador de Salamanca, C/Teso de la Feria 2, **t** 923 26 87 00 (*expensive*). Just across the Roman bridge, and with a fine view of the city's enchanting skyline. One of Spain's newest *paradores*, it has a very enjoyable pool and garden.

****Palacio de Castellanos, C/San Pablo 58, **t** 923 26 18 18 (*expensive*). In the centre, in a late 15th-century palace, with a lovely patio and plush, modern and pricey rooms.

Hotel Amefa, C/Pozo Amarillo 18–20, **t 923 21 81 89 (*moderate*). A luxurious charmer well-placed in the centre of town, but with rooms still at mid-range rates.

*Hs Tormes, Rúa Mayor 20, **t/f** 923 21 96 83 (*inexpensive*). Stands out with its great location, between Plaza Mayor and University; rooms are clean and pleasant, and you can eat cheaply in its small **restaurant**.

Day 4: Through Brown Castile to Segovia

Morning: Take your time the next morning, and maybe visit some of Salamanca's sights you couldn't fit in the previous day (next in line might be the Casa de las Conchas, a Renaissance mansion with a façade covered in shells that now houses the tourist office, or the Torre Clavero, a belligerent 15th-century tower built as part of a private fortified palace). Then, head up the N620 Valladolid road, but after 37km turn off right onto the C605. This will immerse you in the classic *meseta* landscape of Old Castile, of empty plains beneath giant skies, vivid with flowers after rain but leather-brown in high summer. In the middle of this vast meditative space, after about 65km you will reach **Arévalo**, a walled village that seems scarcely changed since around 1650. Another reason to stop at this remote spot is that it has a renowned restaurant, for classic Castilian country cuisine.

Lunch: In Arévalo, *see* below.

Afternoon: From Arévalo, to keep the rural mood, avoid the main highways that pass a little to the east, and stay on the C605 southeast to **Segovia** (50km). This will also bring you into town along the Eresma river valley, so that you first have an unusual, spectacular view of the bizarre Alcázar, and then circle the walls of old Segovia to come up below the Aqueduct. As usual, deposit the car, before you climb up past this Roman monument into the old town to sample its special atmosphere and see some of the many monuments within a short walk of the Plaza Mayor (*see* p.152).

Dinner and Sleeping: In Segovia, *see* below and p.152.

Day 4

Lunch in Arévalo

Asador Las Cubas, C/Figones 9, Arévalo, **t** 920 30 01 25 (*moderate*). Arévalo may seem like a lost and remote spot but it's something of a place of pilgrimage for lovers of true Castilian cooking for this little restaurant, in an old wine cellar. Roast meats (of course) are the highlight, plus eggy desserts, and the atmosphere has a real country feel.

Dinner in Segovia

Mesón de Cándido Plaza Azoguejo 5, **t** 921 45 59 11 (*expensive*). This has headed the list for 50 years or so, and is situated beside the aqueduct and has a very picturesque exterior (as shown on most of Segovia's tourist brochures). The late Señor Cándido wrote cookbooks on Castilian cuisine – and played host to all the famous folk who ever passed through Segovia (autographed photos on the walls, of course, to prove it). *Open daily 1–5 and 8–11.30.*

Mesón del Duque, C/Cervantes 12, **t** 921 43 05 37 (*expensive*). Consistently one of the best Segovia *mesones*, with delicious traditional roasts prepared with some subtle touches too. To help it all go down, everyone gets a free shot of brandy.

La Oficina, C/Cronista Lecea 10, **t** 921 46 08 04/**t** 921 46 02 83 (*moderate*). Yes, more roast meats, but excellent value and cheaper than some of the grander (kitschier) places.

Sleeping in Segovia

★★★★**Parador Nacional**, Ctra de Valladolid, **t** 921 44 37 37 (*expensive*). 2km out of town and only convenient if you have a car: in a plain modern building, but with fine views of the town, a pool and one of the best **restaurants** of any *parador*.

★★★**Infanta Isabel**, C/Isabel la Católica 1, **t** 921 46 13 00 (*expensive*). Small, elegant, and overlooking Pza Mayor.

★**Hs Plaza**, C/Cronista Lecea 11, **t** 921 46 03 03, (*inexpensive*). Small, clean and enjoyable, and close to Plaza Mayor.

Day 5: Back to Madrid across the Guadarrama

Morning: Head southeast from Segovia on the C601. After 11km call in at Philip V's French palace of **La Granja**, an elegant monument in the rugged mountain land-scape, especially if it's one of the days when the fountains are in operation (*see* p.154; tourist offices have schedules). Beyond La Granja, the road climbs ever more steeply up to the **Puerto de Navacerrada**, at 1,800 metres (6,100 ft), one of the most famous passes across the **Sierra de Guadarrama**, the massive screen of mountains that separates Madrid from Old Castile. In winter, it's a skiing centre, but at other times it's a favourite for walking, with magnificent views; from the top of the pass you can try at least a little of the *Siete Picos*, a well-marked walk west. At the pass or a little below in **Navacerrada** village there are also several places to eat with a view.
Lunch: In Navacerrada, *see* below.

Afternoon: After lunch, you have a choice in exploring what is also known as the *Sierra de Madrid*. A turn north up the minor road from Navacerrada pass will take you into the **Valle de Lozoya**, a superb bowl in the mountains with the village of **Rascafría** and monastery-hotel of El Paular, a base for fairly hard walking. Or, a turn west from Navacerrada village leads to **Cercedilla**, a charming mountain village (also reached by train from Madrid, *Cercanías* C-8b), with plenty of easy walks, such as the one along the *Calzada Romana*, the old Roman path across the sierra. A very helpful information centre has maps. Otherwise, it's a short drive back to Madrid.
Dinner and Sleeping: In Cercedilla or Rascafría, *see* below.

Day 5

Lunch at Navacerrada
Asador Felipe, C/Mayo 3, t 918 56 10 41 (*inexpensive*). In the village, with a terrace and the area's best beef, lamb and suckling pig.
Restaurante Felipe, Av Madrid 2, t 918 56 06 36 (*inexpensive*). Across the road: excellent fish; wild mushrooms in autumn and winter.
La Fonda Real, Ctra Madrid–Segovia Km 53.5, t 918 56 03 05 (*inexpensive*). A restored 18th-century hunting lodge near the pass now offering traditional Castilian cooking: look uphill towards the Puerto de Navacerrada and you'll see fabulous views.

Dinner in the Sierra de Guadarrama
Briscas, Plaza España 13, Rascafría, t 918 69 12 26 (*inexpensive*). Very friendly, bargain restaurant on Rascafría's main square, with a very warming atmosphere if you arrive after a healthy walk.
El Chivo Loco, C/Pontezuela 23, Cercedilla, t 918 52 34 39 (*moderate*). A bar-restaurant that offer both great *tapas* and more substantial Castilian favourites, including suckling pig or roast lamb.

Sleeping in the Sierra de Guadarrama
★★★★Santa María de El Paular, C/El Paular, t 918 69 10 11 (*luxury–expensive*). An upscale option, but with a touch of austerity, this is in the converted wing of an ancient Benedictine monastery, replete with fitness centre and pool. The severe building still has something of a monastic feel, but it all adds to the tranquillity.
★★★★Arcipreste de Hita, Ctra M-601, Km 12, t 918 56 01 25, (*moderate*).On the main Navacerrada road, this hotel has excellent facilities, including a sports and fitness centre and a pool.
★★Hostal Longinos, C/Emilio Serrano 71, Cercedilla, t 918 52 15 11 (*inexpensive*). Cercedilla's main hotel: this very popular little place has snug, comfortable rooms, as well as a likeable bar. Be sure to book, above all for summer weekends.

Touring from Madrid 2:
South: Toledo and La Mancha

Day 1: Flowers and Anís in Aranjuez and Chinchón

Morning: Exit Madrid (as with route 1, first get to the M30, then find the N-IV road south, the Carretera de Andalucía. After about 15km you leave Madrid's sprawl behind and things get calmer. You enter **Aranjuez**'s oasis-like pocket in the Tajo (Tagus) valley beside riverside gardens. Get to the Palacio Real (*see* p.155) and check when guided tours are leaving; if you can, join one round the Casita del Labrador, Charles IV's indulgent folly of a summer house, with whole walls clad in porcelain. The great glory of Aranjuez, though, is a walk around the delicious gardens. It's often fiercely hot here, but in these gardens there are always wonderfully cool, shady places, with hypnotic changes of light and shade.

Lunch: In Aranjuez, *see* below and p.155.

Afternoon: If it's hot, especially, a long lunch is in order. Afterwards, head up the 20km to **Chinchón** for instant contrast: in place of the daintiness of Bourbon Aranjuez, this is a real piece of old-world Castile. Wander round its extraordinary Plaza Mayor and the tight, narrow streets, and try some strong *anís*, the town's fiery aniseed liqueur. It should put you in a mellow mood for a rich Castilian meal.

Dinner and Sleeping: In Chinchón, *see* below and p.155.

Day 1

Lunch in Aranjuez

Casa José, C/Abastos 32 (*expensive*). One of the most enjoyable places to sample Aranjuez's specialities - like the famous strawberries – beautifully and imaginatively prepared.

La Rana Verde, C/Reina 1, **t** 918 91 32 38 (*inexpensive*). A very pleasant place to eat by the river, with fish or game specialities as well as a rather plain *menú*.

Dinner in Chinchón

Mesón Cuevas del Vino, C/Benito Hortelano 13, **t** 918 94 02 85 (*moderate*). A well-known and liked *mesón*, built in centuries-old caves, signposted up the hill from Plaza Mayor.

Restaurante La Columna, Plaza Mayor, **t** 918 94 05 02 (*inexpensive*). No views over the square, but an extremely pretty galleried patio inside; worth visiting for its great, reasonably priced, *menú del día*.

Bar Los Huertos, C/Generalísimo 3 (*inexpensive*). A bar with a big courtyard with a fountain and spreading fig tree – the perfect place for a glass of *anís*.

Sleeping in Chinchón

****Parador de Chinchón**, Av Generalísimo 1, **t** 918 94 08 36, *chinchon@parador.es* (*expensive*). Exceptional *parador*, with a sense of cool serenity pervading every nook of the stunning 17th-century monastery; its lovely box-scented garden is filled with roses and fruit trees. Pretty rooms too, with simple tiled floors and painted bedsteads.

Hs La Cerca, C/Cerca 9, **t** 918 94 13 00, *www.hotel-lacerca.com* (*moderate*). Uphill from Plaza Mayor, on the way to the town's swimming pool: it's quite plain, but always neat and clean.

Hs Chinchón, C/José Antonio 12, **t** 918 93 53 98 (*inexpensive*). As close to the Plaza Mayor as you can get: welcoming and spotless; all rooms have TV and a/c, and room 1 has a spectacular view over the square and the hillsides beyond. Plus, it also offers a baby rooftop pool, bar and **restaurant**.

Day 2: Three Cultures: Toledo

Morning: Return the way you came through Aranjuez and take the N400 road for **Toledo** (65km). All access roads to this legendary city tend to bring you to the same entry point into the old town, the Puerta de Bisagra on the north side, and, once again, a car is spectacularly useless inside the old town, so drop it off somewhere (at your hotel, or there are big car parks around the walls). Walk up through the Bisagra gate and a second, inner wall gate, the Puerta del Sol, and follow the winding street up to Plaza de Zocodover, hub of the city, stopping to look at the very ancient mosque of Cristo de la Luz. Stop in the Zocodover to get your bearings, and try to take in some of the cathedral before lunch (for all Toledo sights, *see* pp.156–60).

Lunch: In Toledo, *see* below and pp.156–60.

Afternoon: Toledo has a great many sights, so few people manage to fit many of them into one day: the old town's cobweb of narrow alleys is a sight in itself, and everybody first has a fun time trying to find their way around at first. As well as the giant monuments, it's good to experience the town's quiet corners, like the **Judería**. Don't miss the Museo Sephardí in the Sinagoga del Tránsito, a fascinating display that opens up the era when Toledo was the 'city of three cultures' – Christian, Islamic and Jewish. Head back to the Zocodover around 6pm, after the tours head back to Madrid, to experience the sudden blast of extra tranquility. And then take a walk around the outside of the walls or across the river, for golden sunset views.

Dinner and Sleeping: In Toledo, *see* below and p.156.

Day 2

Lunch in Toledo

El Ábside, C/Marqués de Mendigorria 1, **t** 925 21 32 02 (*expensive*). A fine combination of a modern-ish style and Castilian standards such as venison and roast suckling pig.

La Abadía, C/Nuñez de Arce 3, **t** 925 25 11 40 (*inexpensive*). Hectic but charming.

Dinner in Toledo

La Lumbre, C/Real del Arrabal 3, **t** 925 22 03 73 (*expensive*). Local cooking shares the menu with French-inspired dishes; and there's plenty for vegetarians: onion tart, leek pie and mushroom-stuffed artichokes.

Hs del Cardenal, Pso Recaredo 24, **t** 925 22 08 62 (*moderate*). An excellent hotel-restaurant: Toledan stuffed partridge is a speciality, well hung and gamey – the way *Toledanos* like it.

Venta de Aires, Paseo Circo Romano 35, **t** 925 22 05 45 (*moderate*). Comfortable restaurant that also serves traditional Toledano fare.

Sleeping in Toledo

****Hotel Doménico, Cerro del Emperador, **t** 925 20 01 01 (*expensive*). Like the *Parador* (*see* p.157) this hotel overlooks the old city from a certain distance and is artistically decorated and surrounded by olive groves and gardens.

***Carlos V, C/Trastamara 1, Plaza Horna Magdalena, **t** 925 22 21 00, *www.carlosV.com* (*expensive*). This hotel has more good views (particularly from the roof terrace bar, and some rooms); it's elegant and correct, tucked away on a quiet street in the old city near the Alcázar and Plaza Zocodover – and correspondingly pricey.

P. Santa Úrsula, C/Santa Úrsula 14, **t 925 21 33 25 (*inexpensive*). Just downhill from Pza El Salvador, this small budget hotel is relatively new, good value and very friendly.

Hs Nuevo Labrador, C/Labrador 10, **t 925 22 26 20 (*inexpensive*). Not the most beautiful of places, but its rooms are spacious and comfortable, and have all the essential services, and there's usually a vacancy.

Day 3: La Mancha: Ciudad Real and Almagro

Morning: Leave Toledo going south on the N401, and carry on, and on: the yellow-brown, rolling hills and crags of New Castile have the power to hypnotize anyone. **La Mancha**, just to the south, is one of the most famous parts of Spain thanks to *Don Quijote*, but remains an 'empty quarter' of the country, with very little population around its ruined 11th-century castles – which gives it an other-worldly fascination. About 120km south of Toledo is **Ciudad Real**, La Mancha's main town, which is still sleepy (despite being on the AVE Madrid–Seville train route) but is also an atmospheric little city to walk around, with old squares and a fine medieval gateway, as well as a kitschily ornate 19th-century casino or gentlemen's club.

Lunch: In Ciudad Real, *see* below.

Afternoon: A minor road leads 24km east to **Almagro**, another Castilian town that was very wealthy in the 16th century, but later seems to have come to a dead stop. Hence, it has retained a lovely, colonnaded stone Plaza Mayor, several old monasteries and its greatest treasure, the Corral de las Comedias theatre. This is rather like Shakespeare's Globe, except that it's no reconstruction, but an original, entirely intact 17th-century theatre. Spanish Golden Age theatres were quite like English ones of Shakespeare's day, with an open 'pit' and boxes round the outside, but square, not round; the *Corral* is now used for a theatre festival of suitably classic theatre each summer. Almagro is also a lovely place to stay, with delightful hotels.

Dinner and Sleeping: In Almagro, *see* below.

Day 3

Lunch in Ciudad Real

For good *tapas* bars try around Pza Mayor (especially **Mesón el Ventero**, Plaza Mayor 9), Plaza del Pilar (including the longstanding **Casa Lucio**, C/Dulcinea del Toboso, off C/Montesa), C/Palma and around Av Torreón.

El Real, C/Tinte 3, t 926 22 85 45 (*moderate*). Very comfortable restaurant in a hotel (the Santa Cecilia) with a good Manchegan classics like partridge.

Miami Park, Ronda de Ciruela 34, t 926 22 20 43 (*moderate*). Oddly-named but quite likeable, modern-looking restaurant, with all the necessary *tapas* and a *menú*. *Closed Sun eve.*

Dinner in Almagro

Mesón El Corregidor, Plaza Fray Fernando Fernández de Córdoba 2, t 926 86 06 48 (*moderate*). Almagro's best restaurant, in an old house in the centre. *Closed Mon.*

Abrasador, C/San Agustín 18, t 926 88 26 56 (*inexpensive*). A new restaurant set next to the Teatro Municipal, using home-grown produce to offer typical Manchegan dishes, especially hams.

Airen, Plaza Mayor 41, t 926 88 26 56 (*inexpensive*). A pleasant place on the plaza to *tapa*, or make a meal of it with *raciones*, the tasty pizzas (try the *pisto* topping) or the *menú*.

Sleeping in Almagro

★★★★**Parador de Almagro**, Convento de San Francisco, Ronda de San Francisco 31, t 926 86 01 00 (*expensive*). Set in a restored 16th-century convent in the centre, this is one of the loveliest (and best value) *paradores*.

La Posada de Almagro, C/Gran Maestre 5, t/f 926 26 12 01, www.laposadaalmagro.com (*moderate*). A recently and tastefully converted 16th-century inn, with simple, attractive rooms arranged around a lovely inner courtyard. The **restaurant**, lined with enormous vats, has an (*inexpensive*) *menú*.

★★**Hospedería de Almagro**, Convento de la Asunción, Ejido de Calatrava, t 926 88 20 87, f 926 88 21 22 (*cheap*). Simple, clean rooms in a wing of a monastery, with a shady patio.

Day 4: Don Quijote-land to Cuenca

Morning: The vast stretch of little towns and villages northeast of Almagro is the actual home of *Don Quijote*, and many scenes and places associated with the Don are easily visible, if you don't mind wandering about the countryside a little. From Almagro, follow the road north to **Daimiel**, and get on the N420 north to **Puerto Lápice**, a lovely little village with a fantastic old, very Cervantes-esque inn (see below). It may be too early for more than a few *tapas*, so carry on east along the road, past Alcázar de San Juan to **Campo de Criptana**, site of La Mancha's largest remaining set (10, in a row) of 16th-century windmills. A turn left off the main road just beyond there will lead in an empty 15km to **El Toboso**, named in *Quijote* as the home of his romantic idol the peerless Dulcinea, and so now with a clutch of small museums (*open Tues–Sun 10–2 and 4–6; closed Mon; adm*).

Lunch: In one of the La Mancha villages, *see* below.

Afternoon: By now time may be running on, so from El Toboso cut back to the N301 road and then rejoin the N420 road for the 150km to **Cuenca**, one of Spain's most spectacular small cities. Arriving from the south you see why: it's built above a gorge of the River Huécar, and its famous *Casas Colgadas* ('Hanging Houses') stand right along the rim, by a sheer drop. All are carefully preserved and several are put to cultural uses, one being the Museo de Arte Abstracto Español (*open Tues-Fri 11–2 and 4–6, Sat 11–2 and 4–8, Sun 11–2.30, closed Mon; adm*), with very 20th-century art.

Dinner and Sleeping: In Cuenca, *see* below.

Day 4

Lunch in La Mancha

Venta del Quijote, C/Molino 4, Puerto Lapice, t 926 57 61 10 (*moderate*). The Venta is set in an 18th-century inn in the centre of Puerto Lapice and serves splendid food. It has the most authentic atmosphere you'll find – give or take a century or two.

Dulcinea, C/Clavileño 1, El Toboso, t 925 19 73 11 (*inexpensive*). A fine choice of local dishes.

Dinner in Cuenca

Mesón Casas Colgadas, C/Canónigos, t 969 22 35 09 (*moderate*). Stunningly situated in a 14th-century hanging house, with inspiring views over the Huécar gorge.

Posada de San José, *see* right (*inexpensive*). Yet more gorge(ous) views, a terrace and reasonably priced *castellano* food.

Figón de Pedro, C/Cervantes 15, t 969 22 45 11 (*expensive–moderate*). The best new-town restaurant for classic Castilian cuisine, with a wide range of specialities.

Sleeping in Cuenca

★★★★**Parador de Cuenca**, Paseo Hoz del Huécar, t 969 23 23 20, *www.cuenca@parador.es* (*expensive*). Perched on a cliff across the Huécar gorge in the restored former Convento de San Pablo, with a pool.

★★★**Leonor de Aquitania**, C/San Pedro 60, t 969 23 10 00 (*moderate*). An upmarket *casa colgada* conversion, overlooking the Huécar gorge, but not costing the earth. There are marvellous views from the *cafetería* and the more expensive suites.

★★**Posada de San José**, C/Julián Romero 4, t 969 21 13 00, *www.posadadesanjose.com* (*moderate*). A 17th-century labyrinth of a convent, which has been atmospherically converted with a winning mix of white-washed walls and polished terracotta floors; some of the rooms have terraces which overlook the gorge, while the nuns' cells (which have shared baths) are much cheaper. There's also a good-value, home-made buffet breakfast, and the **restaurant** (*see* left) is worth a detour too.

Day 5: Through the Alcarria to Guadalajara

Morning: The next morning, take a walk around Cuenca's Plaza Mayor, with its distinguished 18th-century Ayuntamiento, before leaving along the N320 road north,
through more rugged, empty scenery. After about 80km the road is lined on the
south side by a giant reservoir, the Mar de Castilla or 'Sea of Castile'. The area west of
here, the Alcarria, was renowned for its rustic remoteness, despite being so close to
Madrid. A turn off south on the CM200 will take you to **Pastrana**, its main centre. A
timeless old town, founded by the Romans, it has a remarkable collection of fine
buildings along its cobbled streets: a Gothic Colegiata church with a museum with
15th-century tapestries (*open daily 10.30–1.30 and 4.30–6.30;adm*), and the Palacio
de Mendoza, once home to the grandee clan of the same name. Now a popular
weekend escape for Madrileños, it's a very pleasant town for easy walks.

Lunch: In Pastrana, *see* below.

Afternoon: From Pastrana it's a short ride to **Guadalajara**, back on major highways.
Civil War battle damage has meant that this is not as big an attraction as the other
historic Castilian towns, but it has its charms, as well as a very genuine atmosphere.
Like Pastrana it was a base for the Mendoza family, who built its greatest monument, the 1460s Palacio de los Duques del Infantado (*open Tues–Sat 10.15–2 and 4–7,
Sun 10.15–2, closed Mon; adm*), with superb carving. It also has a very likeable evening
paseo, as a change from all the bustle in Madrid.

Dinner and Sleeping: In Guadalajara, *see* below.

Day 5

Lunch in Pastrana

Hostería Princesa de Éboli, Convento de los
Monjas de Abajo, Pastrana, **t** 915 55 72 72
(*moderate*). A *pensión* and traditional
mesón-style restaurant in a converted
convent: the generous meals are excellent,
and it's packed at weekends. *In winter, open
only Sat, Sun and hols.*

★★★Hospedería Real de Pastrana, Convento
del Carmen, Pastrana, **t** 949 37 10 60
(*moderate*). Another of Pastrana's convents,
a Franciscan one near the entrance to the
town: it's food is as good as that of the
the Princesa de Éboli, and served in as lovely
a setting. *Open all year.*

Dinner in Guadalajara

Places to seek out local specialities such as
cabrito a la barreña (spit-roast kid), garlic soup,
and *bizcochos borrachos* (rum babas) are plentiful around the **Plaza Mayor** and **Plaza
Bejanque**.

Miguel Angel, C/Alfonso López de Haro 4,
t 949 21 22 51 (*expensive*). Miguel Angel has
run this restaurant for many years, and
offers creative variations on classical cuisine
using the finest ingredients.

Casa Victor, C/Bardales 6, **t** 949 21 22 47
(*moderate*). Castilian favourites rule the
menu here: they're consistently high-
standard, and it's a favourite with locals.

Sleeping in Guadalajara

★★★★Tryp Guadalajara, Carretera Nacional
Km55, **t** 902 44 66 66 (*expensive*). A modern
hotel a bit outside the centre, with all the
mod cons provided by the Tryp chain.

★★★Green Alcarría, C/Toledo 39, **t** 949 25 33 00,
(*moderate*). One of the best of the smallish
bunch of mid-range options, with very good
facilities and located towards the outskirts
of Guadalajara.

★España, C/Teniente Figueroa 3, **t** 949 21 13 03
(*inexpensive*). A good-value budget hotel, in
a much-altered 19th-century palace and
with the advantage of being right in the
centre of town.

Costa Blanca and Costa Cálida:
Alicante and Murcia

08

The practice of calling bits of the Spanish coast *costas* was invented way back in the early 1900s by a Catalan journalist called Ferran de Pol, at the very dawn of the tourist era, when most travellers were ladies and gentlemen in big hats and buttoned-up linen jackets. Inspired by the success of the French, who had recently come up with the *Côte d'Azur*, he decided the Catalan coast needed marketing too, and so thought up *Costa Brava*, 'rugged coast', for the idyllic coves near Palafrugell (*see* pp.81–5). However, it was not until Spain's real tourist boom ignited in the 1950s that labels were given to every bit of coastline, beginning with the Costa del Sol and the Costa Blanca, two beach-zones that gained a Europe-wide popularity they've never lost. The Blanca, centred on the ancient port of Alicante and stretching round a rocky triangle of land jutting east into the Mediterranean, is one of the most naturally favoured of Spain's shorelines, with long, long sandy beaches running away to the north, through the legendary fleshpot of Benidorm, giving way to more intimate rocky coves around the point of Cap de la Nau. South of Alicante towards Torrevieja are yet longer, ever-more developed beaches against a much more arid landscape. In the north, the sun shines down and temperatures get hot, but rarely too hot; as you will almost certainly read somewhere while you're here (since it's become a bit of a local mantra) a UN report has stated that the northern Costa Blanca has the healthiest climate in the world, with the optimum combination of sun and cooling breezes.

The Costa Blanca is also part of the Valencian region or *Comunitat Valenciana*, another of Spain's bilingual regions. Once one of the richest parts of Moslem Spain, it was conquered in the 1230s by Jaume I of Aragon, who repopulated it with Catalan-speakers – although it retained a big Moslem population right up until the 16th century, who left many traces behind them. This complex history is reflected in charming historic towns, many of them on the coves of the northern costa, like Altea or Dénia. València is also the land of oranges and rice, and the home of the arch-famous national dish, *paella*, which tastes better here than anywhere else. Alicante itself is a real, vibrant Spanish city, with a strong, tangy character, grand architecture, a buzzing little maze of an old town and no-holds-barred nightlife – as well as more miles of beaches, just a bus-ride from the centre.

South of Alicante province lies Murcia, an all-Spanish speaking area that is one of the places that, in ever-regionalized Spain, isn't really part of anywhere else, and so in the 1980s became an autonomous region all on its own. In magazine polls, with questions like 'Who would you like your daughter to marry?' Murcians always come out at the bottom, and they're the local butt of the how-many-does-it-take-to-change-a-lightbulb jokes pitched at anyone around the globe who is considered a bit out of it in the modern world. Murcia has been a dusty backwater; it and the neighbouring Andalucían province of Almería are the hottest, driest places in western Europe, with its only true deserts. Most recently, though, this self-same heat that used to drive people away (combined with some essential irrigation) has led it to become the fastest-growing holiday region in Spain, with huge new developments along the endless beach of La Manga. In the process it has acquired a new identity as the Costa Cálida, or 'Warm Coast' – although this could just be translated as 'hot'.

Alicante (Alacant)

Alicante, or Alacant in Catalan, is the air gateway to the Costa Blanca, and many of the millions who fly in here every year treat it just as that and no more, and head off to their resort or beach villa without ever taking a look inside the town. This is to miss out, for it has a lot to offer – unlike all the small resorts nearby, Alicante is a proper city, with a history stretching back to Carthaginian times, and an ongoing life of its own along its seaside promenades and narrow back streets. Its particular mixture of urban life and beach life makes for a very enjoyable combination.

The Castle, Cathedral and Around

Alicante was the mightiest citadel of the medieval Kingdom of Valencia, and judging by the powerful **Castillo de Santa Bárbara** (*open Tues–Sat 10–2 and 5–8, Sun 10–3; closed Mon; access by lift from Paseo Gomis, behind the tourist office on Platja del Postiguet; runs summer daily 7.30–12 and 5.30–8.30; winter daily 7.30–12.45 and 5.30–8.30; adm*) that crowns the city, it still is. An English garrison spent much of Spain's War of Succession here; Philip V blew castle and troops up in 1707, but it was restored, and is fun to explore, for itself and for the stunning views it commands. The castle now contains the sculptures of the Fundació Eduardo Capo, one of the largest collections of contemporary Spanish sculpture in the world, set in galleries within the castle and along the gardens and paths that wind across the summit of the hill.

Below the castle is Alicante's lively and sparky old quarter, **Santa Cruz**, around the 1662 **Catedral San Nicolás de Bari** (*open daily 7.30–12.30 and 5.30–8*), a strong, well-proportioned church, covered with red graffiti. The interior has been restored since its destruction in the Civil War, but remains dour and unwelcoming. Alicante was the last place in Spain held by the Republic at the end of the war in 1939; some 15,000 refugees waited on the docks in vain for ships to rescue them from Francoist reprisals, and several hundred committed suicide. Behind the cathedral, on C/San Agustín, is the **Museu de Belenes** (*open summer Tues–Fri and Sat am 10–2 and 5–8; winter Tues–Fri and Sat am 10–2 and 4.30–7.30; closed Sat pm, Sun and Mon; adm*), a nativity museum with a dizzying collection of Christmas figures (some for sale) from Spain and around the world, including a winsome red set from Japan.

The **Ayuntamiento** (*open for visits Mon–Fri 8–3*) has an elegant Baroque façade and is near the **Museo de la Asegurada** or museum of 20th-century art, off pedestrian C/Mayor. It's housed in an elegant 17th-century former granary – the oldest civic building in the city – and displays works by Picasso, Braque, Gris, Miró and others (*open summer Tues–Sat 10–2 and 5–9 (winter afternoons 4–8), Sun and hols 10.30–2.30*). The museum overlooks the tiny **Plaza de Sant María**, named after the florid Baroque **Church de Santa María** (*open daily 7.30–12.30 and 5.30–8*) which looms over it. Begun in the 13th–14th centuries, the church features an extraordinary golden Plateresque altar, with a resplendent Virgin peeking from a heavily gilded cave. There's more Baroque architecture at the **Palacio Maisonnave** (*C/Labradores 9; open Mon–Fri 9–2, Sat 9–1; closed Sun*), an 18th-century aristocratic mansion that now houses the municipal archives, built on the remains of a Roman necropolis.

The city's latest attraction is the **MARQ**, a state-of-the-art **archaeology museum** (*open Tues–Sat 10–2 and 4–8, Sun and hols 10–2; adm*) behind the castle of Santa Barbara on Plaza Doctor Gómez Ulla. It's very engaging, with finds from prehistory up to the Middle Ages, all given 21st-century pep with audiovisuals and buttons to push.

For a delightful evening stroll, head up the steep streets of the old quarter towards the tiny **Ermita de Sant Roque**, with its revered painting of the Gipsy Christ above the altar, and carry on up through narrow, stepped passages overflowing with flowers in bright blue ceramic pots to the 18th-century **Ermita de Santa Cruz**, which has spellbinding views across the rooftops and out to sea.

Getting to Alicante

Alicante has many scheduled and charter flights from the UK: **Bmibaby** flies from East Midlands and Cardiff; **easyJet** (ex-**Go** routes) from Stansted, East Midlands and Bristol; **mytravellite** from Birmingham; **Monarch** from Luton and Manchester; and **British Airways** and **Iberia** from Gatwick. For details, *see* p.13.
Airport flight information: t 966 91 91 00.
Bmibaby: t 902 10 07 37.
British Airways: t 902 11 13 33.
easyJet: t 902 29 99 92.
Iberia: t 902 40 05 00.
Monarch: t 966 91 91 00.
mytravellite: t 914 53 42 38.

Getting from the Airport

El Altet airport is 12km south of the city. **Bus** C-6 runs from the airport into Alicante around every 30 mins, daily 6.55am–11.10pm (from Alicante, 6.30am–10.20pm); in town, the route ends and begins at Plaza Puerta del Mar, by the harbour. The trip takes about 40 mins and costs €1.05. A **taxi** from the airport will cost about €10–€16 and take about 20 mins.

Getting Around

As in many Spanish cities, there are national and local **train** services. The main Spanish railways (**RENFE**) station is on Avda Salamanca, on the west side of the city centre. The Valencian regional railway, the **FGV**, has a handy line, known as *El Trenet* ('the little train'), which chugs up the coast to the north. The station is by El Postiguet beach; trains run each hour on the hour for **Altea**, daily 6am–8pm, and every two hours go on to **Dénia**.

Alicante's **bus** station is also near the centre, on C/Portugal. There are frequent buses all along the Costa Blanca and south towards Múrcia, and to long-distance destinations.

Central Alicante is compact enough to walk around, but transport is handy for getting to beaches and the Albufereta. Local **bus 21** runs along the seafront all the way to Platja de Sant Joan, approximately every 15mins, and all night on summer weekends. There's also a **tram** that hugs the bay and the beaches. It leaves from Platja del Postiguet, near Plaza Puerta del Mar, and stops at the FGV station.

A **taxi** from the centre to the beaches should cost around €6–7. For a radio cab, call **t** 965 10 16 11 or **t** 965 25 25 11.
Train information (RENFE): t (national) 902 24 02 02, (local) 965 92 02 02.
Train information (FGV): t 965 26 22 33.

Car Hire

For car hire in Spain in general, *see* pp.17–18. Most companies have offices at the airport.
Auriga Rentacar, C/Segura 21, **t** 965 20 64 00.
Local company based near Plaza Luceros.
Avis, Explanada de Espana 3, **t** 965 14 46 66.
Europcar, Hotel Melià Alicante, Platja del Postiguet, **t** 965 21 02 27.
National-Atesa, airport, **t** 965 68 25 26.

Tourist Information

Alicante: Municipal Office: Pza Ayuntamiento 1, **t** 965 14 92 80, *www.alicanteturismo.com*; Provincial Office: Explanada de España 2, **t** 965 20 00 00; at bus station, C/Portugal 17; Rambla de Méndez Núñez 23, Platja del Postiguet and Platja Sant Joan (*the latter opens summer only*).

Alicante's Beaches

Most visitors, when they're not lounging on Alicante's fine beaches, are strolling down the shady harbourfront **Explanada de España** with its flamboyant mosaics. The **Platja del Postiguet**, at the end of the Explanada, can get very, very crowded (and none too clean) in summer, and sometimes it seems as many people take the bus or train to bigger and cleaner **Platja de Sant Joan**, next to Alicante's beach suburb on the other side of the jutting cape (the Cabo de las Huertas). The little coves at the end of the Cape are favourites with nudists, while the big beach that swoops along the southern side of the cape, **Platja de la Albufereta**, is more family-orientated. You can

Shopping

The best streets for shopping head off from the main drag, especially **Avenida Maisonnave** and **Calle Gerona**. For local specialities like the delicious *túrron*, or date liqueur from Elche, try **El Túnel**, C/Sant Lorenç 34, or **Toní y María**, C/San Nicolas 10. For fresh produce, head straight for the delightful Art Deco-ish **Mercado Central** on Av Alfonso X el Sabio.

Where to Stay

Alicante ✉ 03000

The most popular hotels are near the Explanada – and the cheapest are around Santa María church, a great area for nightlife.

Luxury–Expensive

★★★★★Sidi San Juan, C/La Doblada, Cabo de la Huerta, **t** 965 16 13 00, *www.hotelessidi.es* (*luxury*). Big, modern hotel with all the luxuries imaginable, and great beach views.

★★★★Meliá Alicante, Platja del Postiguet, **t** 965 20 50 00, *melia.alicante@solmelia.es* (*expensive*). A big chain hotel in a self-contained complex overlooking the beach, complete with **restaurants** and shops. Rooms have amazing views and private terraces.

★★★★Hotel Mediterránea Plaza, Plaza del Ayuntamiento 6, **t** 965 15 61 85, *medplaza @teleline.es* (*expensive*). A smart, well-equipped hotel in a renovated old building, with grand views over the Town Hall.

Moderate

★★★NH Hotel Cristal, C/López Torregrosa 9, **t** 965 14 36 59, *www.nh-hoteles.es*. A few blocks from the Explanada, with an eye-catching crystal façade to match its name. Rooms are attractive, if a bit small, with a/c.

★★Hs Galicia, C/Arquitecto Morell 1, **t** 965 22 50 93. More reasonably priced; two blocks from the bus station, in a modern building.

Inexpensive–Cheap

★★Montecarlo, C/San Francisco 20, **t** 965 20 67 22. A good budget *hostal*, close to the town centre and near the beach.

★Hotel Marítimo, C/Valdés 13, **t** 965 21 99 85. Well-priced and a block from the Explanada, with big, airy rooms and friendly staff.

★P. Les Monges, First Floor, C/Monjas 2, **t** 965 21 50 46. A truly special place: behind the Ayuntamiento, it's charmingly run and has prettily decorated rooms, eccentric art, and satellite TV, music, a/c and parking. Some rooms (*moderate*) even have jacuzzis.

★P. Versalles, C/Villavieja 3, **t** 965 21 45 93. A fantastic bargain: spacious rooms around a jasmine-scented, vine-canopied courtyard. Shared bathrooms and kitchen; very mellow atmosphere.

Eating Out

Expensive

Delfín, Explanada de España 12, **t** 965 21 49 11. Alicante's best restaurant: delicious Alicantino versions of Valencian rice dishes, innovative international dishes and excellent seafood, all served with fine sea views.

Dársena, Paseo del Puerto, just off the Explanada, **t** 965 20 75 89. In an even more scenic location with a bright and shiny interior, this is a favourite with Alacantinos. The speciality is rice dishes; there are more than a hundred varieties to choose from.

get to all three beaches by bus, tram or FGV Trenet train (*see* p.175); the FGV up the coast also passes some **quiet coves** along the way. It's possible to explore on the ride: just keep your eyes peeled, and be prepared to jump off quickly whenever a nice beach catches your fancy.

A short way inland from Platja de Sant Joan, you can visit the **Monasterio de La Santa Faz** (*open 9–12 and 4.30–sunset; take bus C3 from Plaza Puerta del Mar*), built to enshrine the supposed handkerchief that Santa Veronica loaned to Christ as he carried the Cross – although for authenticity it has to compete with a similar handkerchief in the Vatican.

Nou Manoulin, C/Villegas 3, t 965 20 03 68. Housed in old brick wine cellars close to the ancient centre of town: delicious local delicacies and cosy traditional atmosphere mean booking is essential.

Piripiri, C/Oscar Espla 30, t 965 22 79 40. Elegant eaterie serving good regional dishes. Try the *fideos*, a paella-like dish using noodles instead of rice, but save room for the delicious *mousse de Jijona túrron*. There's a popular *tapas* bar here, too.

Moderate

La Goleta, Explanada de España 6, t 965 20 03 38. With a sea view from the terrace: specializing in seafood rice dishes and mixed grills.

O'Pote Galego, Plaza Santísima Faz 6, t 965 20 80 84. Just off an attractive square, the Galician specialities here are a must: lovely grills and *merluza a la gallega*.

Bar Luis, C/Pedro Sebastián 7, t 965 21 14 46. Cool and elegant with a grand wine cellar and unusual dishes created with real flair. Try the lasagne with spinach, prawns and salmon, or excellent *tapas*. *Closed Sun*.

Restaurante Alebrije, Pza Gabriel Miró 11, t 965 21 68 14. A swanky and sophisticated new restaurant with minimalist décor, contemporary cuisine and a fashionable clientele.

Inexpensive

Regina, Av Niza 19, t 965 26 41 39. A great bargain: good *tapas*, *paella* and seafood.

Mesón Labradores, C/Labradores 19. Good *tapas*, and typically Alicantan with *azulejo* walls crammed with pictures and ceramics. If it's full, try its smaller branch around the corner on C/San Pasuel 3. *Closed Mon*.

Restaurante Mixte Vegetariano, Pza Santa María. Cosy, friendly, mainly veggie

restaurant with a perfect setting opposite the old church of Santa María.

Rincón de António, Patronato de Santa Cruz, just above Pza del Carmen. In the old Santa Cruz quarter, tourist-free and a local favourite. No menu, but the friendly owner will be happy to give you a good selection.

Bodega Las Garrafas, C/Major 33. Tiny and very unusual *bodega* squeezed between modern convenience cafés, and filled with all things ancient: a cash till on the counter, oil lamps, cow bells and even a British police helmet hanging from the ceiling. The walls are covered with pictures of the owner with famous visitors over the last 50 years.

Entertainment and Nightlife

The area around Plaza del Carmen, known as **El Barrio**, comes alive after 1am – every street is crammed with bars and clubs. One of the strangest is **Celestial**, C/San Pascual, stuffed with kitsch décor and religious knick-knacks. Around Plaza Quijano and C/Carmen you'll find **Agustito**, **Yatevale** and **Pisamorena** – along with hundreds of others. At the corner of C/Labradores and C/San Isidro is the small, hip **Austin** bar, with tables on the street. If jazz is more your speed, try **Armstrong's**, C/Carmen 3, with live acts at weekends. Just behind the Explanada, C/San Fernando has plenty of lively bars, mainly popular with a teenage crowd, as well as the big disco **Bugatti**.

In summer the place to be is **Sant Joan** beach, which is overrun with all-night bars and discos. Buses run all night, and there are also extra FGV trains to help you get there.

Alicante

Archaelogical Museum

CALE DOCTOR SAPENA

PLAZA DOCTOR GÓMEZ ULLA

PLAZA DOCTOR MAS MAGRO

C. VÁZQUEZ DE MELLA

CUESTA DE LA FABRICA

C. VIRGEN DEL SOCORRO

To Playa del Albufereta and Cabo de las Huertas

AV. JAUME II

El Trenet Station

C. TENIENTE DAOIZ

Castillo de Santa Bárbara

Ermita de Santa Cruz

PLAZA VIRGEN CARMEN

C. SAN ROQUE

C. P. SEBASTIÁN

C. CARMEN

PLAZA QUIJANO

Museum of 20th-Century Art

Lift to Castle

AV. JOVELLANOS

P

Catedral San Nicolás de Bari

C. SAN PASCUAL

PLAZA MONJAS

C. VILLAVIEJA

PLAZA SANTA MARÍA

Santa María

PLAZA SANTÍSIMA FAZ

C. SAN AGUSTIN

C. SAN NICOLÁS

Ayuntamiento

PLAZA AYUNTAMIENTO

C. MAYOR

C. JUAN BAUTISTA LAFORA

Tram Station

PASEO GÓMIZ

C. RAFAEL ALTAMIRA

PLAZA PUERTA MAR

Playa del Postiguet

P

DE ESPAÑA

PLAZA PUERTO

Marina

Mediterranean Sea

N

300 metres
200 yards

Day Trips and Overnighters from Alicante

Benidorm

The undisputed giant of the Costa Blanca, Benidorm is even more a symbol of a larging-it, loud and very likely loutish good-time package holiday than other modern legends like Torremolinos and Mallorca's Magaluf. Its 6.5km of beautifully curving, wide sandy beach are obviously at the root of its fame, one of the finest strands on the Mediterranean and the thing that first drew people here in the 1950s. Behind this wonderful natural asset, Benidorm decided to go for broke and build on a scale seen in no other holiday town in Spain, with an awesome ensemble of skyscrapers huddled together in a dense forest – now topped off by the tallest hotel in all Europe, the 52-floor **Grand Balí**, opened in 2002. All this brash touristic overkill, though, gives Benidorm a verve most other costa resorts lack – as well as many more clubs, theme bars, vaguely-Vegas-y shows and other forms of fun than anywhere else in the region.

Getting There

The FGV *Trenet* local **train** (*see* p.175) is the most enjoyable way to get up the coast, reaching Benidorm in just over an hour from Alicante. In summer, trains run up and down the coast all night.

By **car**, simply follow the N332 coast road north from the city (40km). The A7 motorway runs parallel to it, but is scarcely necessary unless you're in a real hurry.

Tourist Information

Benidorm: Av Martínez Alejos 16, t 965 85 32 24.

Where to Stay

Benidorm ✉ 03500

It's easy to get back from here to Alicante, but if you get into the mood you may want to stay over. Benidorm has hundreds of hotels, but they can all be booked up in August; off-season you can get excellent rates. Budget accommodation tends to be clustered in the centre, away from the sea.

***Los Alamos Av Gerona, t 965 85 02 12 (*moderate*). In the heart of Benidorm near the beach, with a pool and garden.

*Hs Nacional, C/Verano 9, t 965 85 04 32 (*inexpensive*). Not stylish, but centrally located and with its own pool. *Open April–Oct.*

Eating Out

Tiffany's, Av del Mediterráneo 51, t 965 85 44 68 (*expensive*). The poshest place in Benidorm for dining out, serving high-class international cuisine. *Closed 7 Jan–7 Feb.*

I Fratelli, Av Dr Orts Llorca 21, t 965 85 39 79 (*expensive*). As expensive as its food is delicious: Art Deco-style décor and an interesting menu, throwing in a few regional dishes as well as fine Italian.

La Caserola, Av Bruselas 7, t 965 85 17 19 (*moderate*). Serves international cuisine; it has a good atmosphere, and a lovely terrace.

L'Albufera, C/Girona 3, t 965 86 56 61 (*moderate*). There's an excellent range of *tapas* in the busy bar, and the restaurant has all manner of Valencian rice dishes.

Entertainment and Nightlife

Benidorm counts its pubs, clubs, and discos by the score; there are close to 100 discos alone. Most stay packed all night, disgorging the crowds only when the need for a fried egg breakfast grows too strong. Otherwise you can choose any kind of entertainment you fancy: from English to German and Scandinavian pubs, American-style bars, naff-flamenco nightclubs and establishments in which to let loose with your own karaoke version of *Una Paloma Blanca*.

At the same time, lately the town's authorities, conscious of the reputation their burg had acquired, have struggled to carry it upmarket, and while this hasn't entirely come off Benidorm now has smart, high-standard eating places as well as chip shops and bratwurst bars, and its prom has been neatly landscaped. And its many facilities for good times have been added to with a new star attraction, a full-size, global-scale theme park just north of town, **Terra Mítica** (*see* below). Not far away are two older but also hugely enjoyable family attractions, a **funfair** and **Aqualandia**, a great water-park with slides, whirlpools and other thrilling rides for cooling off when the heat gets up (*open May–June, mid-Sept–mid-Oct daily 10–6; July, early Sept daily 10–7; Aug daily 10–8; adm, discounts for 3–12s, free under-3s*).

Behind Benidorm (seen clearly from the *autopista*) there is a peculiar mountain with a neat, square notch taken out of it – shaped exactly like the islet off the coast. A legend recounts that a giant once lived near Benidorm, and that after years of loneliness he found a lady-love. She fell ill, and said she would die that day at the moment the sun went down. In despair, the giant watched the sun sink down behind the mountain; then, at the last minute, he wrenched out a piece of it and hurled it into the sea to give his beloved another minute of life. True or not, geologists have confirmed that islet and mountain are indeed made out of the same kind of rock.

La Vila Joiosa (Villajoyosa), just south of Benidorm, is a quieter resort, with a pretty white nucleus of an old town. There are some quieter coves beyond the packed main beaches, and those with a sweet tooth can indulge themselves at **Valor**, best-known of the many local chocolate-makers, with a pretty *modernista*-style chocolate shop.

Terra Mítica

The Costa Blanca's own full-on theme park opened in 2000, and gives no ground to its competitors in the European mega-park league in terms of scale and state-of-the-art rides. Like others it is part-run by a US corporation (Paramount). The 'themes' though, stay close to the Mediterranean, the 'Mythical Lands' of the title being Egypt, Greece, Rome, Iberia and 'The Islands', so that in the Egypt zone, for example, you get an all-splashing **Cataracts of the Nile** ride, or can cruise on the **Barge of Luxor**. The big highlights for thrill-junkies are in the Roman zone, a vast roller-coaster called the **Magnum Collosus**, built of wood just like the roller-coasters of ancient Rome (and the largest wooden roller coaster in the world), and the **Flight of the Phoenix**, a stomach-amputating sheer 60m drop, not obviously of ancient origin but which probably would have been used by the Romans for tormenting captives had they had the technology. Naturally enough, inside the park there are also plenty of places to eat.

Getting There

Terra Mítica has its own station on the FGV *Trenet* local **train** line to Altea (*see* p.182), which gets there in an hour from Alicante. Tickets can also be bought in advance at any FGV train station, in which case the train to the park is free. By **car**, follow the N332 or the A7 motorway (exit 65-A).

Park Information

Terra Mítica: **t** 902 02 02 20, *www.terramitica. es. Open Mar–June, mid-Sept–Oct daily 10–8; July daily 10–9; Aug–mid-Sept daily 10–midnight. Adm exp; tickets available for one, two or three days, discounts for 5–12s and over-55s; free under-5s.*

Getting There

There are **trains** hourly to Altea from Alicante on the FGV *Trenet* line (*see* p.175; services are more frequent in summer), which reach Altea in about 1hr 20mins. By **car**, follow the N332 past Benidorm (50km).

Tourist Information

Altea: C/Sant Pere 9, **t** 965 84 41 14, *www.alteadigital.com*.

Eating Out

The best area for atmospheric open-air dining is around Plaza de la Iglesia.
Raco de Toni, C/La Mar 127, **t** 965 84 17 63 (*expensive–moderate*). Excels in traditional rice and fish dishes.
Sant Pere 24, C/Sant Pere 24, **t** 965 84 49 72 (*moderate*). Cool and pleasant, specializing in splendid rice dishes: like *arroz de langosta*.
Bella Altea, C/Concepción 16, **t** 965 84 08 84 (*moderate*). Small, rustic and very welcoming restaurant serving international cuisine.

Altea

Altea is just 10km north of Benidorm but couldn't feel more different. Located on a natural balcony over the sea, it's the beginning of the Costa Blanca of small, intimate bays, winding, shore-hugging roads and spectacular vistas of yellow-rock cliffs falling sheer into the sea, in sharp contrast to the long open beaches to the south. Altea itself is one of the most charming spots on the Costa Blanca; artists discovered it in the 1960s and 1970s and the steep, stepped streets of the old hill town are packed with craft shops and artisans' studios.

It has certainly embraced tourism, and around it there are plenty of *urbanizaciones* of neat villas mostly owned by foreigners. There's also a very large permanently-resident, mostly-British foreign community, especially of older people who have come here to take advantage of the *costa*'s famously balmy and life-preserving weather. Even so, however much the town may have been prettied up for its new audience, it has never abandoned its own sleepy charm. The old church, right at the summit of the village, has a fine blue-tiled Valencian dome, and is surrounded with plenty of enjoyable bars and restaurants; down below by the water, there's a likeably low-key seafront promenade, and a small fishing harbour. Altea's beaches are stony rather than sandy, but they're divided into an attractive series of sheltered coves, one of which is a nudist beach. The others are family favourites.

Elche (Elx)

Elche, or just Elx (pronounced *Elsh* in Catalan), 20km west of Alicante, makes two claims on the world's attention. First, Spain's most famous piece of ancient art, *La Dama de Elche*, now in Madrid's archaeology museum, was unearthed here. Secondly, it has the only date-palm grove in Europe. The Moors planted the first palms, and now the trees – some 200,000 of them – nearly surround Elche. Although they produce a crop of dates (no other palms in Europe do), they are economically more valuable for their fronds, which are tied up to bleach a pale yellow and then shipped throughout Spain for Palm Sunday. Often you'll see one tied to a balcony, not because the owner has forgotten to take it down after Easter, but because the fronds are widely believed to ward off lightning. The palms are best seen in the **Huerto del Cura** (*C/Federico*

García Sanchis; open daily 9–9; www.huertadelcura) just east of town, where you can pay your respects to the seven-branched Imperial Palm, thought to be 150 years old. It's an immaculate town, with scattered monuments between the pristine apartment blocks; a tourist office leaflet shows a circular walk that goes around most of them.

The Lady of Elche bust was discovered in 1897 in **La Alcudia** south of town. Since then further excavations have revealed nine successive civilizations, documented by a small **museum** on the site, two kilometres from town on Carretera Dolores (*open April–Sept Tues–Sat 10–2 and 4–8, Sun 10–2; Oct–Mar Tues–Sat 10–5, Sun 10–2; adm*). In the centre, the blue-domed **Basílica de Santa María** has an elaborate 17th-century Baroque façade; ask to climb the tower for the view across the palm plantations. If you miss Elche's famous mystery play (*see above*), the little **Museu de la Festa** (*open winter Tues–Sat 10–1 and 4.30–8.30; summer Tues–Sat 10–1 and 5–9; closed Mon; adm*), which is the starting point for the ceremony, gives an audiovisual taste of the performance. Just behind the Basílica are the **Arabic baths**, converted into a convent in the 14th century (*open April–Sept Tues–Sat 10–1.30 and 4.30–8; Mar–Oct Tues–Sat 10–5; closed Sun and Mon*). Just north of the cathedral, in a restored 15th-century palace on the edge of the municipal park, another **archaeology museum** (*open Tues–Sun 10–1 and 4–8; closed Mon*) contains a copy of *La Dama de Elche*, along with finds from prehistoric, Phoenician and Roman times. There's also a Greek headless torso of Venus. On Plaza de Arrabal a small **Museum of Contemporary Art** (*open Tues–Sun 10–1 and 5–8; closed Mon*) contains paintings, sculptures and ceramics by modern Valencian artists. The stolid Gothic **Ajuntament** (Town Hall) has been in use since 1445, and just off the square in front of it is the charming **Calendura Tower**, with two mechanical figures that have been chiming the hours since the 18th century.

For the beach areas south of Alicante around **Torrevieja**, *see* p.194.

Getting There

Most RENFE **trains** going south towards Murcia and Andalucía from the main station in Alicante stop in Elche. **Buses** run by the Molla company from Alicante bus station go to Elche every half-hour from 7am to 9pm (Mon–Fri) and hourly from 8am to 9pm (weekends). By **car**, take the coast road south and then turn right onto the N340 (19km).

Tourist Information

Elche: Plaza del Parc, t 965 45 27 47.

Festivals

Elche: Misteri d'Elx, *mid-Aug*. A medieval mystery play is still performed each year in Elche's basílica.

Eating Out

Els Capellans, Porta de la Morera 14, t 966 61 00 11 (*expensive*). The restaurant of Elche's *parador* (the **Huerto del Cura**) is one of the town's finest, with views over the palms; some of the desserts are made with the local dates. The hotel itself is lovely, with rooms scattered around a palm grove.

Restaurante Parque Municipal, Psg de l'Estació s/n, t 965 45 34 15 (*moderate*). Specializing in rice dishes under the palms in the city's central park; there's even a terrace with tables scattered around a fake bust of *La Dama de Elche*.

Mesón El Granaíno, across the river at C/Josep María Buch 40, t 965 46 01 47 (*moderate*). Decked out in traditional style and serving varied *paellas*, *cocidos* and a local speciality, *tarta de almendra*, almond tart. *Closed Sun*.

Touring the Costa Blanca

Day 1: Two Sides of the Costa: Benidorm and Altea

Morning: Make your way north out of Alicante on the N332 coast road (if making this trip from Murcia, take into account a 75 km journey from Murcia city, or 70km from San Javier airport). For some sightseeing, turn left by Sant Joan d'Alacant (8km out of Alicante) onto a winding road up to the hill village of Busot and the **Cava dels Canalobres** (*open 1 Oct–20 June daily 11–5.50; 21 June–31 Sept daily 10.30–7.50; adm*), a dramatic cave full of strange rock formations, where concerts are held in summer. Afterwards, depending on the time of year, you'll be pretty hot: the beach may just make you hotter, and **Terra Mítica** theme park (*see* p.181) demands a full day, but a quicker, cheaper blast of fun and coolness can be had at **Aqualandia** (*see* p.181). Then, head to Benidorm to find a terrace for a pre-lunch drink (not hard).

Lunch: In Benidorm, *see* below and p.180.

Afternoon: Post-lunch – by which time, if you eat in proper Spanish fashion, it will be at least 4pm – take a walk along Benidorm's seafront: marvel at the skyscrapers, and take note that the town is not nearly as tacky as you might be expecting. Then make the short trip up to the contrasting world of Altea (*see* p.182), and wander around its old town souvenir shops, or down to one of the small beaches for another swim.

Dinner and Sleeping: In Altea, *see* below and p.182.

Day 1

Lunch in Benidorm

Tiffany's, Av del Mediterráneo 51, t 965 85 44 68 (*expensive*). Benidorm's smartest restaurant has a certain glitzy look, and serves high-class international cuisine, naturally making good use of the local seafood as well. *Closed 7 Jan–7 Feb.*

I Fratelli, Av Dr Orts Llorca 21, t 965 85 39 79 (*expensive*). As expensive as its food is delicious: Art Deco-style décor and an interesting menu, throwing in a few regional dishes as well as fine Italian.

La Caserola, Av Bruselas 7, t 965 85 17 19 (*moderate*). Serves international cuisine; it has a good atmosphere, and a lovely terrace.

Dinner in Altea

Monte Molar, outside Altea on Ctra València, t 965 84 15 81 (*expensive*). One for gourmets; delicate, very imaginative dishes – snails and wild rice, duck in bilberry sauce – are served on a terrace overlooking the sea.

Sant Pere 24, C/Sant Pere 24, t 965 84 49 72 (*moderate*). A cool and pleasant restaurant in the old town that specializes in splendid Valencian rice dishes, like *arroz de langosta*, more-or-less lobster paella.

La Capella, C/San Pablo 1, t 966 68 04 84 (*inexpensive*). One of the best of Altea's *tapas* bars, and very enjoyable.

Sleeping in Altea

★★★Cap Negret, Ctra València, t 965 84 12 00 (*expensive*). A luxurious hotel right on the beach, with a big range of facilities including a very nice pool.

★★Hotel Altaya, C/Sant Pere 28, t 965 84 08 00 (*moderate–inexpensive*). Also on the beach, but a lot more modest: a pleasant and very comfortable small hotel, with helpful and friendly service and sea views from its rooms.

★Hotel San Miguel, C/La Mar 65, t 965 84 04 00 (*inexpensive*). Delightful, pristine little hotel overlooking the seafront, and extremely good value.

Day 2: Rocks and Relaxation: Calpe to Jávea

Morning: Before leaving Altea, especially if you haven't done so the night before, take a look around its rocky coves, and maybe pick one for a swim before carrying on the short way (11km) to **Calp** (Catalan) or **Calpe** (Spanish) – many towns here have alternative names in the two languages, which both turn up on signs, brochures and so on. It's a bigger resort than Altea, with longer, sandier beaches, and a buzzing nightlife scene. Its spectacular feature, though, dominating the view, is the **Penyal d'Ifach**, a massive, 332m-tall sugar-loaf of rock that looms out of the sea just to the east. A path, part of it through a tunnel, allows you to make a wonderful – but steep – walk to the top, past slopes covered in fragrant Mediterranean herbs. From the summit the views are breathtaking, and on a good day you can see Ibiza; allow two hours for the walk, there and back, after which you'll be in need of refreshment.

Lunch: In Calp/Calpe, *see* below.

Afternoon: From Calp, follow the minor road past the Penyal d'Ifach, to stay with the coast. This is the loveliest part of the Costa Blanca, lined with snug coves that are enormously popular with British people for second- and retirement homes. They run into **Xàbia** (Catalan)/**Jávea** (Spanish), as pretty as Altea, with a shoreline of small bays, still guarded by the remains of medieval watchtowers, and a historic old town on a hilltop just inland, a maze of steep streets clustered around the fine Gothic church of **San Bartolomé**. However well-touristed, it's a charming, relaxing place.

Dinner and Sleeping: In Xàbia/Jávea, *see* below.

Day 2

Lunch in Calp/Calpe

Los Zapatos, C/Santa María 7, **t** 965 83 15 07 (*expensive–moderate*). Good local specialities with an Arabic twist, and an excellent selection of regional wines.

La Cambra, C/Delfin s/n, **t** 965 83 06 05 (*moderate*). Basque meets Mediterranean in this delightful restaurant.

Bora Bora, Av del Puerto, **t** 965 83 31 77 (*inexpensive*). Incredible variety of pancakes.

Dinner in Xàbia/Jávea

Olé, C/Bonaventura 9, **t** 966 46 23 76 (*moderate*). In an old mansion, serving delicious *tapas* and a very good wine selection.

Azorín, C/Toni Llidó, **t** 965 79 44 95 (*inexpensive*). At the centre of the action near the port: huge plates of shellfish for a nice price.

Tasca Tonis, C/Mayor 4, **t** 966 46 18 51 (*inexpensive*). A down-to-earth neighbourhood restaurant, always filled with locals enjoying the local dishes at very reasonable prices.

Sleeping in Xàbia/Jávea

★★★★★Villa Mediterranea, **t** 965 79 52 33, *www.hotelvilamed.es* (*luxury*). The most exclusive choice in town, with just 10 luxuriously appointed rooms and two suites in a stunning white Mediterranean-style villa with magnificent views – as far as Ibiza on a good day. An elegant terrace overlooks the huge pool.

★★★★Parador de Jávea, Platja del Arenal, **t** 965 79 02 00, *www.parador.es* (*expensive*). A modern, not a historic, parador, but beautifully situated, with a lovely pool and a palm-filled garden, and a first-class **restaurant** emphasizing local dishes.

★★Hotel Miramar, Plaza Almirante Bastarreche 12, **t** 965 79 01 00 (*moderate*). An attractive hotel near the seafront, with pretty, pine-decorated rooms and friendly staff. Go for the rooms with sea views.

★★Hs Xàbia, Pío X 5, **t** 965 79 54 61, *www.javea.net* (*inexpensive*). Small, friendly and central.

★Hs La Favorita, C/Magallanes 4, **t** 965 79 04 77 (*cheap*). The best budget choice.

Day 3: At Home with the Borgias: Dénia to Gandia

Morning: After breakfast, take a look around **Cap Sant Antoni** (San Antonio), northern-most of the two capes that shelter Jávea harbour. The steep rocky coves here have (mostly) been protected from development, so it's one of the best places for beach-squatting hereabouts. After a couple of hours, head off up the 9km to **Dénia**. This is one of the most historic towns on this coast; it was founded by the Greeks, and its name comes from a temple to the Roman goddess Diana, while the ruins of an Arab **castle** still loom over the town from the top of a crag. There are yet more fine beaches, and it's the liveliest of the Costa Blanca's harbours, with ferries to Ibiza.

Lunch: In Dénia, *see* below.

Afternoon: **Gandia**, 27km north, is usually thought of as the northern boundary of the Costa Blanca. Like most towns here it was built on a hilltop, but some way from the sea, so that its modern beach resort, **El Grao**, is over 2km away (buses run between the two). It was the seat of the Borja family, Dukes of Gandia, who, Italianized as Borgia, provided the most notorious of Renaissance Popes, Alexander VI, and his daughter Lucrezia. A later duke, perhaps to redeem the family name, became known for his piety and was made a saint; his home, the Palacio Ducal (*open summer Mon–Fri 11–12 and 6–7, Sat 11–12; winter Mon–Fri 11–12 and 5–6; closed Sun; adm*) is now a Jesuit school, but its glittering Baroque chambers, and fine collection of local ceramics, can be visited. Around it, old Gandia is an untouristed, characterful town.

Dinner and Sleeping: In Gandia, *see* below.

Day 3

Lunch in Dénia

Most of Dénia's **restaurants** are on Platja Les Rotes; the town's cuisine has got the best reputation on the Costa Blanca:

El Poblet, Ctra Las Marinas Km2, El Poblet 43, t 965 78 41 79 (*expensive*). One of the best in the area, with a renowned chef, and great dishes using Dénia's equally renowned prawns. *Closed Mon exc. in July and Aug.*

Gavila, C/Marqués de Campo 55, t 965 78 10 66 (*expensive*). Among the best rice and other local delicacies to be found. *Closed Sun eve.*

L'Olleta, Av d'Alacant 19, t 966 42 09 52 (*expensive*). Good for a splurge; thoughtful Mediterranean cuisine. *Closed Sun.*

El Trampoli, Platja Les Rotes, t 965 78 12 96 (*moderate*). Delicious rice and seafood.

Dinner in Gandia

Most of the **restaurants** are on the beach.

L'Ullal, C/Benicanena 12, t 962 87 73 82 (*expensive–moderate*). Probably the best food in town; a charming and attractively decorated restaurant that serves imaginative Mediterranean dishes with striking fresh flavours. *Closed Sun.*

La Gamba, on the Ctra Nazaret-Oliva s/n, t 962 84 13 10 (*moderate*). Just outside of town, with a garden terrace and delicious seafood. *Closed Mon and Nov.*

Sleeping in Gandia

****Bayren I**, Pso de Neptuno 62, t 962 84 03 00, www.hotelesbayren.com (*expensive*). Of the swanky category, with a pleasant pool, dancing in the evening and a perfect seaside location.

***La Casa Vieja**· C/Horno 2, Rugat (14km from Gandía), t/f 962 81 40 13, lacasavieja@ xpress.es (*moderate*). A truly delightful choice, in a tiny village inland (take the Cv-60 road, signposted for Ontinyent). There are just five rooms and one suite in this tranquil, attractively converted little 17th-century farmhouse; the welcome is friendly, and the views over the orange groves are glorious.

Day 4: Urbane Pleasures in Valencia

Morning: Make an early start to head off up the 60km to Valencia, and find a car park. There's enough in Spain's third-largest city to occupy you for some time, but a day walking around is a good taster: begin at **Plaza de la Reina**, heart of the old city, with the **cathedral** (*open daily 7.30–1 and 4.30–8.15*) begun in 1262, and next to it its very unusual, minaret-like 15th-century belltower, **El Miquelet** (*open daily 10.30–12.30 and 4.30–7; adm*). Climb up its 200 steps for a fine overview. Take a look behind the cathedral at the lovely **Plaza de la Vírgen**, and then walk back across Plaza de La Reina and past a 17th-century tower, the **Torre de Santa Catalina**, to find the **Museo Nacional de Ceramica** (*open Tues–Sat 10–2 and 4–8, Sun and hols 10–2; closed Mon; adm*), a dazzling collection of Valencian ceramics housed in a Baroque palace.

Lunch: In Valencia, *see* below.

Afternoon: Having taken advantage of the old city's eating opportunities, walk past the cathedral again to Valencia's river, the **Turia**, and a surviving part of its medieval walls, the **Torre de Serranos**. The once-tatty river banks have been landscaped into parks, ideal for a post-lunch stroll. This will prepare you for the **Museo de Bellas Artes** (*open Tues–Fri 9–2.15 and 4–7.30, Sat, Sun and hols 9–2;*), on the north bank, the biggest arts museum in Spain after the Prado, with great works by Goya, Velázquez, Bosch and others as well as quite a lot of routine paintings. After that, you'll need another stroll before sampling Valencia's celebratedly funky nightlife.

Dinner and Sleeping: In Valencia, *see* below.

Day 4

Lunch in València

San Nicolas, Plaza Horno de San Nicolás 8, **t** 963 91 59 84 (*expensive*). Refined seafood on a pretty square; choose from a huge variety of local fish, then decide how you'd like to see it cooked. *Closed Sun eve and Mon.*

Chicote, Av Neptuno 34, **t** 963 71 61 51 (*moderate*). On Levante beach, with fine rice and seafood: try *arrós a banda*, rice cooked in fish stock. *Closed Mon and 15 Nov–15 Dec.*

Serranos, C/Blanquerías 5, by the Torres de Serrano, **t** 96 391 70 61 (*inexpensive*). Good, cheap, and authentic *tapas* bar, with a bustling interior full of young Valencians tucking into a big range of perfect *tapas*.

Dinner in Valencia

Seu-Xerea, C/Conde de Almodóvar 4, **t** 963 92 40 00 (*expensive*). Here, innovative Mediterranean cuisine takes on some influence from the Far East, in a fashionable, pleasantly relaxed setting.

Casa Carmina, C/Embarcadero 4, El Saler, **t** 961 83 02 54 (*moderate*). Universally acknowledged as one of the best for Valencian rice dishes; it's not much from the outside, but always packed with local families.

La Carme, C/Sogueros 8, **t** 963 92 21 46 (*inexpensive*). Delicious, imaginative local dishes at very reasonable prices in this prettily decorated, family-run restaurant.

Sleeping in Valencia

★★★Hotel Inglés, Marqués de Dos Aguas 6, **t** 963 51 64 26 (*expensive*). Perfectly located, in a frilly mansion opposite the ceramics museum. Plenty of style and atmosphere, and at night the street is very quiet.

★★★Hotel Ad Hoc, C/Boix 4, **t** 963 91 91 40, *adhoc@nexo.net* (*expensive–moderate*). Perhaps the nicest place to stay in the city, in a converted 19th-century house with beamed ceilings. The charming **restaurant** offers a well-priced *menú del día* at lunch.

★★Hs Continental, C/Correos 8, **t** 963 51 09 26 (*inexpensive*). Well located, with airy rooms.

Day 5: Back to the Coast via the Peak of Guadalest

Morning: Extricate yourself from Valencia's urban sprawl, going south, and after 15km leave the motorway or the N332 to take the CV41 road that runs almost due south through orange groves down to **Xàtiva** (50km), the most scenic of València's small towns, with a main square, Plaza de la Seo, dominated by a cathedral, the Colegiata, which is even bigger than Valencia's. Also on the square is the lovely Hospital, with a 16th-century façade, while a walk uphill to the castle takes you past a second, older cathedral, San Félix. Carry on to the castle (*open Tues–Sun 10–2 and 4.30–8*) for sweeping views. Take a look too at the town museum, in a 16th-century granary, the Almudí (*open Tues–Sat 10–2*). Xàtiva's eventful history includes having been the actual birthplace of the Borgia pope, and later being near-destroyed in 1707 for its resistance to King Philip V; hence, his portrait is hung in the museum upside-down.

Lunch: In Xàtiva, *see* below.

Afternoon: Go south from Xàtiva for about 50km to Alcoi, and then look for a turn left (east) onto the CV-70, to climb into the most spectacularly rugged scenery around the Costa Blanca. Its centre is the extraordinary village of **Guadalest**, with its Moorish castle perched atop a sheer pinnacle – King Jaume I said his troops needed wings to take it. Although often hugely crowded in summer, it's still a magical place, with quite stupendous views. There are some fine places to eat nearby, in wonderful settings, or you can drive straight down the slope to Benidorm or Alicante.

Dinner and Sleeping: In Guadalest and Benidorm, *see* below and p.180.

Day 5

Lunch in Xàtiva

Hosteria de Mont Sant, C/del Castillo, **t** 962 27 50 81 (*expensive*). This hotel occupies a former Cistercian monastery, with magnificent views from its garden and swimming pool. The restaurant is equally lovely, and has a high reputation for its refined Valencian cuisine. Service is very smooth.

Casa de la Abuela, C/Reina 17, **t** 962 28 10 85 (*moderate*). A local favourite, 'Grandma's house' appropriately serves traditional home cooking, but has a sophisticated side too, and has won awards for its fine versions of classic Valencian rice and seafood dishes and stout grilled meats.

Dinner around Guadalest

Restaurante Nou Salat, Ctra de Callosa Km 11, **t** 965 88 50 19 (*expensive*). Up the winding road south towards Callosa d'en Sarrià, this country restaurant is very popular locally for its no-nonsense cooking and friendly feel.

Restaurante Mora, C/del Sol 1, **t** 965 88 50 87 (*moderate*). A popular restaurant in the middle of Guadalest village, with good traditional cooking. Touristy, but enjoyable.

Hostal-Restaurante Trestellador, Benimantell, **t** 965 88 52 21 (*moderate*). A hotel-restaurant in a restored farmhouse just west of Guadalest, which – like so many buildings in this area – is in a spectacular location atop a cliff, with great views from the dining room.

Sleeping in Benidorm

★★★Los Alamos Av Gerona, **t** 965 85 02 12 (*moderate*). In the heart of Benidorm near the beach, with a pool and garden.

★★Hotel Don José, Ctra Del Alt, **t** 965 85 50 50 (*moderate*). Further from the seafront, but attractive and good value. *Open Mar–Oct*.

★★Hotel Los Ángeles, C/Los Ángeles 3, **t/f** 966 80 74 33 (*moderate*). Very nice, friendly little hotel down a narrow street in the old city.

★★Hotel Mayor· C/Mayor 16, **t** 965 85 18 19 (*inexpensive*). Renovated rooms in an old hotel which even has its own pool.

Murcia

However much other Spaniards from cosmopolitan haunts like Madrid or Barcelona may dismiss it and its supposedly backwoods inhabitants, Murcia is a congenial little city. Very appropriately for Spain's most desert-like provincial capital it was founded by the Moors, in 825, as *Mursiya*, on the site of a much smaller Roman outpost. They were attracted by one of its most distinctive features, the *huerta* or fertile plain of the Segura river, a pocket of watered land, just like a North African oasis, that stands out in this often bone-dry region and which, the Moors naturally recognized, could if carefully tended and watered be highly productive. The Moorish water-management systems have formed the basis of Murcia's agriculture for most of the centuries ever since, indispensable in the cultivation of the red peppers that for Spaniards go with Murcia as much as turkeys do with Norfolk in England.

Murcia was taken from the Moslems in 1243 by the greatest of the kings of medieval Castile, Alfonso X *el Sabio* ('The Wise'). While never a very prominent city, Christian Murcia had its times of prosperity and opulence, notably from the 16th to the 18th centuries, when it acquired many of its fine buildings. Today, the streets of the old quarter still follow the twists and turns of the ancient Moorish town, dotted with a rich collection of Renaissance and Baroque churches, many converted from former mosques. The **cathedral**, not far from the river, is easy to find by its unusual **tower** (*ask the museum custodian to open the door if you'd like to climb up*), built by four different architects between 1521 and 1792. The cathedral itself has a fine Baroque façade and Gothic portals on either side. The interior, in a mixture of styles, is notable for its 15th-century **Vélez Chapel**, an exuberant Plateresque national monument. An urn on the main altar contains an odd relic: the innards of Alfonso the Wise. In the cathedral **museum** (*open daily 9–1 and 4–8*) a Roman sarcophagus relief of the muses shares space with a collection of religious artefacts.

From the cathedral head up the pedestrian C/de Trapería, where, at the first block, stands the **Casino**. Just about every town in Spain acquired a 'casino' in the 19th century, which here meant not a gambling hall but a very respectable club for the gentlemen of the locality and their ladies, but none has anything quite to match Murcia's for over-the-top grandeur. Inaugurated in 1847, it manages to combine exuberantly a dozen eclectic styles: there's a Moorish patio vestibule, an English-style reading room and, most extravagant of all, a florid Louis XV ballroom, dripping with monstrous, glittering chandeliers and frescoes. Ladies, above all, should not miss an opportunity to visit the *Tocador de Señoras*, or Ladies' Powder Room, covered with a sea of primping nymphs in a fresco supposedly on the subject of the goddess Selene. The Casino has been undergoing major restoration, but it's still possible to explore several of its salons and patios. Just off C/de Trapería is the **Teatro Romea**, on a large, pleasant square. This 19th-century theatre has already been incinerated twice – and a local legend predicts a third fire, because this temple of frivolity was built on a monastic graveyard. Nearby, Trapería passes through Plaza Santo Domingo, surrounded by all of three grand old churches, **Santo Domingo**, **Santa Ana** and the monastery of **Santa Clara la Real** – the last of these begun in the 14th century on top

Murcia

RONDA NORTE

AVDA GENERAL PRIMO DE RIVERA

AVENIDA LIBERTAD

PLAZA CIRCULAR

RONDA DE LEVANTE

PLAZA JUAN XXIII

RONDA DE LEVANT

AVDA RECTOR JOSE LOUSTAU

Jardin de La Fama

PUERTA NUEVA

GRAN VIA ALFONSO X EL SABIO

AVDA DE LA CONSTITUCIÓN

Museo Arqueológico

AVDA JAIME I

GENERAL GUTIERREZ MELLADO

DR JOSE TAPIA SANZ

Jardin de la Constitución

Jardin El Salitre

PLAZA FUENSANTA

Jardin de San Esteban

CALLEJON BURRUEZO

ACISCLO DIAZ

Monasterio de Santa Clara la Rea

Santa Ana

P. STA ANA

ENRIQUE VILLAR BAS

SANTO CRISTO

PASEO MENENDEZ PELAYO

University

Museo de Bellas Artes

OBISPO FRUTOS

SAN ANDRES

SANTA TERESA

GRAN VIA ESCULTOR SALZILLO

MAESTRO ALONSO

SANTA CLARA

Teatro Romea

PLAZA JULIAN ROMEA

PLAZA SANTO DOMINGO

Santo Domingo

SANTO SAAVEDRA FAJARDO

PLAZA EUROPA

VICTORIO

Museo Salzillo

PLAZA SAN AGUSTIN

GARCIA ALIX

Bus Station

BOLOS

PLAZA SAN ANTOLIN

SAGASTA

PLAZA MAYOR

San Nicolás

SAN NICOLAS

PLAZA SANTA ISABEL

PLAZA SANTA CATALINA

PLAZA DE LAS FLORES

MADRE DE DIOS

PLATERIA

TRAPERIA

RADIO MURCIA

INFANTES

Casino

PLAZA CETINA

PLAZA SANTA EULALIA

PLAZA SIMON GARCIA

PLAZA CEBALLOS

Bu Rin

JUAN DE LA CIERVA

Mercado Verónicas

Muralla Arabe

VERONICAS

Almudi

Ayuntamiento

PLAZA MARTINEZ TORNEL

PLAZA FONTES

AZUCAQUE

Museo de la Catedral

PLAZA CARDENAL BELLUGA

PLAZA DE LOS APOSTOLES

Cathedral

Palacio Episcopal

PLANO DE SAN FRANCISCO

GLORIETA DE ESPAÑA

PUENTE VIEJO

PUENTE PASARELA

AVDA TENIENTE FLOMESTA

PASEO DE GARAY

Jardin Botanico

River Segura

Murcia Parque

JUMILLA

PLAZA DE CAMACHOS

RICARDO CORBALAN

AVENIDA RIO SEGURA

PUENTE NUEVO

River Segura

AVENIDA COLON

GLEZ CEBRIAN

Jardin de Floridablanca

PLAZA GONZALEZ CONDE

CARTAGENA

TORRE DE ROMO

FLORIDABLANCA

N

250 m
250 yds

Train Station

AVDA JUAN ANTONIO PEREA

INDUSTRIA

of the foundations of a Moorish palace, some remains of which can still be seen. The street then changes into the broad boulevard of the Gran Vía Alfonso X el Sabio, which leads up to Murcia's **Museo Arqueológico** (*open Mon–Fri 9–2 and 4–8, Sat 10–1.30; closed Sun*),housing a varied collection of Iberian artefacts and Roman sculptures and coins, and some relics of Murcia under Islamic rule.

Not far from here is the 17th-century **convent** that now houses Murcia's **university**, but has retained it's pretty double-decker cloister. This is one of the most animated parts of town, with dozens of *tapas* bars and terrace cafés. Just to the southeast is the **Museo de Bellas Artes** (*open summer Mon–Fri 9–2, Sat 11–2; winter Mon–Fri 9–2 and 5–7.30, Sat 11–2; closed Sun; adm*), with a collection of paintings some of which date from the 15th century, and works by several Golden Age Spanish masters including a *St Jerome* by Ribera.

Getting to Murcia

Murcia's airport is some 30km away at **San Javier**, much closer to the beaches of La Manga (6km) than to the city. Therein hangs a tale; San Javier was actually a military airbase, and was only adapted for civil flights when nearby beach resorts began their boom and Alicante airport became seriously overloaded. Today, it has scheduled flights from Britain with **Bmibaby** from East Midlands and **Buzz** from Stansted, and is ever-more popular for charters. It also has Iberia domestic connections with Madrid and Barcelona.
Airport flight information: t 968 17 20 00.
Bmibaby: t 902 10 07 37.
Buzz: t 917 49 66 33.

Getting from the Airport

There are no buses or other regular public transport from the airport, so **taxis** are the only way into town or to La Manga. A cab to Murcia city will cost around €8–10, and take about 30mins; to La Manga should cost under €5, and take about 15–20mins.

Getting Around

The **RENFE** (Spanish railways) train station is south of town, on C/Industria; local buses **9** and **11** will take you there from the centre. Murcia is on the line between Alicante and Almería and Granada.There is also a **local rail line (FEVE)**, which runs from the same station down to **Cartagena** and **Los Nieto**s, on the Mar Menor near Cabo de Palos. It runs every 1½hrs,

complemented by hourly FEVE buses between Cartagena and Cabo de Palos.

Murcia's central **bus** station is on the west side of town on C/Bolos and C/Sierra Nevada. Buses run throughout the day to every part of the region, and there are also many long-distance routes. Within Murcia city, it's easy to walk, but **taxis** are plentiful and quite cheap.
Train information (RENFE): t 902 24 02 02.
Train information (FEVE): t 968 50 35 92.
Bus information: t 968 29 22 11.

Car Hire

For car hire in Spain in general, *see* pp.17–18. Most companies are based at the airport, rather than in Murcia.
Avis, airport, t 968 57 20 21; C/Industria, by RENFE station, t 968 34 23 82. One of few companies with an office in town.
Europa Rentacar, airport, t 902 11 97 26.
Europcar, airport, t 968 12 30 10.
National-Atesa, airport, t 968 57 35 04.

Tourist Information

Murcia: Regional Office, Palacio González Campuzano, Plaza Romea, t 968 27 76 76 (*open Mon–Fri 10–2 only*);
City Office, Plano de San Francisco 8, t 968 35 87 20, *www.ayto-murcia.es/turismo*.

Festivals

Murcia: Semana Santa, *Easter*. The city's Holy Week processions are among the most elaborate and ornate in Spain.

On the far side of the Gran Vía Escultor Salzillo, Murcia's main street, you'll find the **Museo Salzillo** (*open Sept–June Tues–Sun 9.30–1 and 4–7, closed Mon; July and Aug daily 9.30–1 and 4–7; adm*), dedicated to the works of Murcian sculptor Francisco Salzillo (1707–83) who made many of the *pasos*, or floats, used in Murcia's Semana Santa processions, which make them some of Spain's best. Nearer the river are the plazas of Las Flores and Santa Catalina, two of the prettiest in the city, surrounded by elegant Baroque buildings occupied by dozens of bars, restaurants and cafés. Just by the river itself is the 13th-century **Almudí** (granary) now used as a municipal gallery, and a stretch of Moorish walls and one of the ancient look-out towers that used to ring the city – also now a gallery of local art. Opposite is the **Véronicas market**, piled high with glistening fresh local produce, naturally including Murcian red peppers, and the famous fresh prawns from the Mar Menor (*see* p.193).

Where to Stay

Murcia ✉ 30000

★★★★**Hotel Conde de Floridablanca**, Corbalán 7, **t** 968 21 46 26, *www.hoteles-catalonia.es* (*expensive–moderate*). Delightful Baroque palace in the old town, with air-con.

★★★★**NH Rincón de Pepe**, Plaza Apóstoles 34, **t** 968 21 22 39 (*expensive*). More modern, also with a/c (a big plus here when the torrid *leveche* wind blows in summer) and nice rooms. It has a fine **restaurant** (*see* below).

★★★★**Arco de San Juan**, Plaza de Ceballos 10, **t** 968 21 04 55, *www.arcosanjuan.com* (*moderate*). Modern, elegant and comfortable.

★★★**Hispano II**, C/Radio Murcia 3, **t** 968 21 61 52, *www.hispano.com* (*moderate*). Pleasant rooms with a/c at decent prices. Its cheaper, scruffier sister round the corner (**P. Hispano I**, C/Trapería 8, **t** as above) is only worth it if you're on a budget. The main hotel **restaurant** (*moderate*) is a local favourite.

★★**La Huertanica**, C/Infantes 3–5, **t** 968 21 76 68, **f** 968 21 25 04 (*moderate*). A central option; as a hotel in general it's a bit bland, but note that the top-floor rooms have amazing views.

★★**P. Segura**, Pza Camachos 19, **t** 968 21 12 81 (*inexpensive*). Over Murcia's old bridge: comfortable, basic rooms.

★**P. Perro Azul**, C/Simon Garcia 19, **t** 968 22 17 00 (*inexpensive*). You can't miss 'the blue dog': it's painted bright cobalt blue. Decent rooms, a good bar downstairs and a good, central location for partying in the bars

around Plaza las Flores. There's a laid-back, mellow bar downstairs, with reggae accompanying the *tapas*.

Eating Out

The **hotel restaurants** of the **Rincón de Pepe** (*expensive*), **Hispano** (*moderate*) and **Arco de San Juan** (*expensive*) all have excellent reputations; Rincón de Pepe's is the best in town (*see above for phone numbers*).

There are several good areas In Murcia for *tapas*: try around the cathedral, where there are several traditional places. Perhaps the best is the stylish, elegant **La Muralla** at the Hotel Rincón de Pepe, which has incorporated a stretch of the Moorish walls. Also good, but a bit more down to earth, are the bars around Plaza de las Flores. There are several lively, younger-oriented *tapas* bars – and plain old drinking bars – around the university.

Los Apóstoles, Pza Apóstoles 1, **t** 968 21 77 79 (*moderate*). Touristy but decent. Traditional local cuisine, with the menu changing daily and pretty brick décor. *Closed Aug.*

Paco Pepe, C/Madre de Dios 15, **t** 968 21 92 76 (*moderate*). Solid Murcian dishes at this very popular little local restaurant, which does a good *menú del día* (*inexpensive*).

Bocatta's Todo 100, C/Platería 44 (*cheap*). Small kiosk in a square, run by nice people and with a friendly atmosphere, serving very cheap, fuel-stop sandwiches.

Alegría, Pza San Antolín 4, **t** 968 29 09 10 (*cheap*). Health-food shop near the bus station – gorgeous wholemeal seed bread.

Day Trips and Overnighters from Murcia

La Manga

The biggest draw of this region and the 'Costa Cálida' is not at all the city of Murcia but instead this fast mushrooming tourist zone, right next to the airport at San Javier. In the first decades of Spanish tourist development, Murcia and La Manga were scarcely noticed, but they took off like a rocket in the 1990s. The centre of attraction is the Mar Menor or 'Little Sea', a broad, shallow saltwater lagoon of 170 square kilometres, very high in mineral content and, because it is so shallow, always balmily warm. Separating it from the sea is a long, narrow, beach-lined strip of sand called La Manga ('the sleeve') del Mar Menor, where you can choose between calm, warm beaches on the lagoon, or cooler waters along the Mediterranean. It's now ever-more lined with holiday developments, more often villas than hotels, centred around the very grand **La Manga Club**, the biggest integrated sports resort in Europe, with three championship-standard golf courses, a five-star hotel (*see* below), ranks of opulent villas and, among all kinds of world-class sports facilities, a specialized football centre now used by clubs and national teams from all over Europe for winter training.

Long before these modern luxuries were ever thought of, Moorish kings used to come to the Mar Menor for their ritual 'nine baths'; today some of the ancient mud pools are still used at **Lo Pagán**, not far from the airport in **San Pedro del Pinatar**, for

Getting There

Buses from Murcia bus station run fairly frequently to La Manga, and up and down 'The Sleeve' between San Pedro Pinatar and Cabo de Palos. Another route runs to San Javier and then down the west side of the Mar Menor, through Los Alcázares. By **car**, from Murcia city, follow the airport road (C3319), and La Manga is impossible to miss.

Tourist Information

Los Alcázares: C/Fuster 63, t 968 17 13 61.
La Manga del Mar Menor: Urb. Castillo del Mar, San Javier, t 968 14 18 12.
San Pedro del Pinatar: Parque de los Reyes de España, t 968 18 23 01.

Where to Stay and Eat

Mar Menor ✉ 30380

Like all resort areas La Manga has plenty of restaurants, to suit all budgets, and lots which have terraces on the seafront.

*****Hyatt La Manga, La Manga Club, t 968 33 12 34, *www.lamanga.hyatt.com* (*luxury*). For a real splurge it has to be this one, the only hotel in the La Manga club complex: very luxurious, in an international style, and with some of the world's best sports facilities within walking distance.

****Cavanna, Gran Vía de la Manga, t 968 56 36 00, f 968 56 44 31 (*expensive–moderate*). Excellent facilities including a pool, tennis and children's activities between the two seas. Rooms have a/c. *Open May–Sept.*

**Hotel Corzo, Av Aviacion 8, Los Alcázares, t 968 57 51 31 (*moderate*). A smart option; decent rooms and close to the beach on the quieter side of the Mar Menor.

**Hotel Los Narejos, Av de la Constitución, Los Alcázares, t 968 57 56 34 (*inexpensive*). Very reasonably priced for the area: not much charm, but a decent base if you're going to be out all day at the beach.

Miramar, Paseo del Puerto 14, Cabo de Palos, t 968 58 30 33 (*moderate*). Excellent seafood is served in local rice-based specialities; the *menú del día* (*inexpensive*) is very good value, and there are great views too.

rheumatism therapy. The holiday developments begin around there too, and run on down the 'sleeve' without too many interruptions, through **La Manga del Mar Menor** itself, not so much a village as a purpose-built resort, and the main nightlife-hub. The road ends at **Cabo de Palos**, which remains at least in part a pretty old harbour village with a fair bit of charm, and also has more fine beaches. There are also resorts along the landward side of the Mar Menor, which are particularly popular with Spanish families. The smooth waters of the inland sea are ideal for sailing, and at **Santiago de la Ribera** there is a popular sailing and watersports centre; further south, **Los Alcázares** is a low-key beach town overlooked by a Moorish tower. In addition, because of its warmth the Mar Menor is also used as a great prawn nursery, where Spain's favourite snacks may be harvested right up to the beginning of winter.

The Southern Costa Blanca: Torrevieja, Santa Pola and Orihuela

Thanks to its location and the light traffic on the local roads Murcia-San Javier airport is increasingly popular as an entry point not just for Murcia's own resorts but also for those of the southern stretch of the Costa Blanca, across the line in Alicante province. Like their neighbours of the Costa Cálida, these towns were largely passed over at the time when the resorts of the Costa Blanca-proper were first making themselves famous in the 1960s, in part because they were thought of as too hot and too dry, but they too have really taken off since the '80s, and **Torrevieja**, especially, is now ringed by a growing swathe of golf courses and villa developments, the hub of a huge market in second- and retirement homes for northern Europeans.

In contrast to the northern Costa Blanca, the landscapes south of Alicante are more like those of Murcia, mostly flat and not especially attractive, although in February blossoming almonds provide a pretty lace edging. Of the resorts, **Santa Pola**, furthest from Murcia and closest to Alicante, has good beaches and a landmark, fortified **Isla de Tabarca**, which you can visit on an excursion boat. It is surrounded by an underwater reserve, and the old Governor's residence has been converted into the only hotel on the island (*see* p.194). Behind Santa Pola are salt flats that are home to flamingos and many other birds, and have been made a nature reserve (*guided tours available; check with the information office*). Further south, **Guardamar del Segura** is more scenic than Santa Pola, with palms and pines, while **Torrevieja** has been transformed in a very short time into the biggest centre on the coast. The rocky bay at the centre of the town has been turned into an amazing swimming pool, and there's a long, lively street market which draws big crowds for the evening *paseo*. Between there and San Pedro in Murcia there are some quite tranquil beaches, as yet not too developed, belonging to Orihuela. Known collectively as **Las Playas de Orihuela**, the best and easiest to get to are Playa La Zenia and Playa Cabo Roig.

Just inland from this coast and 18 kilometres from Murcia is **Orihuela**, a prosperous oasis of a town set in its own very fertile *huerta*. Ferdinand and Isabella held court here in 1488, and it remained an important city long after; there are plenty of reminders of its illustrious past scattered among the narrow streets, including the idiosyncratic **cathedral** (*open Mon–Fri 10–1.30 and 5–7.30, Sat 10–1.30; closed Sun; adm to museum*). Finished in 1355, its interior is a fantasy of spiralling pillars and corkscrew-

Getting There

The Costa Azul company's **buses** run about every two hours from Murcia bus station up to Santa Pola via Torrevieja; there are also frequent services from Alicante. Torrevieja is also the last stop on a RENFE local **train** line, from Alicante via Elche. By **car**, the best route from Murcia city is to take the N340 northeast to Orihuela, and then the CV910 for Torrevieja and the coast; from San Javier airport, just follow the coast road north.

Tourist Information

Orihuela: Francisco Díez 25, t 965 30 27 47.
Santa Pola: Pza Diputación 6, t 966 69 22 76.
Torrevieja: Pza Ruiz Capdepont, t 965 71 59 36.

Where to Stay and Eat

**Hs Rey Teodomiro, Av Teodomiro 10, Orihuela, t 966 74 33 48 (*moderate*). The only choice for a hotel in the town itself: it's set in a bland, modern building not far from the station, but the management is kindly, and the rooms are spacious and well equipped.

**Hotel Casa del Gobernador, on Isla de Tabarca, t 965 96 08 86, f 965 11 42 60 (*moderate*). The only hotel on the island; perfect for divers or bird-watchers who want an early start, or anyone who wants to cut off from the hubbub of the coast for a while.

Hotel Patilla, C/Elche 29, Santa Pola, t 965 41 10 15, (*hotel and restaurant moderate*). A well-located hotel with a great, original **restaurant that's eccentrically kitted out like the interior of a ship.

**La Cibeles, Av Dr. Marañón 26, Torrevieja, t 965 71 00 12 (*moderate*). A pleasant beach *hostal* situated near the sea and the heart of things in Torrevieja.

Palomar, Playa de Levante s/n, Santa Pola, t 965 41 32 00 (*moderate*). One of the town's most enjoyable restaurants, with a magnificent terrace right on the seafront and good local rice and seafood specialities, and a well-priced *menú del día*.

rib vaulting; the **cathedral museum** has a Velázquez and other masters. Perhaps the town's most over-the-top monument is the **Church of Santa Domingo** (*open Tues–Sat 9.30–1.30 and 5–8, Sun and hols 10–2*), which became a university in 1569. It has two large cloisters; a subdued Renaissance one with gardens, and a frilly Baroque one added in the 18th century. The old refectory contains some of the finest examples of Valencian *azulejo* tiling, but the *pièce de résistance* is the church itself, a dizzying swirl of sublimely kitsch cherubs and gilt which cover every inch of the walls and roof.

A little further out of town, well beyond the university, is **El Palmeral**, Orihuela's own palm grove, one of the largest in Spain. Back in town, the Gothic **Church of Sant Justa y Rufina** (*open Mon–Fri 10–1.30 and 5–7.30, Sat 10–1.30; closed Sun; small donation requested*) prickles with gargoyles, including a small fleet taking wing from the square belltower, built in the 14th century. There's another fine example of Catalan Gothic in the little **Church of Santiago** (*open Mon–Fri 10–1.30 and 5–7.30, Sat 10–1.30; closed Sun; small donation requested*) just opposite the tourist office. Orihuela also has a host of smaller museums, including two dedicated to the town's biggest festivals: the **Museu de Semana Santa** (*open Mon–Fri 10–1 and 5–7, Sat 10–1; closed Sun*), with pictures and costumes from the Holy Week processions; and the **Museu de la Reconquista** (*open Mon–Fri 11–1 and 5–7; closed Sat and Sun*), with exhibits dedicated to the battles between the Moors and the Christians which are enacted annually in the middle of July. The former home of the Communist poet **Miguel Hernández** (*open Tues–Sat 10–2 and 5–7, Sun and hols 10–2; closed Mon*) has been opened as a small museum; if on the other hand you want to see one of the grander mansions of the era to find out how the other half lived, visit the **Palacio de Rubalcava** (*open Tues–Fri 10–2 and 5–8, Sun and hols 10–2; closed Mon and Sat*). Apart from housing the tourist office, it has magnificent tiling, as well as furniture, pottery, sculpture and paintings dating back three centuries. If you get the chance, visit the **Teatro Circo**, a fanciful, circular theatre from the late 19th century, designed for circuses as well as regular theatrical performances, which has been prettily restored.

Cartagena

Cartagena was the major city of the Carthaginians in Spain, who honoured it by naming it after their own capital, as 'New Carthage'. It prospered by dint of its gold and silver mines, and it was a major blow to Hannibal when Scipio Africanus besieged and captured it. It next made history when Francis Drake raided the port and snatched its guns in 1585. Later on, it became a hotbed of radicalism; a revolt by radicals in Cartagena in 1873, who briefly declared it an 'autonomous canton', contributed to the downfall of Spain's first Republican Government. The Civil War inflicted more damage; nor does the presence of a naval base improve its appearance.

Cartagena's port is dominated by its **Arsenal** (1782) and decorated with an early (1888) submarine, Isaac Peral's big white torpedo called the *Cartagena*. The old town is clustered around the woebegone, ruined 13th-century cathedral, where a path twists uphill to give a wonderful bird's-eye view of the remarkable **Roman theatre**, considered one of the finest in the whole of Spain. From here you can climb further to admire the views from the **Castillo de la Concepción**, which was built during the 13th century with stones recycled from the amphitheatre. The town is thickly studded with Roman ruins: walls, doorways and stretches of old Roman roads appear in the most unlikely places, and what the medieval builders left of the amphitheatre has been discovered beneath the shabby bullring. Behind the port, the **Calle Mayor** is the place to stroll during the evening *paseo*; it's dotted with florid *modernista* buildings, like the pink-domed **Ayuntamiento**, and the **Casino**, a popular place to stop for a drink. A hiking path, about 12 kilometres long, leads up over the cliffs of the Sierra de la Muela for dizzying views down into tranquil coves.

Getting There

The **FEVE** local **train** line runs from Murcia RENFE station down to **Cartagena** and **Los Nietos**, on the Mar Menor near Cabo de Palos, every 1½hrs. There are also more frequent **buses** from the main bus station. By **car**, follow the N-301.

Tourist Information

Cartagena: Puertas de San José, Plaza Bastarreche, t 968 50 64 83, *www.ayto-cartagena.es*.

Eating Out

Los Habaneros, San Diego 60, t 968 50 52 50 (*moderate*). At the entrance to the old city, this hotel-restaurant has a varied menu of high-standard local dishes, including some delicious seafood possibilities (*menú del día inexpensive; menu dégustacion is only verging on expensive*).

La Tartana, Puerta de Murcia 14, t 968 50 00 11 (*inexpensive*). An excellent place to get a taste of Cartagena, whether in a full meal in the restaurant, or in the big choice of delicious *tapas* at the bar.

Andalucía:
Málaga and Jerez

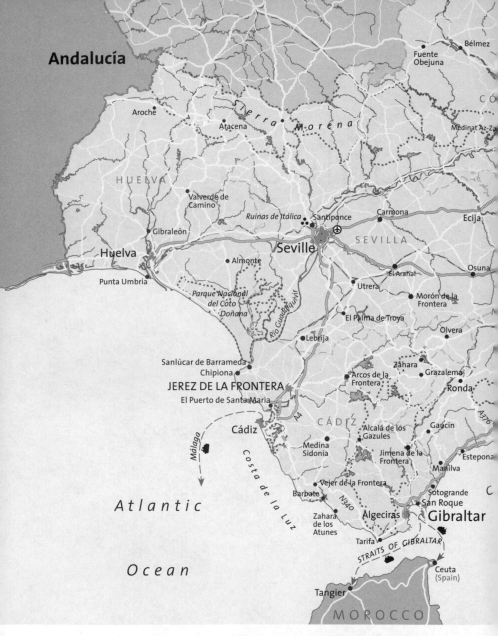

Andalucía

The ghost of Islamic al-Andalus still haunts southern Spain; a more graceful and delicate spirit could not be desired. In gardens, palaces and white villages, this lost civilization is a separate reality that shines through centuries of Spanish veneer. Shorn away from this refined heritage, Andalucía fell under the hand of one of the most useless and predatory aristocracies Europe has known. Today, though, the new Andalucía, after all its troubles, oppressions and inquisitions, is looking pretty well, thank you, with its exuberant life and culture, and a fun-loving population of generally sane and friendly people, as much of an attraction as the land itself.

Andalucía is a minefield of unexploded stereotypes: sequined matadors, flamenco, hot-blooded gypsies, orange blossoms and jasmine. They may be hard to avoid, but why try? Few regions have been blessed with such stereotypes. Visitors never weary of them, and nor it seems do Andalucíans, who cultivate them with care. Andalucía also contains a remarkable diversity of landscapes – from alpine mountains to rolling hills covered with olive trees, Europe's biggest wetland reserve and patches of desert. And no other part of Spain can offer so many fascinating cities. Andalucía is a world unto itself; it has as many delights to offer as you have time to spend.

Málaga

Much-maligned Málaga, capital of the Costa del Sol and also of a certain amount of sleaze in southern Spain, is making a determined effort to improve its reputation and attract more of the tourists who are all around it. In the past, a brief visit to its shops was often the only reason tourists spent any time here at all, between the airport and the beach. To miss Málaga, however, means to miss the most Spanish of cities, certainly on the Costa del Sol. It is alive and real: ungainly cranes and elegant palm trees compete for dominance of the skyline; police cars roar by as pretty girls toss their skirts and stamp their heels to flamenco, to a private audience in a public square; elegant old Spanish ladies, scented with *Maja* soap, sit and reminisce, and tattooed gypsy boys flash their double-edged smiles to lure you into a shoeshine. From its billboards and walls splashed with political slogans to its parks overflowing with exotic fauna, Málaga is a jamboree bag of colours, aromas and sounds.

Málaga cannot compete with Sevilla or Granada for wealth of cultural distractions, but the *malagueños* are proud of their fun-loving metropolis. To experience a real local *juerga* (spree), have an afternoon ramble through the many and famous *tapas* bars, where you will encounter more Spaniards in one afternoon than in a week in Torremolinos. Unfortunately, the old quarters of Málaga have been treated ruthlessly by town planners, and **El Perchel**, once the heart of Málaga's flamenco district, has lost a lot of its personality and charm. The Avenida de Andalucía cuts through this old district and then becomes the Alameda Principal and Paseo del Parque. The essence of Málaga is within this limited area, from the elegant Alameda to the seedy, teeming neo-Moorish market on the Calle Atarazanas.

You may find it hard to decide whether to love or loathe this city – will you notice the snarling drivers impatient for a green light, or the old gentlemen sipping sherry by the door of a cool, dark *bodega*, hung with Serrano hams and lined with wine casks?

The Heart of Málaga

As the Avenida de Andalucía, the main road from the west, crosses the dry rocky bed of the Guadalmedina river it becomes the **Alameda Principal**, a majestic 19th-century boulevard. North of the Alameda is the **Plaza de la Constitución**, the heart of the commercial centre, and the **Pasaje Chinitas**, an all-and-sundry shopping arcade. One of the clothes shops bears a commemorative plaque – it's the original site of the Café Chinitas, where bullfighters and flamenco singers gathered in the old days; the spirit of it was captured by García Lorca. The Alameda continues into the Paseo del Parque, a tree-lined promenade that runs along the port area, and leads to the city's **bullring**, built in 1874, and very much in use today. Nearby is the **English cemetery**. William Mark, the 19th-century consul, so loved Málaga that he described it as a 'second para-dise', and encouraged his fellow countrymen to join him here. In 1830 he founded this cemetery, allowing a decent burial to Protestants who had previously been buried on the beach. Hans Christian Andersen declared he could 'well understand how a splenetic Englishman might take his own life in order to be buried in this place'. Its sea views, however, have long since been blocked by concrete buildings.

Just off the Paseo del Parque, steps lead up to the Moorish **Alcazaba**. Under the Moors, Málaga was the most important port of al-Andalus, and from contemporary references it seems also to have been one of its most beautiful cities. King Fernando thoroughly ruined it in the conquest of 1487, and after the final expulsion of the Moors in 1568 little remained of its ancient distinction. Little too remains of the Alcazaba, except a few Moorish gates, but the site has been restored to a lovely series of terraced **gardens** (*open Wed–Sun 9.30–7*). At the top is an **archaeological museum**, containing relics from the Phoenician necropolis found on the site and some Moorish architectural decoration salvaged from the ruins. The top of the Alcazaba also affords fine views over Málaga. There is a half-ruined **Roman theatre**, recently excavated, on the lower slopes of the hill, and from the Alcazaba you may climb a little more to the **Gibralfaro** (*open 9–9*), the Moorish castle that dominates the city, now a *parador* (*see p.204*). But be careful – there have been reports of robberies on this path.

Back on the Paseo, note the chunky Art Nouveau **Ayuntamiento**, one of the more unusual buildings in Málaga. On the opposite side of the Alcazaba is the **Museo de Bellas Artes**, C/San Agustín 8, in a restored 16th-century palace. It is currently being turned into the city's Picasso museum. Picasso was a native of Málaga, although once he left it at the age of 14 he never returned. Much of the museum is given over to the works of other late 19th-century *malagueño* painters who made up in eccentricity what they lacked in genius; one of them, Antonio Múñoz Degrain, was Picasso's first teacher. The artist's birthplace, **Casa Natal Picasso**, which now incorporates the **Municipal Picasso Foundation**, on Plaza de la Merced, is open for visits and holds occasional exhibitions (*open Mon–Sat 11–2 and 5–8, Sun 11–2; adm*).

Málaga's **cathedral** is a few blocks away on Calle Molina Lario. It's an ugly, unfinished 16th-century work, immense and mouldering. Known as *La Manquita* (the one-armed lady), its only interesting feature is the faded, gaudy façade of the **sacristy**, left over from the earlier Isabelline Gothic church that once stood here (*open Mon–Sat 9–6.45, closed Sun; adm*). Further west and next to the usually-dry river bed, the **Museo de Artes Populares** on Pasillo de Santa Isabel (*open 10–1.30 and 4–8 in summer, 10–1.30 and 4–7 in winter; closed Sat afternoon and Sun; adm*), occupies a restored 17th-century inn, and has a collection of household bric-a-brac.

Outside Málaga, The **Jardin Botánico Historico** (*open 9.30–7; adm*), an old farm 7km north of Málaga on the new road to Granada (N-331), has been transformed into one of Spain's most important botanical gardens. They were founded in the mid-19th century by Amalia Loring, who encouraged ships' captains to bring her plants from around the world. The gardens passed on to the Echevarria family, who eventually could no longer afford their upkeep, and by the time Málaga city council bought them in 1990 they had grown into a virtual jungle. After much pruning, they were re-opened in 1994 and display a variety of plants from around the world, including a 700-year-old Canary Islands Dragon Tree (which could live up to 2,000 years).

For some reason the tourist industry has neglected the areas east of the city. There are a few resorts strung out along the coastal highway, notably **Torre del Mar**, but they are all rather grim-looking places: little bits of Málaga that escaped to the beach. Nearby are some scanty remains of a Greco-Phoenician settlement called **Mainake**.

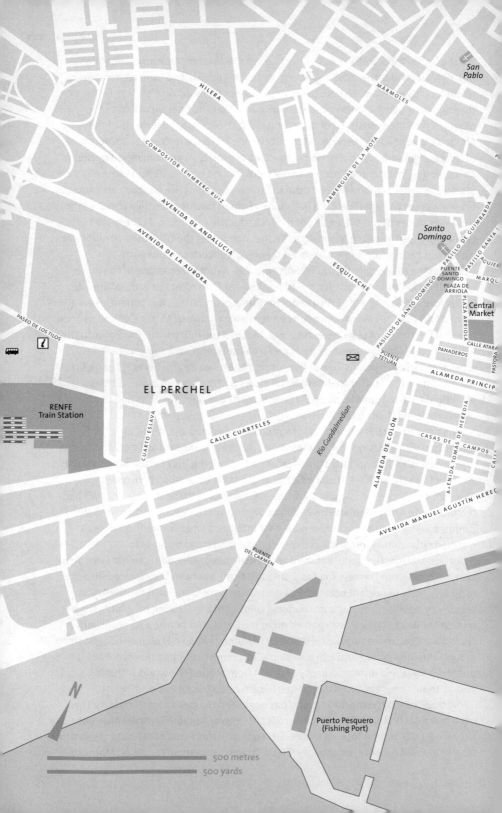

HILERA

MÁRMOLES

San Pablo

COMPOSITOR LEHMBERG RUIZ

ARMENGUAL DE LA MOTA

AVENIDA DE ANDALUCÍA

Santo Domingo

PASILLO DE GUIMBARDA

AVENIDA DE LA AURORA

ESQUILACHE

PUENTE SANTO DOMINGO

PASILLO SANTA

PASILLO ACUJE

MARQL

PLAZA DE ARRIOLA

Central Market

PLAZA ARRIOLA

PASTORA

PASEO DE LOS TILOS

PASILLOS DE SANTO DOMINGO

CALLE ATARA

PANADEROS

EL PERCHEL

PUENTE TETUÁN

ALAMEDA PRINCIP

RENFE Train Station

Río Guadalmedian

ALAMEDA DE COLÓN

AVENIDA TOMÁS DE HEREDIA

CASAS DE CAMPOS

CALL

CUARTO ESLAVA

CALLE CUARTELES

AVENIDA MANUEL AGUSTÍN HERE

PUENTE DEL CARMEN

Puerto Pesquero (Fishing Port)

N

500 metres
500 yards

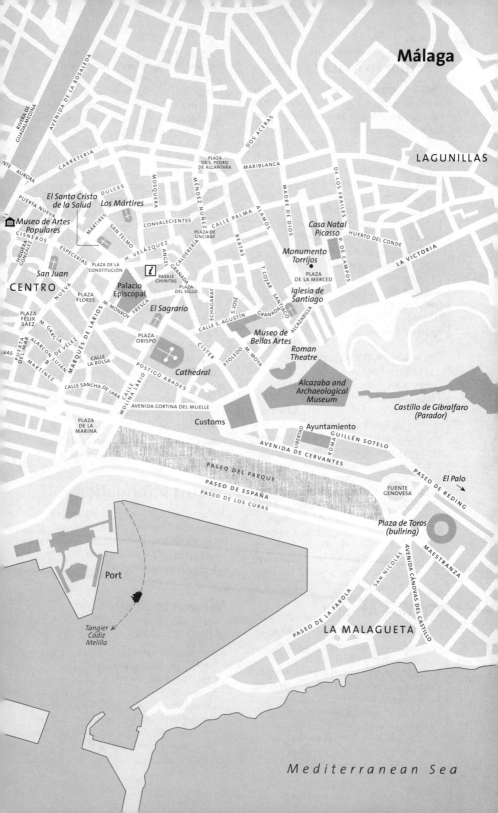

Málaga

LAGUNILLAS

AVENIDA DE LA ROSALEDA

RIVERA DE GUADALMEDINA

AVENIDA DE LA SALUD

PTE. AURORA

CARRETERIA

PLAZA DE S. PEDRO DE ALCÁNTARA

DOS ACERAS

MARIBLANCA

DE LOS FRAILES

DULCES

MOSQUERA

MÉNDEZ NÚÑEZ

MADRE DE DIOS

HUERTO DEL CONDE

El Santo Cristo de la Salud

Los Mártires

PUERTA NUEVA

MÁRTIRES

SAN TELMO

CONVALECIENTES

CALLE PALMA

ÁLAMOS

Casa Natal Picasso

P. DE CAMPOS

LA VICTORIA

Museo de Artes Populares

CISNEROS

ESPECERÍAS

H. VELÁZQUEZ

PLAZA DE UNCIBAY

BEATAS

Monumento Torrijos

HIGUERA GONZÁLEZ

ÁNGEL

GRANADA

CALDERERÍA

PLAZA DE LA MERCED

San Juan

PLAZA DE LA CONSTITUCIÓN

PASAJE CHINITAS

PLAZA DEL SIGLO

T. CÓZAR SANTIAGO

Iglesia de Santiago

CENTRO

NUEVA

Palacio Episcopal

M. MONROY

FRESCA

CALLE ECHEGARAY

GRANADA

ALCAZABILLA

PLAZA FLORES

El Sagrario

CALLE S. AGUSTÍN

S. JOSÉ

PLAZA FÉLIX SÁEZ

M. GARCÍA

ALARCÓN DE VÉLEZ

MARQUÉS DE LARIOS

PLAZA OBISPO

CÍSTER

Museo de Bellas Artes

Roman Theatre

PUERTA DEL MAR

M. LUJÁN

CALLE LA BOLSA

P. TOLEDO

M. MOYA

MARTÍNEZ

POSTIGO ABADES

Cathedral

Alcazaba and Archaeological Museum

Castillo de Gibralfaro (Parador)

CALLE SANCHA DE LARA

CALLE MOLINA LARIO

AVENIDA CORTINA DEL MUELLE

PLAZA DE LA MARINA

Customs

LIBERTAD

ROMA

Ayuntamiento

GUILLÉN SOTELO

PASEO DE REDING

El Palo

AVENIDA DE CERVANTES

PASEO DEL PARQUE

PASEO DE ESPAÑA

PASEO DE LOS CURAS

FUENTE GENOVESA

Plaza de Toros (bullring)

SAN NICOLÁS

MAESTRANZA

Port

AVENIDA CÁNOVAS DEL CASTILLO

Tangier
Cádiz
Melilla

PASEO DE LA FAROLA

PASEO DE LA FAROLA

LA MALAGUETA

Mediterranean Sea

Getting to Málaga

Málaga's airport, 11km southwest, is one of Spain's busiest – so much so that congestion has been a problem in peak holiday seasons, but a recently built terminal has relieved pressure a bit and reduced baggage delays. As well as frequent charters, it has many scheduled flights from the UK: **Bmibaby** flies from East Midlands; **easyJet** (including ex-**Go** routes) from Stansted, East Midlands, Bristol, Gatwick, Liverpool and Luton; **mytravellite** from Birmingham; **Monarch** from Luton and Manchester; and **Iberia** from Heathrow.

For airline details, see p.11.

Airport flight information: t 952 04 84 84.
Bmibaby: t 902 10 07 37.
easyJet: t 902 29 99 92.
Iberia: t 902 40 05 00.
Monarch: t 952 04 83 50.
mytravellite: t 914 53 42 38.

Getting from the Airport

The airport has a station on the RENFE *Cercanías* local **train** line between Málaga and Fuengirola via Torremolinos: from Arrivals, go up a floor to the Departures area, go out of the Terminal and follow the *Ferrocarril* signs to the right. Trains run every 30 mins, at 15 and 45 mins past each hour, daily 7am–11.45pm (from Málaga, 5.45am–10.30pm). For the city centre, get off at the end of the line, **Centro-Alameda**, not at **Málaga-RENFE**, the mainline railway station. **Buses** also run from the airport to the city bus station, every 30 mins daily from 6.30am–11.30pm. A **taxi** from the airport costs about €12–€16 and takes about 20 mins; cab drivers here have been known to overcharge, so try to check the rates, posted at the rank.

Getting Around

The main RENFE **train** station is about 15min walk west of the city centre. The *Cercanías* local line to Fuengirola is very handy for getting up and down part of the Costa del Sol (for timings, see above). There are also direct *Regional* services to Córdoba and Seville, and several daily to Madrid, Barcelona and other destinations. An eccentricity of rail travel in Andalucía, though, is the **Bobadilla** effect: because different parts of the network were originally built by separate companies, they meet (but do not actually connect) only at the strange little junction of Bobadilla, near Antequera. Because of this some journeys (notably Málaga–Granada) involve changing trains there, which can drag out the journey. In these cases, buses are often faster.

The **bus** station is just north of the train station, on Paseo de los Tilos. Buses run fairly frequently to all destinations in the region, and especially Ronda and places on the coast.

Most places of interest in the city are within a walkable area, but there is a decent bus service, and **taxis** are cheap. You can call for a cab on t 952 34 52 04.

Train information: t (national) 902 24 02 02, (local) 952 36 02 02.
Bus information: t 952 35 00 61.

Car Hire

For car hire in Spain in general, see pp.17–18. All companies also have offices or will deliver cars at the airport, and there are many hire companies in all the towns along the costa.
Autopro Rentacar, Carril de Montañez 49, t 952 17 60 30. Good-value local company; cars can be picked up at the airport.
Avis, Cortina del Muelle 13, t 952 22 49 49.
Europcar, Carril de San Isidro 3, t 952 17 37 77.
National-Atesa, RENFE station, t 952 35 65 50.

Tourist Information

Málaga: Compositor Lehmberg Ruiz 3, t 95 228 83 54. *Open Mon–Fri 9–1.30 and 5–7.*

There are branch offices at Pasaje Chinitas 4, just north of the Alameda and at the airport, and booths at the bus and train stations.

Where to Stay

Málaga ✉ 29000

Expensive–Moderate

****Parador de Gibralfaro**, Castillo de Gibralfaro, t 952 22 19 02, *gibralfaro@parador.es*. Up in the old Moorish castle above the city; with a lovely pool, it offers the very best view of Málaga, and is one of the most enjoyable places to stay. Lunching on its terrace is unforgettable.

****Larios**, Marqués de Larios 2, t 952 22 22 00. Well appointed, extremely comfortable and good value (cheaper rates at weekends).

****Málaga Palacio**, Avda Cortina del Muelle 1, t 952 22 06 98. Part of the AC chain, with an excellent location at the top of the Alameda, and sweeping views over the port. Try to get a room on an upper floor.

*****Hotel Don Curro**, C/Sancha de Lara 7, t 952 22 72 00. Excellently placed behind the Alameda, a short walk from the cathedral.

Inexpensive

Any place on or around the Alameda will be decent, but avoid the really cheap budget dives around the train station.

***Alameda**, Casa de Campos 3, t 952 22 20 99. In the south of town, a pretty basic but decent value budget hotel.

Castilla, C/Córdoba 5, t 952 21 86 35. Along with the Guerrero, which is in the same building, this is a well-run establishment.

Casa Huéspedes Bolivia, Casa de Campos 24, t 952 21 88 26. Spotlessly clean and central.

Eating Out

El Compá, C/La Bolsa 7, t 952 22 97 06 (*expensive*). An excellent restaurant, albeit sometimes a little pricy, specializing in fresh local fish and with a big wine selection.

Méson Astorga, C/Gerona 11, t 952 34 68 32 (*moderate*). A really atmospheric *malagueño* restaurant that's on the up and up – a good place to enjoy a long late lunch.

Antonio Martín, Paseo Marítimo, t 952 22 21 13 (*moderate*). *Malagueños* flock to the Paseo Marítimo and El Palo district east of town on Sundays to fill up the restaurants that line the beaches in this former fishing district. This one is a favourite: fish and rice dishes as the basis of the menu, and try scrambled eggs with baby eel and salmon, or gilthead bream cooked in salt. *Closed in winter.*

El Cabra, C/Copo 21, Paseo El Pedregal, t 952 29 50 70 (*expensive*). Another restaurant in this area, with a pricier range of seafood.

Casa Pedro, C/Quitapenas 57, El Palo, t 952 29 00 13 (*moderate*). You may well be deafened by the din while you tuck into skewered sardines or Sierra-style angler fish. *Closed Mon evenings.*

Café Cosmopolita, C/Marqués de Larios (*inexpensive*). Start your day with breakfast at this café, with tables spilling onto the pavement from around the wooden horseshoe bar. Service is outrageously slow, but this allows you to relax over your paper.

Cafetería Horizonte, t 952 22 56 23 (*inexpensive*). Fine *tapas*, cakes or ice creams.

Antigua Casa de Guardia, Alameda 18 (*inexpensive*). For sherry, prawns and a marvellous atmosphere come here to choose from one of 20 or so barrels lining the bar, with names like *Pajarete 1908* and *Guinda*.

Bar Lo Güeno, C/Marín García 9 (*inexpensive*). Head here for *tapas* – it's literally a hole in the wall, serving imaginative *raciones* and a decent selection of wines.

Orellana, C/Moreno Monroy (*inexpensive*). One of the city's oldest and most classic *tapas* bars (they still offer a free *tapa* – or 'lid' – with your first glass of sherry).

Meson la Aldea, C/Esparteros 5, t 952 22 76 89 (*inexpensive*). A great *tapas* restaurant, with a speciality you won't find anywhere else in Málaga: *carne el curry*. Try also the *flamenquin de carne*, a cheese and ham dish.

Rincon de el Tillo, C/Esparteros, t 952 22 31 35 (*moderate*). A more upmarket *taberna* opposite Meson la Aldea.

La Arkesama, C/Cervantes 10, t 952 21 79 26 (*inexpensive*). Full of hams, cheese and atmosphere, at a reasonable price.

Nightlife

Málaga has a buzzing summer club scene. On Friday or Saturday nights, it's hard to move through the streets between Plaza de la Constitucion and Plaza de Siglo, as hundreds of trendy Spaniards spill out of a bewildering variety of street bars and clubs. Some of the best bars are in and around Plaza de Uncibay, C/Granada and Plaza Merced. A few bars and disco bars can also be found down by the bullring. In summer, the action moves out to the beaches, particularly Pedragalejo and El Palo.

Bar Pim Pi, C/Granada. A good place to start nocturnal wanderings – a small doorway leads into a courtyard with rooms off every angle – cellars, patios, balconies – where beautiful *malagueños* come out to play.

Day Trips and Overnighters from Málaga

Torremolinos

All sources agree about Torremolinos: the oldest and biggest resort town on the Costa del Sol, it has become a hyperactive, unsightly holiday inferno. In other words, it has character. Torremolinos isn't interested in anyone's opinion, as it's been doing well for years with its endless blocks of bars, shopping centres and concrete hotels. For those who want to spend a bit of time in the fast lane, in a raucous, international, synthetic environment, this is the place. In summer, tourists, hustlers, gypsies, drug-pushers and an assortment of others mingle in the streets and the movement is fast and furious. The predominant language is English, but a dozen others can be heard in the space of a few steps. To escape this horde step down to one of the beach cafés: if your luck is in, you'll be treated to some of the local street performers sharing their talents: an *anís*-soaked troubadour mangling an aria, or a transvestite flamenco dancer, whirling between passing cars. Welcome signs on the outskirts proclaim this to be the 'City of Tourists', and each August it becomes the third largest city in Andalucía, when 36,000 residents are joined by some quarter of a million tourists. In recent years the city, like Benidorm, has also made attempts to cloak itself in green, and in among the concrete blocks there are now leafy spaces. The tree-lined **Paseo**

Getting There

Torremolinos and **Fuengirola** (the end of the line) are both stops on the *Cercanías* local **train** line from Málaga. Trains start from Centro-Alameda in the middle of Málaga (with a stop at Málaga-RENFE) every 30mins daily 5.45am–22.30pm, and leave from Fuengirola 6.33am–23.15pm. The full trip along the line takes 40mins. The Portillo company runs **bus** services all along the Costa del Sol from Málaga bus station, which in busy areas (such as all the way from Málaga to Fuengirola) operate almost like city buses, stopping every few hundred metres, so that some take a very long time; there are also 'express' buses that stop less often, so check.

For **Mijas**, there are direct buses from Málaga, or take a train to Benalmádena and get one from there (which may be quicker).

By **car**, take the N340 west. Once notorious as the 'death highway' because of its accident rate, most of this road has been upgraded into a near motorway-standard *autovía*, which has greatly reduced congestion and the number of blind bends. Also, from Fuengirola to Estepona it is flanked by a part of the A7, a full-scale, toll *autopista*.

Tourist Information

Torremolinos: Plaza de la Independencia, **t** 952 37 42 31.
Fuengirola: Avda Jesús Rein 6, **t** 952 46 76 25.
Mijas: Plaza Mayor, **t** 952 48 59 00.

Eating Out

Carihuela in Torremolinos and Los Boliches in Fuengirola are beachside areas where you can eat fresh fish at low prices.

Torremolinos

Mar de Alborán, Hotel Alay, Avda Alay 5, Benalmádena Costa, **t** 952 44 64 27 (*expensive*). Highly recommended. Basque and Andalucían cuisine. *Closed Sun and Mon.*
Casa Guaquín, C/Carmen 37, **t** 952 38 45 30 (*moderate*). Real local specialities.
Escuela de Hostelería de Málaga, Finca La Cónsula, Churriana, **t** 952 62 24 24 (*moderate*). In an old mansion, and an interesting experience. Hotel school students prepare lunches with subtle *andaluz* recipes. Booking essential.
La Chacha, Avda Palma de Mallorca (*inexpensive*). A real old-style *comedor* where you can

Marítimo – an uninterrupted 6km stretch leading to Puerto Marina at Benalmádena – makes a pleasant stroll. The marina is Torre's less plush answer to Marbella's Puerto Banús, a quayside spot for dining and yacht-gazing. **Benalmádena** itself claims an ancient history back as far as the Phoenicians, and so has the **Castillo del Bil Bil** – of Moorish origin and now used for concerts – a bullring, and a **Pre-Colombian Museum** (*open Mon–Fri 10–2 and 4–7*), with artefacts from Latin America.

Fuengirola and Mijas

Another 21km west, Fuengirola was once a typical whitewashed Spanish fishing village. It's still white, but hardly typical, and even less Spanish. With miles of *urbanizaciónes* around it, it would be easy to be hard on Fuengirola, except that everyone here seems to be having a good time. The town, and adjacent **Los Boliches**, are places where you see signs in shop-windowsreading '*Se habla español*'. The Costa del Sol is by far the most popular place for British people buying homes in Spain, joined by many from other parts of Europe, and Fuengirola (or 'Fungaroller') is one of their favourite spots. The shops of the old village have been transformed into pubs, English bookshops, travel agencies and Swiss, Chinese, Italian, Moroccan and even Spanish restaurants. Spaniards still live in most of the town, sunbathing on their flat roofs or balconies; the foreigners drive in from the *urbanizaciónes* for pub-hopping or to shop

choose from *gambas* and *pulpo* as you sit at the bar.

Bodega Quitapeñas, by the beach (*inexpensive*). Sit outside this *bodega* in town for a cheap aperitif – everybody passes this way.

Fuengirola and Mijas

Portofino, Edificio Perla 1, Paseo Marítimo, Fuengirola, t 952 47 06 43 (*expensive*). Italian-based restaurant. *Closed Mon*.

Valparaíso, Ctra de Mijas, km 4, t 952 48 59 75 (*expensive*). Outside Fuengirola on the road to Mijas, this is one of the most popular in the area, with bars, terrace, pool and a varied menu. It's chi-chi (women get menus without prices), but it's a favourite haunt of local expats. *Closed Sun except July–Oct*.

Blanco, Plaza de la Constitución 2, Mijas, t 952 48 57 00 (*moderate*). Family-run restaurant with Basque fish specials; one of Mijas' best.

Casa Navarra, Ctra de Mijas (by Valparaíso), km 4, near Fuengirola, t 952 58 04 39 (*moderate*). Navarrese cuisine, including steaks and fish that you choose yourself. *Closed Tues*.

La Cepa, Plaza Constitución, Fuengirola (*inexpensive*). The place to come for some pub-style grub while you observe the movements on the plaza.

Hermanos Blanco, Paseo Maritimo, Fuengirola (*moderate*). Typical of the great-value *chiringuitos* in the Los Boliches area.

Nightlife

The very name **Torremolinos** is a byword for hedonistic fun, but the party has moved on, and it's never tried to keep up with places like Ibiza in the hip stakes. The best action is 3km away at Puerto Marina in **Benalmádena**. Torre is also, of course, awash with English-style bars, up and down C/San Miguel and Plaza de la Independencia. **Fuengirola** has never rocked as much as its neighbour, but has its share of brash bars and discos. In the centre they're concentrated around Plaza Constitución. Off Paseo Maritimo, C/Martinez Catena has bars, clubs and restaurants vying for punters.

El Botijo, C/Capitán, Fuengirola. One of several stylish cocktail bars.

The Palladium, Avda Palma de Mallorca 36, Torremolinos. In town, and in the style of a Roman bath, complete with pool.

Piper's, Avda Palma de Mallorca, Torremolinos. Possibly the biggest club in Spain, with seven dancefloors and six bars.

in the vast hypermarkets. Unlike in other resorts on the Costa, there are also some things to see – the Moorish **Castillo de Sohail** above town, a bullring, even a **Roman temple**. In Roman times there were important marble quarries in the mountains near here, and off the coast divers recently discovered a wreck with these stones.

Just inland from Fuengirola is the **Sierra de Mijas**, with (originally) small hill villages that are now a location of choice for home-buyers looking for views, cool breezes and a quieter atmosphere than on the *costa*. Its centre is **Mijas**, to which visitors drive by the coachload to find a typical Andalucían village, which it hasn't been for years. By dusk it returns to the hands of its foreign residents, nearly half the population. Yet, it's still a pretty place, with a promenade with views out to sea, a shrine to the Virgin, pine woods, souvenir shops and 'officially licensed *burro* taxis' to take you around.

Marbella and Puerto Banús

Marbella finds herself in the middle of the stretch of coast said to be the fastest-growing area in Europe, so it is not without its growing pains. Until recently, zoning laws were permissive to the point of being totally ineffective, and so eager developers

Getting There

There are frequent Portillo **buses** to Marbella from Málaga bus station (get an *expreso*, with only a few stops). Marbella is 60km from Málaga; by **car**, you can get there fast on the A7 (toll) from Fuengirola, which has left the old N340 coast road, now also of a good standard, as a slightly more peaceful 'scenic route'.

Tourist Information

Marbella: Glorieta La Fontanilla, t 952 77 14 42, and Plaza Los Naranjos, t 952 82 35 50.
Puerto Banús: Avda Principal, t 952 81 74 74.

Eating Out

Marbella naturally has a wealth of eating spots to suit all tastes, although, once you're here, it seems only right to go for the luxurious. For inexpensive eating it also has excellent *tapas* bars, in the old town and the streets behind the Alameda. Many of the inexpensive *chiringuito* beach restaurants that run the length of the coast are open year-round.
Hostería del Mar, Avda Cánovas del Castillo 1A, t 952 77 02 18 (*expensive*). Summer dining on the patio by a pool, and cosy inside in winter. Specialities include chicken and prawns Catalan-style. *Open evenings only, closed Sun.*

La Meridiana, Camino de la Cruz. t 952 77 61 90 (*expensive*). Marbella's most expensive and glamorous restaurant, offering designer dishes such as salad of angler fish marinated in dill. *Open evenings only*.
La Torre, Club de Mar, Puerto Banús, t 952 81 15 61 (*expensive*). On the marina, with superb views and excellent seafood, but at a price.
Villa Tiberio, Ctra Cádiz, t 952 77 17 99 (*expensive*). An Italian restaurant with affordable prices, soft music and luxurious surroundings. Your host will kiss you (if you're female) on both cheeks, whether or not he's ever clapped eyes on you; it's that kind of place.
Dalli Pasta Factory, Avda Fontanilla, t 952 77 67 76 (*moderate*). Toni Dalli has a mini-empire around Marbella, offering delicious fresh pasta at very reasonable prices.

Nightlife

Most action will be found in Puerto Banús, with its late bars, discos and piano bars. The best bars in the old town are on and around Plaza de los Naranjos, and Plaza de los Olivos, and near the Paseo Marítimo.
Sinatra's, at the main entrance to the port. The classic hang-out of the see-and-be-seen set.
Atrium, C/Gregorio Marañon 11. A place to investigate for early drinks; super-hip and pricey with outdoor seating and foliage.

could throw up one unattractive building after another. But for every ugly development there is a stunningly beautiful one, carefully preserving Andalucían tradition and landscaped with trees, lawns and flowering shrubs. So, Marbella continues to thrive, as the smartest, most expensive and complex resort in Spain. When you arrive, you might find yourself asking why – its appeal is not obvious. When you get to know it, this in itself is one of Marbella's attractions. The place has been much maligned, but the old quarter is still a delight, as whitewashed and charming as Andalucía can be, without being cutesy or tripperish. If you're in doubt whether any Spaniards live here, come in May when the *feria* is in full swing – an event you're unlikely to forget.

Nonetheless, for the earnest tourist there is not a great deal to see. You can pay high prices here and yet still not get in on the action, which takes place in private clubs, villas and yachts. Besides, few foreigners actually live in old Marbella itself; self-styled artists and flashy bachelors take studios in **Puerto Banús**, golfers head for 'Golf Valley' in **Nueva Andalucía**, and very well-heeled French, Italians and Germans heave-ho at the **Marbella Club** and **Puente Romano**, both a few kilometres west of town. **Puerto Banús** is the brilliantly designed, ancient-looking (but modern) development 6km to the west, with a marina full of gin palaces; don't pass up the chance of spending an afternoon or evening in one of the waterside cafés here.

East of Málaga: the Axarquia and the Costa Tropical

The resorts east of Málaga have no special attractions, except that they're less crowded than the big names to the west, but a turn inland from Torre del Mar will take you to **Vélez-Málaga**, in a fertile valley and with a Moorish castle, **La Fortaleza** (of which a restored tower remains, in pretty gardens) and several fine churches, including **La Encarnación**, which began life as a Visigothic church, was then a mosque, and then became a church again. Vélez-Málaga is also the gateway to the **Axarquia**, a collection of tiny whitewashed villages on the slopes of the **Sierra de Tejeda** national park, a less-explored region than the Serranía de Ronda, but no less beautiful.

To really explore you need a car, as public transport is scarce. Some villages, such as **Frigiliana** and **Torrox**, both a short drive from the coast, have undergone the same fate as Mijas (*see* p.208), and are now ringed by villas. Press on into the hills, however, and you find little gems like Cómpeta and Almáchar, or **Comares**, perched atop one of the highest peaks and with one of the best-positioned hotels in the region (*see* p.210). Comares is known as the *Balcón de la Axarquia*, with views from its main square across the valley to the coast, the other villages like splashes of white paint on a green canvas. It was of strategic importance in Moorish times, and there are the ruins of a Moorish **castle** at its highest point. West of Vélez, **Almáchar** is an exquisite little village of tumbling houses and winding streets, best explored on foot. Leave your car at the top of town and head down C/Eugenia Rios: in spring and summer, the town is a riot of colours, with flowers spilling from every balcony and patio box. Unusually, the uniform white of the houses is broken up with splashes of violet, pink and mauve. From Comares you can press on to **Colmenar**, a dusty town on the borders of Málaga province and a centre for honey production. Another Axarquia route, perhaps less dramatic and a good deal shorter, begins on the coast east of Vélez and winds

Getting There

Portillo or Alsina Graells **buses** from Málaga run to Nerja, Almuñécar and Salobreña, and (infrequent) buses run from these towns to interior villages. By car, take the N340 east to Torre del Mar (35km) and turn inland.

Tourist Information

Frigiliana: Pza del Ingeniero s/n, **t** 952 53 31 26.
Nerja: Puerto de Mar 1, **t** 952 52 15 31.

Where to Stay and Eat

El Molino de los Abuelos, Plaza Mayor 2, Comares, **t** 952 50 93 09, *www.molino-abuelos (moderate–inexpensive)*. Possibly the best-located hotel in the region: an old olive mill beautifully converted into a small hotel. There are five rooms and an apartment: the ones to go for are the front-facing double or the suite, which look right out across the

valley. The atmospheric **restaurant** below serves a fine selection of local dishes.

Hotel Balcón de Competa, C/San Antonio 75, Cómpeta, **t** 952 55 35 35, *www.hotel-competa.com (moderate)*. Nice rooms, fantastic views, a **restaurant**, café and pool, and activities such as riding, hiking and golf.

Hostal Canillas, Canillas de Aceituno. **t** 952 51 81 02 *(inexpensive)*. Canillas, west of Cómpeta, has this one little place to stay, with rooms above a shop on a quiet street. The *duena* also has apartments to let.

Hotel Balcón de Europa 1, Paseo Balcón de Europa, Nerja, **t** 952 52 08 00, *balcon europa@spa.es (expensive–moderate)*. A fabulous location on the 'balcony of Europe' makes the difference at this hotel. It has a lift down to the beaches under Nerja's cliffs.

Meson de la Villa, Plaza F. Ramirez de Madrid, Salobreña, **t** 958 61 24 14 *(moderate)*. The best restaurant in Salobreña, serving up local fish dishes and *rabo de toro* (oxtail). *Closed Wed*. There are also good *chiringuitos* along the beach during the season.

through **Salares** and **Sedella**, two of the prettiest villages in the area. Continue on to **Cómpeta**, a truly lovely old village known principally for its sweet wines. As has happened with many Andalucían villages near the coast, northern invaders have discovered its charm, Brits and Danes particularly. Beyond Cómpeta begin the wilds of the **Reserva Nacional de Sierra de Tejeda**, with plenty of rugged walks. To return to the coast, take the MA-137 through beautiful vine-clad slopes to **Torrox**, another Nordic enclave, from where the road drops down to the expanding resort of **Torrox-Costa**.

To the east along the coast road the scenery becomes more impressive as mountains loom closer to the sea. Eight kilometres on is **Nerja**. A very pleasant resort, its big attractions are the **Balcón de Europa**, a promenade with fountain above the sea, and secluded beaches under the cliffs, either side of the town. A few kilometres east, the **Cueva de Nerja** *(open daily 10.30–12 and 4–6.30; adm)* is one of Spain's fabled grottoes, full of Gaudiesque formations and needle-thin stalactites. This perfect setting is occasionally used for ballets and concerts. A scenic 7km drive north finds **Frigiliana**, a pristine whitewashed village of cobbled streets and, nowadays, a big expat population. The coast road east of Nerja, bobbing in and out of the hills and cliffs, is the best part of the whole Costa. The next resort, **Almuñécar**, is a nest of high-rises, but even this former fishing village has a lot to offer, not least that Laurie Lee immortalized it in *As I Walked Out One Midsummer Morning*, describing his experiences just prior to the Civil War. **Salobreña** is much nicer, although it may not stay that way. The village's dramatic setting, slung down on a steep, lone peak overlooking the sea, is the most stunning on the coast, and has insulated it just a little from big tourism, although *urbanizaciones* are now sprouting fast. The best beaches here are 2km southeast.

Ronda

Away from beaches and inland from Málaga, the biggest attraction for a short trip is Ronda, the only city in the dramatic Serranía de Ronda. It's a spectacularly beautiful place, blessed with a perfect postcard shot of its lofty bridge over the steep gorge that divides the old and new towns. Its monuments are actually surprisingly few, but the views from the top of the city alone are worth the trip. One of the best places from which to enjoy them is the **Alameda del Tajo**, a park on the edge of the **Mercadillo**, as the new town is called. At its north end is the 16th-century **Convento de la Merced**, where nuns will sell you sweeties. Next to it, Ronda has one of Spain's most picturesque bullrings. The 1785 **Plaza de Toros**, the 'cathedral of bullfighting', stages only about three *corridas* a year – including *La Goyesca* each September, in 18th-century costume – but has great prestige: the art of bullfighting was developed here. There's a small **museum** (*open daily Nov–Feb 10–6, Mar–Oct 10–7; adm*) which has pictures, costumes and photos, including those of Orson Welles, who wanted his ashes scattered here, and Hemingway, who mentions it in *Death in the Afternoon*.

Ronda's other landmark, the **Puente Nuevo**, was built at the second try in 1740 – the first one immediately collapsed. Its two thick piers descend almost 92m (300ft) to the bottom of the narrow gorge. The main square, **Plaza de Socorro**, is where most of the town comes out before dinner. Crossing the bridge into the **Ciudad** (old town), a steep path heads downwards to two 18th-century palaces: the **Palacio de Salvatierra**, a Renaissance mansion still used as a private house (tours are available), and the **Casa del Rey Moro** (*open daily 10–8; adm*), built over Moorish foundations. From its garden

Getting There

Portillo company **buses** run fairly frequently from Málaga bus station to Ronda. It is also a stop on the Granada–Algeciras train line, with about four trains daily in each direction, but to get there from Málaga you must change in Bobadilla. Travelling by **car** from Málaga, follow the A357 road west, and then the A355 through Coín (80km).

Tourist Information

Ronda: Paseo de Blas Infante, opposite the bullring.

Where to Stay and Eat

See also pp.218 and 242.

★★★★**Parador de Ronda**, Pza de España, **t** 952 87 75 00, *ronda@parador.es* (*expensive*). This *parador* preserves the façade of the old town hall, but is modern inside. It is the flag-ship of the *parador* chain; comfort and service are excellent, and the views from the duplex suites are matchless. The **restaurant** has an excellent-value menu.

★★★★**Reina Victoria**, Avda Fleming, **t** 952 87 12 40, **f** 95 287 10 75 (*expensive*). A fine and handsome old hotel, built by the British in the 1900s as a retreat for the military in Gibraltar. It has lovely views over the cliffs; the German poet Rilke stayed here for a season in 1912,; his room 208 is preserved as a museum. The hotel has recently been refurbished by the Husa chain.

Hostal Hnos Nacias, C/Pedro Romero 3, **t** 952 87 42 38 (*moderate*). In an excellent location between the bullring and the main square. Comfortable en suite rooms with air-con and heating; excellent **restaurant** attached.

Doña Pepa, Plaza del Socorro (overlooking the square), **t** 952 87 47 77, *restopepa@ronda.net* (*moderate*). A good bet around the Mercadillo, with quail sautéed in garlic, and partridge.

there is a stairway – 365 steps cut out of the rock, called the **Mina** – that takes you
down to the bottom of the gorge. Here there is a **Moorish bridge** and well-preserved
remains of a **Moorish bath**. Further down from the Casa del Rey Moro you reach the
Puente Viejo and the Puente de San Miguel, beyond which the city walls start; you can
walk along them, with views out over the *vega*. Across the Puente Viejo, to the north,
is the Gothic-*mudéjar* **Convento de San Francisco**, founded by Ferdinand and Isabella
in 1485. From here, a very pleasant walk back up to town runs via the **Jardines Ciudad
de Cuenca**, tiered viewing platforms on the side of the gorge.

In the old town, **Palacio de Montragon**, Plaza Montragon (*open Mon–Fri 10–7,
Sat–Sun 10–3; adm*), is one of Ronda's most beautiful palaces, which today is the
town's museum. Just east of here is the main church, **Santa María La Mayor** (*open
daily 10–8; adm*), still retaining the mihrab and minaret of the mosque it replaced.

Granada

The first thing to do on arrival is pick up a copy of Washington Irving's *Tales of the
Alhambra*. It was Irving who put Granada on the map, and established the Alhambra
as the essential romantic pilgrimage of Spain. Granada, in fact, might seem a disap-
pointment without Irving. The modern city underneath the Alhambra is a stolid place,
with little to show for the 500 years since the Catholic kings put an end to its ancient
glory. As the Moors were expelled, the Spanish Crown replaced them with Castilians
and Galicians, and even today *granadinos* are thought of as a bit foreign by other
Andalucíans. Their Granada has not often been a happy place, and in the last hundred
years, particularly, has been full of political troubles. At the start of the Civil War, the
reactionaries who controlled Granada exerted their will over those who disagreed
with them with a large-scale massacre. One of their victims was Federico García
Lorca, the *granadino* who has come to be recognized as one of the greatest Spanish
dramatists and poets since the 'Golden Age'. If Irving's fairy tales aren't to your taste,
consider Lorca, for whom Granada and its sweet melancholy are recurring themes.

First Iberian *Elibyrge*, then Roman *Illiberis*, this town did not make a name for itself
until Muslim Al-Andalús broke up into small emirates called *taifas* in the 11th century.
In the 1230s, while the Castilians were seizing Córdoba and preparing to polish off the
rest of Moorish Spain, an Arab chieftain called Mohammed ibn-Yusuf ibn-Nasr established himself around Jaén. When that town fell in 1235, he moved his capital to the
town the Moors called *Qarnatah*. Against the grain, Ibn Nasr and his descendants the
Nasrid dynasty enjoyed great success, and by 1300 this last Moorish state left in Spain
extended from Gibraltar to Almería – although this achievement had come almost
entirely at the expense of other Muslims, for the Nasrids long kept up a more cooperative relationship with the kings of Castile. Qarnatah at this time is said to have had a
population of 200,000 – almost as many as now – and its arts and industries were
strengthened by refugees from the fallen towns of al-Andalus. In the relatively
peaceful 14th century, Granada's civilization reached its height, with the last flowering of Arabic-Andaluz poetry and the stunning architecture of the Alhambra.

This state of affairs lasted until the coming of the Catholic kings. Queen Isabella's religious fanaticism made the completion of the Christian *Reconquista* the supreme goal of her reign. In 1490, King Ferdinand mounted a final attack, and after a two-year siege the last Muslim king Boabdil surrendered under terms that guaranteed his people the use of their religion and customs; he handed over the keys of the city on

Getting There

There are **trains** between Málaga and Granada, but this is the one route where the rail network remains most illogical. There is no direct line, so you have to change at the dusty junction of Bobadilla. There are about 10 possible connections each day, but with some you have a long wait, making the total journey over 4 hours (quicker connections are closer to 2½–3). Check before travelling. **Buses**, with the Alsina Graëlls company, are faster; there are usually four or five daily.

By **car**, take the N331 north from Málaga – a fast, modern road, though it still has to climb mountains – and after 35km follow signs right on to the N359 and A92 for Granada (130km).

Tourist Information

Granada provincial tourist office: Plaza Mariana Pineda 10, **t** 958 22 66 88. Smaller offices at Corral del Carbón, C/Libreros 2, and in the Alhambra, on the Avda del Generalife.

Where to Stay

Granada ✉ 18000

The centre is full of hotels, but many are dreary. Fortunately, there is also a good choice around the Alhambra and older parts of town.

*****Parador Nacional San Francisco, t 958 22 14 40, *granada@parador.es* (*luxury*). In the Alhambra itself, this is perhaps the most famous of all *paradores*, housed in a convent where Queen Isabel was originally interred. It is beautiful, expensive (though worth it), and small; you must book well in advance

***Palacio de Santa Inés, Cuesta Santa Inés 9, **t** 958 22 23 62, *www.lugaresdivino.com* (*expensive*). A 16th-century Albaicín palace with murals attributed to Alejandro Mayner, Rafael's disciple. Nine rooms – some with views of the Alhambra – and an art gallery.

Casa del Aljarife, Placeta de la Cruz Verde 2, **t/f** 95 822 24 25, *most@mx3.redestb.es* (*moderate*). This 17th-century Moorish house is one of a handful of hotels in the Albaicín, and one of the most delightful places to stay in the city, with a view of the Alhambra that you won't better elsewhere. Only three rooms, so be sure to book in advance.

Landázuri, Cuesta de Gomérez 24, **t** 958 22 14 06 (*inexpensive*). A likeable budget option on the hill between the Alhambra and the Puerta Nueva, with a **restaurant** and small roof terrace.

Eating Out

Granada rivals Seville for *tapas*, and has a fine tradition of serving up mini-meals for the price of a drink. Areas to explore are the roads off the top end of Gran Via, and, around the cathedral, Plaza Bib-Rambla and C/Pescaderia are particularly good places to look.

Sevilla, C/Oficios 12, **t** 958 22 12 23 (*expensive*). The best-known, best-loved restaurant in Granada, where Lorca often met fellow poets. Its character has been preserved, and the specialities are still the local dishes of Granada. *Closed Sun evening*.

Ruta del Veleta, Ctra de la Sierra, Km 5, **t** 958 48 61 34 (*expensive*). Some of the finest cooking in Granada is found here, in innovative, traditional-with-a-twist dishes like partridge with onion ragôut; It's 5km outside the city, towards the Sierra Nevada.

Mesón Antonio, C/Ecce Homo 6, **t** 958 22 95 99 (*moderate*). There is no better place in Granada for agreeable dining in a snug, warm atmosphere than this family-run restaurant; international meat and fish dishes are served. *Closed Sun, July and Aug*.

Cepillo, Calle Pescadería (*moderate*). Everyone's favourite rock-bottom, filling *menú* is served up at this tiny restaurant. One of the few places where you can get a paella for one – order fish or squid.

2 January 1492. This agreement was kept to until the arrival in 1499 of Cardinal Cisneros, the most influential cleric in Spain, who began a creeping persecution that intensified through the next century. A revolt in the Alpujarras in 1568 was followed by a rising in the city, in the Albaicín. Finally, between 1609 and 1614, the last Muslims were expelled, including many who had outwardly converted to Christianity (known as *Moriscos*). Such a history, though, does not easily wear away, even after centuries.

In spite of everything, more of the lost world of al-Andalus can be seen in Granada even than in Córdoba. Granada stands where the foothills of the Sierra Nevada meet the Vega de Granada, the greenest stretch of farmland in Andalucía. Two hills extend into the city. One bears the **Alhambra**, the fortified palace of the Nasrid kings, and the other the **Albaicín**, most evocative of the 'Moorish' neighbourhoods of Andalucían cities. How much you enjoy Granada tends to depend on how successful you are in ignoring the new districts, in particular three ugly 19th-century streets: the **Gran Vía Colón**, the **Calle Reyes Católicos** and the **Acera del Darro**. Before these were built, the centre of Granada was the **Plaza Nueva**. The handsome building that defines its character is the **Audiencia** (1584), built by Philip II for royal officials and judges. From there the ascent to the Alhambra begins, winding up a narrow street called the **Cuesta de Gomérez**, past guitar-makers' shops and gypsies selling trinkets, ending abruptly at the **Puerta de las Granadas**, a monumental gateway erected by Charles V.

The Alhambra and the Generalife

The grounds of the **Alhambra** (*open daily Mar–Oct 8.30–7.45, Tues–Sat evenings 10pm–11.30pm; Nov–Feb open daily 8.30–5.45, Fri and Sat evenings from 8pm–9.30pm; adm*) begin with a bit of the unexpected. Instead of the walls and towers, not yet even in view, there is a lovely grove of great elms, the **Alameda**. Take the path to the left – a stiff climb – and you'll arrive at the **Puerta de Justicía**, the real entrance to the Alhambra. The orange tint of the fortress walls explains the name *al-hamra* (the red). From the gate, a path leads up to a broad square. Here are the ticket booth, and the **Puerta del Vino**, so called from a long-ago custom of doling out free wine from this spot. To the left are the walls of the Alcazaba, the fort at the tip of the Alhambra's promontory, and to the right the huge Palacio de Carlos V; signs point to the entrance of the Casa Real (Royal Palace), with its splendid rooms that are the Alhambra's main attraction. Visit again after dark; seeing it under the stars is the treat of a lifetime.

Not much remains of the oldest part of the Alhambra, the **Alcazaba**, the citadel that probably dates back to the first Nasrid kings. Its walls and towers are still intact, but only the foundations of the buildings that once stood within it have survived. The **Torre de la Vela** at the tip of the promontory has the best views over Granada and the *vega*. The Albaicín, visible on the opposite hill, is a revelation; its rows of white, flat-roofed houses on the hillside, punctuated by palm trees and cypresses, provide one of Europe's most exotic urban landscapes. The natural point to head for, though, is the **Casa Real** (*palace visits limited to 30 mins, the time must be specified when ticket is purchased*). Words cannot communicate the experience of this greatest treasure of al-Andalus. One of the most unusual features of this palace is its modesty. What you see is what the Nasrid kings saw; your imagination need add only a few carpets and tapestries, some well-crafted wooden furniture inlaid with ivory, some screens, and round braziers of brass for heat or incense, to make the picture complete.

Like so many old royal palaces, it is divided into three sections. The small **Mexuar** was where the kings would hold their public audiences; its **Patio del Mexuar** is one of the finest rooms of the Alhambra, with a small fountain in the centre to introduce an important element in the architecture – water. Present everywhere, in pools, fountains and channels, water is as much a part of the design as wood, tile and stone. Next comes the grand **Patio de los Arrayanes** (Court of the Myrtles), which, with its long goldfish pond and lovely arcades, was the centre of the second section of the palace, used for state ceremonies; directly off it is the **Sala de la Barca** (Hall of the Boat), so called after its hull-shaped wooden ceiling, and the **Salón de Embajadores** (Hall of Ambassadors), where the kings presided over all important state business. The views and the decoration are some of the Alhambra's best, with a magnificent cedarwood ceiling and plaster panels. A half-hidden doorway leads into the third and most spectacular section, the kings' private residence, built around the **Patio de los Leones** (Court of the Lions). Here the plaster and stucco work is at its most ornate, the columns and arches at their most delicate; the rooms around the patio, such as the **Sala de los Abencerrajes** and the **Sala de las dos Hermanas** (Hall of the Two Sisters), also have exquisite decorations, with extravagant domed *muqarnas* ceilings. The **Sala de los Reyes** (Hall of the Kings), opposite the court's entrance, is unique for the paintings on its ceiling, works that would not be out of place in any Christian palace of medieval Europe. Follow the arrows, out of the palace and into the outer gardens, the **Jardines del Partal**, a broad expanse of rose terraces and flowing water.

In abrupt contrast to this Moorish masterpiece is the **Palacio de Carlos V**, driven into the Alhambra in the 1520s; anywhere else this elegant Renaissance building would be an attraction in itself, but here it seems pompous and oversized. It contains two museums, the **Museo de Bellas Artes** (*open Tues 2.30–6, Wed–Sat 9–6, Sun 9–2.30*), a forgettable display of religious paintings, and the **Museo Nacional de Arte Hispano-Musulmán** (*open Tues–Sat 9–2*), perhaps Spain's best store of Moorish art. Behind the palace a street leads to the remnants of the town that once filled much of the space within the Alhambra walls, now largely given over to restaurants and hotels.

The **Generalife** (*Djinat al-Arif*: high garden; *opening hours same as for the Alhambra; adm inc. in Alhambra ticket*) was the summer palace of the Nasrid kings, built on the height they called the Mountain of the Sun. Many visitors to the Alhambra never notice it, and pass up a chance to see the finest garden in Spain. To get there, it's a five-minute walk from the Alhambra along a lovely avenue of tall cypresses. The buildings hold few surprises if you've just come from the Alhambra, but they are older than most of the Casa Real, which was begun around 1260. The gardens are built on terraces on several levels along the hillside, and the views over the Alhambra and Albaicín are transcendent. The centrepiece is a long pool with a great many water sprays that passes through beds of roses. A lower level, with a promenade on the hill's edge, is broken up into secluded bowers by cypress cut into angular shapes of walls and gateways. The overall effect is intoxicating.

The City

The hillside neighbourhood of white-washed houses and cypresses called the **Albaicín** preserves the feel of al-Andalus more than anywhere else in Granada. From Plaza Nueva, the narrow **Carrera del Darro** leads up the valley below the Alhambra; here the little Darro river has not been covered over, and you can get an idea of how the centre of Granada looked in the old days. Traces of a horseshoe arch can be seen where a Moorish wall once crossed the river; still more curious is the façade of the **Casa Castril**, a flamboyant 16th-century mansion that now hosts Granada's **archaeo-logical museum** (*open Tues 2.30–8, Wed–Sat 9–8, Sun 9–2.30*). Further up the Darro, there's a small park with a view up to the Alhambra; the higher you go the prettier the Albaicín is, and the better the views. At the top, parallel to Cuesta de la Alhacaba, is a stretch of Moorish wall. The heart of the Albaicín is here, around the animated **Plaza Larga**; only a few blocks away the **Mirador de San Nicolás**, in front of the church of that name, offers the most romantic view imaginable of the Alhambra.

For something completely different, strike out beyond the Albaicín to the **gypsy caves of Sacromonte**. Granada has had a big gypsy population for centuries. Some are now settled and respectable, others live in trailers on vacant land, but the biggest community still lives around Sacromonte, in streets of often well-appointed cave homes, where they wait to lure you in for a little display of flamenco. For years, the consensus has been that music and dancing are usually indifferent, and the gypsies' attempts to shake out every euro-cent can make it an irritating affair, but flamenco fans who persevere can sometimes see genuine, fine performances. Hotels sell tours.

South west of the Plaza Nueva is a web of narrow streets that make up the modern shopping district, around the pretty **Plaza Bib-Rambla**, full of flower stands and with an unusual fountain. The alleys leading off it are known as the **Alcaicería**, on the site of the old Moorish silk exchange. Nearby is Granada's **cathedral** (*open Mon–Sat 10.30–1.30 and 4–7, Sun 4–7*). The unique façade, with three tall, recessed arches, is striking, designed by the painter Alonso Cano (1667), but the rest of the cathedral isn't up to the same standard, cavernous but dreary. Far more impressive is the **Capilla Real**, with a separate entrance (*open daily 10.30–1 and 3.30–6.30, Sun 11–1; adm*), built in 1507 as a mausoleum for the *Reyes Católicos* Ferdinand and Isabella, so that they could be buried in the city whose capture they clearly regarded as their greatest achievement, way ahead of sending Columbus to America. It is the finest work of Isabelline Gothic, with a delicate roofline of traceries and pinnacles. Inside, the monarchs lie in Carrara marble sarcophagi, surrounded by sumptous carving.

The part of the city centre south of C/Reyes Católicos is as old as the Albaicín, but was mostly rebuilt after 1492. The only Moorish building remaining is also the only example in Spain of a caravanserai, the type of merchants' hotel common throughout the Muslim world, the 14th-century **Corral del Carbón**, just off Reyes Católicos. Lastly, another attraction of Granada, a little hidden in the northern suburbs, is the gaudiest Baroque chapel in Spain, in the **Cartuja**, or Carthusian monastery, on Calle Real de Cartuja (*open daily except Mon, 10–1 and 4–8*). The 18th-century chapel and sacristy, done in the richest marble, gold, silver and painted plaster, ooze in a froth of twisted spiral columns, rosettes and curlicues, a complete extravaganza of Rococo camp.

Touring from Málaga

Day 1: Andaluz Baroque in Antequera

Morning: Two roads lead north from Málaga: the N331 wil get you to **Antequera** in a hurry, or else take a winding hill road a little to the west through **Almogia**, a dramatic hill town, and **Villanueva de la Concepción**. After the latter, you pass the red crags and unusual rock formations of **El Torcal**, now a regional park (*visitors' centre open daily 10–5*). **Antequera** is a charming town, with a set of monuments from the 16th–18th centuries; the Plateresque Santa María la Mayor, the Iglesia del Carmen, with one of Andalucía's finest Baroque altars, and the pretty Capilla de la Virgen de Socorro, a mix of architecture from Baroque to *mudéjar*. There's even a triumphal arch, the **Arco de los Gigantes**, erected by seldom-triumphant Philip II.

Lunch: In Antequera or Archidona, *see* below.

Afternoon: There are many possibilities for side trips around Antequera. Just outside town, the **Cuevas de Menga** is a collection of Neolithic grave mounds and dolmens (*open Wed–Sun 9–3.30*). A little further east among the olive trees (12km), **Archidona** has one of Andalucía's loveliest squares, the octagonal Plaza Mayor. And just north-west of Antequera, from March to September the **Laguna de Fuente de Piedra** is one of Europe's largest breeding grounds for flamingos.

Dinner and Sleeping: In Antequera, *see* below.

Day 1

Lunch in Antequera or Archidona

El Angelote, C/Encarnación (corner of Coso Viejo), Antequera, **t** 952 70 34 65 (*moderate*). An excellent restaurant in the heart of the old town serving local dishes such as *porra Antequerana*, or *ajoblanco* and roasted offal, which tastes better than it sounds.

La Espuela, Paseo Maria Cristina, Plaza de Toros, Antequera, **t** 952 70 34 24 (*moderate*). The only restaurant in Spain actually located inside a bullring – so *rabo de toro* (oxtail) is usually the dish of the day.

El Centro, C/Nueva 49, Archidona, **t/f** 95 271 48 11. The best restaurant in town, just up from the square, with *tapas* and local wines. Try the speciality *purra*, a kind of thick *gazpacho*.

Dinner in Antequera

Caserio de San Benito, Ctra M-C, km 108, **t** 952 11 11 03 (*expensive*). One of the finest restaurants in the area, highly regarded by Spanish gourmets; the style is traditional, but with a specially high level of quality and skill noticeable in the cooking,

Sleeping in Antequera

★★★Parador de Antequera, Paseo García del Olmo s/n, **t** 952 84 02 61, *antequera@parador.es* (*expensive*). Not one of the historic paradores but a plain, modern building – however, it offers the most comforts in Antequera, including a pleasant pool and garden, and is reasonably priced.

★★Hotel Castilla, C/Infante de Fernando 40, **t** 952 84 32 48 (*moderate*). Set in a completely new building, but in the heart of the old town, this hotel has well-equipped rooms all with air conditioning, bath and satellite TV.

★Manzanito, Plaza San Sebastián, **t** 952 84 10 23 (*inexpensive*). One of the best lower-price-choices in the town centre. The management also runs a good **restaurant** beneath, with plenty of enjoyable traditional Andaluz dishes.

Day 2: Into the Rugged *Serranía* to Ronda

Morning: Leave Antequera on the A343 road southwest for **Alora**, and follow the signs for **El Chorro** gorge. Here, the deep, rugged canyon of the Rio Guadalhorce creates one of Andalucía's natural wonders, with sheer walls of limestone tossed at crazy angles. Just to the north, a series of artificial lakes around the **Guadalhaba-Guadalhorce** dam makes a lovely setting for a picnic, or else seek out the rock-cut basilica of **Bobastro**, recalling the romantic story of Ibn-Hafsun, the Christian emir who made this ruined city the capital of his own little state in the 9th century. Carry on to **Carratraca**, a remote, pretty village that has been a spa since Roman times.

Lunch: In Carratraca or Ardales, *see* below.

Afternoon: Head southwest again from Ardales on a wild mountain road until after 21km you reach **El Burgo**, and join the slightly larger A366, which runs westwards, skirting the edges of the Serranía de Ronda through spectacular scenery. Eventually, it reaches **Ronda**, a gracious and beautiful little city, and home to Spain's oldest bull-ring, built in 1785. Ronda was important in Moorish times, and the church of Santa María la Mayor retains the *mihrab* and minaret of the mosque it replaced. Ronda's most extraordinary attraction, though, is its location: a giant gorge divides the old and new parts of town, spanned by the tall Puente Nuevo; lovely gardens skirt its edges, and you can descend a long stair to the bottom to see the Moorish walls and a baths complex.

Dinner and Sleeping: In Ronda, *see* below and pp.211 and 242.

Day 2

Lunch in Carratraca and Ardales

St Sa Pepe, in Carratraca, **t** 95 245 80 49 (inexpensive). Near the *balus*, a clean and simple place to eat. Around the Serranía there are also many simple roadside *ventas*, with good-value local cooking.

La Posada del Conde, Pantana del Chorro 16 & 18, **t** 952 11 24 11 (*moderate*). A fairly new hotel wonderfully situated on the El Chorro reservoir, with a very enjoyable restaurant attached; great views from the terrace (*moderate*).

Dinner in Ronda

Casa Santa Pola, C/Sto Domingo 3, **t** 952 87 92 08 (*expensive–moderate*). Part of this building is the remains of a 9th-century Moorish mosque, and there's a terrace overlooking the river, and great décor inside; the food is traditional *andaluz* – roast meats and fresh fish. Flamenco show from 9pm on Fridays and Saturdays.

Don Miguel, C/Villanueva 4, **t** 952 87 10 90 (*moderate*). Some of the best meals Ronda can offer, served overlooking the gorge next to the famous bridge; they also have a bar that's actually built into the bridge itself. Take time with your meal, just to absorb that view.

Sleeping in Ronda

★★★Hotel San Gabriel, C/Jose M Holgado 19, **t** 952 19 03 92, *www.ronda.net/usuar/hotelsgabriel* (*moderate*). Probably the loveliest hotel in town in terms of décor, service, atmosphere and value; it was a private house, dating from 1736, before conversion to a hotel in 1998. Wood panelling and old prints line the walls of the individually designed bedrooms, and there's a billiard room, café and a shaded patio.

Hotel Don Miguel, C/Villanueva 8, **t** 952 87 77 22 (*moderate*). Very good value to have such a great location, on the cliff edge and opposite the *parador*. Also has a very nice **restaurant** attached.

Day 3: From Old Andalucía to British Territory

Morning: Start early, and head up in the hills northwest of Ronda, via a right turn off the road for Grazalema, to visit the ruins of the Roman town of **Acinpo**, at a site locals have always called *Ronda la Vieja*, 'Old Ronda'. The remains include an ancient theatre. Or else, start down for the coast, on the spectacular 'scenic route' by turning south on the A-376 road just northwest of Ronda to descend through the Serrania de Ronda from Ronda to **Gaucín**, passing through the villages of **Cortes de la Frontera** and **Jimera de Libar**. Take a detour along the way to the **Cueva de la Pileta** near **Benoaján**, with its 25,000-year-old cave paintings (*open 10–1 and 4–6; the care-taker lives in the farmhouse near the entrance*).

Lunch: In Benoaján or Gaucín, *see* below and p.243.

Afternoon: Continue winding down towards the coast, through many more beautiful, atmospherically remote mountain villages (although now all with their comple-ment of foreign home-owners). Just before you hit the sea, there's **San Roque**, with surprisingly good beaches nearby. If these can't detain you, carry on to **Gibraltar**. Besides the view of the famous Rock, there is much of historical interest here: a Moorish castle and baths, tours of the British fortifications, the Gibraltar Museum (*open Mon–Fri 10–6, Sat 10–2; adm*) and just the strangeness of this piece of British territory in itself. Gibraltar has beaches too, along with tax-free shopping and a casino. And, of course, you can visit the famous apes on the Rock.

Dinner and Sleeping: In Gibraltar or La Línea, *see* below.

Day 3

Lunch in Benoaján or Gaucín

Molino del Santo, Bulevar de la Estación, Benoaján, t 952 16 71 51 (*moderate*). A converted water mill beside a mountain stream, close to the Pileta caves with a spring-fed swimming pool. The kitchen serves excellent *andaluz* cuisine.

El Pilar, opposite petrol station, Gaucín, t 952 15 13 47 (*inexpensive*). A real workman's *comedor*, but with a nobleman's view from the terrace on a sunny day. And it offers an excellent-value set lunch with a quarter-bottle of wine per head.

Dinner in Gibraltar

Da Paolo, Marina Bay, t 76 799 (*moderate*). A favourite place to eat in Gib, with well-prepared fish specialities, such as fillet of John Dory in dill sauce, a particularly good Spanish wine list, and a fine view.

Waterfront Bar/Restaurant, Queensway Quay, t 45 666 (*moderate*). Set in a good spot, right on the marina, with good food at reasonable prices; try the excellent *moules marinières*.

Bull and Bush, 30 Parliament Lane, t 72 951 (*inexpensive*). And for a parting memory of Gibraltar before you cross back into Spain, drop in here.

Sleeping in Gibraltar

****Caleta Hotel**, Sir Herbert Miles Road, on Catalan Bay, t 76 501, *www.caletahotel.com* (*expensive*). If you need a beach, this resort hotel is very modern and recently upgraded. There are rooms with balconies, a pool, and a choice of good **restaurants**

Bristol, 8–10 Cathedral Square, t 76 800, f 77 613, *bristhtl@gibnet.gi* (*moderate*). In the heart of town, with a swimming pool, and TV in all rooms.

***La Campana**, C/Carboneros 3 (just off the plaza), La Línea, t 956 17 30 59 (*inexpensive*). La Línea, just back in Spain, is a lot cheaper than the Rock; this *pensión* is the best bargain in town, with a good little **restau-rant** downstairs with a cheap *menú del día*.

Day 4: The Costa del Sol: Sotogrande to Marbella

Morning: The rest of this circuit is a two-day tour of the Costa del Sol; not a lot of sights to see, perhaps, but plenty of opportunities for golf, water sports or other activities, just sitting on the beach, watching what everyone else is doing, and enjoying the unique, cosmopolitan and amiably synthetic atmosphere of Spain's original holiday Babylon. From Gibraltar, the coastal road leads first to **Sotogrande**, a well-established, somewhat dull British and Germanic enclave that mainlines on golf (with no fewer than three world-class courses). Further on, you can detour inland to **Manilva**, with ruins of a Roman spa, or **Casares**, a typical Andalucían white village with a modest collection of historical monuments. Then comes the first of the big resort towns, **Estepona**.

Lunch: In Estepona, *see* below.

Afternoon: Estepona is a lively place, where the action centres on the Paseo Maritimo promenade, a classic beachfront strip. In the middle there's still the original fishing village around which Estepona grew up, along with more recent attractions like Spain's oldest naturist camp. If there's nothing to hold you here, continue on to the smartest and flashiest resort in the south, **Marbella**, eternally beloved of Spanish gossip magazines. For all its reputation, Marbella is a surprisingly quiet and digni-fied, very Andalucían place; the real action – the big-time shopping , bars and discos—will be found just outside town around the yacht harbour, at **Puerto Banús**.

Dinner and Sleeping: In Marbella, *see* below and p.208.

Day 4

Lunch in Estepona

La Casa de Mi Abuela, C/Caridad 54, **t** 952 79 19 67 (*moderate*). Offers a selection of grills, including Argentinian-style *churrasco*.

El Vagabundo, Urbanización Monte Biarritz, Ctra Cádiz, km 168.5, **t** 952 88 66 98 (*moderate*). A converted tower on the N340, offering a choice of international dishes, including seafood pancakes and roast duck.

Tipico Andaluz, **Bodega Sabor Andaluz** and **Sabor Roceiro**. Three restaurants grouped together at the far end of C/Caridad, all offering wonderful *embutidos* such as *jamón iberico* and *queso manchego* (*all inexpensive*).

Dinner in Marbella

Toni Dalli, The Oasis Club, Ctra Cádiz, km 176, **t** 952 77 00 35 (*expensive*). A special outing in Marbella, this restaurant is housed in a Moorish mansion with a central courtyard and a magnificent view of the beach. The owner Dalli, a retired Italian opera singer, entertains his customers personally with an aria; otherwise there's the regular showbiz band to tap your toes to. Italian food is obvi-ously the order of the day.

Santiago, Pso Maritimo 5, **t** 952 77 00 78 (*expensive*). Try this long-established place for the best *paella* in Marbella, or suckling pig, or white beans with clams – in fact, a wide choice, of some of the best Spanish cooking on the coast.

Casa La Vieja, C/Aduar 18, **t** 952 82 13 12 (*inexpensive*). Likeable little place that serves up good platters of mixed fish

Sleeping in Marbella

★★★★**El Fuerte**, Avda El Fuerte s/n, **t** 952 86 15 00, **f** 95 282 44 11, *www.hotelelfuerte.es* (*expensive*). Very well located next to the Marbella shopping centre, at the end of the promenade overlooking the sea .

★★**Hostal Enriqueta**, Los Caballeros 18, **t** 952 82 75 52 (*inexpensive*). Good value and well located, near the Plaza de Los Naranjos .

Day 5: The Costa del Sol: On to Torremolinos

Morning: From Marbella, head east along the N340 coast road (once known by the label 'highway of death' and other lurid titles, but now much more easy to handle) instead of the motorway. Although this coast has no undiscovered spots, as villa urbanizaciones spread all along it, the view out to sea, with the hills just inland, is still lovely. Just 30km up the coast from Marbella is funky, noisy **Fuengirola**, which can seem a world away from all that upmarket glitz. Fuengirola also has a Moorish castle, and the reconstructed façade of a Greek temple recovered from an ancient shipwreck; plus it has plenty of cheesy attractions for jaded tourists who need a break from Spain: there's a zoo, and an **Aquapark** with water slides.

Lunch: Near Fuengirola, *see* below.

Afternoon: Make a short detour inland and uphill from Fuengirola to **Mijas**, 8km up in the hills, famous for its tiny, square bullring and its '*burro* taxies', for a look at the real expat *costa*. With its neighbours in the Sierra de Mijas, **Alhaurín el Grande** and **Coín**, Mijas is massively popular with foreign home-buyers. Undeniably twee, Mijas also has delicious cool breezes, and superb views. Then, for another abrupt change head down to the beach and the most colourful and hyperactive of them all, **Torremolinos**, a place many Mijas home-owners shun like the proverbial plague. Like Marbella, though, Torremolinos has its posh suburb with a yacht harbour and a casino, at **Benalmádena**, at well as loads of options for a fun time.

Dinner and Sleeping: In Torremolinos, *see* below, or get back to Málaga, *see* pp.204–5.

Day 5

Lunch near Fuengirola

Mesón El Castellano, Camino de Coín 5, **t** 952 46 27 36 (*moderate*). Serves authentic Castilian food: roast meats, especially pork and lamb, and the service is fast and friendly.

Casa Navarra, Ctra de Mijas (near Valparaíso), km 4, **t** 952 58 04 39 (*moderate*). Hearty Navarrese cuisine, including huge steaks, interesting things with red peppers and delicious fish that you can choose yourself. Plus there are also the usual Andaluz fish dishes. *Closed Tues.*

Dinner in Torremolinos

Mar de Alborán, Hotel Alay, Avda de Alay 5, Benalmádena Costa, **t** 952 44 64 27 (*moderate*). Excellent Basque-Andalucían cuisine: chef Alvaro Arriaga knows his craft, and is one of the region's most able cooks. *Closed Sun and Mon.*

Mesón Gallego Antoxo, C/Hoxo, **t** 952 38 45 33 (*inexpensive*). A short walk from the Torremolinos bus station is this very Spanish restaurant with a beautiful interior and charming little courtyard. Galician food is the mainstay, so there's a wide choice of fish and seafood, and Galician crisp white wines.

Sleeping in Torremolinos

★★★★Hotel Cervantes, C/Rió Cañoles 1, **t** 952 38 40 33 (*expensive*). Just a few yards from the heart of the action, this hotel is surprisingly reasonable consideringl the creature comforts it offers, with two pools (one indoor, one out), big rooms with balconies, a disco, restaurant, café and a very good restaurant of the same name .

Victoria, Los Naranjos 103 (opposite the bus station), **t** 952 38 10 47 (*moderate*). Whether staying a few days or just passing through, this *hostal* is a pleasant, conveniently located and reasonably priced place to stay in an often-expensive area.

Jerez de la Frontera

The name is synonymous with wine – via the English corruption of *Jerez* into *sherry* – but besides the *finos*, *amontillados*, *olorosos* and other varieties of that noble sauce, Jerez also ships out much of Spain's equally good brandy. Most of the well-known companies, whose advertising is plastered all over Spain, have their headquarters here, and they're quite accustomed to taking visitors – especially English ones – through the *bodegas*. Don't be shy. Most are open to visitors between 9am and 1pm on Mondays to Fridays, and sometimes weekends, although they're closed in August, and when they're busy with the *vendimia* (harvest) in September. Admission prices are around €3–4 upwards, and nearly always include tasting sessions, of varying generosity. Many *bodegas* are now located a little out of town as land prices in the centre rise. However, booking is strongly advised, especially at the most famous and so most popular bodegas like **Domecq** (*t 956 15 15 00*) – numbers are restricted on the tours, and many people who fail to reserve places are turned away.

Getting to Jerez

Jerex has scheduled flights with **Buzz** from Stansted, and receives a growing number of charters. There are also Iberia and Air Europa domestic flights to Madrid and Barcelona. **Airport flight information:** t 972 18 66 00. **Buzz:** t 917 49 66 33.

Getting from the Airport

The small Jerez airport is 13km north of the city, by the N-IV road towards Seville. There is no regularly scheduled public transport from the airport, so the only way into town is by **taxi.** A cab to Jerez will cost around €12–15, and take about 20mins.

Getting Around

Jerez's stations for **buses** and **trains** are very near each other on the eastern edge of town. There are frequent trains to Cádiz and Seville; other nearby towns are best reached by bus. Buses run frequently to Arcos de la Frontera, Ronda and the other *sierra* towns, and to coastal towns like Rota, Sanlúcar de Barrameda and Puerto de Santa María.

Within Jerez, the best way to get around is to walk – parking can be hard to find. There is a good **local bus** service, and plenty of **taxis**: you can call a cab on **t** 956 34 48 60. **Train information (RENFE): t** 902 24 02 02.

Car Hire

For car hire in Spain in general, *see* pp.17–18. Most companies are based at the airport, rather than in Jerez itself. **Avis,** Hotel Royal Sherry Park, **t** 956 31 41 20. One company that has an office in town. **Budget,** C/del Puerto 5, **t** 956 33 80 54. Also in town, near the Alcázar. **Europcar,** airport, **t** 956 15 00 98. **National-Atesa,** airport, **t** 956 31 41 20.

Tourist Information

Jerez de la Frontera: C/Larga 39, **t** 95 633 11 50/95 633 17 31.

Festivals

Feria del Caballo: One of the most important events of the year in the local horse world, an ultra-Andaluz display of traditions and riding skills (*see* p.225). *First half of May.*

Where to Stay

Jerez de la Frontera ✉ 11400

Jerez has quite a few unremarkable hotels. The two top hotels are close to the centre of town, and both are convenient for the fair and the Spanish Riding School.

One of the most interesting *bodegas* to visit is that of **González Byass**, C/Manuel María González 12 (*t 956 35 70 00, www.gonzalesbyass.es*). The tour includes a visit to the old sawdust-strewn *bodega* that has held sherry *soleras* for two centuries; casks have been signed by famous visitors, from Hispanophile Orson Welles to the Hollywood mermaid Esther Williams. The tour ends at the *degustacion*, where the motto is, 'If you don't have a *copa* at eleven o'clock, you should have eleven at one'. The tour also includes a video of the production process, with cellarmen demonstrating their skill at pouring sherry from a metre or more into the small *copitas* (to aerate the wine). **John Harvey**, C/Arcos 57 (*t 956 15 10 00*), is another *bodega* well worth a visit – watch out for the alligator at the end of the tour. Others include **Sandeman**, C/Pizarro 10 (*t 956 31 29 95*), and **Williams and Humbert**, C/Paul s/n (*t 956 34 65 39*).

Business is not as good as it once was, for sherry sales are falling worldwide, but Jerez is growing, and one of the most prosperous towns in Andalucía. It's an extremely attractive town, at least in the centre, with a lively *paseo* along **Calle Larga** up to the **Alameda Cristina**, and several attractive squares like Plaza Rafael Rivero or

Expensive–Moderate

★★★★**Jerez**, Avda Alcalde Álvaro Domecq 35, **t** 956 33 06 00. Has a pool, tennis courts and lovely tropical gardens, for high prices.

★★★★**Royal Sherry Park**, Avda Alcalde Álvaro Domecq 11, **t** 956 31 76 14. A modern hotel set in a park a little closer to town, with a pool and a good **restaurant**, El Abaco.

★★★**Doña Blanca**, C/Bodegas 11, **t** 956 34 87 61. The most pleasant three-star place in the heart of Jerez; clean and modern, with its own parking – extremely useful in this town.

Inexpensive–Cheap

Several budget hotels are in a cluster on C/Higueras, off Plaza Angustias.

★★**Serit**, C/Higueras 7, **t** 956 34 07 00. In the centre of town, with parking; rooms are comfortable, and prices very fair.

★★**Virt**, C/Higueras 20, **t** 956 32 28 11. A middle-range bargain with air-conditioned rooms.

★**Las Palomas**, C/Higueras 17, **t** 956 34 37 73. An excellent value budget hotel.

★**San Andrés**, C/Morenos 12, **t** 956 34 09 83. Basic rooms for basic prices.

Eating Out

Even in a region known for late hours, Jerez goes a step further. It's not unusual here to sit down to lunch at 3.30pm, and don't even think about dinner until after 10pm.

Expensive

El Bosque, Avda Álvaro Domecq 26, **t** 956 30 33 33/956 30 70 30. Beautifully situated in woods near Parque González Montoria, yet only a short distance from town; formal, elegant, a tad stuffy. The seafood is good; try *langostinos de Sanlúcar*, tortillas of baby shrimps, angler fish in shellfish sauce or strawberry *gazpacho*. *Closed Sun*.

Moderate

Tendido 6, C/Circo 10, **t** 956 34 48 35. Closer to town, by the bullring, Tendido 6 has a covered patio with adjoining dining room decorated on a *feria* theme, and bullfight memorabilia on the walls. The emphasis is on robust helpings of traditional food, and you can gorge to the full. *Closed Sun*.

Gaitán, Gaitán 3, **t** 956 34 58 59. One of the favourite dining places in town, a couple of streets behind the tourist office, Gaitán is the proud bearer of gastronomy awards. Try the very well-aged sheep's milk cheeses (Queso Viejo de Oveja), lamb with honey and brandy of Jerez, or veal sirloin in Paris coffee cream (12,000 pts for two) *Closed Sun eve*.

La Mesa Redonda, C/Manuel de la Quintana 3, **t** 956 34 00 69. Near the Avenida Jerez hotel, this beautifully decorated restaurant has antique furniture and paintings, giving the impression of an old aristocratic Jerez home. The first-class kitchen serves excellent game

Plaza Plateros that are great for café-sitting and people-watching. It also has a few lovely buildings for you to squint at after you've done the rounds of the *bodegas*. Two in particular are worth a look: the **Ayuntamiento** in Plaza de la Asunción, a fine piece of Renaissance architecture from the 16th century, and **Palacio Domecq**, at the start of the Alameda, an 18th-century palace built by the sherry clan. Jerez's prime landmark is **La Colegiata** (also called San Salvador), the town's cathedral, a curious pseudo-Gothic church with a separate bell tower and Baroque staircase; though begun in the 13th century, its façade, largely the work of Vicente Acero, was not completed until 1750. Works inside include a *Madonna* by Zurbarán and sculptures by Juan de Mesa. Nearby, on Plaza San Miguel, **San Miguel** (*open Mon–Sat 8–9, Sun 9–1*), begun in 1482, changes the scene to Isabelline Gothic – a fine example of that style, with a florid *retablo* inside. There is a Moorish **Alcázar** on the Alameda Vieja (*open mid-Sept–April 10–6; May–mid-Sept 10–8; adm*), with a tower and some remains of the baths, a *camera obscura* with wonderful views over the city, an art gallery and a well-preserved mosque. Further north, the **Museo de Arqueología**, opposite San Mateo church on

---

and seasonal specialities, and takes its food seriously. Recommended: probably the best restaurant in Jerez. Reservations essential. *Closed Sun and Aug.*

El Fogon de Mariana, C/Zaragoza, t 956 34 10 19. Set in a huge barn-like space complete with beams, log fire and a huge grill; the emphasis is on meat, and a lot of it – steaks, lamb, pork, you name it – all fresh and at a very good price. They'll even throw in a *jarra* of house wine if you order a *parillada*.

Inexpensive

Bar Juanito, C/Pescadería Vieja. The best of a clutch of tiny *tapas* bars in a passage off the Plaza del Arenal. Try the *alcachofas en salsa* (artichokes in sauce) or *costillas en adobo* (marinaded grilled pork chops). It's a crush here at lunchtime; arrive early in the evening (*opens at 8pm*) if you want a table. Enjoy two or three *tapas* plus wine (around €6).

La Taberna Marinera, Plaza Rivero, t 956 33 44 27. One of a number of good *tapas* bars on this Plaza Rivero, not far from Alameda Cristina. It's small inside but during summer everyone spills out onto the square; try the *carillada iberica* and the *albondigas*.

There are also many street *bodegas*:two central places to try are:

Alcazaba, C/Medina 19.

La Tasca, C/Matadero s/n.

Nightlife

Jerez has great nightlife – if you can find it, as it's spread out all over the city. A good place to start for early evening *copas* is Plaza Canterbury, opposite the Williams and Humbert Bodega, near the bullring on C/Paul. Around this area you will stumble upon a number of bars, clubs and discos, including **Cairo**, C/José Cadiz Salvatierra, a popular spot with young, wealthier locals; and a bit further north, in Avda de Mejico, are **Moet Moet**, where the clientele is a bit older, and **Sala Mol**, a disco. Nearer the centre there are a couple of other discos: **Copola**, in Plaza Aladro, near the Palacio Domecq, and **Oh**, in C/Porvera; expect the usual diet of dodgy Spanish techno.

Jerez is justly famous for flamenco and, unlike in Seville where many *tablaos* will be overpriced and catering for busloads of tourists, here you will find the real thing; but you have to look for it (and don't expect it to happen just because it's advertised; spontaneity/unpredictability is central to the art). Here are a selection of venues:

El Lago de Tio Parilla, Plaza del Mercado, t 956 33 83 34. *Free on Thur, Fri and Sat.*

La Taberna Flamenca, Angostillo de Santiago 3.

El Rincon del Duende, C/Muro 19.

Los Cerinicalos, C/Sanchez Vizcaíno 20.

Los Jerales, Plaza Cocheras 20.

Bar Nochiero, C/Velazquez 20.

Plaza del Mercado (*open Tues–Fri 10–2 and 4–7, Sat–Sun and hols 10–2.30; adm*), contains a number of Greek and Roman artefacts in a pretty restored 18th-century mansion, and near some of the big bodegas on C/Cervantes is the **Museo de Relojes**, also known as La Atalaya from the building it occupies, which strangely enough is one of the finest collections of antique watches in the world (*open Tues–Fri 10–2 and 4–6, Sat, Sun and hols 10–2; adm*). Jerez also has a **zoo** (*open winter 10–6, summer 10–8, closed Mon exc hols; adm*), some way from the centre on the oddly-named C/Taxdirt

Outside town, 4km along the road to Medina Sidonia, is the **Cartuja de la Defensión**, a 15th-century monastery that has the best Baroque façade (added in 1667) in Andalucía – a sort of giant *retablo*, with sculptures by Alonso Cano and others. It still contains a religious community, so you need special permission to go inside. There is not much reason to; the main attraction, an altarpiece by Zurbarán, is scattered to the four winds. Do, however, visit the gardens and patio (*open Tues, Thurs and Sat 5–6.30*).

Horses, Flamenco, Andaluz Ambience

Sherry aside, Jerez is a hub of Andaluz tradition in many other ways. *Semana Santa* here is more intimate than in Seville, but in its way just as splendid. The nightly processions escorting the Saint and Madonna create a city-wide pageant. Late at night, returning home through the back streets, they are serenaded by impromptu solo voices; for the finest singers, the whole procession halts in appreciation. It's also at the centre of Andaluz horse culture. While in Jerez look out for exhibitions at the **Escuela Andaluz del Arte Ecuestre**, Avda Duque de Abrantes. Jerez's snooty wine aristocracy takes horsemanship very seriously; they have some of the finest horses you're likely to see anywhere, and know how to use them. You can see them tarted up like Tío Pepe bottles at the annual **Feria del Caballo** (Horse Fair) during the first half of May. Its origins can be traced back to the 13th century, and events include jumping, classical riding, harness riding and Andalucían country riding. And, being an Andalucían fair, it provides a good excuse for attending the *corrida*, drinking plenty of sherry and, of course, a flamenco extravaganza. There are also the *fiestas de Otoño* in September and October, which include sherry tasting and horse racing in the main square. Every Thursday, too, there is a spectacular 'horse ballet' of dressage at 12 noon at the Escuela Andaluza. The show runs for about 1½ hours, and afterwards you are free to wander through the stables to meet the stars of the show. Additionally, there are tours between 11am and 1pm, weekdays except Thursdays. Check with the tourist information for details of any special shows.

One of Jerez's attractions is its contrasts – as well as being home to some of the wealthiest Spaniards, it also has a big Gypsy population who live in the warren of streets stretching up from the cathedral to the Barrio de Santiago. Here you find the **Centro de Flamenco**, Palacio Penmartín, Plaza San Juan 1 (*open Mon–Fri 9.30–2; closed for two weeks during Aug*), housed in one of the most beautiful buildings of the old part of the city; it hosts activities through the year – concerts, exhibitions, seminars, video shows – to promote the art. You might also be able to locate a flamenco show that hasn't been put on solely for tourists (*see* below). The area's main sight is the 15th-century church of **Santiago**, a wonderfully preserved Gothic pile.

Jerez de la Frontera

Zoo

CALLE TAXDIRT

CALLE ATALAYA

Museo de Relojes

C. CERVANTES

CALLE LEALAS

CALLE

C. LUIS PEREZ

C. PONCE

ANGOSTILLO DE SANTIAGO

Santiago

PLAZA SANTIAGO

C. ANCHA

CALLE

La Merced

CALLE MURO

PLAZA SAN JUAN

PLAZA COCHERAS

CALLE MURO

Centro Flamenco

San Juan

CALLE FRANCOS

RONDA DEL CARACOL

Museo Arqueológico

San Mateo

PLAZA DEL MERCADO

PLAZA BELEN

San Marcos

PLAZA PEONES

PLAZA CARMEN

C. SAN ILDEFONSO

PLAZA DEL ARROYO

PLAZA DE LA ASUNCION

C. PUERTA DE ROTA

C. ESPIRITU SANTO

C. JOSE LUIS DIEZ

Bodegas Domecq

Ayuntamiento

PLAZA VARGAS

CUESTA DE LA CHAPARRA

C. CALZADA DEL ARROYO

Cathedral

C. POZUELO

C. MANUEL MARIA GONZALEZ

ALAMEDA VIEJA

C. ARMAS

Bodegas Gonzalez Byass

Alcazar

C. PUERTO

PLAZA SA MIGUEL

N

200 m
200 yds

GLORIETA C. ALCUBILLA
CUATRO CAMINOS

C. CUATRO CAMINOS

Day Trips and Overnighters from Jerez

Sanlúcar de Barrameda and Chipiona

Sanlúcar de Barrameda, at the mouth of Andalucía's greatest river the Guadalquivír, makes *manzanilla*, most ethereal of sherries. It is also known as the port that launched Magellan on his way around the world, and Columbus on his second voyage to the Indies and third to America, and for its annual horse races on the beach; it was also the birthplace of the artist-writer Francisco Pacheco, Velázquez's teacher. More than that, it and the towns nearby are also known to all Spaniards as keystones of indefinable Andaluz-ness, places that are soaked in local identity even though they've never set out to be so, nor do they put it on for tourists. An extraordinary number of both flamenco performers and popular singers have come from the Bay of Cádiz.

Sanlúcar town has a certain crumbling colonial charm and an exceptionally pretty main square, **Plaza de Cabildo**, with bars and restaurants around it. Off nearby Plaza Roque, where a plaque commemorates Pacheco, is the town's market, a huge, bustling place – one of the biggest in Andalucía and a delight to stroll around to soak up the myriad smells and sounds. From here C/Bretones leads to the church of **Nuestra Señora de la O** (*open Mon–Sat 10–1, Sun 10–12, closed Thurs*) with its fine *mudéjar* portal and 16th-century coffered ceiling. Beside it is the **Palace of the Dukes of Medina Sidonia**, who once owned the town. The building dates from the 16th century and has an extensive private archive including notes on the Armada. Nearby is the 19th-century **Montpensier Palace** (*open Mon–Sat 8–2.30; adm*), with paintings by Murillo, El Greco, Rubens and Goya. To the west, on C/Caballero is the **Palace of Orleans and Borbon** (*open Mon–Fri 10–2; adm*), built by the Duke of Montpensier in the 19th century and now the town hall. Go back east past the church and you will come across the ruins of a 15th-century Moorish **castle**, which is closed for interminable restoration works. Below here lies C/Ancha, the scene of much merriment on 15 August (*see* right).

The town also has sherry houses open to visitors. The biggest is **Antonio Barbadillo**, C/Luis Eguilaz 11 (*t 956 36 08 94*), which makes the bulk of the *manzanilla*; try also **La Guita**, C/Dorantes s/n (*t 956 18 22 20*), another delicious make, and **Herederos de Argueso**, C/Mar 8 (*t 956 36 01 12*). And, although its beaches are not major-league, Sanlúcar has always been a popular summer destination with Spanish holidaymakers for its great cheap seafood. **Bajo de Guía**, the long waterfront, is a very characterful fishing district, and from here you can take a tour over to the **Coto Doñana** reserve for a four-hour trip up the river, including two stops and two guided walks (*two boats daily; tickets from Fabrica de Hielo, Avda Bajode Guia, t 956 36 38 13, open daily 9–7*).

Chipiona, 10km along at the very mouth of the river, is a family resort, full of small *pensiónes* and *hostales*, with a good beach at **Playa de Regla** near the lighthouse, great sea views in the evening –lovely sunsets – and a couple of *bodegas*; **Cesar Florido**, Padre Lerehundi 35–37 (*t 956 37 12 85*), and **Mellodo Martin**, Ctra Chipiona-Nola 3 (*t 966 37 01 97*). This, too, is another town with a strong tradition in the music of Andalucía.

Getting There

Buses run frequently from Jerez bus station to all these towns; there are at least seven daily to Sanlúcar, some of which continue to Chipiona. El Puerto de Santa María is a stop on the **train** line to Cádiz. By **car**, Sanlúcar is 20km away along theA480, Puerto de Santa María 15km on the N-IV.

Tourist Information

Sanlúcar de Barrameda: Calzada del Ejército, **t** 956 36 61 10.
Chipiona: Plaza Andalucia, **t** 956 37 28 28.
Rota: C/Luna 2 (in the Palace), **t** 956 84 61 74.
El Puerto de Santa María: C/Luna 22, **t** 956 54 24 75.

Festivals

Of the fiestas in this area, the most famous by far involves **horse racing** along the beach at Sanlúcar, at the end of August. It's a beautiful sight that has its origins in the middle of the 19th century, when the Spanish aristocracy sojourned here. The town sends a few brotherhoods to **El Rocio** in the Coto Doñana in May, and at the end of that month is the **Feria de la Manzanilla**, which sees horseriding, bullfights, traditional Andalucían dress and sherry; 15 August sees C/Ancha covered with a pretty carpet of faux-flowers (in fact sawdust); a superb flamenco festival takes place in July by the waterfront, called **Noches de Bajo de Guia**; and in mid-October there's a **Feria de Tapas**.

Eating Out

Sanlúcar
Casa Bigote, Bajo de Guía, Sanlúcar, **t** 956 36 26 96 (*expensive–moderate*). A restaurant famous throughout Andalucía for its delicious appetizers, and the best and freshest seafood in all its varieties; the crayfish are a must, and you can try the local *manzanilla* with the day's catch. Get there early or you won't find a table. *Closed Sun.*
Mirador de Doñana, Bajo de Guía, Sanlúcar, **t** 956 36 42 05 (*moderate*). Casa Bigote's main rival on the beach front, this is another popular bar-restaurant on three levels, with a panoramic view across to the Doñana bird reserve. Particularly delicious are: *cigalas* (crayfish), *angulas* (baby eels) and *nido de rapé a la Sanluqueña*, a nest of straw potato chips, deep-fried with monkfish and parsley.

Chipiona
La Panoleta, C/Isaac Peral 4-6, Chipiona, **t** 956 37 21 44 (*moderate*). Specializes in shellfish and *guisos marineros* such as *chocos en salsa*.
Paco, Puerto Deportivo, Chipiona, **t** 956 37 46 64 (*moderate*). Another good place for seafood.
Bar El Toro, Paseo Maritimo, Chipiona (*inexpensive*). A good, honest place which does fabulous *langostinos* and has a wide selection of sherries, all at a reasonable price.

El Puerto de Santa María
La Goleta, C/Babor 5, Puerto de Santa María, **t** 956 85 22 56 (*moderate*). One of the most popular in the Puerto, with simple but well-prepared seafood, especially the fish cooked in salt, the *tosta de salmón* and the pork in brandy. *Closed Mon except in July and Aug.*
Romerijo, Ribera del Marisco 1, Puerto de Santa María, **t** 956 54 12 54 (*inexpensive*). The liveliest place to dine in the Puerto, where you can eat the freshest fish and seafood at the tables outside or have a take-away wrapped in a paper funnel. Everyone throws discarded shells into one of the red buckets on each table, as they eat one of five kinds of prawn on offer. Noisy, and fantastic value.

El Puerto de Santa María

The biggest town on the Bay of Cádiz itself is **El Puerto de Santa María**, across from Cádiz and the traditional port of the Jerez sherry houses, which has quite a few *bodegas* of its own – Osborne, Terry and Duff Gordon among other famous names. It has interesting **churches**, mansions of the Anglo-Spanish sherry aristocracy, and the fine 13th-century *mudéjar* **Castillo de San Marcos**, while the century-old **bullring** ranks with those of Sevilla and Ronda in prestige. El Puerto is not a big resort, but it has bright, bustling streets, excellent restaurants and good beaches (Puntilla especially) on the edges of town, and is another town with a very rich flamenco tradition. **Puerto Sherry** is a modern marina, built in the 1980s.

Cádiz

If Cádiz were a village, the government would declare it a national monument and put up a sign. It's a big, busy seaport, though, and tourism generally leaves it alone. This is a pity, for Cádiz (if you pronounce it any other way but 'Caddy', no one in the locality will ever understand you) is one of the most distinctive Spanish cities, worth spending a few days in even if it has few 'sights'. The city is a small peninsula that comes in colours – a hundred shades of off-white – bleached and faded by sun and spray into a soft patina, which is broken only by the golden dome of a rambling, typically ornate Baroque cathedral.

Cádiz modestly claims to be the oldest city in western Europe. It's hard to argue; the Phoenician city of **Gadir** has a documented foundation date of 1100 BC and, while other cities have traces of older settlements, it would be difficult to find another city west of Greece with a continuous urban life of at least 3,000 years. Gadir served as the port for shipping Spanish copper and tin, and was the base for the now-forgotten Phoenician trade routes with west Africa and England. Cádiz, however, prefers to consider Hercules its founder, and he appears on the arms of the city between his famous pillars. Under Roman rule *Gades*, as they called it, was a favoured city, especially under Julius Caesar, who held his first public office here. The city then remained out of the spotlight until the 16th century, when the American trade and Spain's growth as a naval power made a major port of it once again. Sir Francis Drake visited in 1587 and, as every schoolboy used to know, 'singed the King of Spain's beard'. Later British admirals followed the custom for the next two centuries, calling every now and then for a fish supper and an afternoon's sacking and burning. The years after 1720, when Cádiz controlled the American market, shaped its present character.

This said, the approach to Cádiz is a dismal one, through marshes and saltpans and modern suburbs before arriving at the **Puerta de Tierra**, entrance to the old city on the peninsula. Almost everything about warfare in the 18th-century had a certain decorum to it, and Cádiz's gates and formidable **land walls** (1757), all well preserved, are among the most aesthetically pleasing structures in town. Beyond them is the old city. Neither decaying nor prettified for the tourists, it's great for exploring, a maze of lanes bathed in soft lamplight after dusk, when the cafés fill up with young *gaditanos*. A walk through the myriad cobbled streets, past solid wooden doors and balconies spilling over with flowers, takes you back to the time when mighty Cádiz bustled with commerce as the gateway to the Americas. In an hour or so you can walk entirely around Cádiz along the coast road, past parks like the pretty **Alameda de Apodaca**, and forts and bastions from the 18th century.

From the Puerta de Tierra, the Cuesta de las Calesas leads down to the port and railway station, then around the corner to **Plaza San Juan de Dios**, the lively, palm-shaded centre of Cádiz, in the streets around which are most of the city's restaurants and hotels. Two blocks away, the **cathedral** exercises an ingratiating charm despite its ungainly bulk. Inside, Zurbarán's *Santa Úrsula* stands out among the paintings. The **Museo de la Catedral** (*open Tues–Fri 10–1 and 4–7, Sat and Sun 10–1; closed Mon; adm*) has a lot of ecclesiastical gold and silverware, paintings by Murillo, Zurbarán and Alejo Fernández, and an ivory crucifix by Alonso Cano. A couple of blocks east, on the Campo del Sur, is the **Teatro Romano** (*open Tues–Sun 11–1.30; closed Mon; adm*), a restored Roman theatre dating from the 1st century BC, backing on to a maze of streets and buildings little changed since medieval times.

Continuing westwards to **Plaza Topete**, you'll find yourself in Cádiz's almost excessively colourful **market district**. A few blocks west, the church of **San Felipe Neri** on C/Sacramento (*open Tues–Fri 8.30–10 and 5–7; Sat, Sun and hols 9–1; closed Mon*) is an unprepossessing shrine to the beginnings of Spanish liberty. On 29 March 1812

Getting There

There are around 20 **trains** daily between Jerez and Cádiz; to make more of a ride of it, you can also get off the train at Puerto de Santa María and get a **ferry** across the bay. By **car**, follow the N-IV to Puerto Real and take the N-443 (30km). Parking in central Cádiz is very restricted.

Tourist Information

Cádiz: main office, corner of Plaza de Mina and C/Calderón de la Barca 1, **t** 956 21 13 13; Regional Office: Plaza de San Antonio 3, **t** 956 22 13 08.
City Office: Plaza San Juan de Dios 1, **t** 956 24 10 01 (*open Sat and Sun only*).

Eating Out

El Faro, C/San Félix 15, **t** 956 21 10 68 (*expensive*). Dining, of course, means more fish, and this is generally regarded as the best restaurant in the town. You can explore outlandish varieties of seafood unheard of in English, or more recognizable varieties, such as steamed hake with asparagus, clams with spinach, fried fish *a la Gaditana*, and there's also some meat on the menu.
El Candil, C/Javier de Burgos 19, **t** 956 22 19 71 (*expensive*). If you feel you really can't look at

another fish, try this place in the heart of town. Its garlic chicken is sensational.
Achvin, C/Plocia 15, **t** 956 25 36 13 (*moderate*). A venerable restaurant, popular with locals, and specializing in Basque and Andalucían dishes; just off Plaza San Juan de Dios.
Restaurante Grimaldi, C/Libertad 9 (in the market district), **t** 956 22 83 16 (*moderate*). Delicious fresh fish and seafood from the Bay, at very reasonable prices.
Café Bar Madrileño, Plaza Mina 1, **t** 956 22 51 63 (*inexpensive*). One of several good spots around Plaza Mina for reasonably priced seafood; an excellent place to try the city's classic dishes, fried fish, in *tapas* or *raciones*.
Casa Paco, Plaza San Agustin 5, **t** 956 28 54 51 (*inexpensive*). Excellent *tapas* and strong Voll Damm beer, on tap in the bar; full meals are served in the delightful restaurant just alongside.

Nightlife

Cádiz abounds with bars; the best area to find a bit of *marcha* outside summertime is around the university buildings, particularly **Pza San Francisco** and **Pza Espana** and the streets off and between them, including **C/San Francisco** and **C/Rosario**. Over the summer months the nightlife shifts to the beach area in the new part of town, particularly along the **Paseo Maritimo**.

refugees from Napoleon's occupation of the rest of Spain gathered here as a free *Cortes*, or parliament – since King Fernando VII was a prisoner of the French, and so out of the picture – and wrote Spain's first constitution, proposing full political and religious freedom. This constitution was short-lived, but it was a notable beginning in Spain's struggle towards democracy, and this Cádiz Cortes also gave the world the word 'liberal' as a political concept. Inside is an *Immaculate Conception* by Murillo.

Around the corner, Cádiz's municipal museum, the **Museo de las Cortes de Cádiz** *(open Tues–Fri 9–1 and 4–7, Sat and Sun 9–1; closed Mon and hols; adm)*, has a huge Romantic-era mural depicting the 1812 event. Its star exhibit is a 15m **scale model of Cádiz**, made of mahogany and ivory by an unknown obsessive in 1779. Among a collection of portraits of Spanish heroes is the Duke of Wellington, who in Spain carried the title Duke of Ciudad Rodrigo. It's a short walk from here to the **Torre Tavira** *(open winter 10–8; summer 10–6; adm)*, with a *camera obscura* giving fine views of the city.

In the northwest corner of Cádiz's peninsula is the Plaza de Mina. On this lovely square are the tourist office and the **Museum of Fine Arts and Archaeology** *(open Wed–Sat 9–8, Tues 2.30–8, Sun 9.30–2.30; closed Mon; adm)*. The archaeology section has Phoenician, Roman and Greek finds, but best are the paintings, including some Murillos and portraits by Zurbarán. Moreover, while the **Oratorio de la Santa Cueva** is closed for renovation, the museum is also graced with Andalucía's only Goya frescoes.

Seville

Apart from the Alhambra of Granada, the place where the lushness and sensuality of al-Andalus survives best is Andalucía's capital. Seville may be Spain's fourth-largest city, but it is a place where you can pick oranges from the trees, and see open countryside from the centre of town. Come in spring if you can, when the gardens are drowned in birdsong and the air becomes intoxicating with the scent of jasmine and a hundred other blooms (if you come in summer, you may melt). The pageant of Seville unfolds in the shadow of La Giralda, still the loftiest tower in Spain. Its size and the ostentatious play of its arches and arabesques make it the perfect symbol for this city, full of the romance of the south and delightful excess.

One of Seville's distinctions is its long historical continuity. Few cities in western Europe can claim never to have suffered a dark age, but Seville flourished after the fall of Rome – and even after the coming of the Castilians. Roman **Hispalis** was founded on an Iberian settlement, and became one of the leading cities of the province of Baetica. Seville was an important town under the Visigoths, and after the Moorish conquest was second only to Córdoba as a political power and centre of learning. For a while after the demise of the western caliphate in 1023 it was an independent kingdom. The disaster came for Muslim **Isbiliya** in 1248. The conquest of the city by Ferdinand III of Castile is not a well-documented event, but it seems more than half the population found exile in Granada or Africa preferable to Castilian rule. Despite the dislocation, the city survived, settled by Christian incomers, and found a new prosperity as Castile's window on the Mediterranean and South Atlantic trade routes.

Getting There

There are six to eight **trains** daily from Jerez to Seville, taking just over an hour. Santa Justa station in Seville is northeast of the centre. By **car**, you can take the A4 *autopista* (toll) or the N-IV. Distance to Seville is about 95km.

Tourist Information

Seville: Avda de la Constitución 21, **t** 954 22 14 04; Parque María Luisa, Paseo de las Delicias 9, **t** 954 23 44 65; Also information desks at the airport and at Santa Justa station.

Festivals

Semana Santa, *Holy Week*. Between Palm Sunday and Easter Saturday, 57 *cofradías* hoist up their *pasos* (floats) and process through vast crowds from their church to the cathedral, amid sonorous music and occasional *saetas*, flamenco hymns. Good Friday is the high point of the Festival

Feria, *April*. The solemnity of Semana Santa erupts in a week-long party, with sherry-drinking and dancing in ornate tents (*casetas*) and extravagant riding displays, leading up to a giant fireworks display on the last Sunday.

Where to Stay

Seville ✉ **41000**

Hotels are quite expensive here, so book ahead. High season is March and April; for Semana Santa and the April *Feria* all rooms need to be booked months (or a year) ahead.

★★★★★**Alfonso XIII**, C/San Fernando 2, **t** 954 22 28 50 (*luxury*). Built for the Exhibition in 1929, this is the grandest hotel in Andalucía, attracting celebrities, and tourists who want a unique experience, albeit at a price. The **restaurant**, San Fernando is impressive.

★★★★**Los Seises**, C/Segovias 6, **t** 954 22 94 95 (*expensive*). Hidden in the Santa Cruz Quarter, this 16th-century archbishop's palace contains Roman artefacts, Arabic columns and later antiques; each room is individually styled. There is a rooftop pool too, and an acclaimed **restaurant**.

★★★**Hotel San Gil**, C/Parras 28, **t** 954 90 68 11 (*moderate*). Near the Andalucían parliament is this beautiful old ochre building, with a shady courtyard with palm trees, fabulous mosaics and *azulejo* tiles, and lofty ceilings.

★★**HsR del Laurel**, Pza de los Venerables 5, **t** 954 22 02 95, *host-laurel@eintec.es* (*moderate*). Overlooking a slightly touristy square, this is an engagingly quirky hotel with turrets and terraces that once attracted Romantic poets.

From 1503 to 1680 Seville enjoyed a legal monopoly of trade with the Americas, and for a time was the biggest city in Spain. The giddy prosperity this brought, in the years when the silver fleet ran full, contributed much to the festive, incautious atmosphere that is often revealed in Seville's character. Seville never managed to hold on to much of the American wealth, and what it did grab was often spent in showy excess. It was in this period, of course, that Seville was perfecting its charm. Poets and composers have always favoured it. The prototypes of Bizet's *Carmen* rolled their cigars in the Royal Tobacco Factory, and for her male counterpart Seville contributed Don Juan Tenorio, who evolved through Spanish theatre to become Mozart's *Don Giovanni*.

In the 17th and 18th centuries the city stagnated, and although many industrial programmes were started up over the years, any economic 'take-off' was always hesitant. With the return of democracy in the 1970s, Andalucíans took advantage of the new mood to create an ever-more active regional government. In 1992, crimped and primped, Seville opened her doors to the world for **Expo '92**, a vainglorious display that attracted 16 million visitors, and gave the old city some unheard-of – but now sadly under-used – contemporary architecture.

*Hs Nuevo Picasso, C/San Gregorio 1, t/f 954 21 08 64, hpicasso@arrakis.es (*inexpensive*). One of the nicest *pensiones* in this district, with a plant-filled entrance hall, a green courtyard hung with bric-a-brac, and attractive rooms.

Eating Out

Tapas bars are an intrinsic part of daily life in Seville, and even the smartest restaurants often have excellent *tapas* bars attached.

Corral del Agua, Callejón del Agua 6, t 954 22 48 41 (*expensive*). Seasoned travellers usually steer clear of cutesy wishing-wells, but the garden here is a haven of peace and shade, perfect for a lazy lunch or an unashamedly romantic dinner.

La Judería, C/Caño y Cueto, t 954 41 20 52 (*moderate*). Tucked away in the old Jewish quarter, with brick arches and terracotta tiles. There is an almost bewildering range of richly flavoured regional dishes like *cola de toro*, game in season, fish dishes and home-made desserts. *Closed Tues and Aug*.

La Mandrágora, C/Albuera 11, t 954 22 01 84 (*moderate*). In a country where meat and fish reign supreme, it's a nice surprise to discover La Mandrágora, a friendly vegetarian restaurant with an excellent and wide-ranging menu. *Closed Sun*.

Bodegón Torre del Oro, C/Santander 15, t 954 21 42 41 (*inexpensive*). The rafters here are hung with dozens of different hams. There's a great-value three-course set meal with wine, and the *raciones* are excellent.

El Rinconcillo, C/Gerona 42 (*inexpensive*). The oldest bar in Sevilla (from 1670), this is reputedly where the custom of topping a glass with a slice of sausage or a piece of bread and ham – the first *tapas* – began.

Bar Manolo, Plaza de Alfalfa (*inexpensive*). The best of several *tapas* bars on the square. It's lively at breakfast as well as at night.

Nightlife

The Pza del Salvador fills up quickly in the evenings, so start at the **Antigua Bodeguita**, or **Los Soportales**. Many of the liveliest bars are around **Pza de Alfalfa**. Seville is of course a fine place to experience quality **flamenco**. The tourist office has a notice board with details of flamenco shows; a few venues are listed here:

El Simpecao, Paseo Nuestra Senora de la O.

La Carbonería, C/Levies 18. Near-legendary flamenco bar.

El Tamboril, Plaza Santa Cruz. Come here for *sevillana* dancing; it's as popular with *sevillanos* as it is with tourists.

The Giralda, Cathedral and the Alcázar

You can catch the 97m tower of **La Giralda** (*open Mon–Sat 11–5, Sun and hols 2–6; adm*) peeking over the rooftops from almost anywhere in Sevilla. This great minaret, with its brickwork arabesques, was built under the **Almohads**, from 1172 to 1195, 50 years before the Christian conquest. The surprisingly harmonious spire is a Christian addition; on the top of their spire, the Christians also added a huge, revolving statue of Faith as a weathervane, and **La Giraldillo** – the weathervane – has given its name to the tower as a whole. The climb to the top is fairly easy: instead of stairs, there are shallow ramps – wide enough for Ferdinand III to have ridden his horse up for the view after the conquest in 1248. For a while after that, the Castilians who repopulated Sevilla were content to use the great Almohad mosque, built at the same time as La Giralda. But, at the turn of the 1400s, it was decided to build a new **cathedral** (*opening hours as for Giralda, both are visited with one ticket*), the biggest Gothic cathedral in the world. The exterior, with its great rose window and double buttresses, is as fine as any Gothic cathedrals in northern Spain, if you could only see it. On the west, especially, facing Av de la Constitución, the buildings close in; walking around its vast bulk is like passing under a steep and ragged cliff. The ground plan of this monster, roughly

122m by 183m, probably covers the same area as the original mosque. On the northern side, the **Patio de los Naranjos** (Court of the Orange Trees) preserves the outline of the mosque courtyard. The cathedral's cavernous **interior** overpowers the faithful with its size more than any grace or beauty. Just behind the Large Chapel (**Capilla Mayor**) and main altar, the Royal Chapel (**Capilla Real**) contains the tombs of Ferdinand the Saint, conqueror of Seville, and of Alfonso the Wise. In the southern aisle, four stern pall-bearers support the **tomb of Christopher Columbus**.

Parts of Seville's cathedral were public ground, used to transact all sorts of business. A 16th-century bishop put an end to this, but prevailed upon Philip II to build an **Exchange** (*Lonja*), next to the cathedral for the merchants, and Philip sent his favourite architect, Juan de Herrera, to design it. In the 1780s, Charles III converted it to hold the **Archive of the Indies** (*open Mon–Fri 10–1; closed Sat and Sun*), the repository of all the documents the Crown had collected in the age of exploration.

Next comes the **Alcázar** (*open summer Tues–Sat 9.30–7, Sun and hols 9.30–5; winter Tues–Sat 9.30–5, Sun and hols 9.30–1.30; closed Mon; adm*). It's easy to be fooled into thinking this is simply a Moorish palace; parts of it could have come straight from the Alhambra. Most of it, however, was built by Moorish *mudéjar* craftsmen for **King Pedro the Cruel** of Castile in the 1360s, suggesting the possibility that al-Andalus might have assimilated its conquerors rather than been destroyed by them. The Alcázar is entered by the little gate on Plaza del Triunfo, on the southern side of the cathedral. The first courtyard, the **Court of León**, has beautiful arabesques; this was the public court, where visitors were received, as in the Mexuar at the Alhambra. Much of the best *mudéjar* work can be seen in adjacent halls and courts. Off the Court of León is the **Hall of Justice**, with a star-shaped coffered ceiling, where Pedro I passed a death sentence on his brother, who had had an affair with Pedro's wife. Behind, the secluded **Patio de Yeso** survives largely from the Moorish palace of the 1170s, itself built on the site of a Roman *praetorium*. Another courtyard leads to the **Salón de las Embajadores** (Hall of the Ambassadors), a small domed chamber that remains the finest in the Alcázar despite the jarring addition of carved balconies from the time of Philip II. Spanish kings couldn't leave the Alcázar alone, and Charles V added his own **palace**, which has spectacular **Flemish tapestries**. Within its walls, the Alcázar also has extensive **gardens**, with reflecting pools, avenues of clipped hedges, and oranges and lemons everywhere.

Barrios: El Arenal, Triana, Santa Cruz

Av de la Constitución is Seville's main street. Between it and the Guadalquivir is **El Arenal**, once the bustling port district. Today it is quiet and tranquil, without the distinction of the Barrio de Santa Cruz, but with an earthy charm of its own. Heading down to the river, you will pass one of the surviving rampart gates, the **Postigo del Aceite** (Gate of Olive Oil), a 16th-century remodelling of an old Moorish gate. Behind a colourful façade on C/Temprado is the **Hospital de la Caridad** (*open Mon–Sat 9–1 and 3.30–6.30, Sun 9–1; adm*), built in 1647. It still serves as a charity home for the aged, and visitors come to see the art in the hospital chapel, eight paintings of saints by Murillo. A little beyond it on the riverbank is the **Torre de Oro**, the 'Tower of Gold' (*open*

Tues–Fri 10–2, Sat and Sun 11–2; closed Mon and Aug; adm), so named because of the gold and *azulejo* tiles that originally covered its exterior, and built by the Moorish Almohad rulers of Seville in 1220. In times of trouble a chain was stretched from the tower across the Guadalquivir; in 1248 the chain was broken by an attacking fleet, the supply route with Triana was cut off and Seville fell. Inside, a **Museo Marítimo** displays models, documents, weapons and maps. On the river just north of the tower is **La Maestranza bullring**, perhaps the most prestigious of all *plazas de toros*.

Across the Guadalquivir from La Maestranza is **Triana**, an ancient suburb that takes its name from the Emperor Trajan. It still has picturesque white streets overlooking the river, and, along its banks, the charming **Paseo Nuestra Señora de la O** hosts a colourful, cheap produce market. Triana also has a reputation for being the 'cradle of flamenco', and the streets around C/Castilla and C/San Jorge are still some of the best for finding Triana ceramics; all Seville's *azulejo* tiles are made here.

Back across the river is the district of **San Eloy**, full of raucous bars and hotels. On C/San Roque is the **Museo de Bellas Artes** (*open Tues 3–8, Wed–Sat 9–8, Sun 9–2, closed Mon; adm*), an excellent collection in the 1612 **Convent of La Merced**, with major works by the archetypal *Sevillano* painters, Murillo and Zurbarán, plus others by Jan Brueghel, Caravaggio and Mattia Preti. A few streets east, **Calle Sierpes** ('Serpent Street') is the heart of Seville's business and shopping area, a sinuous pedestrian lane lined with every sort of old shop. Just east stands **El Salvador**, a fine Baroque church now picturesquely mouldering. Around it, narrow, half-timbered houses jostle for space in the old merchant district while, to the south, **Plaza Nueva** marks Seville's modern centre, embellished by the Plateresque façade of the **Ayuntamiento** (1564).

From Plaza Nueva or the Giralda a few steps will take you into the **Barrio de Santa Cruz**, most famous of Seville's districts. If Spain envies Seville, Seville envies Santa Cruz, a tiny, exceptionally lovely quarter of narrow streets and whitewashed houses. It appears to be the true homeland of everything *sevillano*, with flower-decked court-yards and iron-bound windows, though there is something unnervingly pristine about it. Before 1492, this was the Jewish quarter; today it's the most aristocratic part of town. In the old days it was walled; today you can enter through the Murillo Gardens, C/Mateos Gago behind the cathedral apse, or **Patio de las Banderas**, a pretty square next to the Alcázar. Also amid the peaceful, eastern fringes of the old city is the **Casa de Pilatos** (*open Wed–Mon 9–7, Tues 1–5; adm*), a 16th-century mansion built for the Dukes of Medinaceli and, the story goes, modelled on Pontius Pilate's official residence in Jerusalem. The **Patio Principal** is laced with 13th-century Granadan deco-ration, tiles and rows of Roman statues, a perfect introduction to the dukes' collection of ancient sculpture, and there are delightful **gardens** and **courtyards**.

Around old Seville there are also two areas that were reconstructed in the 20th century. In the 1920s, Seville and Spain decided on promoting themselves with an international exhibition, held in 1929, To house it, the entire southern end of the city was turned into an expanse of gardens and grand boulevards, at the centre of which is the **Parque de María Luisa**, a paradisiacal half-mile of palms and orange trees. Two of the largest pavilions now house museums, the **Museo Arqueológico** (*open Tues 3–8, Wed–Sat 9–8, Sun and hols 9–2; closed Mon and Aug; adm*) and the **Museo de**

Artes y Costumbres Populares (*open Tues 3–8, Wed–Sat 9–8, Sun and hols 9–2; closed Mon; adm*), Andalucía's attic, with everything from ploughs and saucepans to exhibits from the city's fiestas. The biggest construction for 1929, though – to show that excess was still a way of life in Seville – was the **Plaza de España**, with its Baroque towers, fancy bridges and immense colonnade, a piece of World's Fair architecture at its most outrageous. Then, 60 years later Seville sought to top this with Expo '92, for which a huge area on the river's west bank, the isle of **La Cartuja**, was transformed. Since then it has become seedy and run down; some of the pavilions are used for trade fairs, while another bit is **Isla Mágica** funfair (*open Mar–Oct daily 11–11; adm exp*).

Córdoba

There are a few places around the Mediterranean where the presence of past glories becomes almost tangible. It occurs in Istanbul, in Rome, or Egypt, and it occurs here on the banks of the Guadalquivir, at Córdoba's southern gate. Looking around, you can see reminders of three defunct empires: a Roman bridge, a triumphal arch built for Philip II and Córdoba's Great Mosque, more than a thousand years old. The first reminds us of the city's beginnings, the second of its decline; the last scarcely seems credible, as it speaks of an age when Córdoba was one of the most brilliant metropolises of all Europe.

Roman *Corduba*, built on a prehistoric site, was almost from the start the leading city of interior Spain. It gave Roman letters Lucan and both Senecas, testimony to its prominence as a city of learning. Córdoba became Christianized at an early date. When the Arabs arrived, they found it was still an important town, and it became the capital of al-Andalus when Abd ar-Rahman established the Umayyad emirate in 756. For 300 years, Córdoba enjoyed the position of unqualified leader of al-Andalus, a city without equal in the West as a centre of learning. If proof were needed, it would be enough to mention two 12th-century contemporaries: **Averroës**, the Aristotelian philosopher who contributed so much to the rebirth of classical learning in Europe, and the Jewish philosopher **Moses Maimonides**. At its height, it was a city of bustling markets, great palaces, schools, baths and mosques, with 28 suburbs and the first street lighting in Europe. When **Ferdinand III** 'the Saint' captured the city in 1236, most members of the population chose flight over putting themselves at the mercy of the priests, although history records that he was unusually tolerant of the Jews. It did not last. Three centuries of Castilian rule sufficed to rob Córdoba of all its glories and turn it into a depressed backwater. Only in the last hundred years has it begun to recover.

La Mezquita

La Mezquita is the local name for Abd ar-Rahman's **Great Mosque** (*open summer Mon–Sat 10–7, Sun 1.30–7; winter Mon–Sat 10–5.30, Sun 1.30–5.30; adm*). *Mezquita* means 'mosque' and even though the building has officially been a cathedral for more than 750 years, no one could ever mistake its origins. **Abd ar-Rahman I**, founder of a new state, felt it necessary to construct a great religious monument for his capital.

Only about one-third of the mosque belongs to the original, for successive enlarge-ments were made by Abd ar-Rahman II, al-Hakim and al-Mansur. Expansion was easy; the mosque is a simple rectangle divided into aisles by rows of columns, and its size was increased simply by adding aisles. After 1236, it was converted to use as a cathe-dral without major changes. In the 1520s, however, clerics convinced the Royal Council to allow the construction of a choir and high altar, typical of Spanish cathedrals.

Before entering, take a few minutes to circumnavigate this somewhat forbidding pile of bricks. Spaced around its 685m of wall are the original entrances and windows, of which those on the western side are best. The only entrance to the mosque today

Getting There

There are four **trains** daily from Jerez to Córdoba, via Seville, and the journey takes about two hours. There are also fairly frequent trains from Málaga. Córdoba station is about 1½ km from the town centre. By **car**, continue on the N-IV past Seville (Córdoba is 230km from Jerez). Parking is a nightmare here; if possible, get a hotel with a car park.

Tourist Information

Córdoba: Regional Tourist Office, C/Torrijos 10, next to the Mezquita, **t** 957 47 12 35; Municipal Office, in the Judería on Pza Judá Levi, **t** 957 20 05 22. It's worth a visit to get a map to Córdoba's labyrinthine old quarter.

Where to Stay

Córdoba ✉ 14000

★★★Posada de Vallina, C/Corregidor Luis de Cerda 83, **t** 957 49 87 50 (*expensive*). One of the nicest new hotels to have sprung up recently, opposite the Mezquita. An old inn dating from Roman times, it has just 15 rooms, all tastefully designed, some with mosque views, others facing the patio. Attached is a great **restaurant**.

★★Lola, C/Romero 3, **t** 957 20 03 05, *hotel-lola@terra.es* (*expensive*). Even newer, this hotel is in the heart of the old Jewish quarter in a lovingly restored old house with many antique fittings and furniture. There are eight rooms, each individually designed, all doubles, but varying in size. Go for the suite, with a superb view and a tiny terrace.

★★Hotel Mezquita, Plaza Santa Catalina, 1, **t** 957 47 55 85 (*moderate*). A converted 16th-century mansion restored with paintings and sculptures, this is fantastic value for its location. A drawback: no garage.

★Hotel Los Patios, C/Cardenal Herrero 14, **t** 957 47 83 40 (*inexpensive*). Fantastic value for its location, opposite the Mezquita. Brand new and sparkling clean, the 24 rooms are set around the hotel's patio, and all have TV, phones and good bathrooms.

Eating Out

El Churrasco, C/Romero 16, **t** 957 29 08 19 (*expensive*). In an old house in the Jewish quarter, this is Córdoba's best-loved restau-rant, and for food and atmosphere perhaps the finest in southern Spain – but it's not grand; it's actually small, and intimate. It specializes in grilled meats. *Closed Aug*.

Rincón de Carmen, C/Romero 4, **t** 957 29 10 55 (*moderate*). Family-run, noisy and full of atmosphere. The local dishes are prepared as well as at any establishment in the city, and the prices are low. It also has a very pleasant (and slightly more peaceful) café attached.

El Tablón, Cardenal González 79, **t** 957 47 60 61 (*inexpensive*). Around the corner from the Mezquita, this is one of the best bargains in the city, with a choice of *menús del día* or *platos combinados*, glass of wine included.

Bodegón Rafaé, corner of C/Deanes and C/Buen Pastor (*inexpensive*). Take it or leave it, this place has true *bodega* food and atmosphere. Sausages drape from barrels, the radio and TV are on simultaneously; *cola de toro* (oxtail) with wine at one of the vinyl-topped tables will cost next to nothing.

is the **Puerta del Perdón**, a *mudéjar* gateway added in 1377, opening on to the **Patio de los Naranjos**, the original mosque courtyard where the Moorish fountain can still be seen amid orange trees. Built into the wall of the courtyard, over the gate, the original minaret has been replaced by a 16th-century belltower. From the courtyard, the mosque is entered through a little door, the **Puerta de las Palmas**.

Here is the first surprise. The building is gloomy only because Spanish clerics wanted it that way. Originally there was no wall separating mosque from courtyard, and that side of the mosque was entirely open. In the aesthetics of this mosque, too, there is more than meets the eye. Many European writers have seen it as un-spiritual, a plain prayer-hall. To the Christian mind it is difficult to comprehend, for the guiding principle is a rarefied abstraction – the repetition of columns is like a meditation in stone, a mirror of Creation where unity and harmony radiate from innumerable centres.

The surviving jewel of the mosque is its *mihrab*, added in the 10th century under al-Hakim II, an octagonal chamber set into the wall and covered by a beautiful dome of interlocking arches. A Byzantine emperor, Nikephoras Phokas, sent artists to help with its mosaic decoration, cubes. Looking back from the *mihrab*, you will see what was once the exterior wall, built in Abd ar-Rahman II's extension, from the year 848. Its gates are as good as those on the west façade, and better preserved. The various 16th-century Christian intrusions into the mosque – now rarely used for services – are not unlovely in themselves, and would not offend anywhere but here. Fortunately the Mezquita is so large that from many parts of it you don't even notice them.

Around the Mezquita

The tatty souvenir stands and third-rate cafés that surround the Great Mosque on its busiest days do their best to re-create the atmosphere of Moorish *souks*, but walk a block in any direction and you'll enter the essential Córdoba: brilliant whitewashed lanes with glimpses into dreamily beautiful patios, each one a floral extravaganza. One of the best is **Calle de las Flores** ('street of the flowers') just a block northeast of La Mezquita, although sadly its charms are diminished by hordes of tourists.Below La Mezquita, along the Guadalquivir, the melancholic plaza called **Puerta del Puente** marks the site of Córdoba's southern gate with a decorative **arch** put up in 1571. The most fascinating area of all in the old city is the Judería, the ancient Jewish quarter, which as in Seville has become newly fashionable, a nest of tiny streets between the Mezquita and Av Dr Fleming. Part of the Moorish walls can be seen along this street, and the northern entrance of the Judería is the old **Almodóvar gate**. The streets are tricky, and it will take some effort to find C/Maimonides and the 14th-century **synagogue** (*open Tues–Sat 10–1.30 and 3.30–5.30, Sun 10–1.30; closed Mon*). From the mosque you can also walk eastwards through well over a kilometre of twisting white alleys, a place where the best map in the world wouldn't keep you from getting lost. Though it all looks much the same, it's never monotonous. Every little square, fountain or church stands out boldly, and forces you to look at it in a way different from how you would look at a modern city. These streets have probably changed little since 1236, but their best buildings are a series of **Gothic churches** built soon after the Reconquista. Though small and plain, most are exquisite in a quiet way.

Touring from Jerez: the White Villages

Day 1: Medina Sidonia to the Beach at Zahara

Morning: From Jerez, the A381 heads south to **Medina Sidonia**, one of the prettiest of the 'White Villages', on a hill in the middle of a picture-postcard landscape. Medina's aristocratic career began in 1440, when it was given to its first Duke, Don Juan de Guzman (a line that continues today). The 16th-century Santa Maria la Coronada has a huge carved *retablo* stretching from floor to ceiling. There are also three well-preserved Moorish gates, and a ruined Moorish castle, with great views.

Lunch: In Medina Sidonia, *see* below.

Afternoon: From Medina Sidonia, the A393 takes you to the coast and **Vejer de la Frontera**, a gleaming whitewashed village moulded around its hilltop like a Greek island town. Like Medina, Vejer retains its Moorish gates and castle; the 13th-century Gothic church, at the centre of its narrow streets, was built on the site of a mosque. There are scant remains of a Roman aqueduct at the lovely nearby village of **Santa Lucía**, and a seldom-visited beach at **El Palmar**, 9km away, just off Cape Trafalgar, site of Nelson's victory in 1805. You might skip the beaches, for there are miles of them to the south at the next stop, **Zahara de los Atunes**, along one of the most unspoiled coastlines in southern Spain (even though that's changing fast).

Dinner and Sleeping: In Zahara de los Atunes, *see* below.

Day 1

Lunch in Medina Sidonia

La Duquesa, on the road to Benalup, km 3, **t** 956 41 08 36 (*moderate*). Set in a converted farmhouse, this restaurant offers superb local cooking with the emphasis on game, including pheasant, partridge and deer, served with fresh vegetables from its own fields. They also whip up some fine home-made desserts.

Cadiz, Pza Espana, **t** 956 41 02 50 (*moderate*). Has a lovely shaded patio and serves some good gamey local dishes including partridge, rabbit and beef stews.

Dinner in Zahara de los Atunes

Sergio, **t** 956 43 94 55 (*moderate*). Just out of the town centre, on the Atlanterra road, and specializing in Segovian-style meats, plus, of course, local seafood.

El Pirato, **t** 956 23 22 55 (*moderate*). Perfectly situated restaurant with a lovely terrace overlooking the beach and Cape Trafalgar.

Los Tangos, C/Gobenardor Sanchoz Gonzalez, **t** 956 43 91 30 (*moderate–inexpensive*). On the beach in the castle walls, with a very nice *terraza*; also functions as a disco.

Sleeping in Zahara de los Atunes

Gran Sol, on the beach at the end of Sanchez Rodriguez, **t 956 43 93 58 (*expensive–moderate*). A good option, with comfortable air-conditioned rooms with TV, a fairly good **restaurant** and a pool.

***Portofirio, Ctra Atlanterra 33, 200m from the beach, **t** 956 44 95 15, *porfirio@arrakis.es* (*moderate*). A delightful hotel built in Andalucian style with patios and 24 rooms arranged around a large pool and set in its own grounds. Bedrooms are with terraces and all mod cons, and there's a good, reasonably priced **restaurant**.

***Doña Lola, Plaza Thomson 1, **t** 956 43 90 09 (*moderate*). The prettiest hotel in Zahara, with rooms set around a patio and overlooking a large pool. Excellent value, and a very pleasant place to be.

Day 2: From Hip Tarifa to Algeciras

Morning: After a morning walk along the beach at Zahara continue on south for the short journey to the southernmost town in Europe, **Tarifa**. Bleached by sun and salt, with a slightly African air to it, Tarifa has for its only sight yet another Moorish castle (10th century, much restored), though the confluence of winds here makes the town better known as one of the top destinations in Europe for windsurfing. There will be a sizeable young crowd in season, with a lively bar scene, and miles of beaches for the less ambitious to sit on. Just west of Tarifa along the beaches lie the ruins of a once-important Roman town, **Baelo Claudio** (*open July–15 Sept 10–2 and 5–9; 16 Sept through June, 10–12.30 and 4–8; adm*); you can make out foundations of temples, basilicas, roads, and the factory that made *garum*, the ancient Andalucian fish sauce shipped from here all over the Empire.

Lunch: In Tarifa, *see* below.

Afternoon: Between Tarifa and **Algeciras**, the coastal road passes through a corner of the **Parque Natural de Los Alcornocales**, an important stopover for migratory birds that also possesses the largest forest of cork oaks in Europe. Algeciras, a big industrial port and fishing centre, has little to charm you into staying the afternoon, but there is another pretty village just up the coast, **San Roque**, with exceptional views and more clean beaches nearby at Puente Mayorga, Los Portichuelos and Carteya; the last one also has ruins of another Roman town.

Dinner and Sleeping: In Algeciras, *see* below.

Day 2

Lunch in Tarifa

Meson de Sancho, Ctra N 340, km 94, t 956 68 49 00, f 95 668 47 21 (*expensive*). One of the best restaurants in the area, attached to a hotel of the same name, near the Hurricane Hotel. Especially pleasing in winter with its roaring fire, it specializes in home-cooked dishes – favourites are garlic soup, *urta* in cream sauce and *rabo de toro*. There are also very good set menus, at much lower prices.

Pizzeria Transito Tropical, C/Don Sancho IV, t 956 68 17 39 (*inexpensive*). Good fresh pizzas at decent prices.

Dinner in Algeciras

Los Remos, at Villa Victoria (on the road out of San Roque to La Línea), t 956 69 84 12, (*expensive–moderate*). The most famous restaurant in the area, long-established and Michelin-rosetted. It has only recently moved to this old house surrounded by lovely gardens, but in a horrible setting – in the shadow of the oil refineries; red-meat-carnivores beware – it serves mostly fish.

Almazar, C/Alfonso 9, t 956 65 74 77 (*moderate*). One of the best restaurants in town, serving *tapas* at the bar and great steaks and fish in the tiny restaurant.

Sleeping in Algeciras

★★★★Reina Cristina, on Paseo de la Conferencia, t 95 660 26 22, (*expensive*). The hotel of the town's bygone elegance, scene of the Algeciras Conference of 1906, which carved up Morocco, and was a hotbed of spies during the Second World War. WB Yeats spent a winter here.

★★★Alborán, Álamo (Colonia San Miguel), t 956 63 28 70 (*moderate*). A wonderful building in classical Andalucian style, very atmospheric and keenly priced, with an indoor patio and porticoed terrace.

Versailles, Montero Rios 12, t 956 54 21 11 (*inexpensive*). One of a cluster of convenient little *hostales* in the back streets behind the Avenida de la Marina.

Day 3: Back into the Mountains and Ronda

Morning: A short 20km around the bay from Algeciras but in another world lies Gibraltar, where there's more than enough to keep you busy for a morning: historical tours, a look at the famous apes or just a visit to a pub (*see* p.219). If you've already had the Rock experience, head on north up the A369 and back into the Andalucía of white villages, through **Jimena de la Frontera** and **Gaucín**, known as 'the most fashionable village in the Sierra' because of the number of foreign celebs who have acquired houses in or around it. Beyond Jimena begins the Serranía de Ronda, where you can take the 'scenic route' from Gaucín to **Ronda**, or detour to Benoaján and the **Cueva de la Pileta**, with cave paintings (*see* p.219).

Lunch: In Benoaján or Gaucín, *see* below.

Afternoon: One of the loveliest cities in Andalucía, **Ronda** is blessed with the perfect postcard shot of its lofty Puente Nuevo, spanning the deep gorge that divides the old and new towns. Its other landmarks include one of Spain's most famous bull-rings (built in 1785, with a small museum, o*pen daily Nov–Feb 10–6, Mar–Oct 10–7; adm*), and the church of Santa Maria la Mayor. The town's museum is in the Palacio de Montragón (*open Mon–Fri 10–7, Sat and Sun 10–3; adm*); more Moorish memories include a baths complex and walls; there are churches and monasteries, and even a museum of banditry. Yet one of the best things to do here is simply walk in the lovely gardens above the gorge, and marvel at the extraordinary views.

Dinner and Sleeping: In Ronda, *see* below and pp.211 and 218.

Day 3

Lunch in Gaucín or Benoaján

Molino del Santo, Bulevar de la Estación, Benoaján, **t** 952 16 71 51 (*moderate*). A converted water mill beside a mountain stream, close to the Pileta caves with a spring-fed swimming pool. The kitchen serves excellent *andaluz* cuisine.

La Fructosa, C/Luis de Armiñán 67, Gaucín, **t** 952 15 10 72 (*moderate*). Known as one of the best restaurants in the area, with modernized *andaluz* cuisine. *Closed Thurs*.

Dinner in Ronda

Duquesa de Parcent, C/Tenorio 12, **t** 952 19 07 63, (*expensive*). The place you can see from the bridge, with three tiered terraces perched above the gorge. This 19th-century house has been sumptuously renovated inside, and features grilled pork and lamb and fish in salt crust as the house specials. It's ideal for an early-evening drink as you watch the sun set over the mountains.

Escudero, Chalet del Tajo, Paseo de Blas Infante 1, **t** 952 43 45 45 (*expensive*). Traditional food such as roasts and grills and with probably the best view in town, behind the bullring.

Sleeping in Ronda

★★★Hotel San Gabriel, C/Jose M Holgado 19, **t** 952 19 03 92, *www.ronda.net/usuar/hotels-gabriel* (*moderate*). Probably the loveliest hotel in town in terms of décor, service, atmosphere and value; a 1736-vintatge private house before its conversion to a hotel in 1998. Wood panelling and old prints line the walls of the bedrooms, and there's a café and a lovely, shaded patio.

★★Hotel Don Miguel, C/Villanueva 8, **t** 952 87 77 22, **f** 95 287 83 77 (*moderate*). Very good value for such a great spot on the cliff edge opposite the *parador*, and with an excellent **restaurant** attached.

★★★Polo, C/Mariano Soubirón 8, **t** 952 87 24 47, (*moderate*). A busy little place in the centre of town, with old-fashioned comfort at a modest price.

Day 4: Hill Villages: Olvera and Zahara

Morning: You might spend part of the morning on a trip up to *Ronda la Vieja*, really site of the Roman town of **Acinpo**, with remains of a theatre (*see* p.219). Or else, carry on exploring the villages of the Serranía: head northwards for **Setenil de las Bodegas**, a curious village with houses lining the walls of a gorge, tucked under the cliffs. Continue on northwards from there up more rocky crags to **Olvera**, once a famous bandits' hideout, and now a beautiful place with a memorable silhouette, formed by its 12th-century castle and 17th-century church, sticking bravely up over the whitewashed houses, and a delightful village to wander around.

Lunch: In Olvera or Zahara, *see* below.

Afternoon: Start on the A382 road back for Jerez, and turn south after **Algodonales** for **Zahara** ('flower' in Arabic) **de la Sierra**, a national monument village crowned by a medieval castle. Here, you are on the edge of the **Sierra Grazalema**, a visually stunning chain enclosed in a national park, with many rare species of plants and animals, and opportunities for walking, hang-gliding, horse riding and more. Zahara is a good base for walks, including one through the superb gorge of the **Garganta Verde**, or you can continue on southwards for **Grazalema**. Full of flowers and surrounded by pine woods, this is the archtypical Sierra village: Grazalema has also been famous for woven blankets since Moorish times, and people here still make them today on big, old wooden looms.

Dinner and Sleeping: In Grazalema, *see* below.

Day 4

Lunch in Olvera or Zahara de la Sierra
Sierra y Cal, Avda Nuestra Senora de los Remedios 4, Olvera, **t** 956 13 03 03 (*moderate–inexpensive*). A good hotel restaurant, and much the best place to eat in Olvera.

Arco de la Villa, Paseo Nazari s/n, Zahara de la Sierra, **t** 956 12 32 30 (*moderate*). A hotel restaurant in a fantastic location built into the cliff edge above the town and below the ruined castle; the setting makes up for the slightly average food.

Dinner in Grazalema
Most food and drink options can be found in the streets leading off Plaza de España.

La Garrocha, Plaza Pequeña 8, **t** 956 13 24 06, *www.grazhotel.com* (*expensive*). Grazalema's best restaurant, featuring *andaluz* dishes of fresh fish, meat and vegetables, prepared in an innovative way. Part of the Hotel Puerta de la Villa.

El Torreon, C/Agua 44, **t** 956 13 23 13 (*moderate*). Another good option in this area, with local trout, steak and chicken featuring on the reasonably priced menu.

Cadiz el Chico, Pza de Espana 8, **t** 956 13 20 27 (*inexpensive*). Back on the main square, offering real bargain menus of local dishes.

Sleeping in Grazalema
★★★★**Hotel Puerta de la Villa**, Plaza Pequeña 8, **t** 956 13 24 06, *www.grazhotel.com* (*expensive*). Recently-opened hotel just off the main square, with light, spacious rooms with outstanding views and all the mod cons, plus a tiny pool, gym and sauna, and the best restaurant in town (*see* left).

Hotel Villa Turistica de Grazalema, C/Olivar, **t** 956 13 21 36 (*moderate*). One of the comfortable, government-run self-catering places, which you pass on the approach into town. Has some apartments with jacuzzis.

La Casa de las Piedras, C/las Piedras 32, **t** 95 613 20 14 (*inexpensive*). The cheaper, functional option, just above the main square.

Day 5: Town on a Crag: Arcos de la Frontera

Morning: Spend the morning walking around Grazalema some more, or explore the park that surrounds it; the scents of wild flowers and herbs in these Mediterranean mountains, even on just a short walk, are utterly invigorating. When you're through, head back for Jerez, passing through Ubrique, a town famous for leatherwork, and **El Bosque**, a town and road junction through which everyone in this part of the Serranía is slightly fated to pass. It's a superb place to stop off to eat in the *sierra*.

Lunch: In El Bosque, *see* below

Afternoon: From El Bosque, the A372 road runs relatively straight for 25km to **Arcos de la Frontera**, in a spectacular site hanging on a steep rock with wonderful views over the valley of the Guadalete. The name comes from the Latin *arx*, or citadel, and this has been an important spot since ancient times. Under the Moors it was briefly capital of its own little kingdom. Its monuments today are its churches: Santa María de la Asunción (*open Mon–Fri 10–1 and 3.30–6.30, Sat 10–1.30; adm*), on the northern side of Plaza del Cabildo, has an impressive Platheresque façade and 14th-century *mudéjar* wall paintings inside. Arcos' most venerated relic, a 17th-century Jesus Nazareno (Christ Carrying the Cross) by Jacomi Verdi lies within yet another shrine, the 16th-century Convent of San Augustín (*open Wed–Mon 10.30–1 and 3.30–6.30*). The 18th-century church of San Pedro (*open Mon–Sat 10–1 and 4–7, Sun 10–1.30; adm*), is perched on a clifftop, with two paintings by Velázquez's teacher, Pacheco.

Dinner and Sleeping: In Arcos, *see* below, or continue back to Jerez, *see* p.222.

Day 5

Lunch in El Bosque

Las Truchas, Avda de la Diputacion , **t** 956 71 60 61 (*moderate*). Situated just outside El Bosque, a delightful little village set amongst verdant forests (providing shady relief from the sun-blasted landscapes of the rest of this area) and the Río Majaceite, which is stuffed full of trout. There is a pool and excellent restaurant specializing in – you guessed it – fresh trout *a la serranía*. There are lots of walking routes possible from this spot, and, for the more daring, paragliding and hang-gliding.

Dinner in Arcos de la Frontera

Meson de la Molinera, Lago de Arcos, **t** 956 70 80 02, (*expensive–moderate*). Specializes in delicious regional meat and game dishes, and also give diners the chance to enjoy fabulous views of the town.

El Convento, Marqués de Torresoto 7, **t** 956 70 32 32 (*moderate*). Offers typical cuisine of the Sierras, such as rabbit and partridge, in a 16th-century nobleman's house.

Los Parra, Ctra Arcos–El Bosque 3, **t** 956 70 41 21 (*moderate*). Another reasonable option, serving mostly pork and game dishes.

Sleeping in Arcos de la Frontera

★★★Parador Nacional Casa del Corregidor, Plaza de Cabilda s/n, **t** 956 70 05 00, *arcos@parador.es* (*expensive*). A lovely *parador*, and pretty popular, so book ahead. Be sure to request a room with a view, and even if you don't stay, sit over a coffee in the café – a picture window looks out over the entire plain.

★★El Convento, C/Maldonado 2, **t** 956 70 23 33 (*moderate*). The place to stay in the old town if the *parador* is full (which it frequently is), sharing the views but at half the price and with a very above-average restaurant attached (*see* left).

★★★Los Olivos, San Miguel 2, **t** 956 70 08 11 (*moderate–inexpensive*). A comfortable and reasonably priced three-star place.

Language

Castellano, as Spanish is properly called, was the first modern language to have a grammar written for it. When a copy was presented to Queen Isabel in 1492, she understandably asked what it was for. 'Your Majesty,' replied a perceptive bishop, 'language is the perfect instrument of empire.' In the centuries to come, this concise, flexible and expressive language would prove to be just that: an instrument that would contribute more to Spanish unity than any laws or institutions, while spreading itself effortlessly over much of the New World.

Among other European languages, Spanish is closest to Portuguese and Italian – and, of course, Catalan and Gallego, the native language of Galicia. Spanish, however, may have the simplest grammar of any Romance language, and if you know a little of any one of these, you will find much of the vocabulary looks familiar. It's quite easy to pick up a working knowledge of Spanish; but Spaniards speak colloquially and fast, and in Andalucía they leave out half the consonants and add some strange sounds of their own. Expressing yourself may prove a little easier than understanding the replies. Spaniards will appreciate your efforts, and if they correct you, they're not necessarily being snooty; they're simply trying to help you learn.

There are dozens of language books and tapes on the market; one particularly good one is *Teach Yourself Spanish*, by Juan Kattán-Ibarra (Hodder & Stoughton, 1984). Note that younger Spaniards increasingly use the familiar *tú* instead of *usted* even when addressing complete strangers.

Pronunciation

Pronunciation is phonetic although some consonants can be difficult to get the hang of for English speakers.

Vowels
a short *a* as in 'pat'
e short *e* as in 'set'
i as *e* in 'be'
o between long *o* of 'note' and short *o* of 'hot'
u silent after *q* and gue- and gui-; otherwise long *u* as in 'flute'
ü *w* sound, as in 'dwell'
y at end of word or meaning *and*, as **i**

Diphthongs
ai, ay as *i* in 'side'
au as *ou* in 'sound'
ei, ey as *ey* in 'they'
oi, oy as *oy* of 'boy'

Consonants
c before the vowels *i* and *e*, it's a Castilian tradition to pronounce it as *th*, but many Spaniards and all Latin Americans pronounce it in this case as an *s*
ch like *ch* in 'church'
d often becomes *th*, or is almost silent, at end of word
g before *i* or *e*, pronounced as **j** (*see* below)
h silent
j the *ch* in loch – a guttural, throat-clearing *h*
ll *y* or *ly* as in million
ñ *ny* as in canyon (the ~ is called a tilde)
q *k*
r usually rolled, which takes practice
v often pronounced as *b*
z *th*, but *s* in parts of Andalucía

Stress
If the word ends in a vowel, an *n* or an *s*, then the stress will fall on the penultimate syllable, otherwise stress will fall on the last syllable; any exceptions are marked with an accent.

If all this seems difficult, remember that English pronunciation is much, much more confusing for Spaniards.

Practise on some of the place names:

Madrid ma-DREED
León lay-OHN
Sevilla se-BEE-ah
Cáceres CAH-ther-es
Cuenca KWAYN-ka
Jaén hai-EN
Sigüenza sig-WAYN-thah
Trujillo troo-HEE-oh
Jerez her-ETH
Badajóz ba-da-HOTH
Málaga MAHL-ah-gah
Alcázar ahl-CATH-ar
Valladolid ba-yah-dol-EED
Arévalo ahr-EB-bah-lo

Useful Words and Phrases

Hello *Holá*
Goodbye *Adios/Hasta luego*
Good morning *Buenos días*
Good afternoon *Buenas tardes*
Good night *Buenas noches*
Please *por favor*
Thank you (very much) *(muchas) gracias*
You're welcome *de nada*
Excuse me *Con permiso/¿Me permite?*
I am sorry (in apology) *Disculpe/Perdon*
I am sorry (in sympathy or regret) *Lo siento*
It doesn't matter *No importa/Es igual*
all right *está bien*
ok *vale*
yes *sí*
no *no*
nothing *nada*
I don't know *No sé*
I don't understand Spanish *No entiendo español*
Do you speak English? *¿Habla usted inglés?*
Does someone here speak English? *¿Hay alguien que hable inglés?*
Speak slowly *Hable despacio*
Can you help me? *¿Puede usted ayudarme?*
Help! *¡Socorro!*
It is urgent! *¡Es urgente!*
How do you do? *¿Cómo está usted?*
 or more familiarly *¿Cómo estás? ¿Qué tal?*
Well, and you? *¿Bien, y usted?*
 or more familiarly *¿Bien, y tú?*
What is your name? *¿Cómo se llama?*
 or more familiarly *¿Cómo te llamas?*
My name is ... *Me llamo ...*

What is that? *¿Qué es eso?*
What ...? *¿Qué ...?*
Who ...? *¿Quién ...?*
Where ...? *¿Dónde ...?*
When ...? *¿Cuándo ...?*
Why ...? *¿Por qué ...?*
How ...? *¿Cómo ...?*
How much? *¿Cuánto/Cuánta?*
How many? *¿Cuántos/Cuántas?*
I am lost *Me he perdido*
I am hungry/thirsty *Tengo hambre/sed*
I am tired (man/woman) *Estoy cansado(a)*
I am ill *No siento bien*
good/bad *bueno(a)/malo(a)*
slow/fast *despacio/rápido(a)*
big/small *grande/pequeño(a)*
hot/cold *caliente/frío(a)*

Numbers

one *uno/una*
two *dos*
three *tres*
four *cuatro*
five *cinco*
six *seis*
seven *siete*
eight *ocho*
nine *nueve*
ten *diez*
eleven *once*
twelve *doce*
thirteen *trece*
fourteen *catorce*
fifteen *quince*
sixteen *dieciséis*
seventeen *diecisiete*
eighteen *dieciocho*
nineteen *diecinueve*
twenty *veinte*
thirty *treinta*
forty *cuarenta*
fifty *cincuenta*
sixty *sesenta*
seventy *setenta*
eighty *ochenta*
ninety *noventa*
one hundred *cien*
five hundred *quinientos*
one thousand *mil*
first *primero*
second *segundo*

third *tercero*
fourth *cuarto*
fifth *quinto*
tenth *décimo*

Time

What time is it? *¿Qué hora es?*
It is two o'clock *Son las dos*
... half past two ... *las dos y media*
... a quarter past two ... *las dos y cuarto*
... a quarter to three ... *las tres menos cuarto*
month *mes*
week *semana*
day *día*
morning *mañana*
afternoon *tarde*
evening *noche*
today *hoy*
yesterday *ayer*
soon *pronto*
tomorrow *mañana*
now *ahora*
later *después*
early *temprano*
late *tarde*

Days

Monday *lunes*
Tuesday *martes*
Wednesday *miércoles*
Thursday *jueves*
Friday *viernes*
Saturday *sábado*
Sunday *domingo*

Months

January *enero*
February *febrero*
March *marzo*
April *abril*
May *mayo*
June *junio*
July *julio*
August *agosto*
September *septiembre*
October *octubre*
November *noviembre*
December *diciembre*

Shopping and Sightseeing

I want, I would like... *Quiero...*
Where is/are...? *¿Dónde está/están...?*
How much is it? *¿Cuánto vale eso?*
open/closed *abierto/cerrado*
cheap/expensive *barato/caro*
money *dinero*
Do you have any change? *¿Tiene cambio?*
bank *banco*
beach *playa*
booking/box office *taquilla*
church *iglesia*
department store *almacén*
hospital *hospital*
market *mercado*
museum *museo*
newspaper (foreign) *periódico (extranjero)*
pharmacy *farmacia*
police station *comisaría*
policeman *policía*
post office *correos*
postage stamp *sello*
sea *mar*
shop *tienda*
supermarket *supermercado*
telephone *teléfono*
theatre *teatro*
winery *bodega*
toilet/toilets *servicios/aseos*
men *señores/hombres/caballeros*
women *señoras/damas*

Accommodation

Where is the hotel? *¿Dónde está el hotel?*
Do you have a room? *¿Tiene usted una habitación?*
Can I look at the room? *¿Podría ver la habitación?*
How much is the room per day/week? *¿Cuánto cuesta la habitación por día/semana?*
... with two beds *con dos camas*
... with double bed *con una cama grande*
... with a shower/bath *con ducha/baño*
... for one person/two people *para una persona/dos personas*
... for one night/one week *una noche/una semana*
elevator *ascensor*
bathroom *servicio/cuarto de baño*

Driving

rent *alquilar*
car *coche*
motorbike/moped *moto/ciclomotor*
bicycle *bicicleta*
petrol *gasolina*
garage *garaje*
This doesn't work *Esto no funciona*
road *carretera*
motorway *autopista*
Is the road good? *¿Es buena la carretera?*
breakdown *avería*
driving licence *carnet de conducir*
exit *salida*
entrance *entrada*
danger *peligro*
no parking *estacionament prohibido*
give way/yield *ceda el paso*
roadworks *obras*

Note: Most road signs are in pictographs

Transport and Directions

aeroplane *avión*
airport *aeropuerto*
bus/coach *autobús/autocar*
bus/railway station *estación*
bus stop *parada*
customs *aduana*
platform *andén*
port *puerto*
seat *asiento*
ship *buque/barco/embarcadero*
ticket *billete*
train *tren*
I want to go to... *Quiero ir a...*
How can I get to ...? *¿Cómo puedo llegar a ...?*
Where is ...? *¿Dónde está ...?*
When is the next (last)...? *¿Cuándo sale el próximo (último)...?*
What time does it leave (arrive)? *¿Sale (llega) a qué hora?*
From where does it leave? *¿De dónde sale?*
Do you stop at ... ? *¿Para en ... ?*
How long does the trip take? *¿Cuánto tiempo dura el viaje?*
I want a (return) ticket to ... *Quiero un billete (de ida y vuelta) a ...*
How much is the fare? *¿Cuánto cuesta el billete?*
here/there *aquí/allí*

close/far *cerca/lejos*
left/right *izquierda/derecha*
straight on *todo recto*
corner *esquina*
square *plaza*
street *calle*

Eating Out

See also 'Menu Decoder' in the **Food and Drink** chapter, pp.36–7.

menu *carta/menú*
bill/check *cuenta*
change *cambio*
set meal *menú del día*
waiter/waitress *camarero/a*
Do you have a table? *¿Tiene una mesa?*
... for one/two? *... ¿para uno/dos?*
Can I see the menu, please? *¿Me da el menú, por favor*
Do you have a wine list? *¿Hay una carta de vinos?*
Can I have the bill (check), please? *La cuenta, por favor*
Can I pay by credit card? *¿Puedo pagar con tarjeta de crédito?*

Some Useful Catalan Words and Phrases

Good morning, Good day *Bon dia*
Good afternoon *Bona tarda*
Good night *Bona nit*
Goodbye *adéu*
Please *si us plau*
Very good, OK, great *molt bé*
thank you (very much) *moltes gràcies*
see you later *fins ara, fins després*
you're welcome *de res*
open/closed *obert/tancat*
entrance/exit *entrada/sortida*
left/right *esquerra/dreta*
I don't understand *no entenc*
I like... *m'agrada...*
change, exchange *canvi*
more *més*
enough *prou*
too much *massa*
bottle *ampolla*
salad *amanida*
omelette *or* trout (so be careful) *truita*

Index

Main page references are in **bold**. Page references to maps are in *italics*.

PARIS
Dana Facaros & Michael Pauls

ROME
Dana Facaros & Michael Pauls

BRUSSELS
Antony Mason

CADOGANguides

Amsterdam
Barcelona
Brussels
Madrid
Paris
Rome
Bruges
Florence
London
Prague

Available Feb 2003
Venice
Milan
Edinburgh

Cadogan City Guides...
the life and soul
of the city

CADOGANguides
well travelled **well read**

Also available from Cadogan Guides in our European series...

Italy

Italy
Italy: The Bay of Naples and Southern Italy
Italy: Lombardy and the Italian Lakes
Italy: Tuscany, Umbria and the Marches
Italy: Tuscany
Italy: Umbria
Italy: Northeast Italy
Italy: Italian Riviera
Italy: Bologna and Emilia Romagna
Italy: Central Italy
Sardinia
Sicily
Rome, Florence, Venice
Florence, Siena, Pisa & Lucca

Spain

Spain
Spain: Andalucía
Spain: Northern Spain
Spain: Bilbao and the Basque Lands
Granada, Seville, Cordoba
Madrid, Barcelona, Seville

Greece

Greece
Greek Islands
Crete

France

France
France: Dordogne & the Lot
France: Gascony & the Pyrenees
France: Brittany
France: Loire
France: The South of France
France: Provence
France: Côte d'Azur
Corsica
Short Breaks in Northern France

The UK and Ireland

London–Paris

Scotland
Scotland: Highlands and Islands

Ireland
Ireland: Southwest Ireland
Ireland: Northern Ireland

Other Europe

Portugal
Madeira & Porto Santo

The City Guide Series

Amsterdam
Brussels
Paris
Rome
Barcelona
Madrid
London
Florence
Prague
Bruges
Venice
Milan
Edinburgh

The Flying Visits Series

Flying Visits Italy
Flying Visits Spain
Flying Visits France

The Buying a Property Series

Buying a Property Italy
Buying a Property Spain
Buying a Property France

Cadogan Guides are available from good bookshops, or via **Grantham Book Services**, Isaac Newton Way, Alma Park Industrial Estate, Grantham NG31 9SD, **t** (01476) 541 080, **f** (01476) 541 061; and **The Globe Pequot Press**, 246 Goose Lane, PO Box 480, Guilford, Connecticut 06437–0480, **t** (800) 458 4500/**f** (203) 458 4500, **t** (203) 458 4603.